CLARK C

CLARK GRIFFITH

The Old Fox of Washington Baseball

Ted Leavengood

McFarland & Company, Inc., Publishers

Jefferson, North Carolina, and London

LIBRARY OF CONGRESS CATALOGUING-IN-PUBLICATION DATA

Leavengood, Ted.
 Clark Griffith : the old fox of Washington baseball / Ted
Leavengood.
  p.   cm.
 Includes bibliographical references and index.

 ISBN 978-0-7864-6386-2
 softcover : 50# alkaline paper ∞

 1. Griffith, Clark, 1869–1955. 2. Baseball players — United
States — Biography. 3. Pitchers (Baseball) — United States —
Biography. 4. Baseball managers — United States — Biography.
5. Baseball team owners — United States — Biography. I. Title.
GV865.G694L43   2011
796.357092 — dc23
[B]   2011017216

BRITISH LIBRARY CATALOGUING DATA ARE AVAILABLE

Front cover image: Clark Griffith, 1919 (Library of Congress)

Manufactured in the United States of America

McFarland & Company, Inc., Publishers
 Box 611, Jefferson, North Carolina 28640
  www.mcfarlandpub.com

For Donna Jean Boxer

Table of Contents

Preface

The older men, many of them former players, gathered in the mornings in Clark Griffith's office area beneath the grandstands of old Griffith Stadium. They came to play pinochle and swap baseball stories with Griffith, the owner of the Washington Nationals. His young grandson, Clark Griffith III, sometimes accompanied the old man to the stadium and the boy watched and listened to the interactions between the men.

Occasionally the group would include famous personages in the game, like Connie Mack or Joe Cronin, men who were in town with their team and wanted to pay their respects to the elder Griffith. "I was always impressed by the way they reacted to him," says Clark Griffith III. There was a deference and respect, because as his grandson now fully understands, "Clark Griffith was a giant of the game."[1]

Clark Griffith III still treasures those moments and decorates his own office with some of the photographs from his grandfather's old office at Griffith Stadium. But one of his most prized possessions, handed down from his grandfather, is the old Winchester rifle given to Clark Griffith senior by A. G. Spalding in 1901. Spalding, more than any other individual, brought the game of baseball from what Bill James calls its "primitive" beginnings to the burgeoning business that emerged during the last two decades of the nineteenth century.[2] Spalding's gift was in recognition of Griffith's hard work in helping to create the American League in 1901.

I knew nothing of the rich tradition of baseball in Washington, D.C. I grew up in southeastern Georgia, and my father and I were limited to minor league baseball when we wanted to go out to the park. One night at Grayson Stadium in Savannah, Georgia, our baseball evening was enlivened by Al Schacht, the Clown Prince of Baseball. Watching his routine I was certain that this comedian — with his slapstick routine of dusting the shoes of the umpires with a big broom, harassing coaches and umpires and generally making a nuisance to the delight of fans — had never been part of major league baseball.

I had no way of knowing who Al Schacht was, nor did my dad fully appreciate the history that he carried with him. For 15 years Schacht was a player and coach for the Washington Nationals. He perfected his comedy routines working the sidelines for Clark Griffith as an extra feature thrown in for free with the price of a ticket to Griffith Stadium. Schacht's career in Washington saw the greatest moments of the Griffith era, and Schacht was an important actor in them. His departure with Joe Cronin in 1934 brought the curtain down on Griffith's best years.

When I encountered the comedian he was an aging performer who took his act to minor league stadiums around the country. What I could not know was that Al Schacht was the last man standing, the lone embodiment of those great Washington Nationals teams that won three American League pennants. Like a Native American performing in a Wild West show, Schacht was a poorly understood final relic of a proud tradition. The Washington Nationals were no more, and Schacht's routine was a last sad remnant.

Schacht's story in baseball began in the earliest years of the impressive baseball edifice Clark Griffith built in Washington. For 23 seasons, from 1912 until 1934, the Washington Nationals finished in the second division only six times. They were in contention for the American League pennant or finished in the first half of the league 16 of those 23 years. It is a record that is hard to imagine from the perspective of today's Washington baseball teams.

Until recently all that Griffith constructed, both literally and figuratively, had been lost. Griffith Stadium was torn down to make way for the Howard University Hospital in the early 1960s after his team was packed up and shipped off to Minneapolis several years earlier. Fans were left with only the debate: Do the old Nationals belong to Minnesota or to Washington? Did the story of presidents throwing out the opening day pitch every year move with the franchise? Did all of the pennant winners and Hall of Fame players leave along with the memories?

When baseball returned to Washington, D.C., in 2005 those debates began afresh. The new Washington Nationals played their first season at RFK Stadium. Outside the main gate to that stadium is a lonely and forgotten commemorative monument to Clark Griffith that was originally placed outside old Griffith stadium in 1956 — the year after he died. Now it stands next to traffic where the years have been no kinder than they were to Al Schacht.

His face, preserved in concrete relief on one side of the monument, has been defaced. The area around the monument is poorly maintained and is so far removed from the pedestrian flow to the stadium that it is unlikely anyone pays it much mind. On the other side of the main entrance to RFK, the one most baseball fans used as they came from the subway, a shiny and well-kept statue to George Preston Marshall — long-time owner of the Redskins — gleams in the sun.

Despite the inattention to his monument, Griffith's legacy stands far above that of the old racist footballer. Clark Griffith gave Marshall his start when he brought Marshall's struggling team from Boston to use Griffith Stadium for their home games in 1937. But professional football never left town, never gave local fans three decades to forget.

Griffith's lonely memorial at RFK Stadium is a squat, four-sided obelisk almost wider than it is tall. On each side are engraved features of his long career. One side outlines his tenure as a player, another as a manager, another as an owner and the last as the head of a family and a member of his community. Clark Griffith is in the National Baseball Hall of Fame in Cooperstown based on the sum of those achievements. He made championship-caliber baseball his hard-won companion whenever possible. Yet it is not Clark Griffith's ability to win pennants and championships that make him a legendary figure in the game.

Mark Armour, in his recent biography of Joe Cronin, said of Griffith, "He had a subversive past. An outspoken critic of the National League's treatment of players … Griffith in 1901 became a key figure in the establishment of the American League."[3] Known as a labor radical and cunning master of his craft on the mound early in his career, Griffith grew into a legend of the game through unmatched "grit." It is the word repeatedly used to describe him. Every inch of the "Old Fox," as he was called, was game to the core.

Yet there was more. There was the quiet integrity and unswerving character that made him a friend to presidents and dedicated him to two very simple things over the course of his long life: baseball and family.

As much as baseball meant to Griffith, he sacrificed much of what he had achieved in baseball to provide security and opportunity to two youngsters he brought into his home. Thelma and Calvin Griffith were plucked from destitution by the Old Fox and made nearly whole. The same can be said of their siblings that Griffith brought to Washington as well. The fourth side of the monument honors the basic humanity of Clark Griffith, but it does not say enough.

There is another monument to Griffith that can be found in Fort Lincoln Cemetery on Bladensburg Road in Washington, D.C. It is the family mausoleum that contains them all — the extended family that Clark Griffith cared for his from the day he plucked them from a failed family life in Montreal, Canada.

The crypt contains his wife and her very extended family, including all of the nieces and nephews he brought to Washington to live. Not the least of those buried so ironically in Washington is Calvin Griffith, the man who took baseball from his uncle's adopted home. It is truly Clark Griffith's last measure of devotion that he gave even Calvin a place among them back in Washington.

This book examines Clark Griffith's life as it unfolded through a changing world of baseball and American culture. Since Griffith remained actively involved in baseball until his death at 85, there are vast amounts of baseball history to cover: the rules changed, the ball changed and the cultural backdrop against which pennants were won and lost became remarkably different.

Researching the life of Clark Griffith required me to learn far more than I knew at the beginning. I learned not only the great stories of Washington baseball, but some of the best ones from the nineteenth century when Griffith's playing days began. It was a great privilege examining all of it and trying to get the details right in the re-telling.

One era in the life of Clark Griffith caused me considerable personal turmoil. The issue of race as it impacted Griffith was quite troubling. I rewrote the chapter on the Homestead Grays numerous times and contacted Brad Snyder to seek his help, which he was gracious in providing. Snyder's book, *Beyond the Shadow of the Senators: The Untold Story of the Homestead Grays and the Integration of Baseball*, takes a particularly critical view of Griffith's role in that era. Ultimately we could not agree completely on how to view Clark Griffith as a historic figure within the game.

One difference in our perspective arises from my own life. I grew up in the South during integration and I experienced racial prejudice as a loud, shrill voice that sought to bully all within earshot and silence was not assent. Clark Griffith was not known to have ever uttered a racist remark and the concerns he expressed in his 1937 interview with Sam Lacy seemed genuine. At first I believed them unbowed by his passive stance in later years.

At the core of Snyder's view is the belief that Griffith's lack of action during the years following Jackie Robinson's breech of the color barrier are culpable. I came to agree that the long inaction and some poorly chosen words were too much to ignore. While Griffith was not an active racist, he did more than stand by silently. He lent support to those whose views were regrettable and he failed the test of time during one of the most important social eras in our nation's history.

I believe that Griffith's precarious economic situation restricted his ability to act meaningfully and I do not share Snyder's belief that Griffith had significant financial room to operate in the post-war years. Regardless the tightness of Griffith's financial strictures, there is no excuse for his inaction. He sided with the racist ownership of the American League when the Cleveland Indians owner, Bill Veeck, provided him an opening to make his voice heard.

Yet, it concerns me to think that Clark Griffith's place in baseball history could by diminished by his failings very late in life. His lion-sized commitment to family, friends and the game itself were always on display throughout his life. That life cannot be diminished by the events that transpired when he was hanging on by a financial whisker and trying to save the family business.

However one comes to view these and other events during Griffith's long life, I can only hope that I open the door for others to discover more about Clark Griffith and the old Washington Nationals. His life deserves greater examination and I can only hope to be another guide ushering fans down the path that Shirley Povich once lit so well during the time that was Clark Griffith's in Washington, D.C.

I would like to acknowledge the help and support of my wife, Donna J. Boxer, whose many wonderful skills include being a fine editor. More importantly, she is an inspiration and the greatest and happiest accident of my life.

I would like to thank the Library of Congress staff for their help whenever it was needed. The institution's historical importance is little understood by most Americans, and even those such as myself who use it cannot fully grasp the depth of its treasures. The National Baseball Hall of Fame Research Library in Cooperstown, N.Y.; the Martin Luther King, Jr., Library in Washington, D.C.; the Montgomery County Library; and the Howard University Library were also extremely helpful and their staffs are just as professional and informed as the more imposing LOC.

My thanks to my numerous friends who have helped me in this venture, including Bill Seedyke — a fine and fair editor — and Rich Lerner, who together convinced me the old Washington baseball team should forever be called the Nationals rather than the Senators. Clark Griffith always honored Tom Noyes' official 1905 declaration that the team be called the Nationals. Over the years, many in the press came to prefer the Senators, but only Calvin bowed to that pressure. Undoing something of Calvin Griffith's should always give Washington baseball fans special pleasure.

Thanks go to Mike Lynch, Dennis Pajot, and Brad Snyder for their help and to Marc Hall for reading numerous chapters of the first draft. Always deserving of thanks are people who provided assistance over the past few years, including Tom Goldstein, formerly of *Elysian Fields Quarterly*, Dr. Joel Cohen, and the Reverend Ed Winkler.

Best of all are my daughters Julia and Claire Leavengood-Boxer. They are still my favorite ballpark companions and while it is great fun being immersed in the writing of a book, nothing can match the memories of those many games we shared over the years.

CHAPTER 1

From Jesse James to Hoss Radbourn

In the fall of 1946, after the final pitch of the baseball season had been thrown, 59-year-old Walter Johnson lay in a Washington area hospital dying of brain cancer. Johnson was visited by many of his teammates and other notable persons from various walks of life. None of his visitors was more diligent and faithful than Clark Griffith, the 77-year-old owner of the Washington Nationals.

The two men who often shared the gloom of that hospital room had brought Washington baseball to the pinnacle of success. Each had dreamed of a World Series victory, but only together had they achieved one. It was joining the burning competitiveness of the two men that made the greatest achievements of Washington baseball history possible.

Every day Griffith visited the "Big Swede" and brought him a single rose that he had picked from his own garden. Clark Griffith told the nurse who put those roses each day into a vase, "I took the earth from the pitcher's box in which Walter Johnson worked so long and made a special rose garden of it."[1]

Griffith sat at Johnson's bedside, often holding his hand and talking even when it was uncertain whether Johnson was fully conscious. Griffith told Walter Johnson the day's baseball news or stories of their past together. Finally, Johnson's family could no longer pay for the extended hospital care. Walter Johnson's long, hard fight for life was draining the family. Clark Griffith quietly gathered up the bills and paid them.[2]

Clark Griffith's dedication to the great pitcher and his supreme sense of loss at his passing can be seen as a measure of his enduring loyalty to his players. Yet it was more than that. There were two men of large heart and much courage in that hospital room, and it was that largeness that was elemental to both men and all they did. Their tenacity of spirit made them both hugely successful winning pitchers. Yet it also kept each of them going, well after others had quit, as they sought the greatest baseball victory they would know together.

Clark Griffith had little of Johnson's unique talent as a pitcher. Never known for the strength of his arm, Griffith won 237 big league games on his brains and grit. Griffith was a small man known more for how he overcame his physical limitations and how sly his offerings to the plate were. Johnson was a large man whose arms hung long at his side, who used his strength and size — especially those long arms — to gain unparalleled leverage with his signature sidearm motion, one that could put more force behind a baseball than anyone who has every pitched.

At Johnson's funeral Clark Griffith was joined by Walter Johnson's teammates, his great friends Clyde Milan and Sam Rice, Bucky Harris, Joe Judge, Ossie Bluege, Muddy Ruel, Roger Peckinpaugh and Tom Zachary. For Clark Griffith the mourners gathered there were almost as close as his own family. From his earliest days Griffith's life had been about nothing except baseball, and he may have spent more time with the players gathered in that room than he had with his rather complicated family.

Despite the broad physical dissimilarities between Walter Johnson and Clark Griffith, there were interesting overlaps as well. Both men were born on the same American frontier, the border between Kansas and Missouri. Griffith was born in 1869, 18 years before Johnson, just a few miles on the Missouri side of the border. Clear Creek, Missouri — Griffith's birthplace — was only 60 miles from Humboldt, Kansas, the nearest town to the family farm on which Johnson was born.

That Kansas-Missouri border was the proving ground for the tensions and hatred that gave rise to the Civil War. When Clark Griffith was born there in 1869 the area remained uncertain territory, haunted by renegades unable to reconcile with the peace reached at the end of the Civil War. Both the Johnson and Griffith families told stories of interacting with the greatest of those outlaws, Jesse James, and his brother Frank. Griffith explained many years after the fact that his father actually knew Jesse James. "One night he slept in our house. The next morning I brought his (James') horse out for him."[3]

Griffith would be marked by those beginnings, by the rugged circumstances of the time, its racial tensions and frontier justice. Playing a game that was capturing the imagination of a nation gave Clark Griffith a chance to perform before a crowd. It gave vent to his natural leadership skills and provided his first chance to lead other men. But more than anything, it allowed him to put behind him the tough times about which he seldom spoke except in folksy yarns that romanticized that early life.

It is likely that those elemental beginnings helped him appreciate the value of the common man and his struggles to survive. It was not just the loud voice on the diamond that made him a gifted leader, but the real concern he expressed for his teammates. It was his understanding of the difficult environment in which the early ballplayers often toiled.

He was called an anarchist and radical by sports writers during his early years because the causes he championed were generally those of working men in their search for a better life. The Major League Baseball Players Association spoke of him reverentially as one of the earliest union organizers in baseball and recognized his contribution to all who played the game.[4]

Several years after Walter Johnson's death, when Clark Griffith was in his last year of life, he told novelist James T. Farrell, "If you started playing baseball as I did when I was seven and still love it at 85, you'll understand what it has meant to me."[5] Griffith's life in baseball was an exceedingly long one, and few began at the professional level at such an early age. Fewer still lived to tell stories about it as one of its premier elder statesmen. Yet there was Griffith at age 85, intently watching a spring training game in Florida, still a central figure in the unfolding story of the season as he regaled Farrell with how he began his life.

The life of Clark Calvin Griffith started inauspiciously. Early in his life he was small and sickly with little to suggest he would become a Hall of Fame professional athlete. Griffith was born to Isaiah and Sarah Anne Griffith as the fifth of six children in Clear Creek, Missouri, on November 20, 1869. His family was of Welsh origins and both his parents had links to wealthy families back east.

Those ties were long forgotten by the time Griffith's father and mother set out from Illinois in a covered wagon for the promised riches of the Oklahoma territory with their young brood of four children. Their hopes remained high until they encountered hungry and disillusioned settlers returning from the frontier. Rather than stretch their own resources to the same breaking point, they staked a claim instead in the Missouri frontier, just east of the Kansas border.[6] Isaiah Griffith — Clark's father — laid claim to a 48-acre farm that provided the support for his family, and he built the log cabin that held his burgeoning family and became the birthplace for his son Clark.

Clear Creek, Missouri, was little more than a rural crossroads adjacent to the frontier town of Nevada, Missouri. Griffith's father kept a muzzle-loading rifle handy and used it to supplement the family table with venison, wild turkey and other game he killed while hunting in the deep woods nearby. He sold some of his kill at Fort Smith, an army post on the Kansas side seeking to tame the lawless nature of that frontier.

A hunting accident ended the life of the elder Griffith when Clark was only two. Coming out of a wooded area, Isaiah Griffith jumped a fence into an open field and was shot by an adolescent neighbor who mistook him for a deer. The loss struck hard at the marginal existence of the Griffiths, but Sarah Griffith was determined to carry on her husband's effort to create a life in the Nevada community. She continued to till the soil, often carrying the young toddler, Clark, as she plowed. She got plenty of help from her neighbors, but the land was not rich, nor was the community of Vernon County.[7]

Sarah Griffith's eldest son Earl tried to take up the slack left by the death of their father by continuing to hunt. As Clark got older he helped by becoming a professional trapper at the age of ten. He shared the same woods his father had died in with his brother Earl as they tried to keep enough game on the table to feed the large family. Clark Griffith restricted himself to simple game like raccoons that he and his dog, Major, would kill together.

Griffith loved telling tall tales about his early life, and he found a willing audience in the sports writers of his day. None were taller than the ones he told about his hunting exploits. Hunting was a necessary part of life on the frontier, of stretching the meager resources the family could force from the land. It remained an important facet of his life for many years.

The young Clark Griffith found release from the rigors of the frontier life in the game of baseball. The game had grown in popularity during the Civil War, played at encampments of soldiers on both sides of the conflict. Soldiers returning home at the end of the war spread baseball through small-town America and brought it to Clark Griffith in rural Missouri.

Clark Griffith had his first experience with organized baseball when he was seven. Griffith described the baseball he played as a kid, making "our own balls ... with a spinning wheel. We wound our own yarn tight and threw buckskin over it."[8] The game was called "One Old Cat" or "Town Ball" at the time. Griffith's childhood friends recalled him years later as the best player in town, who could outrun them all, despite the infirmities that later struck him. When he was ten, he served as the mascot and batboy for the local Stringtown, Missouri, team.

In 1876 the professional player and future sporting goods magnate, A. G. Spalding, came out with a new manufactured baseball that standardized play and gave it a common vernacular that reached down even to rural Missouri. Shortly after the first news of Mr. Spalding's new manufactured baseball, the locals decided that they should benefit from it for an important local game. A collection was taken to buy one of the new baseballs at the price of $1.25. A little-known local man offered to travel to the next town to purchase one for them.

The man did return with a ball, but as soon as play began it became obvious that the ball he supplied back to the Stringtown regulars was of the variety that could be had for two dimes. The crowd concluded that the stranger had pocketed the extra dollar, which was a considerable sum in 1876. The man disappeared, but made the mistake of being caught several days later. The young Griffith, who had witnessed the hand-off of the money to the stranger, next saw him dangling from the Vernon County hanging tree the morning after his apprehension.

"That was my first lesson in the honesty of baseball," Griffith later claimed.[9]

The brutal realities of life on the frontier shaped Griffith in important ways that some say explained the "bewildering paradoxes" of a man who would lead labor revolts in his early adult life before becoming a hard-nosed executive whose wealth made him frequent company for presidents of the United States.[10] As a respected patriarch, not just within the community of professional baseball but also as the head of a large and demanding family, Griffith had little time for those who second-guessed his decisions. He learned early that taking care of a family was a tough business and that there was no knowing when death or financial vicissitudes could shift the ground beneath you.

In 1883, at the age of 13, after numerous bouts of a mysterious fever, Griffith was diagnosed with malaria. His mother decided to move the large family back to Illinois for the boy's health and to get more help from her family with her struggling brood. They moved in with Griffith's uncle, Levi Dillen. Dillen was well-known in the area as a breeder of draught horses used for pulling large wagons. He traveled to France to get the best breeding stock, and his horses were widely sought in southern Illinois and beyond.[11] Dillen's son Frank was also a gifted athlete whose baseball career would take him west where he managed the Los Angeles entry in the Pacific Coast League.[12]

Sarah Griffith got a place of her own for her children when she opened a boarding house and earned extra cash by taking in wash from neighbors.[13] She left Clark with the Dillens so that there was more room for renters at the boarding house.[14] The new surroundings and support from Sarah Griffith's extended family provided important support for the young Clark Griffith, who would consider Normal, Illinois, his home for many years to come.

It did not take the young Griffith long before he was marked as an outstanding baseball figure in his new surroundings. In the Normal-Bloomington, Illinois, area he achieved success for his school team. He started his career as a catcher, but pitched as well, realizing early on that he could bring his mind and increasing knowledge of the game to bear more from the mound than from any other place on the diamond.

The decision to move back to the Bloomington area was fortuitous for Clark Griffith in one very important way. Bloomington was home to Charles "Old Hoss" Radbourn, who was already a star pitcher in the fledgling sport of baseball. Radbourn would go on to the Baseball Hall of Fame as one of the most talented pitchers of his era.

Radbourn's greatest years in the game came during the 1880s. Pitching for the Providence Grays, then of the National League, Radbourn set the record for wins in a single season in 1884 with 59 after winning 48 to lead the National League the year before. The record of 59 wins in a single season will stand without equal in baseball history.

The Providence Grays did not last, and Old Hoss finished his career with the champion Boston Beaneaters in the late 1880s. Charles Radbourn was the formative tutor for Clark Griffith who taught him not only the rudiments of pitching, but also what it took to become a major league pitcher and a skilled one at that. Clark Griffith learned the craft of pitching from Radbourn, but he also learned that baseball was more than a game played for fun. For Radbourn it was a profitable career and Griffith, as one of the best players in the area, took that to heart.

Clark Griffith watched the long hours that Radbourn put into his craft, the endless hours of practice that it took to become a professional. As a young man, Old Hoss threw hundreds of baseballs, aiming each one between two bottles of beer on a split rail fence until he could spot his pitches effortlessly to exactly where he wanted them to go. Later Griffith would say of Radbourn, "He practiced weeks, months, and even years to acquire perfect handling of the baseball."[15]

Radbourn's pinpoint control was an essential part of his genius on the mound. It was an important lesson for the young Griffith, who was wild early in his career. He worked to harness his control by putting a handkerchief on the barn wall and throwing endlessly until he could keep his pitches within that mark. Griffith would never have the speed Radbourn had on his overwhelming fastball. Griffith's control became one of his strongest mound traits, but it took years of work to perfect.

Radbourn's arsenal included several pitches that would become the most important part of Griffith's repertoire. The first was the "slow ball." In his book on Radbourn, Edward Achorn talks at length about the pitch and Radbourn's ability to get a pitch without remarkable speed to achieve as much break as it did.[16] It was Griffith's mastery of important elements of Old Hoss's arsenal that gave him a chance to become a successful pitcher. "I'd say the two greatest things he showed me were the curve ball, how to throw it, how to use it, and the importance of grit."[17]

Grantland Rice said of Radbourn that he was the greatest pitcher he ever saw, better than Mathewson, Waddell and even Walter Johnson.[18] With such a legendary figure to influence him, it is easy to see how a young boy whose family was struggling could look to baseball as a chance for something more, how a mere game could provide not only a career choice, but also an opportunity to become someone of importance who influenced the world around him.

Radbourn's impact on Griffith was that of role model and teacher, and there were few better. Years later Griffith would say of his first baseball teacher, "He was brainy and game to the core," two hallmarks of Clark Griffith's career as well.[19] There is one other Radbourn trait that may have helped define the young Griffith. Old Hoss was a harsh critic of the reserve clause that bound players irrevocably to one team. "He was sort of an anarchist and was never happy unless scoring the magnates for their so-called oppressive measures."[20] When Hoss Radbourn died at the early age of 43, Clark Griffith picked up the mantle of Bloomington's best — all of it — and carried it proudly forward.

When Griffith was only 17, still living in Bloomington, he was offered $10 to pitch for a semi-professional team out of Hoopestown, Illinois, against Danville. He grabbed the money and went out and won his first game as a professional. That small step was the first in his career as a professional baseball pitcher, one that he took without looking back.

Griffith's performance caught the attention of the owner of the Bloomington, Illinois, professional team, Jesse Fell. It was the spring of 1887 that Fell made Clark Griffith a starter for the Bloomington team, and he remained one throughout that season. The team photograph included an unnamed young African-American outfielder.[21] The next year saw Bloomington become part of the Interstate League, and the level of play was at increasingly higher skill levels.

It was while playing for Bloomington that Griffith's place on the mound was cemented. He was playing every day as a catcher and outfielder. But his diminutive size — he stood no more than 5–6 by most accounts — required Griffith to make the most of his skills. During a crucial game the rival Decatur, Illinois, team pushed across several runs early and player-manager Artie Wills knew he needed to make a change. "Griffith, go in and pitch," Wills said. "You could do no worse than your predecessor."[22] Griffith shut down the Decatur team for the remaining five innings and earned a bump in pay in the bargain to $15 a game.

Griffith moved from there to a starting role on the mound. In later years Griffith often recalled his first game as a starting pitcher in the Interstate League. The game was May 1, 1888, pitching for Bloomington against Danville. Not only did Griffith win that first game by a 3–2 score, but his double in the sixth inning knocked in the winning run. His recounting of that game in later years had as much to do with his skill with the bat as the fact that he struck out nine batters and issued no walks.

In Bloomington "Griff" commanded a monthly salary of $50, and he won ten games while losing only four against competition of increased sophistication. Griff's cohorts were older and more mature men who had earned interesting sobriquets during their careers on and off the field. One of the more well-known talents on the Bloomington "Reds" was local wrestling champ. Tom MacMahon. He played second base and served as captain for the Bloomington team when he was not wrestling or driving a beer wagon. Their catcher, "Stockyard" Mathews, was a railroad man who had to be watched before games lest he have one too many snorts of local brew. Another character on the team was first baseman Aubrey "Handsome" Royce, known to friends as "the Dude."[23]

Perhaps it was the rowdy nature of his cohorts and the need to set himself apart, but Griffith tried to learn more than just what great baseball minds had to offer in the late 1880s. He enrolled at Illinois Wesleyan College, but found that the off-season did not provide enough time to sustain a college career. Learning the art of pitching proved to be the intellectual challenge of a lifetime for Clark Griffith.

The central Illinois teams on which Griffith played were strong ones and were often raided for talent by the American Association and the National League teams in the area. Bloomington played an exhibition game against the Milwaukee Brewers of the Western Association in July of 1888. The 18-year-old Griffith started that game, which was won by the Bloomington team. The star pitcher of the Bloomington nine impressed Milwaukee Brewers manager James Hart. He offered Griffith — judged at the time to be the best pitcher in the Inter-state League — a signing bonus of $1,000 and a salary of $225 a month to pitch for Milwaukee. The money was a considerable hike from what he was making in Illinois and lured Clark Griffith from his home in Normal to what was then known as the "Cream City." He finished the 1888 season with Milwaukee, winning 12 games for the "Creams," as they were sometimes called.

He began the next season —1889 — with the Milwaukee Brewers and started 31 games for them, winning 18 and losing 13. His best season there was in 1890 when he won 27 and lost only 7. The Creams played against the Chicago Maroons, the Davenport, Iowa, "Onion Eaters," the Des Moines, Iowa, "Prohibitionists," the Kansas City "Blues," the Minneapolis "Milers," the Omaha "Hogs," the Sioux City "Cornhuskers," the St. Louis "Whites," and the St. Paul, MN, "Apostles."

One of the early highlights of his career in Milwaukee was a return to Bloomington for an exhibition game much like the one in which he had been discovered. This game was in the middle of the 1890 season. As had been the case the previous year, the Bloomington Reds started their ace against the Milwaukee team.

The Reds pitcher was from Griffith's hometown of Normal, Illinois, as well, a young man named Will Darnsborough who pitched a fine game against Milwaukee, much as Griffith had done the previous summer. With the Brewers ahead 3–2 late in the game, Jimmy Deagon of the Reds hit a long drive to center field that looked like a home run that could spoil Griffith's homecoming game. Milwaukee's center fielder was Jimmy McAleer, who would go on to become a major league star for Cleveland in the National League, and later played a prominent role in bringing Griffith to Washington. McAleer ran the ball down in center field that day, and relayed it to the infield where Deagon was tagged out sliding into home to save the game.

While playing in Milwaukee Griffith had his first taste of union activities, something that would mark his career in important ways later. The Players League was formed in 1889 by a union of National League ballplayers called the Brotherhood of Professional Baseball Players. Informally known as the Brotherhood League, it secured financial backing and reached its peak when it had the support of approximately 100 National League players before the beginning of the 1890 season.

The key issue was the reserve clause that bound players to teams, an issue that would haunt major league baseball for another eight decades. Griffith, who would later take a leadership role in union activities, was approached by John Ward of the Brooklyn Players League team and asked to join forces with the Brotherhood. Although Griffith seemed to have some sympathy with the cause and considered the issue for several weeks, he ultimately decided that in 1890 he still had a prosperous arrangement for a young man just starting his career.

Griffith's last season with the Brewers was impressive enough to catch the attention of Charlie Comiskey, manager of the St. Louis Browns, who convinced Griffith to jump to the American Association where the Browns played. The team was a very successful one, unlike the later American League franchise of the same name. They had won the pennant in the American Association for four consecutive years beginning in 1885. The 1890 team was no less strong and featured a roster littered with many of the best players of the time.

Griffith got off to a great start in the league, winning his first game against Cincinnati by a 13–5 margin. A large crowd for the time was on hand for the game — 3,200 fans. Griffith got his chance because the ace of the Browns staff, Silver King, was holding out for more money and had yet to sign a contract in early April. King had led the league in wins with 45 in 1888 and in ERA at 1.63. He had won 35 the previous year and would lead the Players League in 1890 with a 2.69 ERA and manage 30 wins.[24]

Griffith made the most of the opportunity King gave him and won his next four games before losing finally to Louisville and Red Ehret at the end of April. He won 11 games while losing only eight and pitched to a fine 3.33 ERA. Control was still an issue for the young pitcher as he walked almost as many batters as he struck out for the Browns — 58 walks to a paltry 68 strike-outs over 186 innings.

A sore arm halted Clark Griffith's first turn in the major leagues at mid-season and he was released by the Browns. He was picked up by the Boston team and struggled there until the season ended. The American Association disbanded after the 1891 season and left the young Griffith in the lurch.

Griffith ventured west where his cousin Frank Dillen was manager of the Los Angeles team. He caught on at the beginning of the 1892 season with a team in Tacoma, Washington, of the Northern Pacific League. He pitched well and became player-manager for the first time. The Tacoma team and others in the league were having trouble making payroll, however, and there was talk that the league would disband.

Mining companies in Montana were trying to start a league and one firm made the Tacoma team a lucrative offer to relocate to the Montana frontier. Although the Tacoma manager demurred, Griffith gathered the players and put the issue to a vote, encouraging his cohorts with promises of higher pay if they followed him to Montana. The players made Griffith manager at the ripe age of 22 and moved themselves to Missoula. It was a foreshadowing of things to come.

Mining towns in the 1890s were frontier associations of the worst kind, lawless and untamed, where men found entertainment where they could and women only rarely. Baseball was a welcome diversion and the new professional players were welcomed enthusiastically. Griffith described the atmosphere as "scandalous." There was "women, whiskey, wide-open gambling, everything. But what money," he allowed.[25] The pay was often gathered in saloons where a hat was passed, but more money was raised for the ballplayers in Missoula than in Tacoma. Griffith continued to work his way back to form, winning wherever he pitched.

Griffith, no stranger to tall tales, told one about his catcher in Missoula who let a ball get away and roll to the backstop at a key moment in a game. The crowd of miners behind home plate drew guns and told the young catcher it might be wise to take better care of the ball in the future. The wild risks of life on this particular frontier were more than some of the players could handle.

Griffith himself returned to the Pacific coast to play for Oakland of the Pacific Coast League in 1893. Salary issues again intervened and ownership wasn't able to meet payroll consistently. Griffith was at the heart of labor unrest and the team refused to play, sitting down in the infield. A large and rowdy crowd that had paid good money to see a game, however, was not impressed. The tensions were mitigated by a member of the press who explained the situation to the crowd. They broke into applause and Griffith led the players off the field to cheers.

While in the west Griffith developed and honed his showmanship, a trait that he would use with skill throughout his life. In San Francisco Griffith developed an appreciation for players and others who could entertain a crowd. Griffith himself was famous for his saloon acts and swore that he sang for his money during the most desperate times during his western swing.

In the Bay Area one of Griffith's team mates was Joe Cantillon, known during his long career as "Pongo Joe."[26] As a player Cantillon was an adept fielder who could not hit well enough for a professional career. For Griffith and Washington baseball, Cantillon was like a stray who, once fed, continued to show up at the door until he was there for good. This time out both Cantillon and Griffith went bust on the same team.

With the baseball payday an uncertainty, the youthful friends were forced to supplement their funds by performing in bars in parts of San Francisco called the Barbary Coast. In the skit the two men performed, Griffith played a Native American and Cantillon a cowboy, and together they pulled off an act three times a night whereby Cantillon filled Griffith with lead to the guffaws of the barroom crowd.

Similar to what was common for fans in major and minor league ballparks in the day, barroom crowds showered the two performers with vegetables and eggs, although enough gold got thrown their way for Griffith to head back east. Although the shenanigans earned Griffith a reputation as one of the more colorful players around, he still had one of his best seasons while in the Oakland area, with 30 wins and 18 losses. It was that record that drew attention from National League scouts back east.

Griffith had dealt with the owner of the Chicago team in the National League, Jim Hart, while in the Western Association and he convinced Hart to give him a tryout late in 1893. Griffith pitched in four games for the Colts at the end of the 1893 season and while he was not overwhelming, he impressed Hart enough that the owner signed Griffith for the 1894 season. Clark Griffith had found his way to the major leagues and would play for one of the greatest ballplayers of his era.

CHAPTER 2

Playing for Cap Anson's
Chicago Colts

In 1871—two years after Clark Griffith was born—18-year-old Adrian "Cap" Anson set out from Des Moines, Iowa, for Rockford, Illinois, where he would play his first game of professional baseball in a league similar to the one where Griffith got his start. Anson was beginning a career in baseball that would span more than a quarter century. Only a small part of that career would affect a young Clark Griffith, but Anson would give the young pitcher his first success in the major leagues.

Anson's career took him to the Hall of Fame as the most accomplished hitter to play the game in the nineteenth century. Anson's most memorable years in his early career were with the Philadelphia Athletics of the National Association, the first professional league. He returned to the Midwest in 1876 as part of a historic raid on Boston and Philadelphia teams by William Hulbert, a powerful coal merchant who was out to clean up the game and build a championship team in his home town of Chicago. Anson was one of two keys to the raid of eastern talent. The first was Albert Goodwill Spalding, who helped Hulbert organize the new venture.[1]

Hulbert felt that the National Association was played for the financial benefit of east coast owners. His careful procurement of the best and most honorable players in the game shifted the axis of power and gave Chicago its first say in how the game was played. It also produced one of the most powerful lineups in the early history of the game as the White Stockings outscored their opponents in 1876 by an average of five runs per game.

Hulbert's reorganization of the league created a new entity called the National League that survives to this day as the senior circuit. Cap Anson was only 24 years old when he joined Hulbert's White Stockings, and he was one of the seminal figures in establishing the league. He played out the rest of his professional career for Chicago teams, retiring only in 1897 after a 21-year span that saw a remarkable evolution in how the early game was played.

Anson's first manager in Chicago was Spalding, who had jumped from Boston and with whom he had traveled around the globe to popularize the game the year before. Spalding as much as anyone helped standardize the game and the equipment with which it was played.

Spalding and Anson were important supports for Hulbert's efforts to move professional baseball away from the gambling scandals that rocked it in the 1870s, and many of their innovations helped bring the game forward, where it captured the popular imagination of a nation emerging from war and finding a new affluence.

Betting pools were a constant threat to the game and even as late as 1895 gamblers were openly offering bribes to Chicago players like Bill Dahlen who reported their propositions to Anson.

Anson's temper was famous and he had no patience with those who would bring the game down. But Dahlen's account of one episode showed at least one polite exchange where Anson simply escorted the gamblers from the clubhouse and refused their bribes. Anson had no time for throwing games, even when his worst team was struggling. Whatever might be said of him, he fostered the game at its highest level of competition.

During his prime, the White Stockings were a feared team in the National League. After winning the 1876 championship under Anson, they came back in 1880, '81, and '82 to win the league three straight years. They won it all again in 1885 and '86 to establish a unique dominance.

Anson's reputation has been marred in the modern era by a charge that he was not only a notable racist, but one who played a key role in maintaining segregated conditions in the early game. Clark Griffith's legacy has also been examined in light of his role with regards to maintaining segregation of the game, but Anson's role leaves no ambiguity.

In 1883, when rules for racial composition of teams were still fluid, Cap Anson refused to take the field against a Toledo team that used an African-American catcher, Moses Walker. Walker was a college-educated player who had attended Oberlin College and the University of Michigan Law School. Although Walker was physically not able to play in the game scheduled for August 10, 1883, Anson was loudly demonstrative about his unwillingness to share the field with an African American.[2]

The manager of the Toledo team, who had to that point been willing to bench a disabled Walker, became so irked by Anson's behavior that he inserted Walker into the game in the outfield. As he watched the substitution, Anson yelled so that all in the stadium could hear — he was known for a booming voice — that he was taking his team off the field, shouting insults at everyone.

When the Toledo officials informed Anson that his team would lose their half of the gate, Anson's high morality vanished. He played the game but let everyone within earshot know his attitudes.

Cap Anson was the antithesis of Clark Griffith as a player. He was a large man, standing 6 feet tall and weighing 225 pounds. He used his size and strength to become the most accomplished offensive player of his era. When Clark Griffith encountered Anson at the beginning of the 1894 season, the senior ballplayer was known simply as the "Grand Old Man" of the sport.[3] Griffith was only 24, and playing for Cap Anson had to be an honor for the young man who had been singing for his supper in San Francisco all too often.

Griffith spent his first year with the Colts proving himself, but with the team on the downturn, there was plenty of room for Griff to excel. The Chicago Colts were referred to more commonly as "Anson's Colts," at least in the newspaper accounts in the *Tribune*. It was a tribute to the legend and stature of the man, but by 1894 Cap Anson was thought by most to be nearing the end of his career. He was 42 years of age and the only more elder statesman had been future Hall of Fame player Jim O'Rourke, who played his last season in 1893 at the age of 43. Anson was clearly slowing and his numbers were dropping off, but he remained one of the better hitters in the National League and hit cleanup in the Chicago Colts attack.

Jim Hart was the owner of the Chicago Colts who brought Clark Griffith to Chicago. Hart was not overly fond of Cap Anson and considered the older man well past his prime. He encouraged Anson to retire, but the old first baseman would have none of it, and the two men were constantly at odds over the team.

The Players League disruptions that began in 1890 took a toll on Chicago baseball. The Chicago Pirates represented the Windy City in the new league and boasted Charlie Comiskey at first base, and Hugh Duffy and Jimmy Ryan in the outfield. Ryan and Duffy had been stars for the White Stockings in 1889, and Comiskey's team included several other players who jumped ship from Anson's club. Silver King and Mark Baldwin gave the Pirates a formidable mound duo, and the team was a legitimate contender for the affections of the Chicago fan base, finishing fourth in the league.

The labor strife arose from the frustrations that players felt with a plethora of issues in the game. But one grievance specific to Chicago was the monopoly Anson possessed as the manager of the only team representing the city and his unduly stern demeanor regarding his players. For all of the real issues, economic and personal, that led to the formation of the league, it failed financially. When it did, the National League was once again the only game in town. Player salaries once again took a downturn and strife between managers and players escalated.

In 1892 Cap Anson had his worst season, batting .272, one of only three times in his long career that he finished below .300. The anemic offense resulted in the collapse of the team and they finished seventh in the new 12-team alignment of the National League in 1892.

There were personal problems for Anson who suffered the death of his infant son, and team owner Jim Hart had little sympathy for Anson's personal position. Anson was a tough task master with a fiery temper to match what had once been his sandy red hair. He seldom cut any slack for his players, and Hart was not willing to show Anson any better treatment. Hart was almost always on the side of the players and it undermined Anson at every turn.

Team discipline became an open sore for the team and their old-school manager. Griffith's reputation as a labor radical did not make for a long honeymoon with his new boss. Anson was a throwback to earlier days both as a manager and player. Even in 1894 he still refused to wear a glove in the field. Professional ballplayers originally had played bare-handed, but after A.G. Spalding began the mass production of gloves for players, they became commonplace and by 1892, Anson was one of the few who continued to play without one, to the chagrin of fans and his teammates.

Anson was more worried about the more superficial aspects of the player's wardrobe both on the field and off. As part of the mindset that professional baseball players were not rowdies or roughnecks, Anson insisted that his players represent themselves as gentlemen at every opportunity. The team sported colorful uniforms, and they went in style, staying at the best hotels wherever they played. Players were required to wear tuxedos for dinner and wore bathrobes in the locker room. Their uniforms were blousy, ruffled pantaloons and they traveled in formal open carriages to and from the stadium.

The players were not enthusiastic about the carriages as they left them targets for harassment when the team wasn't winning. Fans often threw eggs, tomatoes and other vegetables at players on the field in the nineteenth century, and riding in posh open carriages was an invitation to every hooligan with a good arm.

These superficial accoutrements were in stark contrast to the locker rooms and other accommodations that players enjoyed. Teams other than the Colts stayed in more modest hotels. As late as 1897, Bill Felber reported of the champion Boston Beaneaters, "ball clubs did not necessarily lodge in the city's finest hostelries."[4] Anson always insisted on the best hotel in town, though even in those cases it might mean sharing a single bathroom for all the rooms.

Clubhouses were modest affairs that did not have showers. While they were still in the league, the Washington clubhouse provided nothing more than a barrel set in the floor for players to bathe in. There was considerable room for the sport of baseball to grow, and important changes were afoot that would affect Clark Griffith's career in the big leagues.

To start the 1893 season the pitching configuration on the field was radically altered. Prior to then the pitcher had stood in a box and was required to keep his foot on the back line some 55 feet, six inches from home plate. Newspaper accounts recorded the pitcher as "being in the box," in the same way that they are now said to be "on the mound." The new rules did not bring the mound into play, but made the plate out of rubber and positioned it at 60 feet, six inches, the modern distance.

Adding five feet between hitter and pitcher took considerable heat off the offerings of pitchers. The change resulted in an offensive surge as pitchers like Colts ace Bill Hutchinson lost zip from their fastballs. The additional footage also forced older pitchers to adjust their overall delivery, and such changes came at a point in their careers when it wasn't easy to teach old muscles new tricks.

Hutchinson was just one of the Chicago pitchers who were getting older and having problems with the changes in the game. He and Willie McGill were the only two prominent pitchers from the 1893 team to return for one last try, and only the Yale-educated Hutchinson stuck it out. He had been pitching for Anson since 1889. In 1890 he threw

Clark Griffith was an unproven talent as a pitcher in 1894 (National Baseball Hall of Fame Library).

an astounding 603 innings over 66 starts and led the league in wins with 41. He remained the preeminent National League pitcher until the new pitching rules went into effect.

Using only three starters and pitching them exhaustively was just one of many "old school" traits Anson employed. His overuse of his staff held potential peril for Clark Griffith, just starting his career with what may have been one of the worst managers with whom he could have hooked up. Anson had burned Hutchison out by the 1894 season and his last full year was a very ineffective '95 season that only proved how spent he was.

The other pitcher of note to start the 1894 season was Adonis Terry, who had enjoyed success earlier in his career with Brooklyn until sidelined with a bad arm. Coming back to pitch for Anson may not have done much to extend his career either. Despite the proven pitchers, the *Chicago Tribune* panned Anson's Colts at the beginning of the season, saying that they were too young to compete with the top teams and their veteran talent.

No doubt the *Tribune* had the young Griffith in mind when worried about the unproven talent. But in the field the Colts had two fine players behind Griffith in shortstop Bill Dahlen and right fielder Jimmy Ryan, both of whom were veterans. Neither man had good relations with Anson.

Cap Anson's old-school philosophy was well-suited to the pitching style of Clark Griffith, learned from the great master of endurance himself, Hoss Radbourn. At the beginning of each game, the Colts catcher would take the ball from the umpire and throw it to Cap Anson, who would run it across the surface of the grass and flip it to Dahlen, who would rub it into the infield dirt before tossing it to Griffith. Griffith would administer Radbourn's favorite trick, running the ball across his spikes to add grooves to the surface that allowed for a better grip and aerodynamic features to further baffle the batter.[5]

Clark Griffith added a new weapon to his arsenal in 1894, discovering something akin to the screwball. According to Shirley Povich, Griffith started throwing the pitch after the regular season in 1893 when he was part of a touring team composed largely of the Boston champions. It was a curveball with a different grip that caused the pitch to break in on right-handed hitters and away from the lefties.[6] Griffith said that the pitch was the same used by Christy Mathewson, but that the famous Giants hurler achieved a much sharper break.

Griffith needed a new pitch to confront the offensive explosion that the new pitching rules instigated. Anson's Colts started the 1894 season slowly, their offense unable to gain the advantage others were enjoying. But Dahlen and the others got hot as the season progressed, and the shortstop had a 42-game hitting streak. Anson had a great year at the plate as well, hitting .388, one that saw the Colts' team average spike to .313, fourth in the league behind

Philadelphia, Baltimore and Boston, each of which scored more than nine runs per game.

Adrian Anson played only 87 games in 1894, but proved that he could still perform at the professional level even at 42. In one August game in 1894 the Colts offense pounded the lowly St. Louis Browns for 26 runs, and 34 runs were scored in the 26–8 victory. The total that day was not uncommon. Hugh Duffy, playing for the Boston Beaneaters now, had the highest average ever recorded that year, posting a .440 mark. Duffy led the league with 18 homers and 51 doubles.

Swimming against the incredible offensive tide, Clark Griffith's ERA for the season was 4.92, well behind that of the league leader, Amos Rusie at 2.78.[7] Griffith was the best that the Colts had, though, and he won 21 games. It started a run of six consecutive years that Griffith won 20 or more games. His earned run average was understood more easily given that only two teams posted an ERA for the season below five runs per game.

With Griffith's success on the mound, Anson's misgivings over Griffith's short stature were overcome. Anson preferred hard throwers like Clarkson and believed initially that Griffith could not succeed at 5 feet 6 inches, especially in the new pitching environment of 1894.

Griffith proved Anson wrong and quickly the older man came to admire the younger man, seeing much of his competitive zeal in Griffith, despite their frequent disagreements as manager and player. The Colts continued their mediocre run but Anson's inability to find anyone more skilled than Griffith left the two men at an unhappy draw. They needed each other and learned to make the best of it.

The "old man of the game" introduced Griffith to the rough-and-tumble style of play that predominated during Anson's early years and which he employed until he retired. He would trip players as they rounded the first base bag, shout all manner of insults at the other team, and use whatever means he thought reasonable to intimidate the umpires and his competitors. Griffith was a quick study of Anson's guile and refined his skills.

Anson's old-school approach diminished the Colts in important ways. Teams like the Baltimore Orioles with the young John McGraw began to employ a new brand of baseball. The Orioles employed numerous innovations in how the game was played in the mid–1890s. The most effective was the double steal, where the player on first stole second and, when the catcher threw down to second, the player on third took off for home plate. They also introduced the sacrifice bunt and used the pitcher to cover the first base bag when the first baseman ranged too far for a ground ball.

Charlie Comiskey is given credit for being the initial first baseman to play off the bag and behind the runner. First basemen had served to receive the ball only. As Clark Griffith described it years later, "The first baseman was only a basket. That is, he stood glued to the bag and held out his hands to catch any balls thrown at him. He never thought of moving away from his position. Comiskey changed all that. He made it a fielding position."[8]

Comiskey was the first to play away from the bag and run toward it to catch the infielders' throws. Others took his lead, and great first basemen like Hal Chase made innovations until the infield play of the first baseman began to look increasingly like that of the modern game.

Anson was not impressed with changes in the game and was slow to adjust to them or adopt them. The one change that caused the most trouble for the Chicago Colts was the sophistication of signs used between coaches and players on the field, and between catcher and pitcher. As teams became more adept at stealing signs, it became an increasingly important factor. Anson continued with a simple set of signs that were often pilfered along with second base.

As Anson became increasingly isolated in his old-school world, Griffith appeared to his peers as a polar opposite. Anson's approach was conservative to the point of stodgy. He was the consummate company man with seemingly little respect for players. In contrast, Griffith was the labor radical, known for taking leadership roles in numerous labor disruptions on the west coast. Griff's inclination to side with labor and foment dissent persisted throughout his time with the Colts.[9] Anson was a conservative politically, so it was clear that oil and water were eventually going to go their separate ways.

The only shenanigan in which Anson ever participated was gambling, though of the legal variety. He was forever making loud wagers, many of which he lost. He always bet in favor of his team, however. The bets were preceded by loud predictions that they would contend. Each year the Colts cost Anson significant sums of money from the wagers he made, lost, but always paid. One insignificant wager he would win.

Construction of the Washington Monument began in 1848 and took many years to complete, but in 1884 it was finished and it served increasingly as an attraction for visitors to the city, not the least of which were touring ball players. By 1894 there were numerous discussions about whether anyone could catch a baseball thrown from its top. Opinions varied as to whether the ball would burrow deep in the ground upon landing or be an easy catch for someone standing below. Cap Anson was of the opinion that it was a "can of corn" and had been arguing the point at the Arlington Hotel in Washington with desk clerk H.P. Burney for years.

Griffith — in the same spirit that led him to play an Indian in bars on the west coast — decided to settle the issue with a simple test. Anson was on leave to attend to his seriously ill father in Iowa. Griffith and the team's two catchers, along with other team members and press, went to the monument on August 25, 1894. Burney and several others from the hotel staff were in attendance along with the players who gathered at the foot of the monument while the two pitchers, Hutchison and Griffith, ascended — by elevator — to the top window of the obelisk, more than 500 feet from the ground.

Pop Schriver, the catcher, set up below to catch the ball and Griffith gave it the first heave — being careful to get it far enough out so that it did not strike the side of the monument as it angled outward toward the base of the edifice below. Schriver did not catch the first ball and may have been fearful of the dire predictions of its force. When the ball bounced harmlessly on the ground a few feet from where he was standing, he shouted for another try, and on the second toss from Griffith, Schriver settled under the ball and made the catch to the delight of all in attendance and setting off a furor as word spread of the feat.[10]

It was the most notable success of the season. The Colts ended the 1894 season with 57 wins against 85 losses, good for only eighth place in the 12-team National League. The pitching let the team down as did the defense as they allowed almost eight runs per game, more than all but Washington and Cincinnati.

It was not Anson's overuse of the staff as he employed eight different starting pitchers during the season. Both Terry and Hutchison were spent, however, and Clark Griffith was the best that Anson sent to the mound in 1894, winning 21 games.

The fortunes of Anson's Colts revived in 1895 and '96. Those two seasons were the high points for the Chicago Colts during Griffith's playing days for Anson and a last hurrah for the captain. They also represent two of the best years of Clark Griffith's career as a player.

The Colts finished in fourth place in 1895 and Clark Griffith increasingly became a team leader. He won key games early in the season that saw the team rise to third place only to hit a buzz saw in the Baltimore Orioles. But Griff beat the Orioles in an important mid-season game to provide hope that Anson's club had enough to compete at the higher level.

Griff's leadership brought him into sharper disagreement with his manager. It also made his political leanings an issue that almost led to a fight with his "conservative" catcher during one game. As Griffith and catcher Mal Kittridge took the field one day, their disagreement over presidential candidates boiled over. Griffith was a William Jennings Bryan man and his political discussions about the nature of the looming presidential race reached a fever pitch that outshone their competitive edge, at least during one game. Griffith stood on the mound yelling at his catcher behind the plate who was also standing and yelling back. No blows were thrown, but the two men scowled and grumbled at one another throughout the game.

Verbal heat was clearly part of Griffith's nature, but it was also essential to his presence in the game. His bantam posturing on the mound was as important as anything he put on the ball. Talking to his catcher about political events was made easier because he was used to bantering back and forth with the hitters from the mound. It is easy to understand just how important his psychological war with the hitter was when you examine the statistical tracks of his "stuff." In the early years of his pitching career he annually walked more batters than he struck out, and his strikeouts were certainly one of the more humble statistics throughout his career.

While Griffith may have been perceived as quite different in important ways from Anson, in one area he was a quick study, taking in all that the "old man of the game" could teach. When it came to artful use of profanity or other guile applied to raise the ire of batters in key situations, Griff took his cue from Anson, who was known as a master. On the mound Griffith pitched with measured velocity, but setting up each pitch was the key.

Today's pitchers set up each pitch with a sophisticated knowledge of how the batter's mind works. In 1896 the strategy was quite different. If the hitter was impatient or the situation in the game raised the fever pitch for the batter waiting at the plate, Griffith was a man of leisure, taking his time and even taunting the batter until he had him ready to swing out of his shoes.

They mostly did. He was equally willing to work quickly and was known to "quick pitch" the same batter who had turned his back to urge the umpire to intervene and end the long delays being employed by Griffith. It was this style of play championed by Griffith even in his earliest playing days that earned him the nickname the "Old Fox." Shirley Povich records him gaining the name as early as the 1894 season.[11] According to Povich, Hugh Fullerton said of Griffith during his playing days, "For brains, cunning and ability to mix them all up, Griff was the best."[12]

Another young player making a name for himself in the mid 1890s was John McGraw, who broke in with Baltimore as an 18-year-old in 1891. Anson had seen McGraw play in the minors and liked him, but he was too small by the standards Anson used to judge talent. McGraw became the backbone of Baltimore Orioles teams that won pennants in 1894, '95, and '96. He was a constant source of trouble for Clark Griffith.

When McGraw batted he crowded the plate, and for a pitcher like Griffith who relied on control and placement, giving up any part of the plate to the hitter came at a cost. McGraw was not above sticking his front knee out and taking one for the team as well, and that irked Griffith even more. A well-reported confrontation between McGraw and Griffith affected how the game was played in a key way.

McGraw had remarkable bat control, much as Griffith had control of his unexceptional repertoire. McGraw could foul off Griffith's slow stuff without breaking a sweat. In 1894 the foul ball was not counted as a strike. That year McGraw is alleged to have fouled off so many pitches against Griffith in a game that it held up play for some time. As Griffith recounted the tale in later years, the number of minutes always grew until it reached its limit — fifteen minutes — in the last telling to Shirley Povich. Povich and Griffith claimed that the epic drama between McGraw and the Old Fox led to a rule change as pressure to count foul balls as strikes became overwhelming that year and the rule change was adopted in the National League in 1901, in the American League in 1903. In truth, such prolonged confrontations were relatively commonplace and the one between Griffith and McGraw had no direct casual relationship to the rule change.

Joe Cantillon came to the fore again in Griffith's career and helped to roil the competitive juices that flowed between Griffith and McGraw early as the mid 1890s. Cantillon started a new career as an umpire with Ban Johnson's Western Association in 1895 and moved over to the National League in one of Clark Griffith's favorite stories from his playing days.[13] In this instance McGraw had chewed on umpire Cantillon verbally from the beginning of a game between Anson's Colts and McGraw's championship Baltimore nine.

As the only umpire working the game, Cantillon stood behind the pitcher's box and the pitcher himself— Griffith in this instance. McGraw was on first when Cantillon — standing quietly behind the pitcher — instructed Griffith to pick McGraw off first base. Griffith mimed a move to the plate, but turned and threw to first where McGraw was caught off the bag and tagged out.

McGraw said the move was clearly a balk and should be called as such. But Cantillon refused to hear him. However, when Griffith tried the same move an inning later, Cantillon upheld the balk, letting McGraw know the call the prior inning had been directed personally at him, which only served to further infuriate McGraw.

In 1896 the Colts were once again strong, but Cap Anson was playing a diminishing role with the team as Clark Griffith's became more prominent. In the middle of the 1895 season an incident occurred when Anson took himself out of the game, but put Walter Thornton, a pitcher, into the game to play first base in his stead. Clark Griffith was pitching and was furious that the old man had refused to insert a better player, Tim Donahue, into the game.

Griffith convinced Donahue to start the next inning at first base and when Anson noticed, a shouting match broke out between the two men. Anson yelled to Griffith, "I'm running this club."[14] Anson sent Donahue from the game, but the dustup was indicative of the directions in which the two players were headed.

To start the 1896 season, Anson was sick and allowed George Decker to play first base. The team was winning and drawing good crowds while their captain recuperated. An oft-repeated tale occurred in 1896 where Griffith used his remarkable control — both of his temper and his pitches — to foil the opposition.

The batter was Bill Nash of the Phillies, who was put out both by the pace at which Griff pitched and the balls and strikes being called by the umpire. When Nash turned to argue with the umpire, he continued to stand in the batter's box, but with his back to Griffith and his bat on his shoulders. Griffith threw from the box and the ball struck Nash's bat and rolled into the infield, where Griffith scooped it up and threw to first for the out.[15]

Such smart play was not the rule of the day for the Colts, who slipped into ninth place by mid-summer, and only a strong surge in the last six weeks of the season got them back to fifth place. Clark Griffith was once again the best pitcher on a bad staff, poorly managed by Anson. The discipline on the team was so bad that Griffith left the city of Chicago and the Colts team before the end of the season. He returned to his home in Normal, Illinois, and the event only lost its significance when the last two series of the season were not played because of rain.[16]

The situation was worse with Bill Dahlen when the shortstop was put off the train in the middle of the night and suspended by Anson for the last weeks of the season. He missed no games, but it further exacerbated the rift between the Chicago players and their manager. The rift did not bode well for the 1897, season which proved to be Anson's last. The season started with Griffith holding out for a larger contract. Salaries in the National League continued to fall as the league tightened its monopolistic grip on the sport.

As the best pitcher the team had, Clark Griffith had the Colts by the short hairs, but he played hardball with John Hart and missed pitching the season opener when their contract talks lagged. The difference, according to David Fleitz's book on Cap Anson, was a mere $100.[17] The real difference had more to do with who was running the team, Griffith or Anson. When Opening Day festivities were cancelled because of rain, Griffith and Hart settled in time for Griff to pitch the first game on May 4.

The Colts' play during the last years under Cap Anson was remarkably consistent. The team did not have enough pitching to contend in any season, and Clark Griffith was the workhorse and ace of the staff. Although in 1897 the Colts employed eight other starters and spread the work around, Danny Friend and Nixey Callahan were the only ones that were effective. The team dropped off to their worst finish since 1894 — Griff's first season. Anson managed to log 424 at bats and his numbers were respectable, but at 45 years of age, he was slower than ever. The team finished ninth in the 12-team league.

The worst aspect of that final season was that it left Anson wanting to go out a winner. It took all of the cajoling and wheedling that his old friend A.J. Spalding could do to convince the old man to retire. Even the next year in February, Anson was still thinking of making one more go of it, but he finally hung up his cleats.

The Chicago press, who had always referred to the team not as the Chicago Colts but Anson's Colts, was at a loss. They refused to call the team by the same name and finally settled on the "Orphans" because they were without their longtime leader Anson. They may have been a team cut adrift, but they played better without their old captain in 1898. Clark Griffith had his best season ever, leading the National League with a 1.88 ERA, and one of his best strikeout-to-walks ratio of 97 strikeouts to 64 bases on balls.

With many of the same cast of characters, Bill Dahlen, Jimmy Ryan, and Bill Lange, the Orphans finished in fourth in the National League, 21 games over .500. Nixey Callahan had an excellent season as a 24-year-old and Walter Thornton became a reasonable third starter. The Orphans had the strongest rotation in Griffith's association with the team. Without Anson, the lineup was a bit anemic, however. Bill Everitt took over at first base and hit .319, but with little power.

Tom Burns was the manager, and he had all of the discipline problems that Anson had suffered through as owner Hart continued to support the players in every way except at the pay window. The team slumped in Griffith's last two seasons with Chicago's National League team. But changes were afoot, and when Clark Griffith was elected vice-president of the Baseball Players Protective Association in 1898, historic forces were aligning. The Baseball Players Proactive Association was an anemic players union officially headed by Charles Zimmer as president and Hughie Jennings as secretary.[18] The two men were easily influenced by Griff, the real labor radical and strongest influence on its directions.

From his post within the players union Clark Griffith would have as much influence on the game he loved as any moment he enjoyed in the pitcher's box in Chicago. The young man with all the bluster was about to meet his moment with destiny.

TABLE 1-1. CLARK GRIFFITH PITCHING
STATISTICS, 1893–1900 (NATIONAL LEAGUE)

Year	Team	Games	Wins	Losses	ERA	Innings	Strikeouts	Walks
1893	Chicago	4	1	2	5.03	19.2	9	5
1894	Chicago	36	21	14	4.92	261.1	71	85
1895	Chicago	42	26	14	3.93	353.0	79	91

Year	Team	Games	Wins	Losses	ERA	Innings	Strikeouts	Walks
1896	Chicago	36	23	11	3.54	317.2	81	70
1897	Chicago	41	21	18	3.72	343.2	102	86
1898	Chicago	38	24	10	1.88	325.2	97	64
1899	Chicago	38	22	14	2.79	319.2	73	65
1900	Chicago	30	14	13	3.05	248.0	61	51
Totals		265	152	96	3.40	2188.2	573	517

SOURCE: Baseball Reference.com

Chapter 3

Radical Beginnings of the American League

The birth of the American League in 1901 has been described at length and there is no controversy or disputation about the primary force behind its origin. It was Ban Johnson's "vision for the future of baseball" that guided the making of the new league, forming it out of the labor and management disputes swirling around a sport that was growing in popularity as the population of the nation was expanding.[1] There was room and indeed a need for baseball to extend beyond its early foundations to a wider fan base. The American League became the vehicle for one of the first and most important expansions of the game in the twentieth century.

Ban Johnson crafted, from the old Western League that he had led for six years, a second major league, but he had a talented supporting cast that included many of the best minds in the game at the time, Charlie Comiskey, Clark Griffith, Connie Mack, and financier Charles Somers.

It was as simple as Johnson renaming the Western League in 1900, calling it the American League in a declaration of intent. But no one was willing to grant it "major league" status until the requisite talent was found to take the level of competition between those first eight teams up a notch. To lure the talent away from the existing National League teams took money. Getting them to commit to and believe in the fledging league was a dicey business and it took the concerted efforts of the men who gathered to plot it as early as 1899.

Griffith, Somers, Mack and the rest each brought a unique talent or resource to the task, and it is doubtful that it would have succeeded without the coordinated work of them all. As with Clark Griffith, baseball was an important part of Ban Johnson's early life. Both men played the game in adolescence, but unlike Griffith, Ban Johnson was born into an upper middle class, urbane existence Griffith would not experience for decades. Both Johnson's parents were educated at Oberlin College in Ohio and wanted a professional career for their son. Though he played baseball in college, they discouraged him from pursuing the game further.

His parents preferred that he pursue a career in the law, but Johnson refused and came up with the best compromise he could: sports writing. He showed early acumen for the writing life and became sports editor for the *Cincinnati Commercial-Gazette*. No doubt conscious of his parents' moral standards, an early focus for Johnson was the reputation of the game as an affair for rowdies and brawlers.

Baseball was plagued in the first decades after the Civil War with widespread betting on the outcome of games and generally rough behavior by both players and fans. Umpires were frequently shouted down with profanity and bullied into changing calls. The raucous tenor of games led some to condemn the sport, but the more serious charge was that wagering was leading to games that were played with pre-determined outcomes.

In 1881 the *New York Times* offered that baseball was a sport "unworthy of men and it is now, in its fully developed state, unworthy of gentlemen."[2] Spalding and Hulbert had done much to move the game away from its raw beginnings, but Ban Johnson made further progress in upgrading its image when he assumed the part-time position as the president of the Western League late in 1893. Johnson took over a league that was in disarray, its season suspended at the beginning of 1893 as teams moved about in search of paying markets. But Johnson got commitments from the league's owners that they would support his efforts to revamp the league and clean up its reputation by limiting rowdy behavior from fans and players.[3]

The Western League operated in burgeoning cities including Detroit, Grand Rapids, Indianapolis, Kansas City, Milwaukee, Minneapolis, Sioux City and Toledo. The highest level of professional baseball at the time was played in the National League, 12-team aggregation based in the largest eastern cities, but extending as far west as Chicago and St. Louis. The most prominent rival to the National League had been the American Association, which partially merged into the NL when that senior circuit became a twelve-team league in 1891.

One of the enduring problems for the Western League and Ban Johnson was the raiding of the league by National League teams. John Brush was the owner of the Western League Indianapolis franchise as well as the National League Cincinnati team. Brush used the Indianapolis team as a minor league farm team for his National League franchise, shuttling players to maximize his chances to win the National League pennant. However, he was not above moving players down to Indianapolis to improve that team if Cincinnati was floundering.

Ban Johnson disliked Brush for his less than honorable dealings in acquiring the Cincinnati franchise in 1890. Johnson used his editorial capacity in the Cincinnati sports pages to call Brush out. Brush had not wanted Ban Johnson as the president of the Western League from the beginning, but was convinced that is was better to have him running the league than writing acid columns about him in the newspaper. But when Johnson robbed Brush of his popular manager Charlie Comiskey, the relationship between the two men was irrevocably rent until near the end of Brush's life.

Johnson offered Comiskey the opportunity to buy into and operate the St. Paul, Minnesota, franchise that was moving from Sioux City, Iowa, where it had failed in the run up to the 1893 season.[4] Brush and Johnson would become determined enemies, but the friendship between Ban Johnson and Charlie Comiskey was the first building block of the American League.

The common link between Ban Johnson and Clark Griffith was Charles Comiskey, who finished his playing career as the player-manager for John Brush's Cincinnati Reds in 1894 and was known as the "Old Roman." Comiskey's career as a player ended with the 1894 season. Comiskey began his playing career on the sandlots of Chicago and from there became one of the finest first basemen in the early game. Although content to take a team to Minnesota, his aim was to find a way to assume a similar role with a team in his home town, but that would come later.

Comiskey and Ban Johnson endured John Brush's shenanigans throughout the 1890s as Brush won the Western League pennants in 1895, 1897, and 1899. Brush continued to succeed due largely to his ability to move players between his two teams. But the process of "farming" players, whereby the National League teams bought a player from franchises in the Western and other leagues for only $500, wrought havoc on teams. The St. Paul franchise of Charles Comiskey was particularly hard hit, and Brush's reputation as one of the chief purveyors did nothing to endear him to Comiskey.

The simmering feud between the Western League owners and John Brush and the National League boiled throughout the last decade of the nineteenth century and came to a head in 1900. Clark Griffith assumed a role in the brewing drama when he was named the vice president of the National League players' association known as the Baseball Players' Protective Association. Charles "Chief" Zimmer, respected by all as the catcher for the Cleveland Spiders, was the president of the association. But Clark Griffith was the aggressive voice in group discussions, much as he was on the field.

The feud between baseball team owners and players has forever been about the issues of money and control. It was no less so in 1899 and 1900 as the first century of baseball ended. The players had been underpaid and disgruntled after losing the labor struggle known as the Brotherhood Wars that extended from 1890 through the 1891 season.

The Brotherhood of Professional Baseball Players was formed in 1885 by a player and lawyer, John Montgomery Ward. It was not until 1890, however, that the organization brought their concerns about wages and the reserve clause — that bound a player to one team — to a head.

In 1889 the Brotherhood founded the Players League as a rival to the National League. During the 1890 season, this League fought a running battle against the National League's supremacy within the sport, but finally capitulated leading to a 12-team National League that still ruled the roost in 1900, its owners unchallenged in dictating the course of the game.

When he assumed a leadership role in the labor struggles of the 1890s, Clark Griffith was at the peak of his playing career and few players were able to cross the lines between management and players as well as "Griff." His leadership position with the players' association and his friendship with owners like Charlie Comiskey and James Hart in Chicago served as a crucial alliance for Ban Johnson.

Griffith seemed to have friendships without regard to status within the game. He would exploit those friendships as events in the National League were coming to a head, a fast-moving play of circumstance that would define the rest of Griffith's life. Griffith was just a few footsteps down a path that would make him a wealthy man and provide fame beyond anything he would know as a player.

In 1898 a fierce recession gripped the nation. Attendance fell in many of the National League cities that had been struggling to compete since the league expanded from eight to 12 teams in 1892. Falling revenues led to significant losses by numerous teams, and the league responded by dropping four of its teams at the end of the 1899 season. Washington, Baltimore, Cleveland and Louisville were dropped from the league, leaving an eight-team aggregation once again.

In that same year, Ban Johnson's Western League was joined by a new owner whose purse was not diminished by the recession. Charles Somers bought the Western League's Grand Rapids franchise during the 1898 season. He joined Charles Comiskey in giving Ban Johnson two dynamic owners, but it was Somers who provided the critical mass: the financial backing that was the key to moving the Western League forward into more direct competition with the National League.

Charles Somers was a hugely wealthy coal magnate from Ohio. He wanted to see professional baseball returned to his home town of Cleveland as much as Charles Comiskey wanted to relocate a second professional team to Chicago. Ban Johnson was the organizer behind those two powerfully motivated men. Somers was wealthy enough so that any time money was needed to oil the purchase of land in Boston or Philadelphia, to add a few thousand dollars to the salary offer to a player, he stepped into the breach to make it happen.

Comiskey became one of the initial wedges that Ban Johnson drove into the united front of the National League. The Old Roman had gained a commitment from James Hart, the owner of the Chicago Orphans, to allow a second team in the city, but Hart was certain that he was agreeing only to a "minor" league team. When it became clear that Ban Johnson's league would be in direct competition with the National League, Hart dug in his heels in opposition.

However, when Comiskey promised to locate the new team on the south side of town, close to the wretched smelling stock yards, Hart relented. Comiskey fielded his new American League team in Chicago in 1900, naming them the White Stockings for Hulbert and Spalding's first Chicago champions. The rest of the National League owners were less accommodating than Hart.

There were other baseball men who saw the contraction of the National League as an opportunity. Journalists, including the founder of *The Sporting News* A. H. Spink, along with the former Milwaukee owner Harry Quin, explored the idea of a new major league in September of 1899. They got encouragement from the National League owners — John Brush in particular — when they realized Ban Johnson's intentions.

It was ironic that James Hart's former manager, Cap Anson, became the point person around whom the interest in a rival second new league revolved. Anson wanted to follow the lead of Comiskey and others who parlayed long careers as successful players and managers into team ownership. Anson was named the president of the newly formed "American Association," but instead of trying to confront the National League in a fight for turf, Anson met with the National League owners.

Anson's problem was that he had firm commitments for only six cities in the new league. He needed two others, one of which would be Philadelphia. National League figures tried to help Anson beat Ban Johnson into key eastern cities where the American League's foothold was not yet certain.

Ban Johnson was aiming new franchises at Washington, Philadelphia, Baltimore, Cleveland, Detroit, Milwaukee, Chicago, and Buffalo. Cap Anson's group took aim at Philadelphia and Baltimore as the key battleground locations. Anson failed to deliver when his Philadelphia group fell apart, leaving the American Association with too few competitive locations with which to move forward.

As important as securing financial backing and playing fields in the best cities became, the real linchpin of any expansion of a professional sporting league was the players. Men of wealth cannot grant professional status to a group of players who have not proven themselves. In the second half of the twentieth century, both professional basketball and football expanded and formed new competing leagues, but the effort was facilitated necessarily by well-regarded players who jumped to the new league.

Clark Griffith was the catalyst for gaining reputable talent to commit to the emergent American League. After the formation of the Baseball Players' Protective Association, Ban Johnson approached the nascent union with proposals to address several of their more central concerns. Johnson promised the players that the newly formed American League would feature contracts that guaranteed: (1) suspensions no greater than ten days; (2) a reserve clause not to exceed three years; (3) medical expenses that paid for injuries related to play; (4) and finally, a bugaboo to this day, binding arbitration for player-management disputes.[5]

Before this offer — at the end of the 1900 season — Clark Griffith, the labor radical, instructed the Baseball Players' Protective Association membership not to sign new contracts until word came from the union. After getting remarkable unanimity from the players, a meeting was scheduled with the ownership of the National League, who would be meeting in December 1900. The goal for the players was to determine what the already established league was willing to offer before they contemplated any other moves.

The demands put to the National League ownership included the first and most important demand, a minimum salary of $3,000 that would provide a raise from the existing $2,400.[6] Equally important, however, were demands for an end to the cheap sale of players between minor and major leagues — the practice known as "farming," — and a limit on the reserve clause to three years, the same as provided by Ban Johnson.[7]

The annual National League ownership meetings were held that year in New York City. Johnson and two of his key conspirators prepared to travel to New York to meet with the National League ownership to get a response to their demands. Meanwhile, Ban Johnson, Connie Mack, and Charles Somers met in Philadelphia where Mack was working on obtaining property for a second team there.

Johnson had set forth several proposals of his own for the National League to consider concerning their relationship with the American League as it existed during the 1900 season and moving forward. Johnson was asking for parity between the two leagues but had gotten an icy response at every juncture so far. The decisive point became the labor negotiations. Griffith's group of labor radicals held all the cards for Ban Johnson and his wealthy cohorts.

Johnson, Comiskey and the American League's emerging ownership group waited in Philadelphia for word from Griffith about the players' meeting with the National League. If the National League acceded to the player demands, there would be no pool of disgruntled professional players ready to jump to Johnson's new league that promised better contract terms. If they refused to negotiate, then the game was on. Mack, Comiskey, Johnson and Somers then would swing into action to lock up sites for the new teams as soon as word came from Clark Griffith.

The owners set up a meeting between a sub-group of their members led not by their president, Nick Young, but by the more acerbic and confrontational A. H. Soden, president of the Boston Beaneaters. As Griffith set forth the players' position to the assembled owners, the scene was one of geniality. Yet no commitment was made to Griffith and the players. Rather, Soden agreed to present Griffith's proposal to the full ownership, gathered at a nearby hotel.

Griffith had reportedly been told going in by no less than Nick Young himself, "Son, they ain't gonna give you anything."[8] Griffith's group, perhaps knowing the outcome, adjourned to the hotel bar to wait for word from the owners. As they discussed the earlier proceedings over beer, Griffith noticed Soden making his way furtively through the crowded bar. He waved in a friendly manner and motioned for Soden to join them. The Boston owner assured Griffith that he had delivered the proposal to the owners and that they were talking it over even as the two men spoke.

Griffith claimed in later years that this was the crucial moment in the rebellion. Griffith could see the formal written petition containing the players' demands in Soden's inside coat pocket. He knew then that not only was Soden lying, but that the National League ownership had no intention to accede to their demands. He confronted Soden face-to-face in the bar, but to no avail, and the players left to draft a statement to the press.

Griffith called Ban Johnson at this point and, according to Shirley Povich, said, "Ban, there's going to be a new league."[9] After stiffing the union group, the next move by the National League ownership was to respond to Ban Johnson's group, standing by in Philly in hopes of having their own sit-down with the reigning baseball establishment. To the query from Johnson asking how long before the league would meet with them, the message came back that they could wait "until hell freezes over."[10]

There was no recourse to Ban Johnson and his band of revolutionaries. Griffith was dispatched to talk to his players, and Connie Mack, Comiskey, and Somers began the process of getting the best places to play baseball in the cities they had identified. Griffith enlisted his friend Joe Cantillon and together they began rounding up the names that would convince a curious public what they could expect from this new American League.

The raids began immediately. The most noteworthy player to join the new enterprise was Griffith himself. Comiskey and Ban Johnson promised Griffith that he would be the manager of the newly re-tooled Chicago White

Stockings. But Griffith had to do more than find players for his roster, he had seven other teams to work for as well.

The rosters of the American League were already filled with players who had come over from the Western League franchises, as well as from the four National League teams that had disbanded at the end of 1899. Now the hunt was on for the players with the most recognizable names, the kind that would convince fans that this new American League could provide a brand of baseball on par with its National League rivals.

It was a skeptical public, so Griffith encouraged Johnson to make a public announcement that the league was drafting 40 National League players. The American League brain trust had an actual target of 46 National League players that it sought commitments from, but Griffith assumed that if they could get 40, they would have enough name recognition for public credibility.

Ultimately, Griffith was selling the better contract terms that Ban Johnson was offering, telling the membership of his union that they needed to support the new league or have the National League forever dictate economic terms for their employment. He was nothing less than an early version of Marvin Miller telling his membership they had to hold firm.

The biggest of the early names to come over was Napoleon Lajoie. Lajoie was one of the top batsmen in the National League in 1900, just behind Honus Wagner in slugging and among the league leaders in every category. He played that season with the Philadelphia Phillies of the NL. Now, at Griffith's urging, he came on board with Connie Mack's new Philadelphia Athletics that were still hurriedly trying to find a ball field in which to play.

The National League ownership group filed an injunction to prevent Lajoie and two other players from joining Connie Mack's new team, however, and that became the early test of the new league's status. The hearing to determine where Lajoie would play was not scheduled until late in April of 1901. The issue before the judge was the reserve clause, and the legality of it would not be resolved conclusively for another 75 years. The Curt Flood case that challenged the issue also concerned a player's commitment to the Philadelphia Phillies. This time, however, Napoleon Lajoie took the field as the 1901 season began, happily playing for Connie Mack and his renegade American League team while the judges conferred and baseball awaited their decision.

Although Lajoie was the test case, the issue was mooted by the large number of commitments that Clark Griffith and his friend Joe Cantillon were getting from National League players in January. Griffith was in constant motion during the first three months of 1901, talking to players in their homes as he filled in the rosters of American League teams with well-known National League players. Just weeks after Griffith's travels ended in March, the new league began play, mission accomplished.

In later years Griffith told the tale of his travels during the coldest months of 1901 as he went back and forth across snowy New England, then down to Georgia and out west to Kansas City seeking word from players that they would play in the new league. The second big name Griffith signed was future Hall of Fame third baseman, Jimmy Collins, who had played for the famous Boston Beaneaters. Connie Mack called him the fastest player ever to set foot on a baseball field and he was regarded by many as the greatest third baseman to play the game.[11] He jumped to the Boston AL team — known then simply as the Americans.

Griffith added names like Billy Sullivan, Fielder Jones, and Sam Mertes to his own Chicago roster. Sullivan was one of the best young catchers in the NL, who had played with Boston the prior year, hitting eight home runs in only 238 at-bats. Jones came over from the Brooklyn Superbas where he had hit .310. Mertes had played with Griffith in Chicago for the Orphans. Together they typified the Griffith player: smart, quick players who were good defenders and aggressive on the base paths.

Aside from the players he chose for the new White Stockings team, Griffith was signing the best in the National League. And he took pleasure in raiding the owners who had been the biggest opponents of the league. For example, he got George "Candy" LaChance and Jake Stahl to jump from A. H. Soden's Boston Beaneaters to the American League.[12]

In the end he got a total of 39 players signed for the new league, a remarkable success considering the original target had been 40. Connie Mack and others brought along several players, and only one player refused to sign. He may have been the biggest prize. The one that got away was Honus Wagner, who was on the fence for a while but stayed with Pittsburgh.

The American League began play late in April 1901. The first season was a difficult one to achieve with much of the construction and site selection going down to the wire. But on makeshift fields, none of which would endure, the league started play a full week after the National League on April 24. Charlie Comiskey had his dream of a major league team in his home town of Chicago and he had one of the best managers in the league, Clark Griffith.

That day Griffith's White Stockings hosted Jimmy McAleer's Cleveland Blues. It almost did not matter who won as much as that they were playing. Yet that game set in motion a long line of professional baseball that continues to this day. It all took shape in the cold December of 1900 and was brought to life by the most respected names then in baseball, all now enshrined in the Baseball Hall of Fame.

Although there is little dispute as to Ban Johnson's role as the cornerstone of the effort, history has been less clear in establishing a hierarchy of co-conspirators. Norman L. Macht is one of the more recent to write on the subject.

In his biography of Connie Mack he emphasizes the role of Mack in the process. "Three men were primarily responsible for the early success of the American League," he writes.[13] He identifies the three men as Ban Johnson, Connie Mack, and Charles Somers.

Macht goes on to say that "Mack, Ban Johnson, Jimmy McAleer, Jimmy Collins and Charles Somers were the American League's principal raiders of the National ranks, signing players for other clubs as well as their own."[14] It is a curious turnabout. Griffith goes from co-conspirator, the key player representative taking on the National League ownership in the December meetings, to taking a back seat from there until the first pitch is thrown out on April 24.

In a 1940 article in the *Saturday Evening Post*, Bob Considine and Shirley Povich, viewing the same set of historic events, describe the role of Clark Griffith as crucial, and there is little mention of any central play by Connie Mack outside of Philadelphia, or of McAleer, Collins, or Somers in signing players. There was no hue and cry in 1940 when that version of history was published and one of the principles, Connie Mack, was still very much alive and one of Clark Griffith's closest friends.

An historical analysis of who was likely to have secured the commitments of the players does not favor Somers. Although he may have provided the money, he was not traveling the country with contracts. Griffith's claim in 1940 has more credibility, not because he has unique stature among his peers, but his unique credibility on the issues that led to the formation of the league — money and power. Griffith was alone in his ability to convince players that the new league offered them better money and gave them a bigger voice in deciding their futures. Griffith had been a loud voice on payroll issues throughout his career, and his aggressive role made him a major player in the union. Neither Collins nor McAleer could speak to other players from that perspective.

Clark Griffith knew the concerns of the professional ball player in those first three months of 1901 because he had lived them for a dozen years. He had been shut out of baseball by injury and seen stadiums owned by the wealthy closed down by economic circumstance. He knew the game from the side of the player and was among the loudest voices for their rights.

In the twenty-first century it is easy to forget that once there were unions, but they were in their infancy at the beginnings of the last century and neither Collins nor McAleer are mentioned among those who took the fight for players' rights to the owners in December 1900.

Clark Griffith was Ban Johnson's agent, selling the American League president's commitment to players on a host of issues. Griffith alone could sit across the table from the best players in the game, not only as a peer on the field, but as someone who had spoken out for their rights when it counted.

The other players knew Griff as a canny pitcher who would use whatever it took to win ballgames. He was a feisty player who did not back down on the mound and had never done so in his dealings with ownership. The credibility he had gained by playing for one of the toughest managers in the business — Cap Anson — he took into those negotiations with every player. It was a crucial commodity that could have come from no other source.

Macht is fair to place importance on the new ballpark sites that were crucial in establishing the core rivalries that would feed the public interest in the new league. Charles Somers' investment in expensive new ballparks in prime real estate in eastern seaboard cities was crucial. The *Chicago Tribune*, in its early season reviews, scored this accomplishment among the highlights of what the men of vision behind the new league had been able to accomplish.

But at least equally central is the ever-present story of how money was divided among players and owners. It dates to the beginnings of professional baseball, and figures like Griffith gained their foothold in the early game by exploiting these issues.

Regardless of where emphasis is placed or from what perspective history is viewed, a new league was born from the work of famous men. The competition between the American and National Leagues became the most important force in shaping the business of baseball in the twentieth century. The roles of individual players like Babe Ruth have done much to define the game, as have singular franchises like the New York Yankees. But the competition between the two leagues led to the World Series and the All-Star Game. The championship series between the two leagues slowly rose in stature from its start in 1903 to become the greatest sporting event in American culture. The competition for that title was the ultimate expression of each season's particular vernacular.

Griffith always acknowledged the huge debt that baseball owed to Ban Johnson. Johnson and Comiskey, as baseball magnates comfortable in their plush offices, were an important source of support to Clark Griffith as a manager of the White Stockings, but slowly their support faded in the coming years as Griffith sought to move from player-manager to owner. Comiskey became known as "the dreadful human being whose parsimony would lead to his players fixing the 1919 World Series."[15] In coming years Comiskey would be no more magnanimous to Griffith.

Whatever his faults, Clark Griffith was a loyal friend, and his support for Ban Johnson, Charlie Comiskey and Connie Mack would never waver in the coming years. Regarding Johnson's efforts to clean up the game, Griff later said, "The present high standard of the game, its increasing spirit of sportsmanship, is due more than anything to the organization of the American League under Ban Johnson."[16]

Clark Griffith may not have gotten as much credit as some of the others, but he got something of huge value to him at the time. He became a manager and got one of the things he had never had before — a championship caliber team. In later stories Griffith always put himself at the center, whether it was leading the rebellion of players in Tacoma who took off for Missoula or in leading the sit-down strike for unpaid players in California. In Chicago to start the 1901 season, he made all of those prior claims real as the center-piece of a pennant-winning baseball team.

For his troubles in recruiting players for all of the teams, he got a roster in Chicago that played the kind of baseball he had relished since a teenager. He believed it started with good pitching and defense. As manager of the newly minted Chicago White Sox, Griffith had a team he had almost single-handedly put together and reflected his values as a player. They were fast and smart. It did not matter how big they were, they just had to play good baseball. To start the 1901 season Clark Griffith had his kind of team, one he had sculpted, and it looked like a damned good one. It was the best on which he ever played.

CHAPTER 4

American League Champions

The inaugural season of the American League in 1901 gained as much credibility from its lineup of famous player-managers as from the rosters filled in with recognized stars like Napoleon Lajoie and Cy Young. The lineup was impressive indeed. Clark Griffith and his cohorts were among the best players of their day, men who had achieved stardom on the field and were now leaders on teams that looked increasingly competitive with their National League rivals.

One of the biggest names was John McGraw, who led the Baltimore Orioles again after that team's contraction in 1900 sent him to St. Louis for a single season. Baltimore had been one of the perennial powers of the National League in the 1890s. Hugh Duffy, the player-manager in Milwaukee, was equally prestigious as the heart of the Boston Beaneaters' offense. He had led the National League in 1894 in home runs and a .440 batting average only to see McGraw's Orioles walk off with the championship. Oddly enough, it was not Duffy and McGraw who would grow to be notable rivals, rather it was Clark Griffith who continued his simmering feud with McGraw as the two men emerged as two of the biggest names in the new American League.

There was equal thunder in Philadelphia in Connie Mack, who was managing the Philadelphia Athletics and Jimmy Collins who was carrying on the Beaneaters tradition in Boston. Jimmy McAleer, the fine center fielder, was in Cleveland. The only two managers whose playing careers were less impressive were James Manning in Washington and George Stallings in Detroit.

In the week preceding the opening contests of the American League, the *Chicago Tribune* had a season preview that featured photogravure etchings of each of the managers across the top of the page. The press coverage of sports in general and baseball in particular was expanding, and even during the 1901 season it could be seen taking on new emphasis in major city newspapers. In Chicago the "Sunday Sports" section was gaining separate status as a distinct section of the paper with a lead page that rivaled the front page of the newspaper for graphic presentation.

The *Tribune* offered predictions of the finish for the American League clubs in its preview. The odds were drawn from "reputable" betting establishments. The Chicago White Stockings were accorded the best chance to win, by 13-to-5 odds. McGraw's Baltimore team was second at 5-to-1 odds. Betting on sports was a wide-open affair before the Black Sox scandal would bring the whole business into disrepute. The other sports featured at the turn of the century were horse racing and boxing. Both were heavily wagered and baseball merely followed in line.

Managers played a larger role in the game during the deadball era because strategy was such a huge component of the game before the advent of the lively ball in 1919. Home runs were a rarity and the number of runs scored in an average contest was significantly lower than after 1919. An emphasis on baserunning, defense, and pitching made the game a more cerebral contest, and players and managers like Clark Griffith could excel by bringing their wits to bear as well as their athleticism.

TABLE 4-1. 1901 AMERICAN LEAGUE
TEAMS, MANAGERS, NOTABLE STARS

Team	Manager	Star Players
Baltimore Orioles	John McGraw	Joe "Iron Man" McGinnity, Mike Donlin
Boston Americans	James Collins	Cy Young, Chick Stahl, Buck Freeman
Chicago White Stockings	Clark Griffith	Dummy Hoy, Fielder Jones
Cleveland Blues	James McAleer	Bill Bradley
Detroit Tigers	George Stallings	Kid Gleason
Milwaukee Brewers	Hugh Duffy	John Anderson
Philadelphia Athletics	Connie Mack	Napoleon Najoie, Eddie Plank, Chick Fraser
Washington Nationals	James Manning	Boileryard Clarke

SOURCE: *Chicago Tribune*, Baseball Reference.com

Clark Griffith's skills were well-adapted to the deadball era in which he played. Griffith was described as having intense burning eyes that focused solely on the contest at hand, which during his playing days was the batter. In later years the eyes retained their fire, but shown from behind increasingly bushy eyebrows.

The eyes revealed a man always in the mental moment of the game, searching for any strategic advantage wherever he might find it. He wanted his players fast and athletic, and as the only pitcher among the group of new managers, he may have valued a talented defense more than the others.

The lineup in Chicago lent itself well to Griffith's predilections. The players he brought on board from the National League filled out weak spots that he saw in the White Stockings lineup from 1900. Teams in the new league were limited to only 15 roster slots, and one of the notable differences with the seasons to follow was in the number of pitchers carried by each team.

Pitchers completed 86 percent of their starts in 1901 and even when a reliever was needed, it fell to one of the other starting pitchers to finish for his teammate. Griffith's most prominent addition to the White Stockings staff, Nixey Callahan, provided even more flexibility. Not only was he an accomplished "twirler," as they were called in the earliest days of baseball, but he served as a utility player. He was excellent in the field and at the bat and he presented Griffith with a strategic advantage late in games. He could bring Callahan in as a replacement pitcher and batter.

Griffith's leadership skills played well as a manager in 1901. Griffith had always been about communicating on the field. His reputation was for jawing at umpires or the batter at the plate. But that side of the game was not in keeping with Ban Johnson's "vision for the future." Johnson wanted his managers and players to comport themselves more as management analysts than barroom brawlers. It was a lesson Griffith and McGraw would be slow to learn in 1901. Griffith was still very old school, raised by Hoss Radbourn and Cap Anson in an era that Ban Johnson was trying to bury in the dust of time.

Ban Johnson had faith that Griff could make the change. He had put Clark Griffith in charge of an excellent team in the Chicago White Stockings of 1900. It should be understood that the talent in the newly formed American League did not depend solely on the newly signed players from the National League.

When the National League contracted from 12 teams to eight prior to the 1900 season, many players from those four defunct rosters joined Ban Johnson's teams in the Western League, which he renamed the American League, though it was still regarded for the 1900 season as a "minor league." A total of 200 players manned various American League rosters in 1900, of which half had played in the National League at some point in their careers.[1]

The level of play in 1900 was already at a high level, too good to be considered a minor league, but not quite at a level to be on par with the National League. So the additional National League players signed to start the season were the key to pushing the league's reputation to the higher level.

The best American League team in 1900 was the Chicago White Stockings, who won the pennant. Only four of the White Stockings from that first season in 1900 had never played in the National League.[2] Clark Griffith's team was the best stocked of any team carrying forward for 1901, and he had hand-picked four National Leaguers who he believed would bring with them the kind of baseball Griffith liked.

The infield was defensively strong with Frank Isbell at first, Fred Hartman at third and Frank Shugart at short. Shugart and Hartman had considerable National League experience. Their defensive skills in many respects out-weighed their hitting. They were not sluggers, but pesky hitters who were fast and frequently got on base. Adding National Leaguer Sam Mertes to the infield plugged the hole left by the departure of 1900 captain Dick Padden, who moved back to the National League with St. Louis.

Outfielder Herm McFarland had the least experience, but he turned in a very creditable performance for the White Stockings when Griffith gave him an everyday job. Griffith's additions of Fielder Jones in the outfield and Billy Sullivan behind the plate were the best moves he made. They added punch to a weak lineup. Jones brought great numbers over from his days with the Brooklyn Superbas and gave Griffith's team the one big bat they needed. Sullivan filled another big hole in the 1900 team as a solid backstop who could hit.

Yet for all of the additions, the best player on the team may have been the existing center fielder, Dummy Hoy. Much has been made of Hoy as the first deaf player to succeed at a high level in the major leagues. It overstates how many players of the era had hearing problems they contracted from a variety of childhood illnesses that are treatable today. In 1901 the New York Giants had three deaf mutes on their pitching staff, Bill Deegan, George Leitner and Luther Taylor, all of whom were nick named "Dummy."[3]

For Clark Griffith, Hoy was everything he could have wanted. He was first of all even shorter than Griffith. Hoy was reputed to be 5'5" in height, but was probably closer to 5'4". While it may have been reassuring to Griffith to see someone in his initial lineup who was shorter than he was, the attributes that sold the Old Fox on Hoy was his speed, his ability to run down anything in center field and to turn and throw with remarkable accuracy. Dummy Hoy was one of the fastest players in the league at the start of his career in 1888, and while he may have lost a step or two by 1901, he remained one of the finest defensive center fielders in baseball.

As they say in modern parlance, he had a cannon for an arm. He had the unique distinction to have thrown three men out at the plate in a single game. Hoy could hit and, even better, he could get on base by taking a walk. He had led the American Association League in bases on balls in 1891 and would do so for Griffith in 1901. With Hoy batting leadoff and Fielder Jones second, Chicago had two fine all-around players anchoring a potent lineup.

Baseball rosters had been heavily weighted to Irish Americans in the early years during the nineteenth century. But increasingly more players were being brought in from all walks of life. In the Chicago papers of the day, college teams were highlighted just off to the right of the major league teams, and players with college degrees like Christy Mathewson were becoming more frequent.

Clark Griffith's White Stockings had no college educated pitchers, but it was an excellent staff that would make the team a contender. The attribute that set them apart was their manager. Playing for Cap Anson, Griffith had been the only reliable pitcher on many of those Chicago Colts teams. Now he was the ace of the staff, but he had more help.

Griffith's ability to talk his teammate Nixey Callahan into joining the crosstown rivals proved to be a key acquisition. He was a reliable arm if not overpowering.

The ace of the White Stockings from their first season in 1900 was an excellent young pitcher named Roy Patterson. Patterson came into his own during the 1900 season, but would have his finest year in 1901.

Patterson, Nixey Callahan and Clark Griffith formed what would prove to be an imposing rotation and certainly the best the 31-year-old Griffith had led to date. The *Chicago Tribune* in the middle of the season ran a feature on the three pitchers with etchings of Griffith at the center flanked by the two younger men, claiming they were the best threesome pitching in the American League.

Cobbling together a new league in only months meant that the White Stockings spent a hurried spring training in Excelsior Springs, Missouri. They arrived in Chicago on April 13 and played an exhibition game at Marshall Field while the West Side Grounds on the south side of town was made ready for the home opener. The new stadium and playing field was located at 39th Street and Wentworth Avenue and could be reached by either streetcar or the elevated commuter train. The ballpark could seat only 7,500, which would prove a problem very quickly.

The *Tribune* remarked that new manager Clark Griffith was generally quiet about the team's chances in the upcoming season. He was guardedly optimistic but "there is something behind the half-hidden smile of the little manager."[4] Others in the new league were having more basic problems than Griff. Connie Mack in Philadelphia did not know whether he had Lajoie and the other National League players or not as the legal fight was taken into the courts. National League "agents continued to trail them, using threats or cash to recapture them."[5]

Jimmy Callahan broke his arm in the last exhibition game. Some worried it was an ill omen for the impending season. Before the American League played its first game, the National League season had a week of play under its belt. The additional time allowed to make ready the American League's newest playing grounds was crucial to success, especially for the new teams in Washington and Philadelphia that were slowest to get their parks ready for action.

Perhaps the visitor to the West Side Grounds in Chicago might have noted the odors of the nearby stockyards and the bare amenities to the ball field, but on opening day no one seemed to mind. Chicago mayor Carter Harrison, Jr., and the entire city council were hosted elegantly by Charles Comiskey, fully in command of his proud new venture. A regimental band played patriotic marches for the festive occasion until the mayor tossed out the first pitch to begin the game in the afternoon of April 24.

The White Stockings won the first game of the season against the Cleveland Blues by a score of 8–2 behind the pitching of Roy Patterson, who took the win for the home team. The new league's other openers were not as lucky as rainy conditions prevented play everywhere except in Chicago. When play did finally get under way, the newly constructed stadiums were found wanting and large crowds in Philadelphia were turned away because adequate seating did not exist.

The *Chicago Tribune* continued to refer to the White Stockings with pride as "the Champion White Stockings," and they continued to look like champs, winning the second game 7–3 with a young left-hander named John Skopec on the mound. The only loss of the Cleveland series occurred when Dummy Hoy made an uncharacteristic error. The *Tribune* opined that the "man with the eloquent fingers" had contributed to considerable sloppy play in the 10–4 loss. Jack Katoll started the third game and took the loss.

Griffith waited until the final game of the series to debut on the mound. It was the biggest crowd of the opening series, standing room only to see the Old Fox pitch. Fifteen thousand fans crowded into the park and many were turned away, prompting the Old Roman, Comiskey, to promise that additional bleachers would be added as quickly as they could be built. The fans crowded onto the playing field in the outfields and limited the field of play allowed to the fielders.

The problematic squeeze by the crowds did not diminish Clark Griffith in his first appearance on the field as a White Stocking. He repaid the enthusiasm of the fans by "pitching a masterful game," according to the *Tribune*. He had the Clevelanders at his mercy and "with a cunning of his own made them hit the ball on the ground" rather than allow fly balls that might fall in the reduced outfield expanse where the crowds remained standing throughout the game.[6] Chicago won the game handily by a 13–1 score.

The American League was off to a rousing start and the National League was providing the rival league with every opportunity to upstage it. One of the biggest changes in the game in the first decade of the 20 century was being played out in the National League. The foul ball strike rule was in play in the National League in 1901 and was proving unpopular with fans, which may have been a lightning rod for dissatisfaction as much as National League teams missing key stars from the season before. The foul ball rule would not be used in the American League until 1903.

Before 1901 the foul ball did not count as a strike. Only when a batter swung and missed, or took a pitch called a strike by the umpire, did a strike register. The most egregious practice was the one recounted by Clark Griffith whereby the more talented batters like McGraw could foul off pitch after pitch until, as Griffith would later attest, the pitcher was bone weary.

When fouls counted as strikes, the pace of the game was naturally accelerated as the batter proceeded to two strikes more quickly. Predictably, the rule change led to a shift towards the pitcher and a more defensive-minded game. Batting averages fell off by 40 points; slugging was reduced as was base stealing.[7]

The largest impact was naturally in the number of strikeouts that were up by 50 percent and team batting averages dropped "from near .280 down to the .240-.250 range."[8] The bottom line was a less aggressive and slower paced game that evolved first in the National League while the American League — where the foul strike rule had not been adopted — continued to demonstrate the style of play to which the public had grown accustomed. The huge crowds showing up for American League games may not have been directly attributable to this difference, but it played a significant role as the season progressed.

Baseball attendance was surging generally as new fans were given an opportunity to get to major league contests being played in the new league. Expansion of baseball has always worked to the benefit of fans and ultimately to the benefit of the game and its wealthy owners, regardless of the inevitable disbelief of existing ownership groups.

Attendance for all of the American League in 1901 was estimated at 1.8 million overall, or 230,000 per team.[9] The attendance built on itself, as owners increased the seating capacity of brand new stadiums as quickly as they could to accommodate large and growing crowds.

Numerous sources have credited the expanding popularity of the sport in 1901 and following years to Ban Johnson's American League with its cleaner style of play that promoted attendance by families. Profanity and fights were controlled as tightly as possible on orders of the league president. The atmosphere also attracted more well-attired businessmen as hooligan behavior diminished.

The new American League provided an exciting pennant race in 1901 from the start as well. The Detroit Tigers broke out of the box the quickest, winning all four of their initial games. They held the lead in the American League race for the first few weeks of the season, but the White Stockings were never far behind. In early May, Clark Griffith pitched the team to victory against the Milwaukee Brewers, winning 6–3, and the White Stockings swept a series against the Cleveland Blues in Cleveland. Then Griffith won again on the May 14, 6–2, that kept them apace with Stallings' Detroit Tigers who just kept winning. McGraw's Orioles stayed steadily on pace in third.

On May 25 the White Stockings took over first place for the first time when the Tigers faltered against the Washington Nationals. The following day McGraw's Orioles came to town for the first time and provided a head-to-head match-up between the old rivals, Griffith and McGraw. Griffith pitched the first game against the ace of the Orioles and future Hall of Famer Joe "Iron Man" McGinnity. There were 12,000 fans gathered to watch the contest.

"So sharp and aggressive was the play of both teams that the spectators hardly realized when the finish came," reported the *Chicago Tribune* on April 27. "Griffith, cool, serene, absolute master of himself and the situation, pitched through to the end just as he had commenced."[10]

Clark Griffith had a superstition as a pitcher that a shutout was never a good thing. He believed that he should allow the other team a run in the last inning or so if the lead was indisputable. Against McGraw, however, Griffith did not let up and hung tight until the game was over. The White Stockings won, 5–0, with Griff taking the measure of McGinnity successfully and showing no mercy, superstitions be damned.

The White Stockings took three of the four games against McGraw, then three straight from the Boston Americans. At the end of May their record stood at 24 wins and only nine defeats and they held 3 -game lead over the Detroit Tigers.

As well as the White Stockings were doing, James Hart's rival Orphans were doing just as poorly. The National League was undergoing tremendous upheaval generally, but the Orphans were getting the worst of the situation and were dead last in the league.

John McGraw continued to be an especially prickly thorn in Ban Johnson's garden. McGraw, like Clark Griffith, could not shed his propensity for the game as he had learned it in the raucous '90s. Griffith proved more adaptable to the new game environment ultimately, although there were notable bumps along the way. Griffith was suspended for an altercation that involved McGraw in June, but the worst was yet to come.

On the heels of Griffith's humble apologies to Ban Johnson and his subsequent reinstatement, McGraw ratcheted up the heat against the American League president. McGraw was claiming to have signed Hughie Jennings away from Connie Mack's Athletics. The claim arose after the season began and it continued to fester. Jennings was a strong presence in the Baltimore Orioles lineup during the 1890s along with McGraw. McGraw was claiming that he had signed Jennings for his American League team before Connie Mack. He was offering to provide written evidence.

Jennings ended up playing for the Philadelphia Phillies rather than Mack's Athletics, or jumping to McGraw's team. Jennings was tiptoeing through the mine field trying not to alienate anyone, whereas McGraw was taking a more direct approach. Ban Johnson ruled against McGraw and the fiery manager's claims of foul were aired in every major newspaper.

McGraw would make wider claims of favoritism by Johnson and this was the first major evidence in support of it. With the Jennings affair simmering, McGraw's star pitcher Joe "Iron Man" McGinnity ran afoul of league umpires and was suspended by Johnson.

Several weeks later, Orioles first baseman Warren Hart drew an even harsher suspension. In both instances the issue was treatment of umpires. Hart had little room to complain. He had attacked the umpire and punched him in the face. McGraw was hardly quick to corral his players, rather inciting them more often than not.

But the idea that Ban Johnson was playing favorites had no compelling support. Griffith's suspension countered the claim as did a similar suspension after Milwaukee manager Hugh Duffy struck an umpire. In one of the worst incidents that summer, White Stockings shortstop Frank Shugart had an ugly, physical confrontation with an umpire and the same "indefinite" suspension was handed down by Johnson. The incident in Chicago involved the same umpire, Jack Haskell, who had been assaulted by McGraw's team.

Shugart and White Stockings pitcher John Katoll instigated what could have been called a general riot. It involved spectators who came out onto the field and attacked Haskell, forcing the police to protect him. Police were finally successful in restoring order and escorted Haskell from the park. Shugart's attack split the umpire's lip, and Katoll supported Shugart by picking up the ball and throwing it at the umpire, which resulted in his suspension.

Rough, bullying tactics against umpires were not isolated in the American League. It had been commonplace in the National League and continued apace in 1901. National League Umpire Henry O'Day was set upon in St. Louis in July, and the *Chicago Tribune* described the scene as involving upwards of 400 fans in the fracas. O'Day was kicked and beaten by the angry mob before police could intervene on his behalf. Police drew their revolvers and fired shots into the air to stem the mob.[11]

The *Tribune* opined that Ban Johnson's "infusion of more National League blood into the teams of the new league ... resulted not in elevating the new players to the standard of the American League, but in lowering the American League's standard to that of the National League."[12] The issue came to a head unfortunately for Frank Shugart. Ban Johnson said in meting out punishment of the White Stockings shortstop that he was "throwing leniency to the wind."[13] The suspension for Shugart was not lifted for weeks.

Griffith joined McGraw in protesting the treatment of players by Johnson. Ever the labor radical, Griffith said that if a permanent blacklisting of Shugart resulted, "then every player in the league will walk out."[14] With the talk of labor action in the works, team owner Comiskey intervened and said he would travel with the team for the rest of the season, ostensibly to reign in his feisty manager.

The National League was a stark contrast, not for the lack of confrontations between umpires and everyone else, but for the fractious atmosphere between the owners. Andrew Freedman in New York was the flash point as the *Chicago Tribune* reported ongoing disputes between the "Freedmanites" and other ownership blocs in the NL. John Brush was the leading co-conspirator as the two men fought a rear guard action against the encroachments of the American League. The two men had been the most committed in working to block acquisition of new playing fields for the American League by Charles Somers' group on the eastern seaboard. Now they hatched new plans to pool ownership of all teams in the National League, an ill-fated idea that won no support from the rest of the owners.

Freedman was a Tammany Hall politician and accustomed to using muscle to forge a path wherever he wished to go. However, he and Brush encountered heavy resistance in 1901 and accomplished nothing more than additional bad publicity for their league at a time when it could ill afford it.

The bad behavior of fans and players and the ill-tempered cabal in New York City had its worst effect in detracting attention from the exciting pennant race that came to a head in 1901. The *Chicago Tribune* even gave top billing to the horse racing at the Washington Park Race Track where the cheering crowds could be heard from the West Side Grounds. Clark Griffith would not be deterred by concerns about umpires and hooliganism. He was pitching the best baseball of his career.

And his hitting wasn't bad either. His average was over .300 for the second time in his career. In 1895 he hit .319 and drove in 27 runs. He was in a tight pennant race for the first time as a major leaguer and was ahead by a nose. Whatever he could do to help was just plain smart baseball.

In the second half of June the White Stockings lost five games in a row in Boston as Collins' Americans hit the Chicago pitchers hard in the first two games and embarrassed the league leaders. Griffith pitched the third game and held the Americans even at 1–1 until a costly error by third baseman Hartman let in three runs and he lost the contest, 4–3. The sweep of the extended five-game series gave Boston a share of the lead for the first time all season. It dumped the White Sox into a tie for first, with Detroit tight on Griff's heels in third.

The White Stockings' long road trip continued to Philadelphia, and Griffith's friend Connie Mack was just the tonic Chicago needed. They beat the Athletics and Griffith went against his old superstition again by shutting out the opposition twice, 4–0 and 5–0. It had no ill effects as the team kept on winning, sweeping the Athletics in four games and then returning home to sweep three games from the Cleveland Blues and two more from the Tigers.

The ten-game winning streak put Chicago three games in front of the pack by the Fourth of July holiday. But they were swept in a holiday doubleheader at Cleveland and lost two of three in the Motor City. The team seemed lethargic according to owner Comiskey, who accompanied Griffith and the team to Milwaukee and insisted that Griffith shake up his lineup. Shugart was benched at shortstop.

The prodding by Comiskey worked as the White Stockings set off on another winning streak with Griffith starting and relieving if it was required to win. This time the White Stockings won nine of their next 11 games and beat the Tigers three of four to start August. In the Detroit series Griffith pitched another key shutout. Chicago was back on top as the August heat set in.

Charles Comiskey and James Hart, the owner of what the *Chicago Tribune* had dubbed the "Remnants," continued talks that had started in July concerning a post-season series between the crosstown rivals. The two owners offered to settle whether the new upstart American League was really the better of the two leagues. The discussions sparked an extended column in the *Chicago Tribune* comparing the two teams, player by player. The *Tribune* concluded that the White Stockings had the better catcher, the better outfield, the better pitching and a better team spirit. There was little need to read between the lines. Yet the friendly contentiousness between the two Chicago owners gave expression to a sentiment that was moving baseball forward in the national consciousness.

Casual wagering as to the merits of the two leagues would grow into the World Series two years later. It would spark one of the greatest sports contests in American history. In the late summer of 1901, however, National League owners such as John Brush and Andrew Freedman were too busy feuding within their ownership group and those allied with the American League.

Seeing beyond that to the advantages created by the new rivalry was not within their grasp as yet.

Charles Comiskey was again unhappy with his team in August as they could get no traction against Cleveland and Detroit. The White Stockings won at home and lost on the road, so Comiskey climbed on board again for the next road trip, accompanying the team to Cleveland for a key series. With his owner in the stands, Griffith pitched the team to another victory. But the team split the series and then lost two in Boston to bring the Americans closer still. Griffith won again in Washington, but the team lost the series and limped back home with a meager game and a half lead over Boston.

The first of two crucial series began with four games against John McGraw's Orioles, who were in third place. The first game ended anti-climactically as Nixey Callahan made three errors that allowed McGraw's nine to tie the score at 5–5 when umpire Sheridan called the game because of darkness. The next day, a Saturday doubleheader, had all the more suspense with Boston still just 1½ games back.

Both Saturday games were well played as McGraw's teams always featured good defenders, but Griffith had the better team on the field that day. He got key work from Fred Hartman, who started two double plays just when Baltimore seemed about to rally. He also had the game-winning hit in the second game. The Griffs won both ends of the doubleheader and increased their league lead to three games. Then the White Stockings won the last game of the Baltimore series for a sweep and were ahead of Boston by 3 games.

After winning against McGraw, Chicago could not clinch the deal against lesser foes like the Athletics and Nationals, losing four of seven games. Boston, however, was worse, losing three straight. With the White Stockings still ahead by 3 games, a decisive four-game series against Boston provided Jimmy Collins' Americans a last chance to pull back into contention. The first game was on September 7 in Chicago.

A national tragedy struck on the same day, however, and overshadowed the pennant race. President McKinley was shot by an assassin at the Pan American Exposition in Buffalo. The early reports were that the two bullets that struck the president did not constitute life-threatening wounds, and Americans everywhere breathed a sigh of relief.

Gale-force winds blew in off Lake Michigan for the beginning of the first game with Boston, but they seemed to help Nixey Callahan, who held Boston to a single run as Chicago won, 4–1. The next day the conditions improved and a large crowd was on hand that "crowded every nook and cranny of the stands."[15]

With Collins and Cy Young, most pundits believed Boston could take the White Stockings' measure and indeed Boston had a 3–2 lead going into the bottom of the ninth inning with Young still pitching. Nixey Callahan — Griffith's recruit from the Chicago Orphans — had a pinch-hit single batting for Patterson after a rare error by Jimmy Collins on a routine grounder. There were two aboard and no outs.

Young retired the next two batters and it came down to the final out. Dummy Hoy was the last hope for the Griffs, and he stroked a line drive down the line that scored Callahan and Jimmy Burke. "Ten thousand steam calliopes working night and day would not have made so much noise" as the Chicago crowd, opined the *Tribune* writer.[16] It was a stirring come-from-behind win for the White Stockings that made Clark Griffith's team local heroes.

Clark Griffith, manager of the first American League pennant winner, the 1901 Chicago White Stockings (National Baseball Hall of Fame Library).

The next day Griffith pitched and won a close 4–3 contest in the opener of a doubleheader, and a 6–4 victory in the second game gave the White Stockings a sweep of all four games. The inaugural American League season was all over but the shouting. Chicago had a commanding seven-game lead and had taken all the steam out of Jimmy Collins' and Cy Young's Boston Americans.

There was sad news just as Chicago was bearing down on its first pennant triumph. President McKinley succumbed to his wounds on the September 13 and the nation was in mourning. Teddy Roosevelt, the young vice president, assumed office amid the funereal atmosphere that gripped the country. As the president was laid to rest in Canton, Ohio, the White Stockings went on a five-game winning streak that finished the pennant race.

Clark Griffith won his last game of the season against Connie Mack's Athletics. His record on the mound stood at 24 wins against only seven defeats. The team's final record stood at 83 wins against 53 losses, four games better than Boston.

The *Tribune* analyzed the season as a success for both the Whites Stockings and the new league. But they expressed surprise that Griffith had actually pulled it off. They had no Lajoie or Collins, not a single punishing hitter of that ilk, and Fielder Jones was the best they could offer.

Clark Griffith willed them to win, getting great defense and pitching from a team that would not be able to duplicate its success. The most important member of the team was Griffith himself. He was the rock of the strong pitching staff, and without him they would never have stood up to Boston. Griffith's 2.67 ERA was the second lowest of his career and his five shutouts topped the league. Those shutouts were key wins that came at crucial points in the season when the team's back was to the wall.

Cy Young was better. He was the class of the league with 33 wins and an ERA of 1.62 and 158 strikeouts, all league-leading figures. But Griffith had a stronger team from top to bottom. It was the kind of team he had wanted, a fast athletic outfield, a solid pitching corps and defensive specialists in the infield who could gather timely hits.

With the surprise success of the White Stockings, Clark Griffith arrived as a manager and improved his stock as a leader within the sport. The *Tribune* was much impressed that the Old Fox had been able to bring the first American League pennant home to Chicago. He beat John McGraw and Connie Mack, both of whom would go on to great success as managers. He did it against some of the best names in the game at the time. It seemed to herald the Old Fox as a force to be reckoned with.

Yet for all his triumph in 1901, it would be a long time before Clark Griffith would craft a team as good as the 1901 White Stockings. It would be the year 1924, a future time when the baseball world had long forgotten that Griffith had ever won the American League pennant. He would be up against John McGraw one last time and no one would believe he could win that one either.

CHAPTER 5

Playing Off Broadway

The first season for the American League as a legitimate rival to the more established National League was a very good one. The AL teams drew far better than anyone could have imagined and were generally an economic success. To build on that success many teams expanded their seating areas and bolstered their grandstands looking toward the second season of the new league.

In April 1902, the Sunday *Chicago Tribune* led with a panoramic view of the new grandstands added to the West Side Grounds. It was dramatic proof that American League stalwart Charles Comiskey was intent on building a long-term presence in the city. The other more prosperous teams in American League, Cleveland, Detroit, and Boston, were doing the same.

Although the National League had outdrawn its new rivals over the course of the season, Ban Johnson was certain that the difference could be bridged with more strategic location of American League teams in cities like New York and St. Louis. Moving the Western League into key eastern cities had been Ban Johnson's first goal, and cities like Baltimore had been the targets then. Now he sought to gain a foothold in cities where the National League was most successful.

The National League for its part was determined to win back some of the talent it had lost in the prior winter's raids. Owners like John Brush in Cincinnati and Andrew Freedman in New York were determined to regain the upper hand. As the fight between the two leagues entered a new phase, Clark Griffith played another key role.

Ban Johnson's primary target for a new eastern franchise was New York City. Johnson believed that a competitive nine in the Big Apple was an economic imperative, but Andrew Freedman and John Brush were determined to thwart the plan. Freedman had been unhappy when Brooklyn ceased being an independent city in 1899 and was folded into New York. That annexation meant there was already a second team in New York City, in violation of the National League constitution. Ban Johnson's idea that a third American League team would be added was just a further erosion into what Freedman saw as an exclusive right.

Excepting Brush and Freedman, the skeptics were less common and most assumed the move was just a matter of time. The only question in the minds of the press was the right person to lead the effort. During the winter of 1901–1902, the press openly speculated about whether John McGraw or Clark Griffith was involved in the efforts to win a new team in New York City.

Andrew Freedman took his fight against the American League back to court, but he was upstaged when the Pennsylvania Supreme Court ruled just prior to the 1902 season in favor of the National League by blocking Nap Lajoie's ability to play for Connie Mack's Athletics in Philadelphia. According to the court's ruling neither Lajoie nor four other members of Connie Mack's Athletics would be allowed to play for any team except the Phillies in the state of Pennsylvania. National League owners tried to use the ruling to force all American League players back to their teams. Two of Connie Mack's former Phillies returned to their National League team in Philadelphia.

It was the National League's turn to lose in court as their attempt to reinstate the reserve clause lost in St. Louis. The court there upheld the shift of players from the Brooklyn and St. Louis teams to the American League. Ban Johnson decided that he would shift Lajoie and the other two players to Cleveland — with Connie Mack's approval. Since other courts — one in Washington followed the St. Louis court in ruling in favor of the American League — had ruled in favor of the ability of players to jump leagues, the Pennsylvania ruling was deemed to only apply in that state.[1] The hope was that the ruling could be ignored in Ohio and elsewhere. The American League successfully parried the ongoing attempts by National League owners to reclaim their players. Ban Johnson proved to be a persistent and talented foe.

Given the legal jousting in 1902, Ban Johnson decided that the time was not ripe to move into New York. He decided instead to shift his Milwaukee team to St. Louis to keep the pressure on the National League in at least one arena. By March 1902, Clark Griffith was content to work on another winning season in Chicago as he secured the services of pitcher Ned Garvin from Milwaukee. Garvin would have a good year on the mound, but in his off hours was a bit of a hooligan.

In August 1902, Garvin was at the center of a barroom brawl in a Chicago pub, Flanagan's fittingly enough. Fists were flying and a police officer was called to quiet the disturbance. Garvin pulled a pistol and fired shots at the policeman, who escaped the bullets, but was then struck in the head by the butt of Garvin's revolver. An onlooker rescued the officer and put Garvin to flight. He ran from the bar and jumped on a passing street car to make an exit befitting Hollywood.[2] The fracas ended Garvin's season prematurely with a prolonged jail stint.

The Chicago White Stockings began the 1902 season much the way they had a year earlier, 5-to-2 favorites to win the pennant. The season began in late April and by the middle of May it looked much as it had the prior year with a tight race between Philadelphia, Boston and Chicago, with St. Louis and Detroit also close.

John McGraw's team was further off the pace, but in an early season match-up between his and Griff's teams, McGraw got the best of the deal in Baltimore as Griffith was thrown out of the game for repeatedly arguing close calls. Both Griffith and McGraw were shameless throwbacks to their time in the National League. Ban Johnson could posture that his teams were playing a different kind of baseball in a different atmosphere, but McGraw and Griffith remained two persistent scrappers who fought with umpires in a style more reminiscent of National League play.

McGraw was certain that the contest between himself and Clark Griffith was not over the second American League pennant, but over the right to manage what was sure to be the league's premier franchise, the second team in Manhattan. McGraw knew Johnson wanted to move to New York and knew it would be his Baltimore team that would lose out at the end of the 1902 season.

As the Baltimore manager he considered himself the logical pilot for the new team after it moved. Yet every signal from Ban Johnson regarding John McGraw was a negative one. McGraw concluded that "someone would be left holding the bag and I made up my mind it would not be me."[3]

McGraw was correct is seeing most of the portents in negative terms. There were plentiful indications that McGraw was the less favored of the two most likely candidates. Clark Griffith was tossed from numerous games during the 1901 season and again in 1902 as he fought to shed his National League roots. Yet there was an edge to the McGraw situation that made it different from Griffith's. His arguments were hot and ugly, often escalating quickly to the point that punches were thrown or threatened.

The incident Griffith related where Joe Cantillon as an umpire had targeted McGraw specifically may have been just another tall tale, but the kernel of truth behind it was the passionate dislike by umpiring crews for John McGraw and his team. One of the last incidents occurred early in 1902 in Boston where every manager's least favorite umpire, Jack Sheridan, threw McGraw out of a game. McGraw charged Sheridan and bumped him hard in the vicinity of the first base bag, daring him to retaliate. In the National League in the 1890s it was not unheard of for an umpire to swing at a manager.

Sheridan, however, was content to toss McGraw, though a heated exchange ensued.

The next day, Boston pitcher Bill Dinneen hit McGraw with pitches five times when he came to bat. Sheridan looked on from behind the plate as though nothing had happened. He refused to award McGraw first base and once again there were sparks between the two men.[4]

In a game just a week later in Detroit, McGraw was spiked intentionally in the knee. His knees were weak from numerous injuries and would force him into semi-retirement at the end of the 1902 season. Although the incident may have had no relation to the enmity between McGraw and the larger league representatives, McGraw saw a pattern of disrespect from players, umpires and other managers in the American League. The spike wounds were slow to heal and while they festered, McGraw's anger and resentment toward Ban Johnson did as well.

"Muggsy" McGraw turned his fuming hostility into action in the summer of 1902. McGraw's trips to New York in the winter of 1902 were more likely for meetings with Andrew Freedman to discuss McGraw's shift to the New York Giants. Some have speculated that some or all of McGraw's altercations in 1902 were intentional, designed to get him tossed from the league, to create the conditions for his banishment.

Regardless of whether premeditated or a spontaneous expression of despair, on July 7, 1902, John McGraw demanded his release from the Baltimore ownership and their purchase of his minority stake in the team. When it was granted, Andrew Freedman promptly announced him as the new manager of the faltering New York Giants.

Andrew Freedman was a businessman and not McGraw's abiding friend. He saw in McGraw an opportunity to increase the value of his holdings in the New York team and then be done with the troubling enterprise of baseball ownership once and for all. His partner in crime was again John Brush of Cincinnati.

Freedman arranged to buy controlling interest of the Baltimore Orioles, who were left staggering with the loss of McGraw and other players who were leaving with him. The Baltimore ownership group joined the larger uprising and club president John Mahon sold his controlling interest to Freedman. As owner, Freedman then released four additional players from their contractual obligations to Baltimore. Joe McGinnity and Roger Bresnahan went to New York with McGraw and two others jumped to John Brush's Cincinnati team.

Freedman completed the action by selling his interests in the New York Giants to John Brush for a cool $150,000—a substantial sum at the time. Brush would remain the Giants owner until he died in 1912. During that decade he would back John McGraw to the hilt while he turned the New York Giants into one of the greatest baseball teams in the history of the sport.

When McGraw bolted from Baltimore, he brought along the most important player from his former team, Joe "Iron Man" McGinnity. With McGinnity pitching alongside a 21-year-old named Christy Mathewson, the Giants began to win ball games. McGraw shook up the lineup, releasing four of the Giants to be replaced with his own hand-selected replacements. The resulting New York Giants played quite well during the last half of the 1902 season. It must have sounded all too familiar to Griff, who watched the new Giants lineup start to catch the wind.

On July 6, the White Sox record stood at 37 wins and only 21 losses. The team had a 4 -game lead over second-place Boston. Yet the team had a long east coast road trip from the middle of July until the end of that month. On the road Griffith's team managed only three wins against 11 losses.

The White Sox swoon occurred just as McGraw cemented his hold on the New York City managerial slot. Griffith may have been distracted by events in New York, but they were only a catalyst for the White Sox' losses. Clark Griffith and the White Sox in July of 1902 were up against one of the finest teams in the league when they traveled to Philadelphia.

Connie Mack's ace, Rube Waddell, was one of the best pitchers in baseball prior to Walter Johnson's arrival on the scene several years later. In 1902, for the first time in his career, the big left-hander had a strong team behind him. He had Lave Cross and Socks Seybold who had fine seasons with the bat. Then he had Eddie Plank who joined him to comprise the best starting pitching duo in the AL. Waddell was good with the bat as well and in a crucial game against Griffith in August, it was his triple that beat the White Sox.

Griffith had fine pitching from Garvin, Callahan, Patterson and Piatt, but they could not score runs. Half of the infield — Shugart and Hartmann — left after the 1901 season, but the biggest hole in the team resulted from Dummy Hoy's retirement. The 1901 White Stockings won the pennant behind the best offense in the league, but in 1902 Chicago scored 144 fewer runs than in their pennant winning season. The anemic offense was the real reason the team settled into fourth place at the end of July and failed to rally the rest of the season.

In Griffith's last season with Chicago, he had a 15–9 record and a 4.18 ERA. It was his worst season since breaking in with Cap Anson in the year after the pitching rubber was moved back five feet. There were more good seasons left in Clark Griffith's arm, it just needed motivation. There was no place better to find it than on the other side of town from John McGraw.

As early as August rumors surfaced in the Chicago press that Ban Johnson was moving Clark Griffith to New York. Yet even with the season at an end,

Griffith refused to commit to the move, saying that he would only leave Chicago if Comiskey gave him his release. The *New York Times* printed one of the most compelling indications that another New York team was in the offing in September. The *Times* asserted specifically that Griffith would be the manager, although the names of the players who would come with him were still uncertain.

There was nothing official forthcoming from Ban Johnson, however. Whether Griffith was still in the business of convincing Ban Johnson that only Griffith could get the ballplayers, or whether Comiskey was reluctant to let Griffith leave, is unclear. But for Ban Johnson the successful team Griffith had fielded in Chicago was the key. He wanted a winning team from the start in New York City, and Griffith was the best chance to carve out an American League niche in Manhattan from the first announcement.

That public declaration was finally made in October. The move was made official under the heading, "American League Team Sure Now," in the *New York Evening World*. Ban Johnson promised the press that "the American League will have a team in New York and it will be a winning one."[5]

The way was ultimately paved when a formal accord was signed by Ban Johnson and his American League cohorts with the National League ownership in December of 1902. It explicitly confirmed the move into Manhattan, but there was more drama to come.

By January 1903, Ban Johnson announced the names of the players who were moving to New York as well. Only a handful of players moved from the Baltimore Orioles team that McGraw had abandoned. Johnson confirmed Griffith finally as the manager.

More importantly, Johnson and Griffith had raided Barney Dreyfuss and his Pittsburgh team to provide the foundation for a winning team in New York City. The six players jumping to Griff's American League team included Jesse Tannehill and Jack Chesbro, two of Pittsburgh's better pitchers who had each won 20 games for the pennant winning Pirates of 1902. Infielder Wid Conroy and outfielder Lefty Davis came from Pittsburgh as well. Griff got outfielder Herm McFarland to come with him from Chicago and Kid Elberfeld from Detroit.

Griffith's biggest addition to the offensive lineup was Willie Keeler, who moved across town from the Brooklyn Superbas. Keeler had come to prominence with the Baltimore Orioles during the same years as John McGraw. They had formed a powerful duo in that lineup. He was the kind of player that Griffith loved to have backing him. Standing only five feet, four inches, he was reminiscent of Dummy Hoy of the White Stockings. Known as "Wee Willie" Keeler, he was the best hitter in the National League in the last two years before the contraction of teams in 1900.

Jack Chesbro was a pitcher coming into his prime. He had thrown 286 innings in 1902 for Pittsburgh and had won 28 games against only six losses, a remarkable winning percentage of .824. His ERA of 2.17 stood among the best in the league and he was on his way to the Hall of Fame. Tannehill had an equally impressive background. He had been pitching in the majors since he was 20 years of age and at 29 already had four 20-win seasons to his credit.

The excellent aggregation of talent came for the money. Griffith, as the player-manager, was signed for $8,000. Keeler, Tannehill and Chesbro got $6,000 contracts as the *New York Evening World* put the total salaries for the new Highlanders roster at $60,000. Tannehill and Chesbro left Barney Dreyfuss, who had the largest payroll in the National League, paying $57,000 in an attempt to keep his players happy, but Griffith was offering more and he got two of Dreyfuss's best to jump to the American League.[6]

There was a team and a good one, but no ballpark in which they could play. Tammany Hall was fighting to control ownership of the new team and location of the park. In March 1903, the New York press openly speculated about a variety of possible sites, and Ban Johnson was unable to secure any of them as John Brush, with Freedman's backing, continued to block them at every turn. Johnson, who treasured an image that was opposed to everything that Tammany Hall stood for, was forced to cut a deal. Ban Johnson waved a white flag and immediately a group of Tammany-connected owners emerged with control of a site.

The president of the team initially was Joseph Gordon, Deputy Commissioner of Buildings for the City of New York, a position that would help with the hasty construction of the new ball field. Whatever wealth he brought to the position he owed to his earlier life as a coal merchant. The other backers for the venture were less reputable and regarded as "bushwackers" by Clark Griffith.[7] Bill Devery was a former police chief and lent an air of respectability, but Frank Farrell would emerge as the real power in the ownership group.

Farrell was a former gambler and exactly the opposite of everything that Ban Johnson was campaigning against in his new league. He was known as the "Pool Room King" during his most colorful days and owed every penny he had ever made to wagering.[8] Devery was little better and known more for his ties to protection rackets than to honest police work. The three men were largely inactive within Tammany and its civic corruptions at the time of the purchase, but they were well enough connected to get the job done. Ban Johnson would have his Manhattan ball club and a hastily constructed ballpark. He would beat John Brush in the end game of chess the two men had been playing since 1894.

The overly large sum of $200,000 was being put forward for the construction of the new playing grounds between 165th and 168th Streets, Broadway and Fort Washington Avenues. Trolley lines served it regularly, but it would be several years before a subway stop was added for what would eventually be called Hilltop Park. As late as early April the grounds were littered with huge beams and stacks of lumber with dozens of workers hurriedly putting the grandstands together for a season that would begin in little more than three weeks. Such was the early life of the American League. Much of the money for the construction and salaries was coming from league backer Charles Somers and went into the well-greased pockets of Tammany men.[9]

The peace agreement between the two leagues had wider ranging implications than the location of the American League team in New York City. The intrigue of signing players for the Highlanders had forced other issues to the fore.

Barney Dreyfuss, the owner of the Pittsburgh team that won the National League pennant in 1902, had been a supporter of Ban Johnson at the birth of the American League. He had been fine with targeting other teams in the National League for talent, but once it was his turn, his enthusiasm disappeared. When Ban Johnson came calling to propose a post-season series in 1902 between Pittsburgh and Connie Mack's Athletics, Dreyfuss refused. The first World Series would have to wait for 1903.

Ending the warfare between the leagues and curtailing the shift of players back and forth was in the interest of owners in both leagues. The issue was called by 15 players who had signed contracts with both leagues in the off-season after 1902, most prominent among them Christy Mathewson. A resolution was worked out whereby the owners and managers agreed to split the players, with Mathewson staying with the New York Giants. From the date of that agreement onward, player jumping was not an issue until the Federal League pushed it back to the fore in 1914.

Significant long-term implications came from those meetings that shape the game to this day. The concern was that the game be played uniformly in both the American and National Leagues. The biggest concern was the foul strike rule that was in effect in the National League, but not the American. There was spirited dislike for the idea among Ban Johnson's crowd, but they ultimately gave way.

The catcher was for the first time forced to play at all times behind the batter and could no longer range back several feet. The pitching mound, something that existed only where various groundskeepers had invented one, was given a maximum height of 15 inches. A key owner in negotiating the compromises was August Herrmann who would remain a close friend of Clark Griffith's. Herrmann and Ban Johnson reached a final agreement on the rules changes and roster allocations on March 6 and a formalized written agreement was ratified by the owners of both leagues.[10]

Among those ratifying the new agreement were Charles Comiskey and Connie Mack, who had traveled far from their days on the front lines of the Brotherhood Wars as player radicals. Now they were pillars of the baseball establishment. The effect of the peace agreement these former players helped negotiate between the two leagues was a downward force on player salaries. Clark Griffith was another who was walking away from his ability to organize players to jump leagues. Mack and Comiskey were the establishment and Clark Griffith was firmly in their hire.

Salaries were capped for all intents and purposes and the reserve clause would bind players to their teams with increasing restriction even after a challenge was taken to the Supreme Court in 1922. Players lost that decision as the court ruled that baseball was immune from the Sherman Anti-trust Law and was not interstate commerce.

The reality for Clark Griffith in 1903 was one of a paid employee. He had not risen yet to Comiskey and Mack's stature, but his path was clear. With the labor wars at an end, Griffith set his sights on following in the footsteps of his friend Connie Mack. That avenue was not yet available in 1903. He was locked in combat against John McGraw and the road to fame and fortune lay in winning that contest.

The ultimate dream as a new season loomed for Clark Griffith was of a post-season series that would bring his New York Highlanders team up against McGraw's. But the Giants had a head start on Griff's new team. Christy Mathewson and Joe McGinnity were in great form to start the 1903 season and McGraw's nine was the first out of the gate. They remained in first place in the National League standings through early June.

Griffith's Highlanders team took the field to start the season wearing black uniforms and black hats, perhaps depicting their Tammany roots. But as a team they looked more like an aggregation cobbled together at the last minute and they stumbled in the early going. They sank immediately into seventh place in the American League standings at the end of May. Boston was getting great pitching out of Cy Young. Philadelphia, behind Plank and Waddell, was also near the top of the American League.

In consecutive match-ups against Philadelphia, Boston and Cleveland, Griffith's team lost seven out of ten games. But as he had done in Chicago, Griffith always got the best out of his team against the lower division. Playing Detroit, Washington, and Chicago in the second half of June, Chesbro, Tannehill and Keeler started to put together a run with Griffith adding some excellent pitching as well.

In Chicago on June 27, however, Griffith lost to his old teammates in a close contest and there was some satisfaction in the win as reported by the *Chicago Tribune*. The Chicago White Sox were no longer the strong team that

Griffith had built, and in July the Highlanders won a four-game series with Chicago to get their record for the year above .500 for the first time since early May as they climbed into fourth place in the league. There they would stay until September.

In September, Griffith's squad again had ten games against Boston and Philadelphia. Griffith crowed in the press about the team's chance to climb back into the thick of the race, aiming for second place. The Highlanders could not compete with the attack that Jimmy Collins' Boston team boasted, and the pitching duo of Bill Dinneen and Cy Young were outstanding all season long. They took the two series from the Highlanders and kept New York in fourth place, where they finished 17 games back of Boston.

Boston won its first American League pennant by a commanding 14-game margin over the Athletics. For the Highlanders, Jack Chesbro, Jesse Tannehill and Clark Griffith formed a solid mound crew, but once again Griff's charges lacked enough pop to win the league. Keeler had an off year and second baseman Jimmy Williams led the team in many categories. Clark Griffith at 33 was slowing down. He pitched only 213 innings and spread the work load among his five-man staff with Barney Wolfe and Harry Howell each throwing about 150 innings.

McGraw was in a closer race in the National League with Pittsburgh. Even without Tannehill and Chesbro, Barney Dreyfuss's team had an excellent pitching staff and an offense built around Honus Wagner, the future Hall of Famer who led the league with a .355 batting average. In 1903 the Pirates' Sam Leever was be one of the best pitchers in the National League, with a league-leading ERA of 2.06. The Pirates pulled ahead of the Giants in the second half of the season to take the pennant.

Mathewson and McGinnity were dominating for the Giants, with McGinnity racking up 434 total innings with a 2.43 ERA while winning 31 games. Mathewson was no less impressive, winning 30 games himself and logging 366 innings with a 2.26 ERA. It was one of the best pitching tandems in baseball history, but it was not enough. In August the Pirates won 12 games in a row and despite falling off in the last week of the season, finished well ahead of McGraw's Giants, who held onto second place.

The first World Series pitted Cy Young and the Boston Americans against Honus Wagner and the Pirates. In an eight-game series, Cy Young won twice after losing the first-ever World Series game.

When the season drew to a close Clark Griffith proposed an inter-league post-season series against the Giants. Several other cities sporting two baseball teams, such as St. Louis and Chicago, played short series to determine the best team in the city. It provided a salary bonus to the players. John Brush rebuffed Griffith's proposal to do the same in New York. His players lost out on the money the exhibition series represented and they made churlish remarks in the press, but to no avail.

Griffith saw in the proposed contest with McGraw a way to put extra money in the pockets of his players and reward them for a fine season. It built loyalty and Griffith was always a favorite with players as his ability to recruit them to his cause attested. Despite the gruff rejections of Brush and McGraw, New York City was on the verge of baseball greatness, casting itself as the lead in one of the longest running dramas in sports history. Ban Johnson had given Clark Griffith the star role for the Americans and he was determined to make the most of it in the 1904 pennant race.

CHAPTER 6

Second Fiddle to Muggsy McGraw

As Frank Deford noted in his wonderful book on John McGraw and Christy Mathewson, *The Old Ball Game*, the peaceful resolution of the conflict between the American and National League to begin the 1903 season set in place the beginnings of what became the golden era of baseball.[1] Some have opined that the best years of baseball ended during the Great Depression years, but Deford projects the era as lasting longer.

As the conflicts between John Brush and Ban Johnson slowly gave way to enlightened self-interest, 50 years of stability reigned in baseball during which the same teams waged war in the same cities in front of generation after generation of fans. The idea of a father passing down a baseball legacy to a son or daughter and subsequent generations was born in this historic period, the likes of which have not been seen since.

Whichever school of thought you prefer, the creative works of Ban Johnson, Connie Mack and their cohorts who established the American League set in motion a wonderful run in sports history. Those like Barney Dreyfuss and others in the National League with the foresight to see the powerful dynamic of two competing leagues deserve no less credit. Even the most myopic of owners, like Brush, would temper their harsh attitudes enough for the game to prosper remarkably.

The very successful post-season series in 1903 between the Pirates and Boston Americans provided players with handsome bonuses for their play, and owners saw their coffers filled by swelling attendance for championship games in the newly minted World Series of baseball. Teams in both leagues were anxious for another go at it in 1904.

Clark Griffith's pitching career was on the wane, but he was as eager as a pup to start the spring training period in Atlanta, Georgia, in March of

1904. "Highlanders Will Win American League and Force a Series," was the headline in the *New York Globe*. The story was all about the championship series between the Giants and Highlanders that Griffith foresaw at the end of the season.

Ban Johnson saw the success of his New York City franchise as a key to the ongoing viability of his American League venture. He selected Clark Griffith because of the success he had in Chicago. Griffith knew the challenge was not to beat the rest of the American League as much as it was to win the head-to-head competition for the hearts and minds of New York City fans in the contest against John "Muggsy" McGraw and his Giants. In 1904 Griffith continued to have strong financial backing and overall Highlanders salaries again topped off near $60,000.

The fight for talent that had formed the American League had led to higher salaries, but the contracts that had lured players to jump were now expiring and salaries were coming back to earth such that Griffith's club was spreading twice what many of the other teams were paying in 1904.[2] Yet it was money well spent from the perspective of Ban Johnson and Charles Somers, who knew the importance of the Highlanders franchise to their league.

In retrospect the emergence of the three successful New York City teams, two in Manhattan and one in Brooklyn, seems pre-destined. Yet Griffith knew in 1904 that the issue was anything but settled. He was clawing for a foothold against the walls of established power in Manhattan, and his grasp was anything but certain. Rigging the ship of baseball's most powerful vessel — the New York Yankees — for its maiden voyages may be one of Clark Griffith's most important contributions to the game of baseball — rue it though he eventually came to do.

In baiting McGraw and Brush, Griffith was setting the stage for the historic battles that shaped the game's golden era. No enduring contest did more to frame the perceptions of baseball during the first half of the twentieth century than the struggles between New York City's powerful baseball dynasties. When Griffith portrayed the 1904 season as a contest, not between himself and the defending American League champions in Boston, but between himself and McGraw, the Old Fox was doing all he could to stoke the fires with a new fuel, one that would carry baseball forward until mid-century.

For all of the historic glitter to the contest between New York teams, there was an ugly underbelly. Expectations were higher in New York City than anywhere else and the game was played there with a more deadly seriousness than anywhere else. Frank Farrell and Bill Devery did not like finishing fourth in 1903 and liked even less attendance lagged behind the Giants. The pressure was on Clark Griffith to improve on that fourth-place finish in 1904.

The New York press liked the chances for Griffith's rosy predictions. "Griffith's infield is the fastest ever seen," announced the *Globe* on March 17. In the press Griffith compared his three top pitchers, Chesbro, Powell and Hughes, to McGraw's, Mathewson, McGinnity and Ames, and saw an advantage for his team. It was a brash claim in light of the amazing performances just logged by McGinnity and Mathewson in 1903, but pluck and grit were Griff's strong suit.

The Highlanders traded Jesse Tannehill to Boston during the off-season after 1903 for Tom Hughes. Hughes was a very effective third starter for the World Series champions behind Cy Young and Bill Dinneen. He won 20 games in 1903 against only 7 losses and had an ERA of 2.57. But Hughes had been ineffective in the 1903 World Series, which may have convinced manager Jimmy Collins that he was not a big game pitcher.

In much the same manner, Tannehill did not measure up to expectations in New York. So the two teams were trading pitchers of relative equality, but the numbers seemed to favor Hughes. The more important acquisition was Jack Powell, who came over from the St. Louis Browns. He was an established star who in the prior seven seasons had averaged over 300 innings and nearly 20 wins for a second-tier team.

Hughes would be a huge disappointment in 1904, while Powell would slot in behind Chesbro to give the Highlanders two powerful right-handers. Clark Griffith may have been over-selling his three top "twirlers," but he was not leaving it all to chance.

Jack Chesbro's pre-season workouts were held at Harvard in March 1904. Since Mathewson had come to New York as a college educated man from Bucknell, it may have been intentional on both Chesbro's and Griffith's part to paint his arrival for the 1904 season in ivy-covered hues. Clark Griffith said several years later that at the turn of the century it "was considered more or less disgraceful for a man with a college education to enter baseball." Mathewson, as much as anyone else, changed that.[3]

Chesbro was not studying in the Harvard library, however. He was mentoring with Old Hoss Radbourn, although not directly. Chesbro was laboring to learn the "slow ball" that Radbourn had perfected. Mathewson's arsenal featured Radbourn's "fadeaway," and Chesbro landed in New York for the 1904 season announcing that he had mastered a new pitch that would add to his already impressive capabilities.

He informed the press that he had been working at Harvard on a "slow curve."[4] He described the pitch, saying that he moistened one finger to give the ball far more slip when he released it so that it floated toward the plate ever so slowly before finally diving beneath the batter's swing with a wicked break at the last moment. Chesbro said he first saw White Sox pitcher Elmer

Stricklett throw the spitter, but one can only imagine Griffith imparting the words of Radbourn to his ace as he dispatched him to Harvard for a degree in the aerodynamics of off-speed deliveries.

The 1904 season was a breakout year for Chesbro, and his mastery of the new pitch allowed him to take his already impressive game to the level where he could truly compete with Mathewson. The effects of the new pitch would slowly fade, but in 1904 Jack Chesbro joined the elites in pitching excellence, as he led the league in numerous categories and won a staggering 41 games and pitched 454 innings.

After a 1903 season when Iron Man McGinnity was pitching both ends of doubleheaders and winning them both, Chesbro would best all of McGinnity's marks. The Giants ace won 31 games in 1903 to lead the National League, but now Chesbro saw that and raised him a jaw-dropping ten wins, calmly laying down 41. McGinnity threw 434 innings in 1903, good enough to lead the National League. Chesbro added another 20 to that total as he logged 454 innings in 1904 to lead the American League.

It was statistically reminiscent of the nineteenth century greats like Radbourn, John Clarkson and others when the bench mark for pitching excellence was 40 wins in a season. It was another element in highly publicized competition between New York City teams that would last for decades.

McGinnity was actually the second-best pitcher on John McGraw's team as Christy Mathewson emerged from McGinnity's shadow in 1904. Even in April of 1904, in comparisons of the teams in the New York press, Mathewson was the exceptional talent that tilted the scales toward the Giants.[5]

The comparison between pitchers was not the only one, but it was certainly the best. The *New York Globe* featured large photographs of the Giants' Roger Bresnahan and the Highlanders' Willie Keeler in April before the beginning of the season. They were pictured at the bat, both choking up a good three inches on long, heavy-looking timber. Although the Giants as a team outscored their opponents by a wide margin in 1904, they did it the way McGraw's nineteenth century teams in Baltimore had done: with speed and daring on the base paths.

Bresnahan was not the equal of Keeler with the bat, and it would be Dan McGann, Bill Dahlen, and Sam Mertes who would lead the Giants. Each of them had more than 40 steals in 1904 as they parlayed McGraw's style of play into an amazing record of 106 wins against only 47 losses.

Clark Griffith may have known just how steep the hill was that he set off to climb in late April of 1904, but he, Chesbro, and Keeler believed themselves equal to the task as they set the Boston Americans in their sights. They began the season with three games at home against Jimmy Collins' team starting on April 14.

The Highlanders had been training in Atlanta's Piedmont Park, and the *New York Globe* described the team as fit and ready after long, physical workouts had been established by Griffith in the spring. "Griffith's complexion is dark as tanbark and he looks as spry as a futurity candidate the morning of the race," opined the *Globe*. The team had worked its way up the east coast after a series of exhibition games in New Orleans.

One of those games, scheduled for April Fools' Day, had mischievously advertised a match between McGraw's Giants and the Highlanders, but it had all been an elaborate ruse. The Giants were training in Birmingham, Alabama, where they were too busy to engage in frivolity, and McGraw was seldom in the mood for Clark Griffith's jokes.

The Giants started the season on a long winning streak and would not be headed throughout the summer. The Highlanders, however, were bested in two of their three contests to start the season with Boston. Griffith's primary rivals for the American League pennant took the season-opening series in New York, providing a negative contrast for the local media.

The garrulous Clark Griffith had helped pump enthusiasm into the local rivalry as fans packed both opening day venues in the New York City area. Twenty thousand were on hand at the Polo Grounds to watch the Giants square off against their other cross-town rivals from Brooklyn. Fifteen thousand were on hand to watch the Highlanders.

Griffith's team recovered from their early losses and settled into their season successfully, chasing the Boston Americans. After winning two series against the Washington Nationals, they beat the Americans in Boston two of three and climbed into second place. But Connie Mack's Athletics still had Rube Waddell, who would give the Highlanders an especially tough time in 1904. He struck out 16 in winning the first match-up against Griffith's team in 1904.

There was an overall decline in offense in 1904 which some attributed to the new foul strike rule. Others placed the blame on the spitball. Chesbro was using that extra moisture to add bite to his slow curve and the effects did not go unnoticed in the league as other pitchers used it more freely. Griffith's team seemed well adapted if the new pitch was providing an edge in favor of crafty pitchers.

After losses to the Athletics, the Highlanders dropped to fourth place in May and were playing just above .500 with a 19–15 record when the month ended. The team had numerous injuries, with Kid Elberfeld and Dave Fultz both sidelined. Griffith brought in substitutes, but with two of his best bats out, the Highlanders attack was anemic.

More imposing yet was the oddity of scheduling that put New York on a western road trip the entire month of June. They would play 22 away games before returning home. It was a true test of their mettle and Griffith did a great job of holding his troops together through the adventure. He wrote about it in the *New York Globe*, saying that the contests in St. Louis were like "the fight for San Juan Hill."

The Highlanders responded to Griffith, winning 15 of the contests before returning to New York. The *New York Globe* said of Griffith, "besides being a great ball player, (he) has a pleasing disposition, which accounts for his popularity with his players."[6] It may also have been the salaries that were higher than for any other team in the league, but the western swing put New York back in second place in a tight contest — only two games behind Boston — as the season moved into July.

Besides the offense of Wee Willie Keeler, the most impressive hero during the June run was Jack Chesbro. Starting May 14, Chesbro won 14 straight games including three shutouts. To open July the Highlanders took two of three games from Washington and swept four games from the Philadelphia Athletics. Dave Fultz rejoined the team and added more clout to the offense. Everything seemed to be falling into place for New York. A key series loomed against the champion Boston Americans from July 7–11 and with Chesbro pitching so well, it seemed first place in the American League was again within Clark Griffith's grasp.

This time New York did not get the timely hitting that had put them in such a promising position. Jesse Tannehill, pitching now for Boston, was making the acquisition of Tom Hughes look very bad. He was having his best season. New York lost three of the four games against Boston to fall off the pace again, though it was Tannehill's start that was the only one the Highlanders won.

The possibility of the Highlanders winning the American League pennant had taken on real urgency, despite the team losing the series to Boston. Griff was still pushing for a post-season series with McGraw. The possibility that John McGraw and John Brush would have to play Griff's Highlanders in a post-season series drew a lengthy tirade from McGraw in the press. "Giants Won't Play Americans," read the headline.[7]

McGraw's team was running away with the National League pennant race and would ultimately win 106 games in 1904. But in the July papers they were expressing a willingness to end play without any post-season series, despite the precedent of the 1903 championship. Brush and McGraw were willing to deny their players the substantial bonus money of post-season play rather than submit to a contest against Ban Johnson's champion, especially if it were the New York Highlanders.

McGraw said in an interview with Allen Sangree, "When Johnson got the league going, he thought he could be better by invading Baltimore and

New York."[8] There was considerable bitterness still eating at McGraw as he talked about the persecution by umpires before he left Baltimore that was clearly still fresh in his mind. He said that the choice was his and he would not allow his players to enter into a contest with the Highlanders for the championship.

Griffith's squad could not win the big games and did much to relieve McGraw of any real cause for concern. They were able to win handily against the bottom tier of teams like St. Louis and Washington, but again in July, in head-to-head games with the Chicago White Sox, who were in third place, New York lost three of four. Chicago, Boston and the Highlanders jockeyed back and forth in the American League standings throughout the summer of 1904.

In early August both New York teams appeared in first place on several occasions, and in late August the Highlanders began to play some of their best baseball. They won six straight starting on August 30 and pulled ahead of Boston by a half-game and ahead of Chicago by five games on September 5. John Ganzel was hitting close to .300 and carrying the offense after his slow start in April and May. Elberfeld was back from injury at shortstop and playing extremely well, and Keeler, who had a mid-season injury, was also back in the lineup. Once again, the fates seemed to be aligned. The New York press was comparing the Giants and Highlanders in a series of articles that touted the value of a cross-town World Series match between the two teams.

It all came down to a final five-game series against Boston. Chesbro had been outstanding down the stretch, perhaps even better than during his 14-game winning streak. He started three games in each of the final three weeks of the season and relieved in another. As much as anyone, he was carrying the team.

Though Chesbro was the natural choice to start the final series against Boston, some have questioned whether Clark Griffith pushed Chesbro too much as the Highlanders ace racked up a staggering number of innings. Griffith had seldom ever placed such a heavy burden on a single player, and as a pitcher he knew the costs of overwork. Glenn Stout, in his book *Yankees Century*, claims that Frank Farrell and Ban Johnson were pressing Griffith to use Chesbro, seeing him as the team's only chance to beat Boston.[9]

Regardless of who was calling the tune or why, Chesbro rose to the occasion the seventh day of October with the teams playing a single game in Manhattan. Kid Elberfeld and Willie Keeler put New York ahead in the seventh inning by a 2–1 margin and Chesbro held on as New York won, 3–2. It was a well-played contest that put all of the New York City faithful behind the team. But there was a rotten core.

Frank Farrell and Bill Devery made a fatal miscalculation that came into play at this point. The entire five-game series was originally to be played in New York, giving the locals the clear advantage. But Farrell and Devery had relocated two of the games to Boston early in the season before it became clear that a pennant race between the two teams was shaping up. They had rented out Hilltop Park to the Columbia University baseball team for a single day as a way to eke out a little extra money from a team they saw as still disappointing.

Thus, for two crucial games, the location shifted back to Boston. The Highlanders lost them both and to make matters worse, Chesbro insisted to Griff that he pitch in Boston as well. Griffith had told him to stay in New York to be ready for the final games, but he relented and allowed his ace pitcher to call his own number.

It did not work. Chesbro was beaten in Boston and beaten badly as the team lost his start by a discouraging 13–2 score. Cy Young pitched the second game and beat the Highlanders not only with his arm but also with a key sacrifice fly to score the winning run. The outcome of the season came to rest on a crucial doubleheader to be played back in New York City with the Highlanders needing a sweep to win the pennant.

There was a day off before the doubleheader and Clark Griffith gave the ball to his ace, hoping that he would be sharp again. Chesbro told his manager, "I will trim 'em on Monday if it costs an arm."[10] He not only shut down the Boston team in the first half of the game, but had two key hits to push the Highlanders to a 2–0 lead in the sixth inning.

An error in the seventh inning allowed Boston to tie the game and extended Chesbro's labors to the point that he told Griffith he was done. But Griffith left him in the game after getting advice from catcher Red Kleinow on how much Chesbro had left. In the ninth, Kid Elberfeld made an error on a routine grounder to put Boston's Lou Criger aboard. Boston moved him around to third base, but it took two outs to get him there.

Criger was on third when the fateful event that changed Griffith's career occurred. Chesbro got two strikes on the batter, Freddy Parent. Then Chesbro threw the same spitter he had been throwing all season long. It sailed on him and the catcher who had been catching the spitter all season long, Red Kleinow, could not stop it before it went to the backstop, allowing Criger to score the third and winning run.

Clark Griffith blamed Kleinow for years to come, saying it was a passed ball, though the consensus at the time laid the blame at Chesbro's feet. Fatigue was seen as the guilty party by many. Either way, Clark Griffith was denied another American League championship. It would have been his second in four years and solidified Griff's place as one of the new American League's best managers. It might have been enough to root Griffith to the Manhattan soil, but it was not to be.

John McGraw would not relent and play Boston in a post-season championship and it did not make his players happy to be losing the money. John Brush decided that McGraw was wrong, but not until that winter when Brush worked on a committee that mapped out the rules for post-season play in the future. Baseball history moved onward for both John McGraw, who became a legendary manager for the Giants, and Clark Griffith, who would find his own fame and fortune on the other side of the Hudson, somewhere far to the south of New York.

CHAPTER 7

Losing Ground

Clark Griffith celebrated his 34th birthday shortly after the end of the 1904 season, one that had added luster back to his reputation for bringing winning baseball wherever he went. As a pitcher he was on the down slope of his playing career, but as a player-manager was still regarded as one of the more colorful and successful men in the game. The 1905 season would be one of the first to dim the luster of Griff's star, but again he would learn something in the process, something that would shape the game in new ways.

The 1904 season had been a frustrating one for Clark Griffith. Not only did he fail to deliver on his promise of a pennant winner, but the rancor between the two Manhattan baseball teams, so evident in McGraw's refusal to engage in a post-season series, was a blow as well. It did not prevent him from using the same ploy in the spring of 1905 to fire up the troops. Not three months after the 1904 season ended in a whimper, Griff again challenged New York Giants President Brush to commit to a post-season match in 1905.[1]

Brush "emphatically dismissed" the idea, but would soften on the notion as the 1905 season wore on.[2] His enthusiasm increased as the Highlanders and Clark Griffith's prospects for winning the American League pennant faded.

Griffith's third season in New York City would be his worst. He lost his first baseman John Ganzel, who decided to retire from the majors to devote time to the Grand Rapids, Michigan, team in which he had purchased controlling interest. Ganzel had been a solid bat in the lineup for Griff, but the open spot in the lineup was quickly filled.

Hal Chase, called the "California Comet" by *Sporting Life* magazine in the spring, was heralded as "one of the best youngsters he has ever seen" by no less than Frank Selee, the manager of the Chicago Cubs who had managed the Boston Beaneaters during their prime.[3] Chase was drafted by the Highlanders and joined the team to replace Ganzel. Clark Griffith was excited at the prospect of managing the young star. Chase was faster than Ganzel and a far more talented fielder than anyone who played first base at the time.

It was neither the offense nor Griffith's usually sound defense that failed the Highlanders in 1905, but the pitching. Jack Chesbro pitched in rainy conditions on opening day, came down with pneumonia and did not recover his strength until the middle of June. It may have been the extra weight Chesbro was carrying as well, as he reported in 1905 well over his prior playing weight. Without the Jack Chesbro of 1904, Griff's pitching staff was lackluster, and the team fell into last place early in the year and struggled to rise from the cellar.

Even when "Happy Jack" returned to form, he did not have enough support to right the ship. Kid Elberfeld was injured for a long portion of the season and Hal Chase was out after being hit by a pitch in the face.

Jack Powell, who had been stellar in 1904, failed from the start in 1905. Al Orth, who came on late in the 1904 season, pitched well for the entirety of the 1905 season and was the second-best arm the Highlanders had, giving Griffith hopes for a better year in 1906.

Clark Griffith made his usual contribution, pitching almost entirely in relief, but still logging 101 innings, with a positive record of 9–6. He relieved in 18 games, almost always when the game was on the line and he led the league in closing games. His ERA of 1.68 was the best mark during his long career, albeit in just 101⅔ innings of work. He knew exactly when to insert himself into crucial game situations and perfected the use of the relief pitcher, both as a tool in the manager's arsenal and as a way to extend a career.

He was the lone bright spot on the team in many ways, and the Old Fox would store the knowledge about how an effective relief pitcher could stretch the resources of a weak starting rotation. More importantly he would learn how capable relievers could lengthen the service time of his best pitchers, a lesson he would apply when managing the best pitcher of all time, Walter Johnson, in later years.

As the disappointment of 1905 deepened, Griffith tried to find additional pitching help in the form of Casey Patten of Washington, "Wabash" George Mullin of Detroit, and Harry Howell of St. Louis. He made overtures for them, but he got little support in acquiring them. Frank Farrell and the rest of the Highlanders ownership provided little support for the team and Griffith was left to twist in the wind throughout the tough season.

Although Griffith could not bring any of the best on board, the 1905 season was a banner year for pitchers. Average run production dropped under four runs per game in the American League. The league batting average was only .241 and the "dead ball" was becoming increasingly inert, due in part as well to the advent of the foul strike rule. The difference was more pronounced in the American League however, and the statistical analysis suggests there may have been a fall off in talent after the league was established in 1901.

CHART 7-1. SELECTED AVERAGE LEAGUE
BATTING STATISTICS, PER GAME BY YEAR

	1901		1902		1903		1904		1905	
	Bavg	Runs	Bavg	Runs	Bavg	Runs	Bavg	Runs	Bavg	Runs
AL	.277	5.3	.275	4.9	.255	4.1	.244	3.5	.241	3.7
NL	.267	4.6	.259	4.0	.269	4.8	.249	3.9	.255	4.1

Beginning with the 1903 season, the National League gained supremacy and held the advantage for several years, until players like Ty Cobb and "Wahoo" Sam Crawford tilted the scales back toward the American League.

The Highlanders offense was better than the sub-par league performance levels, but their pitching was decidedly below average. Boston had the pitching tandem of Cy Young and Jesse Tannehill. The Philadelphia Athletics had Rube Waddell and Eddie Plank. All of the top finishers in the American League had at least three highly successful pitchers in 1905. That depth was put to the test when John Brush allowed a playoff championship series at the end of the season. The New York Giants shredded the notion of American League pitching supremacy as Mathewson and McGinnity shut out the Philadelphia Athletics in four of the five games to win the second World Series.

Clark Griffith's squad finished the 1905 season in sixth place. They had clawed their way out of the cellar as the injuries mounted, but it left questions in the minds of team president Farrell as to whether Griffith was still the person to lead the team.

The Highlanders had drawn exceptionally well when they were in the pennant race in 1904, fifth in major league attendance with 438,000 fans for the year. That figure dropped off noticeably as the team fell out of contention early in the 1905 season. Attendance at Hilltop Park in 1905 was 309,000, sixth in the league. It was not enough to impress in the great city of New York.

In June, when the Highlanders' struggles were at their worst, there was talk about consolidating the two Manhattan teams. The talk was quickly squelched, but it was indicative of the tenuous nature of Ban Johnson's hold on the fans of New York City. Yet it was the ability of even a last-place team to draw substantial fans that proved Johnson's proposition that an American League team in Manhattan was essential to the survival of the league.

During the off-season Frank Farrell put down rumors that Ned Hanlon would replace Griffith as the manager in 1906. Instead, Farrell acknowledged that the team needed more talent and promised to give Griffith the money to bolster his roster. Griffith's off-season acquisitions were strictly mundane, however, and whether it was the scale of the budget or just a paucity of available talent, the Highlanders reported to New Orleans for spring training with largely the same squad as the prior year.

Griffith started the spring sessions earlier and stressed conditioning more as a way to address the numerous injuries from the prior season. He was counting on the continuing development of players who had cut their teeth in 1905 like Hal Chase and Bill Hogg. The latter took the third spot in the rotation after Chesbro and Orth. Griffith supplemented them with Doc Newton and Walter Clarkson, who had joined the team late in the 1905 season.

Griffith himself was now 35, and 1906 would be his last season where he took an active role on the field. It would be his 15th professional season, and while he would take the mound a half-dozen times in coming years, those instances would merely be for show, a fond remembrance for Griffith of his long career. He would win only two games in 1906 and they would be his last, moving his record to 237 total wins to go with a respectable lifetime ERA of 3.31.

The 1906 season was one of the few in Griffith's career when he would have a strong offensive club. Hal Chase took his game to the next level in 1906, raising his average to .323. Willie Keeler and Kid Elberfeld both batted over .300 and with Chase they were a formidable core in the middle of the Highlanders lineup. As the offensive drought continued throughout the American League, only the Highlanders and Cleveland Naps managed to score more than four runs per game.

Cleveland had Nap Lajoie, who hit .355 and was near the top of the league in several offensive categories. The Naps also boasted three pitchers with earned run averages under two runs per game, including future Hall of Famer Addie Joss, but they finished a close third behind the Highlanders.

New York's offense carried the team but the pitching came around after its disappointing 1905 season. Jack Chesbro still had one more excellent season left in his arm and he managed 325 innings and 23 wins, despite numerous injuries. But it was the emergence of Al Orth that gave Griffith a reputable staff ace. Orth led staff with 338 innings and won 27 games in what would be his best season in baseball.

Did Orth learn the spitter from Griffith and Chesbro? Orth had pitched for a decade in the major leagues before coming over to the Highlanders in the middle of the 1904 season. Never did he experience the kind of success he had in 1906. The ghost of Old Hoss Radbourn may have cast another shadow for Clark Griffith as the Old Fox tried one more time to compete on an even footing in New York with John McGraw's Giants. Orth and Hal

Chase were Griffith's best, last chance for a World Series championship match-up in New York City.

The Highlanders came out of the gate slowly in 1906, but the offense began to assert itself late in May. The extra conditioning had taken pounds off Chesbro and it seemed to be helping numerous others. *The Sporting Life* opined in June 1906, that Hal Chase was becoming a star and that "to see him play is alone worth the journey up in the sweltering subway."[4] Chase was garrulous and good-looking, quick on his feet with the media and became the team's most popular player.[5]

Clubbing their way to victories, the team won 11 games in a row to pull into first place by June 1. They won 16 out of 17 games from the middle of May until Connie Mack's Philadelphia Athletics finally beat them in the second game of a double-header early in June to break the spell. They won three of those four games against the Athletics, however, and dethroned Philadelphia to make the Highlanders the most popular ticket in town once again. The team was batting a robust .291, well ahead of any other club in the American League.

The press recognized the contribution that Clark Griffith was making even if he was no longer a regular contributor from the mound. William Koelsch, of *Sporting Life,* wrote of Griffith that there was no one more hard working in the game of baseball, no one more conscientious or deserving of success. "In the face of great obstacles and ... discouraging conditions," he gave credit to Griffith for the team's resurgence. He described the Highlanders manager in a way few merited, as "the brainy and courageous exponent of the square deal."[6]

As a full-time manager rarely taking the mound, Griffith found the work more stressful than when he had been able to contribute on the field. By August he was worn to a frazzle and told by a physician that he needed to rest or he would find himself in the hospital. Despite the hard work and worry, the Highlanders were unable to maintain the pace that they set in June. The telling games came in August when they played the White Sox in two four-game series and lost seven of the eight games, tying the other.

The Highlanders' vaunted offensive juggernaut was completely shut down by the White Sox pitching staff that allowed only 10 runs during those games and shut out the Highlanders three times. Charlie Comiskey's team still fea-tured several of the players that had won the first American League pennant under Griffith in 1901. Fielder Jones was the manager and, while he had none of the punch of the Highlanders lineup, he had the best pitching staff from top to bottom.

Roy Patterson was still pitching for the White Sox, but he was plagued by injury. The team was carried by a deep rotation that featured four pitchers.

Frank Owen, Ed Walsh, Doc White, and Nick Altrock all had excellent seasons, and Walsh was just beginning a career in which he would dominate the league several times, most notably in 1908 when he was the last pitcher to win 40 games. Altrock would become a mainstay in the life of Clark Griffith as a third base coach for the Old Fox's Nationals in the coming years.

Griffith's Highlanders team in 1906 was game to the end. They snapped back from their discouraging losses to Chicago by going on another winning streak that exceeded the earlier one. They won 15 in a row going into September and climbed back into contention with the White Sox, but could not close the deal, finishing three games back.

Instead of a World Series between the two New York clubs, the first-ever same-city championship series was held in Chicago between the White Sox and Cubs. There was discussion of a secondary series to be held in New York as both of the New York teams finished in second place in their leagues. John Brush and his manager McGraw both agreed to the idea for such a contest and McGraw quickly laid down the gauntlet to Griffith, describing the beating such a contest would entail for Ban Johnson's favorite.

It was Frank Farrell who declined to participate this time. He said his team was depleted physically from the grueling season, but it may have been the dictates of the two league presidents, who did not wish to diminish publicity for the main contest in Chicago. In the World Series the same White Sox pitching that had shut down the Highlanders' attack had similar success against the Cubs.

Nick Altrock bested Mordecai "Three Finger" Brown in the first game, 2–1, and Ed Walsh shut out the Cubs in Game 3. Ironically it was the offense of the American League champions that delivered the Series win. The White Sox hitters won Games 5 and 6 by scoring 16 runs behind the inspired performance of second baseman Frank Isbell, who had been the mainstay of Griffith's infield in 1901.

The days when Griffith had managed the Chicago championship team and led the New York Highlanders into contention were fading at the end of the 1906 season. He was done as a pitcher and was frustrated by his inability to win the American League pennant. He could boast another second place finish to keep his reputation intact, but second-place was not enough in New York City.

During the off-season Griffith predicted the usual success for his New York American League club and no doubt meant it. He could not know that there would be no more moves by Frank Farrell to bring in the kind of personnel needed to craft a winning team, and Charles Somers was focused on his own team in Cleveland.

The Highlanders drew well all during the 1906 season and Hilltop Park at 165th Street and Broadway brought in 435,000 fans, more than the Polo Grounds during the same season. However, despite successfully establishing an American League team in Manhattan as a viable contender and rival to the Giants, Clark Griffith would learn how harsh expectations in New York City could be. The Big Apple would become one of the most demanding baseball venues over the years, and one of its first victims was Clark Griffith.

William F. Hoelsch, who covered the New York baseball scene for *The Sporting Life*, had been a loyal supporter of Clark Griffith as had the "Old Copy Boy" who had covered the Highlanders for the *New York Globe*. Their enthusiasm waned as both New York teams fell out of contention early during the 1907 season. Kid Elberfeld began to take a leadership role for the Highlanders on the field, confronting umpires and getting himself tossed from games to show that he was not happy with the way the team was being managed. Some saw it, however, as just irrational behavior from a player who was committing far too many errors and on the downside of his career.

Kid Elberfeld was leading the team in hitting in 1907, but most of the old Highlanders were exactly that. The players Griffith brought in to bolster the lineup in 1903 season had been established players then and had been paid accordingly. Now the star of that team, Willie Keeler, was on his last legs and the only new star on the team was Hal Chase, who did not have the same lusty season in 1907 as his breakout year in '06.

The offense under-performed, but the problem at Hilltop Park was again the pitching. Jack Chesbro was a pale shadow of the great pitcher of the 1904 campaign. He managed just over 200 innings as injuries and poor conditioning continued to plague him. Al Orth was effective but had a losing record.

The team played reasonably well early in the 1907 season. They maintained a winning record through May, but the western teams were ascendant that year. Cleveland and Detroit came into New York in June and beat the Highlanders six out of seven games. Griff's team never saw a winning record again for the rest of the season. By August Kid Elberfeld's antics on the field had become the focus of coverage in the press and his behavior was interpreted as an open challenge to Griffith.

On August 3, Frank Farrell backed the Old Fox in his confrontation with Elberfeld publicly, but it was the kind of press coverage that no manager wanted to see. Griffith's long efforts to bring a winner were outlined in the papers, but the bottom line was also stressed. The team was in sixth place, hopelessly out of the race. Griffith was portrayed as a hard-working manager who was as good as any, but he had not been able to win it all, to bring an American League pennant to New York. The implication was that patience was not in infinite supply.

Hughie Jennings, manager of the Tigers, had what every manager needed: a powerful lineup and effective pitching. His team coasted to its first American League pennant behind Ty Cobb, Sam Crawford and a fine pitching staff. Connie Mack's Athletics were a close second. The Tigers began a run of three straight seasons when they carried the colors of the American League into the World Series, and each year they lost.

During the off-season the conflict between Elberfeld and Griffith continued to play out in the press. Elberfeld assured the writers that if Griffith were still in New York to begin the 1908 season, he would not be. Griffith was no longer an active player and Elberfeld was the best on-the-field leader that the team had to offer.

Griffith retired to his Montana ranch in the off-season to ponder his future. He was reported as buying ownership shares in the Montreal minor league club, and it was clear that his thoughts were turning in that direction. The inability to play the game any longer was a frustration, and looking on from the dugout during a season such as 1907 was particularly frustrating. His old friends Connie Mack and Charles Comiskey had parlayed their playing days into team ownership and it was clearly the direction Griffith wanted to go.

The problems with the Highlanders returned almost immediately in the spring of 1908 and did not abate. The true nature of Griff's frustrations came out in mid-season when Rube Marquard made his ascent to the major leagues. Playing for Indianapolis, John Brush's old club, Marquard was seen as one of the great young pitching talents. Griffith recognized that unique ability and made one of the first offers to bring him to New York.

Frank Farrell would not support the bid, whether for lack of funds or other reasons.[7] Marquard would not have an immediate impact in New York, but by 1911 he was a pitching star for John McGraw, teaming with Mathewson to bring the Giants consecutive pennants in 1911, 1912, and 1913. The inability of Griffith to compete for the best young talent behind the ownership of the Highlanders was as much the problem as anything the erratic Kid Elberfeld presented.

The 1908 season was worse than its predecessor. Again, the team played well early, and ended May tied for first place. However, in June the Highlanders established a unique mark for futility. They managed to win only seven of 28 games during June. On June 24, Clark Griffith "quit for the first time in his life."[8] The press reported that owner Frank Farrell went to Philadelphia where the team was playing and tried to talk Griffith into remaining with the team, but to no avail.

Frank Farrell was trying to make the calls in the dugout as he was reputed to have done with Chesbro in 1904. Griffith may have let the owner ruin the

1904 pennant, or at least Chesbro's arm, but in the middle of the 1908 season he decided he had seen enough of the Big Apple. Farrell would not back Griffith when he sought talent like Marquard, and without the top talent there would be no pennant. The long losing streak was just the final straw. The stress of managing in New York and for Frank Farrell had taken its toll, perhaps on Griffith's health as much as anything.

Farrell tried to coax Willie Keeler into stepping in to manage, but he reportedly hid from the owner to avoid having to discuss the subject. Kid Elberfeld was named the interim manager, and Clark Griffith wished him well and returned to his ranch in Montana for badly needed rest.

Griffith sat out the rest of the season, though he was sought out by the press for his assessment of the World Series contest between the Tigers and the Cubs. Griff dutifully picked the American League team as the heavy favorite, but the Cubs proved to have learned something from their match against the White Sox two years earlier. Joe Tinker, John Evers and Frank Chance outplayed their Midwestern counterparts and won the series convincingly in five games. It was the last World Series win for the Cubs franchise.

Upon Clark Griffith's departure from New York, Grantland Rice wrote this poem for Clark Griffith.

LAMENTATIONS OF "GRIFF" THE OLD FOX
By Grantland Rice
Farewell Old Rag, it breaks my heart,
To see you act so shy;
But then the best of friends must part,
So here's a last goodbye,
We've worked for you in sun and rain,
My trusty band so true,
We've battled aye, we've bled in vain,
Farewell, farewell to you.[9]

By November Clark Griffith's departure was characterized as Moses leaving Egypt, setting forth from the oppression of Manhattan for the promised land. It was not an idle comparison. Griff's Canaan turned out to be Cincinnati, Ohio, where he took over for his old first baseman, John Ganzel, as manager.[10] Clark Griffith's attempts to gain the services of Rube Marquard had involved August "Garry" Herrmann, and the two men had a good relationship dating back to the origins of the American League.

The two men had an extensive correspondence that would last for many years. For Griffith it was not so much a return to the National League as it was a return to the Midwest, to home and a sense of belonging. The great majority of his playing years had been in the National League and his family was still in Normal, Illinois, far closer to Cincinnati than New York City, both geographically and philosophically.

The Cincinnati Reds had won the American Association championship in 1882, but after joining the National League in 1890 they had settled into the second division where they had remained comfortably for most of the two decades since. The local press saw the team's problems arising from a lack of discipline, and Griffith was known as a fair boss, but one who demanded conditioning and discipline. Griffith signed only a one-year contract and observers believed he was leery of his chance to succeed where so many others had failed.

Almost immediately Griffith began to make changes in the moribund Reds. Well in advance of the 1909 season, he dispatched catcher Admiral Schlei — a native of Cincinnati and fan favorite — and then moved outfielder John Kane, who had also grown too comfortable at the feeding trough. He got shortstop Tom Downey for Kane and gave Dick Hoblitzell the first base job for the departed player-manager, Ganzel. Griff announced a spring 1909 schedule for his new team that he described as designed to keep them "busier than a colony of red ants around a honeycomb."[11]

He brought in pitcher Art Fromme from St. Louis, outfielder Rebel Oakes to replace Kane, and remade the Reds into his kind of team, one that was fast, played good defense and could pitch. The makeover was not total and he did not have deep pockets behind him as he once did, but the team was better from the outset as the 1909 season began. Most writers thought that the best contribution Clark Griffith would make was the fighting spirit he brought to all endeavors, and one that had been missing from Cincinnati baseball for decades.

Griffith described his new additions as young colts who would push the older nags for playing time. After putting the players through a more strenuous training session in Atlanta, Georgia, the team got off to a fast start, winning seven of their first nine contests to sit briefly atop the National League. They slowly slid backward, but did show brief spurts that had the local fans wondering if Griffith had pulled off a miracle.

The Reds won seven in a row in early June, including a game against the Giants. The head-to-head match-up with John McGraw must have been one of Clark Griffith's delights during the 1909 season. He split the season series until the Reds ventured to New York in July and were unceremoniously swept by the Giants in four games that were hard-fought contests, but losses that hurt the pride of the Old Fox.

The team finished the season a single game over .500, adequate enough for a modest fourth-place and first-division finish few would have predicted. Yet it sounded better than it was. McGraw's team in third place was 15 games better than Griffith's squad, and the Pittsburgh team that won the pennant was 33 games ahead in the standings.

It was no better in 1910 and Griffith was unhappy almost from the outset. The team managed only a fifth-place finish and McGraw's team was clearly on the threshold once again. Clark Griffith was making good money managing in Cincinnati. At $7,500 a year, Griff was making more than the $5,000 Frank Farrell had paid in New York. The Old Fox admired August Herrmann for his largesse, but the chances to win in Cincinnati were bleak and in 1911 the team was even worse, slipping to sixth place.

By the end of the 1911 season Clark Griffith was more discouraged than he had ever been about his prospect to make baseball an enduring part of his life. He retired to his Montana ranch wondering if it was not time to end his baseball career. He had ended his playing days in New York and though he had bought a second chance in Cincinnati, his prospects as a manager were looking increasingly dour. The last two seasons in New York had been a blow to his ebullient spirit, and his inability to put together any kind of winner in Cincinnati was calling his future in the game into question.

It was with some despair that Clark Griffith considered his future. He would always nurse a grudge against New York City and never forget his failure to make the most of his chance there. He had practically guaranteed he would beat his rival John McGraw and had believed he had every chance to follow through, only to be frustrated by his inability to make good on that promise.

He knew that success depended upon having enough control to craft a winner one player at a time, to bring his kind of player into the fold. When he could not convince first Frank Farrell and then his friend August Herrmann of the value of his vision, he knew he needed either a stake in a team or to get out of the game for something else. Ranching was the alternative and he was seriously considering it at the end of the 1911 season. He wanted to follow in the footsteps of his friend Connie Mack, but there were few chances for that on the horizon, nothing more than the red sun setting in Montana.

CHAPTER 8

Clark Griffith
Comes to Washington

There were those in the Cincinnati press that believed Clark Griffith was burning his bridges, but once his days as a wildcat youth on the West Coast were behind him, he never left a situation without kind words for everyone with whom he had been associated. His graceful civility was on display as Griffith pulled out of Cincinnati. He had only kind words for his friend August Herrmann and all of the Reds players, despite the overall lack of success they had experienced together.

The Old Fox had been trying for an ownership stake in baseball dating to his earlier attempts to buy into teams in Montreal, and it continued even to the last days in Cincinnati. His most annoying slight came when Ban Johnson promised him a loan of $10,000 to buy an interest in a team. Griffith was never timid about asserting the unique role he had played in assisting Johnson in getting the American League going and always remembered the promise Johnson never fulfilled. By 1911 his relationship with Ban Johnson had cooled, and for all of the water that Clark Griffith had carried for him in Chicago and New York, there was never the final follow-up Griffith wanted more than anything.[1]

Griffith had been looking for an ownership stake in a baseball team since 1903 when he put an offer forward to S. F. Angus to buy the Detroit team as part of a group. That offer was rebuffed by Ban Johnson who wanted local ownership of the American League team.[2] August Herrmann offered Griffith a limited ownership deal in Cincinnati, perhaps after the initial contact between the Washington baseball club and Griffith was made by Ed Walsh, a limited partner with the Washington Nationals during the 1911 World Series. Yet August Herrmann did not need him as a stock holder or in any other capacity as much as the Washington Nationals. The Reds were a staid and settled team with roots in the early years of the National League.

Washington, by contrast, was struggling to stay afloat in the American League. They had been contracted out of existence by the National League in 1898. They turned to Clark Griffith hoping his reputation as a proven competitor who had built winners in Chicago and New York would prevent extinction again.

The immediate opening for Clark Griffith came about because of a fire at the Nationals' ballpark, Washington Park. A plumber's lamp set fire to the grandstands on March 17, 1911. Before beginning their work, the plumbers had turned off water to the site so there was nothing with which to fight the flames that spread quickly throughout the completely wooden structure. The stadium was totally destroyed along with four surrounding structures.[3]

The team's stockholders needed to raise capital to rebuild the grandstands and refurbish the field.[4] They needed an infusion of $100,000 and were offering common stock to underwrite the construction.[5] Griffith was told of the stock offering and when Tom Noyes and the shareholders agreed to include Griffith, the die was cast.[6]

Griffith recognized not just the ownership opportunity, but the importance of the role he could fill in Washington. Not only would he finally have a significant stake in a team, but he would get the wider influence he had been seeking for years.[7] He sold off all the livestock from his Montana ranch that he had homesteaded in 1906.[8] That sale gave him $7,000 in cash. He then mortgaged the ranch for $20,000 and sank every cent he could lay his hands on — $27,000 — into the fortunes of baseball in the nation's capital.

Griffith later said, "I had enough confidence in myself to think that I could pull out that club, rebuild it and make it into a winner — therefore a big money maker." Griffith saw in the Washington Nationals a chance to buy low and build for the future using his own unique talents as one of the shrewdest men in the game of baseball. He admitted, "Yes, it was a big risk." But Griffith believed that "before I put up my money I knew the situation thoroughly."[9]

Baseball pundits saw Clark Griffith's move to Washington quite differently. It appeared to the press as just another stopover for a former star whose time had come and gone. Griffith himself said that "he knew Washington was the jumping off place in the American League" where old timers went for their last hurrah."[10] No one believed he would stick in Washington much longer than he had in Cincinnati or New York. His star was on the wane and Washington was where they went dark for good.

The Washington Nationals were certainly the worst team with which he was ever associated. The worn-out mantra, "First in War, First in Peace, Last in the American League," was accepted gospel and no one other than Clark

Griffith believed he had any chance to change those fortunes at this point in his career.[11]

He knew better than the pundits the fire burning in his soul. He relished the chance to build a winner from nothing in Washington. It demeans the existing players in Washington to say there was nothing there when Griffith came to town. But it accurately describes the perceptions in the press.

Griffith knew he had two essential building blocks for the ultimate edifice he envisioned. When he began to form his championship team in Chicago in 1901 and later when he moved to New York, he had laid out his specifications for a winning team like an architect explaining his design to the client — in his case Ban Johnson. Johnson had backed Clark Griffith's plan and helped him secure key pitchers like Jack Chesbro and fast outfielders like Dummy Hoy and Wee Willie Keeler. Clark Griffith, master builder, knew he had in Clyde Milan the slick, fast outfielder he needed. In Walter Johnson he had much more, and Griffith knew all about Walter Johnson.

There was no better pitcher in the game than Walter Johnson, and Griffith knew he had in him what John McGraw had found on the Giants roster in Christy Mathewson: pure gold. Griffith believed from the existing foundation he could change the reputation of the Nationals quickly and show the baseball world that he was still a player, someone who could still make magic with the horsehide sphere.

Griffith set about his business in Washington quickly. He began immediately to rid the team of its senior membership. Griffith said, "My first problem was to clean house, to get rid of all the old timber."[12] Griffith believed that the Nationals had young talent being held back by the old timers and he was determined to give the young players a chance to showcase their talents. He would find out quickly which ones could play at the major league level and which ones couldn't.

He liked what he saw from existing shortstop George McBride and considered the threesome of Milan, McBride and Johnson as the "steady, seasoned, capable veterans" around which he could build.[13] Clark Griffith knew something of the Washington Nationals from two excellent sources. Old friends Jimmy McAleer and Joe Cantillon had been the managers in Washington preceding him.

Cantillon, more than anyone, knew the situation and the talent. He had recruited Walter Johnson, convincing the shy man who did not believe he was ready for the big leagues to leave his years as a "Weiser Wonder" behind.

Walter Johnson started his baseball career relatively late as a boy. His family had moved from Kansas to southern California, where Johnson had his earliest success in baseball playing for semi-professional teams. His first professional chance came in Tacoma, Washington, of the Pacific Coast League, but it was a bad experience for the 18-year-old. After the San Francisco earthquake, Bay Area teams dispersed their players to other teams in the PCL, and the Tacoma manager released Johnson in favor of more seasoned players coming from San Francisco.

That experience undercut Johnson's belief in his own potential and he retreated to Weiser, Idaho in the Idaho, State League where he pitched with remarkable success for two seasons. Injured Washington catcher Cliff Blankenship was sent there to scout him for Cantillon. The Nationals were so stretched for resources that Pongo Joe had to use injured players to scout talent.

Cantillon had seen the reports on the young man in Idaho. "This boy throws so fast you can't see 'em ... and he knows where he is throwing the ball because if he didn't there would be dead bodies strewn all over Idaho."[14] Cliff Blankenship convinced Johnson to take a chance on trying out with the Washington Nationals. The 19-year-old took a train across the country from his family home in Southern California to Washington where he would become the "Big Train," coming to town with Joe Cantillon at the throttle. As Johnson's first big league manager, Cantillon became a life-long friend of Johnson's.

Cantillon, more than anyone, was responsible for taking Johnson's huge, but raw talent and providing it a stage on which to develop. Fortunately for Washington baseball fans, that stage was in Washington, D.C. He also recruited Clyde Milan. When Cantillon dispatched Cliff Blankenship to scout on the same west coast trip, his first stop was in Wichita, Kansas, where he watched Clyde Milan playing outfield. One scouting trip landed two of the best athletes that the Washington Nationals had in their first 20 years of play.

Cantillon's tenure with the Nationals ended in 1909 when, despite his ability to recruit young talent, the Nationals continued to occupy the bottom rungs of the American League standings. Griffith and Pongo Joe were old friends and as such Cantillon proved a great source of information on the Nationals players and Griffith's new boss and partner, Tom Noyes.

The other source of information was no more a stranger than Cantillon. Jimmy McAleer had taken over the reigns from Cantillon in 1910 and two years later Griffith was replacing him as manager. Griffith's relationship with McAleer dated to his earliest professional playing days when McAleer was a very talented center fielder when both men played for the Milwaukee Creams. Griff's assessment of the Nationals' talent was well-informed.

Griffith had personal knowledge of two players he encountered on the Nationals roster. Wid Conroy and Kid Elberfeld had been important members of Griffith's New York team in 1904 that made a run for the pennant. Conroy was well past his prime and Griffith cut him. With Elberfeld the relationship had been more intense. He had followed in Griff's footsteps as New York manager in 1908 when the Old Fox had the good sense to leave town.

The Nationals initially offered Elberfeld a contract despite Griff's assertions that he wanted all of the old hands cleaned out. Yet Elberfeld displayed much the same erratic behavior that marked the summer of 1908. He contested the contract offers from the Nationals, asking for more travel money to the training site, while Griffith conditioned all offers on Elberfeld reporting in good shape. That was more than the Kid could bear and he refused to sign. He was sent to Milwaukee of the American Association where that team's management agreed to take him.[15]

After Conroy and Elberfeld, Griffith cut Dixie Walker, the pitcher, and veteran outfielder Doc Gessler. He cut a total of ten players from the 1911 roster and set about building a new team with youth and speed.

The most controversial move Griffith made as spring training approached early in 1912 was trading Gabby Street. Walter Johnson's fastball was hard for hitters to see and had proved a challenge for catchers to handle as well. Street's reputation was that only he among the team's catchers was up to the task.

Griffith said of Street, "he had a big reputation." Griffith wanted new blood on the team and was willing to use Street as a bargaining chip to get it.[16] He traded Street to the Yankees for two players, including catcher Rip Williams. Even Tom Noyes, the owner asked, "who will catch Walter Johnson?"[17] Griffith's answer was Eddie Ainsmith, who would go on to become Johnson's personal catcher for years.

Walter Johnson was particularly fond of Ainsmith, who like himself was a big, muscular country kid, though shorter and more compact. Johnson particularly admired his game nature. "I saw him actually bleeding from cuts, but you couldn't persuade him to let anyone substitute for him."[18] John Henry, a 23-year-old from Amherst College, became the regular catcher when someone other than Johnson pitched. Rip Williams, obtained in the Street trade, became the third catcher — one who hit .318 in 1912 while Street was a bust with the Yankees.

One old timer that Griffith carried forward from the 1911 team was Tom Hughes. Hughes had been with Washington since failing to live up to expectations with the New York Highlanders in 1904. Before the 1904 season Griffith — then the manager for the Highlanders — had traded Jesse Tannehill to the Boston Americans for Hughes. In Boston Hughes had pitched with Cy Young as part of the tandem that carried that team to the American League championship in 1903. He had pitched in the World Series that year. Now he was a 34-year-old pitcher, third in the rotation behind Walter Johnson and Bob Groom.

Griffith informed all hands, young and old, to report for spring training early. Always a believer in the season-long benefits of rigorous conditioning, he began the process "by getting the winter out of every man. I worked off the fat they had gathered, worked out the kinks and stiffness that had come into their bodies, and gave them back the wind that they had lost."[19] He had always sought speed in his players and believed that running countless sprints during the spring would put his players in top form. Pitchers ran for distance and endurance; position players needed speed, so ran sprints.

The team worked out in Charlottesville, Virginia, which some believed too wet and cold for a spring training site. Griffith argued that it was close to the climate in which the players would begin the year just 150 miles to the east in Washington. He had the college gymnasium to work out in on rainy days. If it snowed, the team worked out on the shovels.

Griffith knew that he had a sound pitching staff and good catchers, but after that all he had was Milan and McBride. McBride was the cornerstone of his infield and Milan the outfield, but the Old Fox was challenged to find competitive players to fill out the rest of the lineup.

During the spring he continued to weed out players who did not measure up. He shifted two young ballplayers who had played mostly shortstop in prior seasons. Ray Morgan moved to second base and Eddie Foster to third. He worked both men out during the spring only at their new positions and when the spring concluded they looked good, giving Griff three-fourths of his infield.

In the outfield he tried a 20-year-old, Howie Shanks, who was fast and had a great arm. During the spring Shanks proved he could handle the position defensively. Another young speedster would handle right, Danny Moeller. He had not stuck in two auditions with Pittsburgh, but Griff liked his style and used him to complete his outfield of Milan, Shanks, and Moeller.

There was still a big hole at first base and Griff would not fill it until six weeks into the season. As with every position on the diamond, Griff liked a quick, defensive-minded player, and at first base he wanted someone in the mold of Hal Chase, the youngster who had been so good in New York. Available to Clark Griffith for first were aging utility player Germany Schaefer, who was coming off of one of his best years but was used as a backup at several positions, and John Flynn who came over from Pittsburgh, but his very disappointing sophomore season raised doubts about his ability.

Griff began the season with this aggregation. He was confident and passed that belief on to his players. Before each game he would ask the gathered team, "What pitcher are we afraid of?" To that call the proper response was always, "There ain't none."

Griffith knew who he wanted to fill the hole at first. He — along with many other major league organizations — was watching a young man playing in the International League in Montreal, Canada, named Chick Gandil. Gandil had failed in his 1910 audition with the Chicago White Sox, but was tearing up the minors. Griffith saw in the 24-year-old exactly the kind of player he wanted. Griff said of Gandil, "He can dig nearly any ball out of the dirt, and he is easy to throw to."[20]

While the defense was always a must for Griffith, it was Gandil's bat that made the difference for Washington. On May 26, Griffith purchased Gandil for $12,000 and three players. The money came from Tom Noyes and it would be the best support he ever gave Griffith for the team. Two of the players traded to Montreal — Bill Cunningham and Charlie Becker — had played for the Nationals in 1911, but had been relegated to the bench by Griff. Trading them to Montreal constituted the final phase in the house-cleaning Griffith had started in the spring.

With the team still struggling to play .500 ball, Griffith traveled to Montreal to personally sign and escort his new first baseman to Washington, D.C., afraid that Gandil might yet get away from him. Bringing Gandil back to Washington, Griffith had set in place the second offensive threat in the middle of his batting order. The Old Fox had added new talent by putting young players like Moeller, Shanks and Foster in the lineup. Foster was especially valuable in the number two hole. But now Gandil gave him someone in the middle of the order who could drive in the ever-dependable Clyde Milan. At the end of May, playing his first week with the Nationals, Gandil hit a cool .400 and the Nationals' season was about to take off.

In just a few months, Clark Griffith had totally remade the lineup of the Washington Nationals. The infield of Gandil, Morgan, McBride, Eddie Foster and catcher John Henry, along with the outfield of Milan, Moeller and Shanks, would go into battle together for the next four seasons. That lineup would not change until 1916 when a little known first baseman named Joe Judge would crack it for the first time and signal wider changes to come.

For Clark Griffith the issue of a field leader was an important one. During his playing days he had always been that man, and he appreciated the leadership skills of others when he saw them. He believed George McBride had that talent. Griff said, "I have never seen McBride use tobacco or liquor in any form. He is a very clean-cut chap and very well liked by the men."[21] He became the 1912 Nationals' team captain.

The batting order typically had Moeller leading off, followed by Foster and Milan, with Gandil hitting cleanup. The bottom half of the order was Morgan, Shanks, McBride and the catcher of the day. Griff liked Moeller leading off because he would take a walk and Foster could handle the bat well enough to move him around the bases. He said of Foster that he could handle the bat as well as Willie Keeler.[22] That gave his two best bats a chance to push across enough runs for the Big Train. "The command was speed," said Griffith of his lineup.[23]

It was a formula that began to realize success in a Memorial Day doubleheader against the league-leading Boston Red Sox. Walter Johnson pitched in the second game and struck out 13 Red Sox batters as Washington won, 5–0. The Nationals would not lose another game until June 19, a remarkable run of 17 straight wins. Fifteen of the wins came during a long western road trip, making the feat even more noteworthy. The final win came in Washington against the Philadelphia Athletics.

Fans in Washington were growing to like the change in their baseball fortunes. They gathered in the rain at news stands to read the latest results and box scores as the team swung through the west. When the team returned from the trip, a wild throng of fans greeted the players at Union Station in Washington. President Taft was in attendance for the first game after the team's return.

The surprising run moved Washington from eighth place — the usual position for the team — to second place. The heady new direction set by Griffith had the town abuzz. Ed Grillo, in the *Washington Star,* noted that the Nationals had been "tailenders for so long that other teams were pulling for them to win."[24]

It was the newly rejuvenated batting order that was carrying the team into contention. Gandil, Milan, Morgan, Moeller, and Foster were all hitting over .300 and for the first time the team had something more than Walter Johnson with which to win games. The press was crediting the turnaround to the team's new manager. "Among the factors in this winning streak, Clark Griffith is of course, first and foremost."[25]

Clark Griffith's role in the success of his team was not overstated. Griffith was not content to watch the game from the dugout. He took his position in the coach's box in every game. "I speak to every man as a rule, before he goes to bat."[26] He allowed that he gave his baserunners discretion as to the leads they took, and he allowed them to run on their own. He was counting on their speed to win games and if they saw an opening, they had the green light to exploit it. Griffith also controlled the defense tightly, shifting his players in the field more than most as he knew the tendencies of many players from long experience.

To prove the 17-game winning streak was no fluke, the team embarked on another one to start July. They swept six games from the New York Highlanders — a five-game series played in Washington followed by one game in New York. Gabby Street was proving a bust in New York and made an embarrassing gaffe as he passed one of his team mates on the bases to end a rally. The new Nationals hitting attack was the difference from prior years as the team scored 51 runs against the Highlanders during the six games.

Washington in 1912 scored 4.5 runs per game, good for fourth in the league. They hit only .256 as a team, but they stole more bases than any other team except Cobb's Tigers, and they were a close second to the Tigers' mark of 276 swipes with 273. Clark Griffith's formula for speed was paying off and the July streak saw the Nationals win ten in a row to remain close behind the Red Sox in second place.

The fans were captivated by the exploits of Walter Johnson as well. The Big Train was on a personal winning streak as the season moved into August. On August 20, the Big Train won his 16th game in a row by a 2–0 score, besting Jack Chesbro's American League record of 14 straight wins in 1904.

National Leaguer Rube Marquard had won 19 straight earlier in that year and Washington fans were anxious to see their champion best the mark. After winning his 16th game, however, Johnson's run came to an end on August 26. He came on in relief of Tom Hughes against the St. Louis Browns and lost a tough decision by a 4–3 score, where the decision to give the loss to Johnson was made personally by league president Ban Johnson.[27] It was a controversial call but made moot by Johnson losing his next start against Philadelphia.

Sixteen straight wins was the American League standard, though it would be matched by Smoky Joe Wood in the same 1912 season. For Walter Johnson the 1912 season was one of his best, but for the first time he had an excellent defensive team behind him in the field, and he did not need to shut out the opposition to win games. Clark Griffith — ever the showman — built interest in the Nationals' pennant run using Walter Johnson's huge popularity as every fan's favorite pitcher to make the Nationals every fan's favorite underdog team.

The Old Fox was in the hunt for the first time since leaving New York City. It was as if he were born to strut on a baseball diamond. Muggsy McGraw's Giants were in first place in the National League and the chance once again for a post-season series against McGraw was all the motivation that Griffith ever needed.

The claim that there was a real pennant race was increasingly a tenuous one, but it had resonance in a town suddenly struck with baseball fever. The Boston Red Sox began to put distance between themselves and the Nationals in August and opened their lead to as many as 11 games by the end of the month. Boston was no longer led by Cy Young, who retired in 1912 after a remarkable career. Their pitching staff had a talented ace named Smoky Joe Wood, whose 1912 season was his best. He was close on the heels of the Big Train throughout the season.

Wood had won 13 straight games as a series with the Nationals loomed on the schedule. Clark Griffith told the press that the streak was being fed by his manager, Jake Stahl, who was setting Wood up with easy match-ups. Griff claimed Wood always took his turn against less than the staff ace of other teams. The implication was that he would meet real competition for the first time when confronted by the Washington club — a claim of considerable irony for the perennial cellar dwellers.

The Nationals were scheduled to play four games in Boston early in September, and Griffith dared Stahl to start Wood against Walter Johnson. The two pitchers had notably similar records at the time. Johnson had 29 wins, as did Wood, and both pitchers were allowing fewer than two earned runs per nine innings. The Big Train would lead the league in ERA in 1912 with a 1.39 mark.

Stahl accepted the challenge and sent Smokey Joe out on September 6 to face the Washington Nationals and Walter Johnson. Wood himself recalled the atmosphere at the time, saying, "Newspapers publicized us like prize-fighters."[28] Griffith's much ballyhooed grudge match was won by Wood by a 1–0 score, but the contest was worthy of all the hype. It was not decided until the sixth inning on doubles by Tris Speaker — who would lead the league with 53 doubles for the season — and Duffy Lewis.

Johnson would go on to win 33 games in 1912, eight more than he had won the previous two years before Griffith transformed the team. It was not Johnson's fault that the Nationals faltered. Washington lost the four-game series to Boston, winning only a single contest. They did not win consistently against the best teams in the league and were simply outmatched by Boston. The Red Sox were the stronger team with not only a pitcher to match Johnson, but in Tris Speaker an offensive force paralleled in the American League only by Cobb.

Though the Nationals never drew closer than four games to the Red Sox in the second half of the season, they showed all the grit of a typical Clark Griffith team. After the loss to Wood and the Red Sox, they bounced back to win 11 of their next 16 contests with Bob Groom winning nine games in a row to rival Walter Johnson's streak.

In the final month of the season, Washington was scheduled to play almost all of their games on the road, which tilted the odds even more against the Nationals catching the Red Sox. But Washington fans never gave up hope, and 11,000 fans braved chilly conditions to watch the first game of the Boston series in late September, the only one played in Washington that final month. President Taft was in attendance for the game and the nation's leader offered his counterpart Clark Griffith help in his pursuit of a pennant.

The President noted that "Daredevil" Dan Moeller's shoulder was always being dislocated by his reckless dives for anything hit his way in the outfield. During that game Taft watched as Moeller's shoulder came unhinged and he was forced from the game. Taft was accompanied by a Major Rhoades, a military aid who was also a surgeon. Taft offered Rhoades to the Nationals to perform any necessary surgery to tighten the tendons of Moeller's shoulder to keep it better in place. The surgery was performed in the off-season and for once the unique resources available in the nation's capital were brought to bear on the baseball team.

Washington lost the final two games to the Red Sox and Boston ran away with the pennant. In prior seasons the Philadelphia Athletics normally would have had second place to themselves, but in 1912 Clark Griffith put together a team to match his old friend Connie Mack's. Their contest for second place was the only excitement left in the American League and it came down to final ten days of the season.

Washington played two games against the Athletics in Philadelphia, then three at home against the league-leading Red Sox, followed by a final three-game series in New York against Griff's old team, now called the Yankees. The Athletics still had Chief Bender and Eddie Plank, and Connie Mack's lineup was led by Home Run Baker, who was one of the most feared hitters in the American League.

The first game against Philadelphia ended in a tie, called because of darkness after nine innings. The next day Walter Johnson pitched ten innings of shutout ball in relief of Bob Groom, and scored the winning run as Washington won, 5–4, in 19 innings.

After losing two of three to Boston in Washington, the Nationals and Athletics were tied with 89–60 records. The three games in New York would decide who finished second. Walter Johnson won the first game, 4–3, and the Nationals hung on to win two of the three contests in New York while Philadelphia lost two of three in Boston. The Nationals finished Clark Griffith's first season in Washington second only to the World Champion Red Sox, who did Griffith the favor of beating the Giants in the World Series.

There was a huge sadness to the end of Griffith's first season in Washington. Griffith had been sought out by Tom Noyes to manage and share in the ownership of the team. The two men were friends who shared a common love of the game and a common hope for the Nationals to become pennant contenders. But Noyes died suddenly on August 21 after a short bout with pneumonia. It would prove a major blow to the team although that was not foreseen at the time.

At season's end there was speculation that Griffith would take over for Noyes as team president. It was noted in the press that Griffith's share of the club was the single largest share at the time, but the Old Fox did not have the capital to increase his holdings. The Nationals made a handsome profit of $96,000 for the 1912 season, of which ten percent went to Griffith.[29] Regardless of who was responsible for turning the team around and into a profitable venture, Benjamin Minor stepped forward to take over the role of majority partner for the Nationals, and Thornton Grassley bought heavily into the team to replace Noyes.

Minor and Grassley assumed control of the team and Ed Walsh, who had been second in command to Noyes, took a back seat along with Griffith. Clark Griffith would never have the same support from Minor and Grassley that he had enjoyed from Noyes, nor would the team have the same level of financial support that Noyes had provided.

The new ownership group did provide Griffith a nice raise at the end of the 1912 season. He had taken a cut in pay to come to Washington, receiving only $7,500 compared to the $10,000 that he had been paid in both Cincinnati and New York. Minor and the other directors matched his earlier figure and also provided bonuses to several of the players who had enjoyed good seasons.[30]

The money reflected the improved financial condition of the team. The Nationals had drawn better in 1912 than at any prior point, taking in 350,000 paying customers, 100,000 more than in 1911. The interest in the team would hold in 1913 as well — the team continuing its excellent run of 1912. Their record of 90–64 was good enough to convince the Washington fan base that a welcome change had come to town and its name was Clark Griffith.

Clark Griffith put in place the team that he wanted while he still enjoyed Noyes' backing. What Griff called "his little team" was in the mold of the 1901 White Sox and they stayed together, showing great resilience while finishing second to the Philadelphia Athletics in 1913. The key change in the team was the emergence of 22-year-old pitcher named Joe Boehling, whose record was a solid 17–7 with a 2–14 ERA. Another new pitcher was Joe Engel, who had joined the team in 1912. He would supplant Tom Hughes as the 1913 season wore on and would become a fixture in Washington baseball for 36 years.

The 1913 season was Walter Johnson's best over his long career. He got off to a fast start that year and, after allowing a single run to the Yankees in the season opener, tossed 56 consecutive innings of scoreless baseball including four shutouts. The record stood as a pitching standard for 55 years. The 1913 season was the one in which Walter Johnson wrote his name into the record books and into the hearts of baseball fans in every city where he played.

Ed Grillo of the *Washington Star* wrote of Johnson in 1913, "Unlike most of the other stars of the game, Johnson does not push himself into the limelight."[31] Walter Johnson had a simple grace that endeared him to fans every where. They cheered his accomplishments in Boston as warmly as they did in Washington, although it did nothing to diminish the special spot that Washington fans had for the Big Train. He had as large a following as any man in the game until Babe Ruth came along, and that would be another story entirely.

Much of that admiration came from the dominating season of 1913 when Johnson led the league in almost every category. His ERA of 1.14 stood unequalled until Bob Gibson broke it with a 1.12 mark in 1968. He led the league in wins with 36 and shutouts with 11. He led in strikeouts and innings pitched. It was one of the most dominating performances by a pitcher ever recorded, and upon it his reputation as arguably the greatest pitcher ever to throw rests securely. To complete the wonder of it all, Walter Johnson hit .261 that season with two home runs.

No one admired Walter Johnson more than his manager, Clark Griffith. Griffith used Johnson as a starter and reliever and knew the Big Train was his best weapon. Clark Griffith always wanted to win and as a player would use anything he had to walk off the field on top. Walter Johnson was no less a competitor and the two men conspired together to create the greatest season of Johnson's career. He did not overuse Johnson despite the long innings and the many games into which he threw his ace. He said in 1913, "I am going to win a pennant some day with Walter Johnson, and I am going to keep him in good form until the time comes."[32]

Griffith was always a champion of the player and was no less so with Johnson. Team owner and pinch-penny Benjamin Minor was frequently unwilling to pay Walter Johnson his due, but never Griffith. He was always the big man's fiercest ally even after he became a stockholder.

The two men had great admiration for one another, though Johnson's best friend on the team was Clyde Milan, and their closeness would not fade. In his biography of Johnson, Johnson's grandson Henry Thomas describes the relationship between Johnson the player and Griffith the manager as that between a nephew and an uncle — though a warm and professional one.

Thomas included a marvelous anecdote about their first spring training confrontation in 1913.

Johnson and Germany Schaefer went turkey hunting outside Charlottesville where the team trained in March and April. Griffith had explicitly forbidden the expedition and when the two men returned from the trip, he pulled them up before the kangaroo court of their peers to mete out punishment. The jury ruled against their big star and sentenced both men to two hours of extra practice running down fly balls in the outfield. Milan hit the flies and pushed the two men as hard as he would have anyone else. The Big Train never complained because he was a team player and he held no grudge against his manager for being a fair and disciplined leader.

CHAPTER 9

A Minor Chord

One of the more intriguing stories in 1913 was Clark Griffith's offer to President Frank Navin of the Detroit Tigers for Ty Cobb. It was first reported in August 1913, at a time when Navin was trying to secure right-handed pitcher Tom Hughes from the Nationals. The complicated negotiations for Hughes would send him to Minneapolis, and Navin would get a pitcher, Ralph Comstock. In return Navin would provide something of value to the Nationals.

Griffith liked his lineup and had the team he wanted, with one important exception. He was certain that his team could win the American League pennant and go to war with Muggsy McGraw if his Nationals had just one additional potent bat in the lineup. The inability to get the extra hit, to put that extra pressure on the opposition, ate at Griffith when they could not beat the top teams. So he saw the discussions with Navin as an opportunity to discuss how he could fill that hole.

With the negotiations for Hughes getting nowhere, Griff wrote out a check for $100,000 and gave it to a startled Navin after a game in Detroit in August 1913, saying it was his last offer for Ty Cobb.[1] Cobb was the consummate Clark Griffith-style ballplayer, fast and aggressive on the base paths. Griffith considered Cobb and Tris Speaker to be the best two outfielders he had seen play the game.[2] He had great pride in his own center fielder, Clyde Milan, and put him in the same category, saying, "He can do more stuff than (Joe) Jackson."[3]

As loyal as Griffith was to Milan, he said that while Clyde could hit .300, Cobb could hit .400. He made the statement after Cobb's two league-leading seasons where he hit .420 in 1911 and .409 in 1912. When Griffith made his offer for Cobb, the Georgia Peach looked to have another season at .400 going, though he dropped off to .390 at season's end.

Navin questioned whether Clark Griffith had the money to make good on his check. "You'll have to give me time to work on that check, but if it buys me Cobb, give me two weeks."[4] Griffith got no backing from his fellow owners in Washington, who told Griffith to desist. But the Old Fox would not back off, saying he could sell $1 tickets to Washington fans that would gladly pay to see a great ballplayer like Cobb, and they would likely pay more to watch the Nationals win a pennant.

Ultimately the story is about Clark Griffith's knowledge that his team was one offensive star shy of being able to compete for the American League championship. Griffith said, "I am convinced that if I can get some real offensive strength in that outfield of ours, I can cop the flag, which Philadelphia thinks belongs to Connie Mack."[5]

The story of Ty Cobb has always been a complicated one, even if the issue was a straightforward one to Griff. Cobb had plenty of detractors and he gave them ample ammunition. His objectionable racial views have been well documented and are hardly surprising given his origins in the red clay hills of rural Georgia. His tough style of play is also well known, but many of his peers were willing to look past all of that. They saw only the fierce competitor who won games and pennants. Not the least of those with such a view of Cobb were Clark Griffith and Walter Johnson.

Cobb said of Johnson, "We were friends at all times, on the diamond or across a poker table," and the feelings were mutual.[6] The two men went hunting together during the off-season, Walter Johnson knew that many others held opposing views. The less sanguine opinion saw in Cobb a man who was disliked even by his own teammates.

Joe Judge in later years told a story about Cobb coming over to the Nationals' dugout to file down his spikes in an obvious attempt to intimidate the opposing players. Judge picked up a bat and advanced on Cobb with clear intent, and Cobb took his spikes and his file back to his own dugout.[7] But Clark Griffith came down on the positive side of the Ty Cobb equation. He wanted to win a pennant and play in the World Series, and if Cobb was the vehicle to make that happen, then he was willing to make the deal with the relatively benign devil he saw in Cobb.

The press saw Griffith's gambit to bring Cobb to Washington in regional terms. Washington was one of several major league cities, like St. Louis and Cincinnati in the Midwest, which played to a southern fan base. Clark Griffith was showman enough to know that Cobb would help his cause in two ways. First, he was the added ingredient needed for a pennant champion, and second he was a natural draw for Griffith the stockholder.

Benjamin Minor and the other directors demanded the offer be rescinded.

The incident underscores the very different directions in which Minor and Griffith were headed. Griffith wanted a world championship team and knew he was very close to having the ingredients on hand. Benjamin Minor was happy to be making money on what had been a losing proposition since his early years as a minority shareholder under Tom Noyes. Minor was what Clark Griffith had once called a "bushwacker," back when he and Connie Mack were starting the American League.

Griffith was none too kind in describing them as a group. "The man who has learned the game on the field will fight to the finish, but the ones who regard the game as an investment are the first to pull out."[8] Norman Macht, in his book on Connie Mack, agreed and described them as "these new capitalists who knew nothing of the game and would run when the red ink flowed."[9] Nothing could have described Minor more accurately. He was afraid that signing a top tier player like Cobb ran the risk of red ink in a town like Washington. Ultimately, he just did not have the confidence in his own fan base. Clark Griffith believed that a championship team was necessary to build a loyal fan base.

The risk Minor perceived was coming from the possible labor strife posed by the Federal League. He believed it would negatively impact the bottom line for the Nationals by pushing salaries higher. Although both men were probably correct, Minor's belief would soon come to the fore and take Clark Griffith's mind off Ty Cobb and bring it down to more immediate concerns such as how to keep his existing team together.

As early as spring of 1914 there were rumors of defections from the two major leagues to the nascent challenger, the Federal League. After the founding of the American League, team owners had quickly returned to their penurious ways, using the reserve clause and the other tricks of their trade to whittle away at player salaries.

By June of 1914 the Federal League was a real enough venture — with eight teams — that it challenged the two existing leagues to a championship game after the World Series.[10] James Gilmore, the president of the new league, offered a reward of $20,000 to the winner of a contest between the Federal League champion and that of the two established leagues. The additional post-season money was just another seed of monetary attraction sown with players who had seen their earning power drop off steadily for more than a decade.

The other important event that occurred in 1914 was the beginning of the First World War. Just days after the challenge of Gilmore to the established leagues, Archduke Ferdinand was assassinated on June 28 in Sarajevo, setting in motion the events that would engulf Europe in conflict, and then ultimately bring the United States into the war. Although President Woodrow Wilson would declare American neutrality after the European powers chose up sides, the possibility that the country would be pulled into the conflict was ever-present.

There had never been a war that impacted the game of baseball, but as the conflict in Europe became more serious and protracted, speculation began as to whether players would be pulled into the fighting. Clark Griffith would play a large part in that discussion, but first he had the matter of Walter Johnson and the Federal League to confront.

Clark Griffith started the 1914 season without Ty Cobb. He fielded the exact same lineup as in the prior two seasons, but the club suffered a systemic batting slump. Team captain George McBride managed to hit only .203, Shanks slumped to .224 and Gandil lost almost 60 points on his average that slumped to .259.

Walter Johnson had another excellent season and got reasonable support from Doc Ayers, Jim Shaw, and Joe Boehling. Griffith had hoped the young pitcher Joe Engel would develop into the kind of secondary hurler that the Nationals needed to complement Johnson, but it did not happen. Joe Engel would never reach the early potential some saw in him, but would become a treasured member of the Nationals' scouting and coaching staff.

As the disappointment of the 1914 season wore on, Walter Johnson began hunting more than turkey. After his best friend Clyde Milan married early in the season, Johnson began a courtship of Hazel Roberts, daughter of Nevada's Congressman Edwin Ewing Roberts. Johnson was married in June. Neither Clark Griffith nor any of his teammates who had watched the shy man since his arrival in the American League could have begrudged him a minute of the time he spent pursuing the attractive young woman. And it had no effect on his pitching. Indeed, after a rough start to the season, the Big Train finally got untracked after the wedding and pitched as well as ever.

The Washington offense struggled through to the end of the season, but it was not the only one that slumped. It was a down year for hitters in the American League generally. There was only one team that could hit in the AL, and that was Connie Mack's Athletics. They outscored the opposition by a run per game and coasted to the pennant. The Nationals finished in third behind the second-place Red Sox, but it was a respectable showing and the fan base continued to grow.

Walter Johnson won 28 games in 1914 and saw a modest rise in his earned run average to 1.71. He was still one of the most admired men in the game, and Clark Griffith knew his value to the team as well as anyone. During July of that season, Griffith commented on Johnson's place in the history of the game, "Cy Young and Amos Rusie ... were right with Matty and Johnson. Young and Rusie could be worked more frequently than Matty, but not more than Johnson. Johnson is the greatest pitcher today."[11]

As a newly married family man, Walter Johnson was thinking at the end

of the 1914 season about his future and his financial situation. He had negotiated a one-year contract at the beginning of 1914 for $12,000.[12] It was a
$5,000 bump from the previous years, but before 1914 he had played under
a three-year contract that he signed with Tom Noyes in 1911. Also, $2,000 of
the overall sum was said to be "an option on his services for the following
year."[13]

Benjamin Minor was far more budget conscious than Noyes and saw as his
biggest concern *not* the health or happiness of his best player, but the amount
of money he was owed. In the fall of 1914, the ownership of the Nationals
"seemed curiously passive about signing their star."[14]

Clark Griffith was neither passive nor unaware of what was occurring.
As much as anyone in the game at the time, Clark Griffith knew the pressures
ball players were under from the threat of a new league. Griff was concerned
about the position in which his star pitcher found himself and started an
ongoing dialogue with the Big Train that would prove crucial. Johnson said,
"I know Griffith will pay me what I am worth, and I don't believe we will
have any trouble coming to terms."[15]

The Federal League had positioned itself well during the 1914 season.
They played a competitive standard of baseball and *Baseball Magazine* survey
of readers at the end of that season found that by a ten-to-one margin fans
were favorably impressed by the level of play, believing it to be on a par with
the National League.[16] Their editors expressed the common belief at the time
that there were more cities that could support major league teams than were
currently represented in the two leagues, and they offered their readership's
assessment of the Federal League as proof.

Joe Tinker was the biggest name to jump to the Federal League to begin
the 1914 season, and he managed and played on the Chicago team. Mordecai
Brown was another familiar name and he managed the St. Louis entry. The
league drew well enough and seemed at the end of their first season as a major
league — 1914 — to provide a legitimate chance for players to seek better opportunities and for fans to see a higher standard of play in other cities.

Walter Johnson was first approached in July 1914, by the owner of the
Brooklyn Federal League team, George Ward. Ward, owner of Ward Baking
Company, was one of several financial backers for the league. No formal contract was offered, but Ward provided background information and "painted
the opportunities in the Federal League in an attractive light."[17]

Clark Griffith knew of the Federal League's overtures to his star pitcher
and discussed the situation with Johnson shortly after his meeting with Ward.
Griff knew that Johnson wanted to stay in Washington, but wanted a fair
salary. From his own experience with the beginning of the American League,
Griff knew he had to proceed carefully.

Griffith first asked Johnson for a salary figure that he could live with. Johnson did not provide specifics, but Griffith told Johnson that he believed he could get $16,000 for Johnson with the possibility for $18,000 for part of a five-year contract.[18] Both men at that point seemed confident that there was no threat of Johnson jumping ship.

Johnson penned an article for *Baseball Magazine* on his reasons for considering the Federal League. The magazine devoted an entire issue to the Walter Johnson saga. In his own words, Johnson explained that the issue was money and that while he felt considerable loyalty to the team and the fans in Washington, he had to consider his family and his ability to provide for them in the future. He asserted that it was fair of him to attempt to maximize his earnings during his peak playing years.[19]

Clark Griffith approached Johnson again at the end of the season, this time hoping to settle the issue. He pressed Johnson to give him a final figure. Exactly how much did his star want? Johnson relented and told Griffith he wanted $20,000 a year. That figure was not pulled from thin air, but came from Griffith's old friend Fielder Jones, who had been one of the stalwarts on Griffith's 1901 White Sox team and had managed it to a World Series win in 1906.

Fielder Jones, managing the St. Louis entry in the Federal League, made the offer to Johnson on a train ride the two men took to Coffeyville, Kansas, where the Johnson clan had moved after leaving southern California. Jones told Johnson that "St. Louis will pay you $20,000 annually for three years."[20] Johnson replied that he believed it an attractive offer, but that the Nationals had made commitments to pay him a fair salary and he believed he would sign there.

Griffith had taken the issue to Benjamin Minor as the heat was being applied by the Federal League. The next time money was discussed between Griffith and Johnson, Griff had to report that he had taken the matter to Minor and gotten only three years at $16,000. Johnson reported, "There was no more mention of $18,000 for a single year."[21]

Johnson wrote directly to Benjamin Minor, requesting $18,000 a year for three years, structuring it the same as his most recent contract, $16,000 with a $2,000 per year bonus for each following year — the reserve clause. Minor's response was to offer only $12,500 on a multi-year deal. Furthermore, he implied that Johnson was legally bound to accept that offer as he had taken the $2,000 reserve clause bonus as part of his prior year's salary.

The counter offer from Minor not only undercut the bargaining position of Griffith, but told Johnson that the Washington ownership did not care that he had a much better offer. He admitted that the Minor letter made him "sore."[22] Johnson had said that "other things being anywhere near equal, I would always give Washington the preference."[23] Johnson wrote to Griffith but received no reply. Clark Griffith was in no position to go over the head of Minor and his cohorts on the board.

At this point Joe Tinker of the Chicago Federal club contacted Johnson and the two men met in Coffeyville. Tinker offered $17,500 for three years and a signing bonus of $6,000 against the salary. Weighing that offer against Minor's and feeling an anger that was uncommon for him, Johnson signed with the Feds.

Shortly after Johnson's signing with Tinker, Griffith sent a reply to the earlier entreaties from Johnson assuring his star pitcher that he could get something more from Minor. "Griffith refused to give up."[24] Johnson said later that if he had gotten this letter earlier he would never have signed with Tinker, such was his confidence in Griffith.

Griffith sent a mutual friend, Fred Clarke, who managed the Pittsburgh Pirates, to meet with Johnson. Clarke went to Coffeyville and made an impassioned plea to the Big Train on behalf of Washington. Clarke was also representing the two major leagues at the time, but he made a very emotional case to the star and paved the way for Clark Griffith, who followed close on his heels with a trip to Coffeyville.

Griffith met Johnson and his new wife Hazel at the Coates Hotel in Coffeyville. He pleaded with Johnson as a friend to stick with the Washington Nationals, assuring the much larger man that he would get more money out of Minor and that if he signed for $12,500 he could do better in the following year. He was completely honest, saying that he — Griffith — had all of his money tied up in Washington baseball and that if Johnson left the team, Griffith's chances to build a winner were kaput. Griffith's future was on the line and he knew it. It was the first time when everything was on the line for the Old Fox, when everything was up for grabs. Walter Johnson steamed into the station right on time, and it would not be the last time that he came through for Griffith.

Johnson admitted, "I had unwittingly got into a position where whatever I did was wrong. I had to choose between two evils."[25] Johnson had to go back on his word to someone and he was not happy about it, but if he was going back on his word, he did not want to wound the Washington Nationals, his friends and teammates. Johnson's ultimate decision was a poignant one, based solely on his respect and fondness for his manager and teammates. "I never wanted to leave you or Washington," a teary-eyed Johnson told Griffith.[26]

After Johnson made the decision to remain in Washington, he had to get out of his contract with the Federal League or suffer the consequences. He was uncertain whether the threats coming from President Gilmore of the Federal League to take him to court were real, but he decided to ride them out.

The largest impediment to Johnson reporting to Charlottesville the following spring was the $6,000 that Tinker had given him as a signing bonus. In typical Walter Johnson fashion, he had given the money to his brother Leslie, who had committed the money to building a garage.

Griffith set out to get the money back for the man who had just saved his baseball future. Griff went to the one source that truly owed him. He asked Ban Johnson for the money. Johnson was initially no more responsive to Griffith's request than he had been when Griff wanted $10,000 to invest in the team. Now, however, the American League's biggest star and a box office draw in every city needed money to keep him in the league.

Johnson's first response was a negative one, but Griff persisted, reminding the league president that the league had a rainy day fund of $450,000. There was no bigger natural disaster than allowing Walter Johnson to walk, but Johnson held firm, saying the money was not for individual player salaries.

Griffith then sought out the other American League founding partner, old friend and tight-wad, Charles Comiskey. Griffith informed the Old Roman that if Johnson did not relent, Walter Johnson would be pitching for the Federal League in Chicago. Comiskey was unmoved by any loyalty to an old friend, but understood that Johnson would give the Chicago Federals a real toe-hold in his city. Suddenly $6,000 seemed like a pittance to how much damage the Big Train could do to ticket sales.[27]

Finally Griffith was able to get the commitment from Comiskey, according to Shirley Povich, and the payback of the money to Tinker. That remittance was the final piece of the puzzle that kept Walter Johnson in Washington.

Walter Johnson was not pursued further by President Gilmore of the Feds, and the Big Train remained a very large piece of the puzzle that Clark Griffith was putting together in Washington, D.C. Griffith learned how difficult it was going to be to realize his dreams with Benjamin Minor running the show. Although Griffith was able to deliver on his promise to get the extra money for Johnson, it was a very different set of circumstances getting cooperation out of Minor and Grassley than it had been with Tom Noyes.

As a stockholder, though, Clark Griffith understood the new demands on owners. He saw financial structure of the game changing in 1915 and an increasing need for capital. The ability to field a competitive team required more money though the payoff was greater as well.

Griffith commented on the issue in an article, saying that in little more than a decade the costs for the Polo Grounds had tripled. "In the old days it used to cost us $10,000 a year for traveling expenses to pay for out-of-town games. Today the average bill is $27,000," said Griff.[28] The status of players had increased and they demanded first-class accommodations that would have been unheard of in the first few decades of the professional games. Griffith had seen baseball go from a semi-professional sport to a serious money-making enterprise in his lifetime. Now the scale of the costs was headed for new levels.

In an era when costs were rising, baseball in Washington, D.C. was increasingly hobbled by the short-sightedness of those who bankrolled it. The team that Clark Griffith had put together to make the run at the pennant in 1912 and 1913 had played itself out by 1915. Increasingly Griff was looking for new talent, but not finding the backing he wanted when it came to signing it.

With Walter Johnson in tow and the same strong lineup that had kept the Nationals in the pennant race for the past three years, 46-year-old Clark Griffith lined up in the first base box again to coach another season, to shout encouragement to the same group of loyal troops that he had led into battle for three years.

Walter Johnson reported late for spring training in March of 1915 and when he finally showed up he earned his nickname, the "Big Train." The *Washington Post* reported that "a storm prevented the Big Train from reaching these parts on time."[29] The writer, Stanley Milliken, used the phrase again several times in his reporting from Charlottesville that month and a new nickname was born. The picture of a big train delivering the mail fit perfectly and fans loved it as much as the man himself.

Griffith's band played well in 1915, but could put together no protracted pennant push. Clyde Milan and Chick Gandil led the way, though neither man batted over .300. Walter Johnson was now joined by Bert Gallia who in his first season as a regular turned in a good performance. It was Johnson, Gallia and Doc Ayers, though Ayers pitched more in relief and left-hander Joe Boehling continued to provide solid starts.

There was great change afoot in the American League. Connie Mack's Athletics had been so good for so long, but the Federal League played havoc with the team when team captain Danny Murphy jumped from Mack's team to the new league.[30] Attendance was down sharply in the two major leagues as a whole in 1914. Attendance went from 6.4 million fans in 1913 to 4.5 million in 1914, and it can only be attributed to the Feds. The trend continued into 1915 as the Federal League threat went into its second year.

Benjamin Minor, Connie Mack and other owners were afraid of the impact of the Federal League on their players. They were reluctant to commit money to players who could jump ship. And the impact of war on baseball was unknown as well. Players could be drafted to serve and baseball itself shut down. The warfare spreading through Europe was like none that had ever been seen before with submarines sinking American merchant ships and bringing devastation to the shores of the United States.

Though the war would greatly impact the city of Washington, D.C., the team played well, finishing with 85 wins and 67 losses. Yet up and down the lineup the 1915 season saw a slow dropoff in the team's offensive performance. They finished in the first division, fourth behind the Red Sox, Tigers and White Sox. The diminishing state of the team presaged changes to come.

As Clark Griffith contemplated how to shake up his team, there was a one-man shifting paradigm emerging within the game. A young Red Sox pitcher named Babe Ruth played his rookie season in 1915. He had an immediate impact as part of an impressive Boston pitching staff. Oddly enough they could all hit. Dutch Leonard, Smoky Joe Wood, and Rube Foster hit well enough to play the field, but there was something different about the Babe. He hit .315 with four home runs that season and after Tris Speaker was the best bat on the team though he was rarely used other than as a pitcher.

For the Nationals there were two big changes. In the spring of 1915 Griffith went to Buffalo, New York, scouting talent. At the time, managers like Clark Griffith wore every hat that a penurious owner like Benjamin Minor could get them to accept. Griffith was head scout, manager, and general manager in charge of signing talent.

Although Griffith was known as a keen talent evaluator, he landed two of his best players as lucky afterthoughts. In early 1915 he was in Buffalo scouting a center fielder named Charles "Kid" Jameson. While there he noticed a young first baseman named Joe Judge. Griff offered $7,000 for Jameson and asked the Buffalo owner to throw in Judge as part of the deal. He got both men for $7,500.[31] Then in the summer a debt of roughly $500 owed to Griffith by D. H. Leigh — the owner of the Petersburg, Virginia, minor league team — was satisfied serendipitously when a pitcher named Sam Rice was used to balance the books.

Sam Rice and Joe Judge both joined the Nationals' major league roster in 1915 and from there they became the centerpieces of every team that Griffith would field over the next 18 seasons. Signing these two players began a slow turnover in the Nationals' lineup Griffith had built to begin the 1912 season. It would evolve over the next few years and would mark the pinnacle of achievement for Clark Griffith and the Washington Nationals, one that was unseen before or after.

CHAPTER 10

This Is My Home

Sam Rice's story was a sad one made more compelling by the late start he got in professional ball. At age 21 he was trying to make his first minor league roster for the Galesburg, Illinois, team. Edgar "Sam" Rice was married and had a small family that he had left behind in a little town named Watseka, Illinois — near the Indiana border, but not far from Clark Griffith's adolescent home in Normal, Illinois.

Rice made the Galesburg team and had started his first minor league season when a tornado struck his family's home. It killed seven members of his family, including his wife, his two young children, his mother and two siblings who died immediately. Sam's father died from injuries suffered during the storm a week later. The only member of Sam Rice's family left alive was an older sister. Surrounded by nothing except grief, Rice gave up baseball to join the Navy.

He spent two years in the Navy where he played for Navy teams. He was stationed near the end of his term in Norfolk, Virginia, and he signed on to play for a nearby minor league team, the Petersburg Goobers. It was there in 1915 that he encountered his future in the form of Clark Griffith.

Rice was a pitcher initially, and it was his talent on the mound that first impressed Griffith. Always on the lookout for a hard thrower, the Old Fox was impressed with what he saw in Sam Rice. The Nationals had no real shortage of pitching talent. After Walter Johnson there was still Doc Ayers, Bert Gallia and Joe Boehling. It was the best overall pitching staff in the American League at the end of the 1915 season with an ERA of 2.31.

Rice was already 25 years old when he signed with Washington, so it was a make-or-break audition. He pitched in two games to end the 1915 season and then five games to begin the 1916 season, starting one game. He was a talented if inconsistent pitcher, but he could hit better than he could pitch. After one particular rough outing on the mound that spring, Rice is reputed to have said, "I'm no pitcher, give me an outfielder's glove."[1]

Clark Griffith did just that, moving Rice to the outfield in July, where he hit .299 over the rest of the season. The mark was the best on the team, 25 points higher than Clyde Milan in center. Rice became an excellent defensive outfielder whose speed allowed him to track down almost anything. And his pitcher's arm made him one of the best at cutting down runners at the bases. He had to learn how to steal a base, but he became a league leader in that category as well. Griffith called Sam Rice "the best all-around ball player we ever had."[2]

Joe Judge was a sharp contrast to Sam Rice as a man, but on a baseball diamond was equally in the Clark Griffith mold. Judge was a small man at 5'7", just an inch or so taller than his manager. He played first base and around the bag was about as adroit as anyone, and was fast afoot on the base paths. He was compared early in his career to Hal Chase, considered the best at the position in the early twentieth century.

Unlike either Rice or Griffith, Judge grew up in the ethnic melting pot of New York City, an Irish immigrant whose parents tried to break him from his habit of doing everything with his left hand. The trait helped him from the beginning of his baseball career with the Edison nine — his father's workplace team. He played alongside grownups on that team at the age of 16 and moved up to semi-professional ball the next year where John McGraw scouted him and deemed him too small.

After Judge's signing with Washington near the end of the 1915 season, Clark Griffith was adequately impressed with his new first baseman to sell Chick Gandil to Cleveland. Judge performed well in his first taste of the big leagues, hitting .415 in 12 games in which he managed 41 at-bats. The 1916 season was his rookie year and it did not go as well.

The 1916 season was the first losing season for Clark Griffith in Washington and his worst for many years to come. The abysmal Philadelphia Athletics cushioned the fall as Connie Mack's team lost 117 games that year and allowed the other teams in the American League to pad their records. The Nationals were only a game under .500 with a record of 76 wins and 77 losses, but they finished in seventh place just a notch above Philadelphia in the standings.

Joe Judge fell off in his first full year to a batting average of .220. Across the infield, George McBride was in his last year as a starter. The 35-year-old captain of the team hit only .227, and the Nationals batting average of .242 was lowest in the league.

Once again the team was paced by Walter Johnson and Clyde Milan. Moeller and Shanks started the season in the outfield, but Rice took over for Moeller, whose average dropped off to .246. Ray Morgan and Eddie Foster dropped off in the infield as well. Clark Griffith's team played with vigor and energy in the first two months of the season, occupying first place through Memorial Day.

In June they began to look more like a team that was just a player away from competitiveness and in July they collapsed at the end of the month, losing first five in row, then six, and 18 of 23 overall as they tumbled to seventh place. In truth an era was drawing to a close in Washington baseball. War was inching ever closer and the old gang was getting older and swimming against the tide of time.

In 1917 the speedster Danny Moeller was gone from the outfield and the other corner outfielder, Howie Shanks, moved to third base for Eddie Foster, who moved over to shortstop for George McBride. Complementing Sam Rice in right was Mike Menosky in left field. It was a patchwork lineup of new-comers and old stalwarts. It failed to mesh.

The team finished in fifth place and had a losing record once again. The baseball situation in Washington, D.C. was starting to look like all of Clark Griffith's prior teams. In Chicago, New York and Cincinnati, he had pumped new life into the lineup and led the team to surprising success only to watch a drop off in subsequent years before heading out of town. Griffith was deter-mined to turn that trend around in Washington.

In 1917 the young pitcher Babe Ruth was on the upswing and starting to look like he might have a career as impressive as Walter Johnson's. In head-to-head match-ups between the two men, Ruth was getting the best of the Big Train, winning six games against Johnson, three by 1–0 scores.[3] The Nationals finally beat Ruth in the final weeks of the season, but it was a hollow win as the team looked more and more like the 1908 Highlanders.

The difference was Joe Judge and Sam Rice. They had breakout years in 1917 with Rice topping .300 for the first time in what would be a long run of such seasons. Judge hit .280 and with Clyde Milan the offense had more punch than at any time since 1913. Rice and Judge would become friends in much the same way Clyde Milan and Walter Johnson did. The two young players became neighbors and shared their rich if somewhat disparate family life styles.

Even in a down year, Walter Johnson won 23 games and threw 326 innings with a 2.21 ERA. So rather than showing signs of collapse as had the Highlanders, the Nationals were showing signs of growth, weak though they might have seemed. Clark Griffith saw them and wanted more, but it was not the time for making changes.

With victory over Germany seeming more certain in 1917, the United States entered the war in April with a formal declaration of war. The Selective Service Act was passed in May 1917, to mobilize the manpower for an army that was at skeleton strength. A national lottery was established and the

Secretary of War, Newton Baker, drew the first number from an enormous jar.

The issue of the draft and how it would affect baseball players was a major concern and it hung over the season from the very beginning when war was declared. When the lottery was established it was clear that some final word on the status of baseball players needed to be asserted. An exemption from the draft was granted to men in the newly established Hollywood entertainment field. The position of Ban Johnson and the governing board of the game was that baseball players were entertainers as well

The War Department under Secretary Baker had more important issues to consider than baseball in 1917 and allowed the season to play itself out without resolution of the issue of deferments for players. In the off-season, Ban Johnson pressed the issue of player draft status with General Enoch Crowder, the head of the Selective Service Board. Ironically, the test case that decided the player's situation was that of Walter Johnson's favorite catcher, Eddie Ainsmith.

In July 1918, Secretary Baker promulgated the "Work or Fight" rule that allowed local draft boards to order draft-age men to either enlist or take specific jobs that supported the war effort. Baseball was not deemed a job in support of the war. Ainsmith appealed his draft order as far as possible, but lost on July 19 as Secretary Baker denied his appeal within days of his Work or Fight order. Ainsmith and others were able to line up jobs in shipyards and other essential work areas that gained them exemptions from direct enlistment.

Clark Griffith attempted to present a patriotic front for the sport from the very beginning. He "requested that the Army assign drill sergeants" to each team during spring training in 1918 so that the teams could be prepared not just for the upcoming season, but for war if necessary.[4] The Old Fox telephoned Ban Johnson to tell his old friend that he would attempt to intercede with General Crowder personally, assuring Johnson that he had a close relationship with the man.

Clark Griffith was always a man of remarkable tact and had demonstrated his ability to cross lines of class and authority during the founding of the American League. Those skills were on display once again. When the War Department issued the Work or Fight rule, Ban Johnson decreed unilaterally in July of 1918 that baseball would comply with the new order by shutting down the game for the rest of the year. The owners were not convinced that such a drastic move was necessary, and Griffith and his old friend, Cincinnati owner Garry Herrmann, convinced Johnson to relent on the idea.

Griffith met with Secretary of War Baker as well as with Draft Director Crowder in 1918. "He pointed out ... the leagues were already drilling their eligible players," and requested a deferment that would allow baseball to play on until Labor Day of 1918 and then take a hiatus until the World Series was played.[5] He requested and was granted a 15-day window for the tradition of a championship series to be honored. The games began on September 5 and Babe Ruth pitched the Red Sox to victory over the Cubs in six games, ending on the 11th.

Griffith was able to intervene successfully to allow the World Series tradition because of his early posture of support for the war effort. He started a truly remarkable campaign to portray baseball in the most patriotic terms possible, called the "Clark Griffith Ball and Bat Fund." Griffith first wrote to President Wilson in May of 1917 concerning the fund, shortly after war was declared. He suggested that if every baseball fan contributed a quarter — 25 cents — to a fund, then balls and bats could be provided to units overseas for their use "in training camps."[6] Griffith remembered the stories from his youth in Missouri when men talked of their earliest memories playing baseball during the Civil War. Woodrow Wilson gave his quarter and urged everyone else to help, and Griffith raised $40,000 for the fund.

Although it raised baseball's profile as a supporter of the war effort from the earliest moments of the war, it was the victim of a conflict that struck in new and tragic ways. When the bats and balls were finally purchased and shipped overseas for use by sailors and soldiers, the merchant vessel carrying them was sunk by a German submarine.

As F. C. Lane stated in an issue of *Baseball Magazine* devoted to the war effort by baseball, World War One was the first foreign war to involve the whole nation in the war effort. Victory demanded the efforts of every citizen, and baseball players were no less involved than anyone else. Forty-eight major leaguers would serve in the war, four from the Nationals. The Philadelphia Athletics would contribute ten men to the effort, the most of any team and more than 20 percent of the total. A veritable all-star team could have been constructed from the ranks of those who served. In many cases they became the stalwarts for teams formed from their active units.

Clark Griffith was 48 years old and a senior citizen in the game, and during World War One he became a leading voice for the sport of baseball, one who could lobby in Washington, D.C. better than anyone else. His posture as voice of the game in the nation's capital was one that baseball came to appreciate in 1918 and increasingly with time.

The First World War would have far more affect on Washington, D.C. than on most other major league cities. The war created a burgeoning bureaucracy to direct the fight and resulted in an upsurge in population for the small southern city. Those new arrivals became ardent supporters of the Nationals in the post-war period.

There were new faces but some of their champions missed much of the action. Sam Rice's breakout year in 1917 was followed by a fallow one. He was pressed hard by his local Army enlistment board in Watseka, Illinois, from the outset of the war. He applied for an extension of his exemption from service, but was denied in a hearing in March 1918.[7] He reported for service at the end of April and was assigned to the Army's 68th Artillery unit that was scheduled for overseas deployment. He was granted leave from duty during the season several times and managed 23 at-bats and a .348 batting average, but another year of Sam Rice's career was lost.

The 1918 season was a good one for the Nationals despite the loss of Sam Rice. The team won 72 games during the war-shortened season. One player untouched by the draft was Walter Johnson, who turned 30 after the end of the 1917 season — just at the upper end of eligibility. He had a resurgent campaign in 1918, throwing exactly the same number of innings in the shortened season of 1918 as he had in the full year before. He won 23 games, the same as in 1917. His earned run average is indicative of his return to dominance as he allowed only 1.27 runs per nine innings, a mark almost equaling his 1913 season.

The 1918 season was the first when Babe Ruth played the field more frequently than he pitched, as his bat became a more important weapon than his arm. His 11 home runs led the league and he batted .300, showcasing his remarkable prowess with the bat that in the years to follow would mean his complete retirement from the mound.

The war did not help the pocket books of major league baseball's ownership. Overall attendance plummeted by almost two million fans. For the owners of the Nationals, who operated on tight margins from the beginning, the war was a devastating blow. Despite the third-place finish, attendance was almost half what it had been in prior years — 231,000 in 1918 as compared to 431,000 in 1916 before the war.

The economic distress left the Nationals cash-strapped to begin the 1919 season, and though Clark Griffith implored the owners to spend more to bolster the lineup, they were only marginally supportive. He had an opportunity to purchase the rights to a young ballplayer from Norfolk named Pie Traynor, but Griffith was unable to complete the deal after the price was raised.[8] Whether they had no further reserves or just did not believe in the team, Clark Griffith was more isolated from Benjamin Minor and the other owners of the team during the 1919 season than at any previous period.

Griffith lost second baseman Ray Morgan and Eddie Ainsmith from his 1918 team. That season's version of the Nationals had been cobbled together with established players like Frank Schulte and Burt Shotton, brought in to play the outfield in place of Mike Menosky and Sam Rice, who were drafted.

They returned in 1919 but the holes left by Morgan at second and Ainsmith behind the plate were not filled.

The 1919 season was the team's worst showing during Griffith's tenure to that point. They finished in seventh place and the .400 winning percentage was more in keeping with the teams that predated Clark Griffith's time as manager. Despite the lack of support from ownership and the despair of finishing so poorly, Griffith made two important discoveries that year. The first was a find by Joe Engel in his first scouting assignment. Engel had failed as a pitcher, but he remained a trusted member of the Nationals team.

The Old Fox dispatched him as a scout late in 1919 to Binghampton, New York to evaluate a pitcher named Pat Martin. While there he saw a feisty second baseman named Stanley "Bucky" Harris, who was playing for the opposing Buffalo team. Harris got in a fight during the game with a larger man, and Engel liked his makeup.[9]

Harris had played the preceding year with Joe Judge on a shipyard team and Judge provided Clark Griffith with a personal recommendation after Engel filed his report. Griffith was concerned that Harris could hit enough to play in the majors, but relented after Judge's recommendation and traveled to Binghampton with Engel for a second look. They watched a doubleheader during which Harris went six-for-eight, with a walk and a hit by pitch.

When Griffith approached Harris in the clubhouse after the game, the young man was untaping two fingers, one of which was broken. He had played through the injury, perhaps knowing that big league scouts were watching. Griffith was suitably impressed with the young man's game nature, and the next piece of the puzzle was locked in place by a $2,500 signing bonus.[10]

Harris, like Judge, was a Clark Griffith kind of player. Standing only 5'9" tall, he was aggressive on the diamond, a man who pushed his own talents and the other team's defense. He had speed and could handle the bat. He was an excellent defender as well, with "tremendous range at the position ... (and) no peer at pivoting for the double-play."[11] His batting average and overall offensive profile in the majors would exceed that of his minor league career, justifying Griffith's grudging vote of confidence in his abilities.

Griffith would say of Harris, "I never saw a competitive spirit the equal of his, not even Cobb's. He was the gamest ball player I ever saw in 50 years of baseball. He was the smartest I ever had."[12] Harris played only a few games during the 1919 season, but played well enough to cement a spot in Clark Griffith's 1920 lineup.

The other find was Tom Zachary. He was the kind of player Connie Mack loved to recruit. Mack liked his players to have a college background. Though from a farming family, Zachary attended a small Quaker school in North Carolina, Guilford College. He projected the air of a professor and may have been the best educated player on the team, reading continually even through the season. He would become a useful complement to Walter Johnson on the pitching staff, something Griffith had struggled each season to find.

Clark Griffith was putting the pieces together, but Benjamin Minor was more involved in a fight with Ban Johnson over direction of the American League that had surfaced during after Johnson's decree that the season would end in the middle of 1918. Minor relished his role as one of the ownership group, and his energy for intrigues with Charlie Comiskey and Harry Frazee far exceeded his competitive fire for the game. Most importantly, he perceived the price for continuing to attend the baseball meetings each December as a high one, convinced by the team's losses during the war that investment in Washington baseball was not a wise financial move.

With no forewarning, a sudden and joyous announcement appeared on December 14, 1919: "Washington Club Sold to Clark Griffith — A. L. War More Bitter," read the headlines.[13] The press had been so caught up in the war between Ban Johnson and insurgents led by Comiskey, Frazee and Minor that they missed any sign of the latter's decision to sell the Washington Nationals to Clark Griffith. Ironically, Griffith would abandon Minor's position and support Ban Johnson, though that fight would rage unchecked for a while. The heart of the story was Clark Griffith's ascension to ownership of the team that he had managed since 1912 and unsuccessfully attempted to mold into a champion. It was great news for Washington and for baseball in general.

Griff had tried unsuccessfully to buy a majority share in the team in 1917 with the backing of John Wilkins, a native of Washington and a coffee importer. When negotiations lagged, he broached the subject with Branch Rickey, offering his former teammate with the New York Highlanders a quarter share if he could raise the funds.[14] Rickey was frustrated with his shrinking role with the St. Louis Browns and was certain that he could find and develop baseball talent. A partnership between the two men would have drastically altered baseball history in Washington, but the scheming was brought to an unfruitful end when Rickey moved on to the St. Louis Cardinals.

To support the deal with Wilkins, Griffith sold his ranch in Craig, Montana for $35,000 to leverage his participation in this venture. His holdings were substantial: 4,000 acres of land that he owned directly and another 5,000 acres over which he had grazing rights. He sold it all and was proud that he got a good price.[15]

Though he had sold all of his cattle to support the original Washington Nationals stock purchase in 1912, he still had 70 horses on the land. He turned them loose and in so doing turned his back on an important part of his life. The pictures of Griffith riding a horse in western garb and the tall tales about his hunting prowess dating to his earliest days in Missouri were all real.

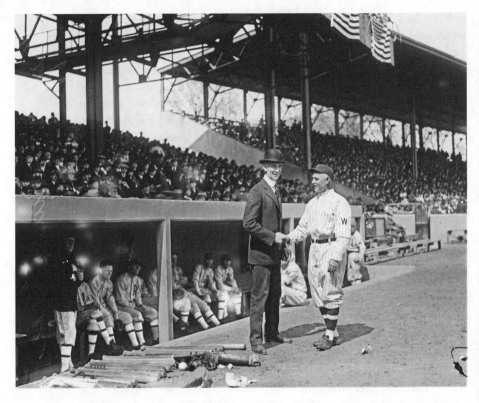

Connie Mack and Griffith. Mack facilitated Griff's purchase of the Nationals by introducing him to William Richardson (Library of Congress).

Clark Griffith wanted to change directions, but in 1917 the time was not right to purchase a baseball team. The economic uncertainties surrounding the game of baseball after war was declared undermined Griffith's deal with Wilkins, who lost interest in owning a baseball team if the war was going to put an end to the games.

In 1919 Clark Griffith was 50 years old. He had sold his ranch two years earlier and in doing so had changed direction irretrievably, seeking to become an urbane man of the city who spent more time taking law school classes to improve his grasp of contract law than riding horses.

Connie Mack had been long aware of Griffith's interest in ownership. Mack was in many ways the role model for what Griffith had wanted since the founding of the American League. Mack had bought half ownership in the Philadelphia Athletics in 1901 with the backing of Charles Somers, who then transferred his shares in the club to Mack a year later.[16] That transfer made Mack an equal partner with wealthy Philadelphia businessman

Benjamin Shibe without ever investing any substantial amount of money in the deal.

He tried to find a similar situation for Clark Griffith. Mack introduced Griffith to William M. Richardson, a wealthy grain merchant from Philadelphia who was the primary business partner of Benjamin Shibe. Mack and Griffith convinced Richardson that the Washington baseball team was seriously undervalued after the war and that it represented an attractive investment, especially with Griffith available to bring it back to competitive status.

The economic distress of the war era and the failure of the team in 1919 left Benjamin Minor without any confidence that Clark Griffith could resurrect the fortunes of baseball in Washington, whereas Richardson saw an opportunity to buy into the opportunity for change. Minor's long relationship as an owner of the team — dating to 1905 — was noted in press accounts describing the sale of the team. He had seen much adversity during his time with the club and now he welcomed a chance to be bought out at a competitive price.

Richardson and Griffith purchased approximately 80 percent of the 20,000 outstanding shares in the team. Griffith owned 2,700 at the time of the purchase and he borrowed $87,000 from the Metropolitan Bank in Washington to buy enough to make him a majority stock holder with Richardson.[17]

They bought the shares owned by the heirs of Tom Noyes, Minor, and everyone except for small shareholders who had not been convinced yet to sell, but Griffith assured the press that no owners were being forced out. The acquisition had been strictly a friendly arrangement of mutual benefit.

Benjamin Minor was quoted in the *Washington Post* accounts as supportive of Griffith. "I know of no better man for the job," Minor stated when asked about the new club president.[18] He pointed out that no team in the American League had a better record since Griffith had taken over in 1912, with the exception of the Boston Red Sox.

Richardson announced that he had no interest in running the team and was ceding that job completely to Griffith as president of the team, taking over that office from Minor. Richardson would occupy the office of Secretary-Treasurer, and Clark Griffith would continue as the on-field manager only until a suitable replacement could be found. The relationship between the two men would remain amicable until Richardson's death and he never interfered with Griffith's position as the chief operating officer of the enterprise.

Clark Griffith said of the purchase, "I am planning on giving Washington a real ball club," acknowledging his ongoing frustration with Minor and his cohorts. "Mr. Richardson and I will make every effort to land the players we

need to strengthen the Nationals and put Washington in the race for the pennant."[19] It was the first time since New York that the Old Fox had such serious
backing in a baseball venture. Not since Ban Johnson had given Griffith every
player he could pry loose to support the move into New York had Griff had
as broad a mandate as Richardson was now providing.

Griffith assured the fans of Washington that his co-owner's status as a
native of Philadelphia should be of no concern. The interests of the club "will
be conducted for Washingtonians first, last and all of the time." Griffith said,
in an emotional acknowledgement of the roots he had sunk in the city, "This
is my home. It always will be I hope. All my interests and the greatest of my
friendships are here."[20]

Clark Griffith's life had started in precarious circumstances on the Missouri frontier before he moved as an adolescent to Illinois. He spent only five
years in Bloomington before leaving to pursue a career in baseball. His adult
life had known so many different locales — San Francisco, Tacoma, Montana,
Chicago, New York City, and Cincinnati. At the end of the 1919 season he
had spent almost eight years in Washington, D.C., as lengthy a period as he
had spent anywhere since leaving Chicago and the Midwest.

Clark Griffith was admitting that he considered Washington his real
home now. He and Addie, his wife of almost two decades, had no children,
but the depth of their commitment to Washington, D.C. would be made
clear in coming years. Every other situation in Clark Griffith's life had been
at the service of another. Now, the Old Fox finally had a home that he owned.
It was a simple thing, but it was what Clark Griffith had been struggling for
most of his adult life. He finally had it and he had only to use his unique and
unmatched knowledge of the game he loved to keep it.

CHAPTER 11

Putting the Pieces Together

Clark Griffith had been chasing a dream since leaving his home in Bloomington, Illinois, to play for Milwaukee in the Western Association. He wanted to follow in the footsteps of Hoss Radbourn, to become a great pitcher who commanded respect for his achievements on the mound. He had realized that goal, and more importantly, put his own distinctive stamp on the game as a player, known almost as much for being a radical who led labor insurrections as for being a wily and winning pitcher.

His reputation derived from an early realization of his leadership potential. He not only took on situations where players were wronged, but he succeeded in making a difference. He seldom made empty boasts even as a young man. His ability to lead his fellow players grew until he became one of the most successful on-field managers in the game. At every stop on his journey, intelligence and character won those around him to his cause.

The greatest prize had eluded him, however, and until he came to Washington he was on the verge of giving it all up. He considered abandoning baseball in 1911 and going home to his Montana ranch and making a living there. He lost confidence in his abilities as a dugout manager in Cincinnati, in his ability to turn around a team. Writers like Bob Considine and Shirley Povich attributed his failure to his unease with the National League, that his natural element was the American League. It was a deeper malaise than that and Griffith was happy to be redeemed by his success in Washington.

He came to Washington for many reasons, but clearly he wanted more than additional success as a manager. Clark Griffith wanted to be what was known in the day as a "baseball magnate." It was his greatest hope from the moment he reached the pinnacle of his playing career in Chicago and could see its downside in the none-too-distant future.

In the lowly fortunes of baseball in Washington, he found a perfect fit. The city needed a gritty bulldog to wrestle its fortunes away from those lacking

Clark Griffith, baseball magnate (Library of Congress).

the vision to lead it. The city had never known a winner, but in his first year, Griffith had brought them one. He was a legendary figure in the game, and when he bought the team, it became known more commonly in the press as the "Griffs" than as the Nationals. It was his team and his adopted home and they had no reason to be impatient as he sought to build a winner.

The town and the team took to the transition immediately. "The donning of a new outfit — the three-piece suits and his ever-present cigar — seemed to bring about a change even in Griffith's countenance, the furrowed brow and piercing eyes replaced at times now by a gracious, grandfatherly smile."[1]

Griffith knew well enough from his tenure with the New York Highlanders that patience is a finite commodity, even in Washington, and he wanted a championship in his new home town. Like any new owner, he set about refurbishing, hammering here and banging there until the walls came to suit his very individual tastes, until the place took on the trappings of the man and his time. There were pictures from his days in New York and Chicago and the Winchester rifle that A.G. Spalding gave him in 1901 hung on the walls of his office.

The real work was building a championship team of his own making for the first time. He was no longer looking to Ban Johnson as he had in Chicago and New York. There were no other owners now. Clark Griffith alone would have the power to buy the talent, to cajole the best players into wearing the "W" on their Washington baseball caps.

There was an immediate irony to the 1920 season as Clark Griffith submerged himself in the business of baseball ownership. The sale of Babe Ruth for $125,000 led the players to believe that there was money in the coffers of ownership, and the Nationals players were among many who were reluctant to renew their contracts for 1920. Clark Griffith set a firm position in negotiations and the former labor radical said he was offering increases in salary only to players who deserved them and that no one could report to spring training in Tampa without a signed contract.

Griffith was active among the ownership club and made a proposal at the owners' meeting to require no player to be sold for more than the waiver price. The proposal was strengthened to prohibit any sale or trade from July 1 until the conclusion of the World Series. Ban Johnson and the owners approved the proposal that created the first trading deadline in the major leagues.

Clark Griffith's first year in the front office did not get him off the field of play. He continued to manage the team on the field while operating it off the field as well. Complicating matters further was Walter Johnson's worst year in his long career. Johnson contracted what was probably influenza, possibly even pneumonia, on the trip north at the conclusion of spring training. He tried to pitch in the numerous exhibition games along the eastern seaboard as the team traveled north and did not rest enough to shake the illness.

On opening day he went out to face the Boston Red Sox in Fenway Park. Had Harry Frazee not sold Babe Ruth to the Yankees, Ruth would have been in the lineup, making matters worse, but a weakened Walter Johnson lasted only two innings.

Though he was not able to resolve questions about his health, Walter Johnson took his regular turns on the mound with few exceptions that year. On July 1, again at Fenway Park, he had his best stuff. It was a remarkable irony that in his worst season he had what could have been his best game. He threw his only no-hitter that day against the Red Sox, a gem preserved by a fine fielding play by Joe Judge on the final out. Only a Bucky Harris error kept him from throwing a perfect game.

After the game Johnson's overall condition worsened. His arm hurt, he had strained a groin muscle, and he reported to Clark Griffith that he could not go in his next start — a game against the Yankees and Babe Ruth back in Washington. Shortly thereafter Johnson gave in to the obvious and went home to Kansas to recuperate from his battered physical condition.

Filling in for Johnson in the game against New York was Al Schacht. The future "Clown Prince of Baseball" had his three seasons as a legitimate major league pitcher with the Washington Nationals from 1919 to 1921. His greatest service to the Nationals was as a first base coach, batting practice pitcher and general clubhouse presence. He and Nick Altrock, the third base coach who had been a 20-game winner for the White Sox in 1905 and 1906, teamed as a comedy duo on and off the field.

It was a testament to the generous nature of Clark Griffith that he allowed Altrock and Schacht to showboat before games as the stadium filled and during the pre-game festivities. Griffith had been an entertainer both on and off the field himself. As a pitcher he had "acted" a part to infuriate the hitter with quick pitches, then changed abruptly and stalled with endless lamentations from the mound that were intended only to bait the batter into poor choices. He was no longer the faux thespian on the Barbary Coast entertaining for nickels, now he could sit back and enjoy the show that Altrock and Schacht provided.

It was one of the few days that Schacht's mound presence had greater value than his presence on the sidelines. He beat the Yankees that day. Walter Johnson would only start two more games after his no-hitter and was unable to complete either. He had a pitcher's nightmare, a seriously sore arm. He went to Rochester, Minnesota, for further medical testing and the general verdict there was good, but the doctors prescribed rest and he did not pitch for the rest of the 1920 season.

The best pitcher for Clark Griffith in 1920 was Tom Zachary. Both he and second baseman Bucky Harris were in their rookie year and showed the potential that would make them stars for the team in coming years. The offensive numbers jumped for every batter in the lineup. Sam Rice, Joe Judge, Clyde Milan and Bucky Harris all hit .300 or better.

The Nationals batted .290 overall, but the American League hit .283 in 1920, 15 points higher than the .268 average in 1919. The biggest statistical anomaly was in home runs. In 1919, 240 home runs were hit, a figure that was up from prior years. In 1920, 369 home runs were hit, a remarkable one-year jump. The new offensive explosion had multiple parents. The biggest change was to the condition of the ball that was in play. In 1920 new balls were introduced into play as soon as the first ball was deemed unplayable.

The stingy nature of the owners — Charlie Comiskey in particular — would lead to the Black Sox scandal. Now they decided to spring for a supply of baseballs that would allow a new ball to be introduced frequently during the game. The effect of that change allowed home runs to be hit with greater frequency.

That change led to a charge that a more "lively ball" was in play. The charge was true only insofar as the changing of the ball kept the ball livelier. The other big change in the 1920 season that affected the offensive surge was the banning of Clark Griffith's old friend, the spitball.

Griffith had been lobbying for a change, and the rules were officially altered to ban the spitball, the emery ball and other alterations to the surface to allow the pitcher to gain an undue advantage. Griff believed that existing pitchers who had crafted careers from the pitch should not be penalized and should be allowed to throw the pitch as long as they continued in the major leagues. That position was upheld by the owners and Burleigh Grimes was the last pitcher to benefit, retiring in 1934 while he was still allowed to throw the spitter.[2]

Griff first wrote proposing the ban in 1917. Griff believed that Jack Chesbro's quick falloff in performance was not a function solely of his added weight and poor conditioning, but his reliance on the spitball. Griffith claimed to have never used the spitball that was in use during the second decade of the 20 century, but admitted, "I guess I was the first person to employ the principal that made the spitball so effective."[3]

Griffith went on to explain, "If one side of the ball is smoother than the other, the ball can be released in such a way as to completely alter its proper rotation ... this rotation is what gives the ball its peculiar break...."[4] The spitball pitcher accomplishes this end by wetting one side of the ball so that it slips away from his fingers with the least possible amount of friction." He explained exactly what Chesbro had done when he returned from his sabbatical at Harvard learning mastery of the pitch before his record-breaking 1904 season.[5]

Griffith said of the spitball and emery ball, "The same results could be accomplished in a general way by roughening one side of the ball." He was describing his own repertoire and the tricks of the trade that he had learned from Radbourn and others. Griffith had used his spikes to rough up the ball, but now pitchers were using an emery board to. As long as one side of the ball was slippery smooth and the other rough, a pitcher could achieve much the same effect. He admitted as much in an article for *Baseball Magazine*.

Griffith's opposition to the pitch was on three grounds. He believed the alteration of the ball would lead to other alterations such as to the bat. He insisted the next step logically would be to "have a batter take a plane with him and shave down one side of the bat."[6] Although it is uncertain how a flat bat surface would help, Griffith posed the extreme possibility to make a point.

He also believed the spitball affected fielders who got the ball in the infield. And lastly, now that Griffith was a modern magnate, he wanted the batter to have a more competitive position in the game. Griffith wrote of the dangers of the spitball and emery ball, saying that pitchers could not control the flight of the ball nearly as well when seeking the radical break of the spitball. Chesbro's famous wild pitch that cost the Highlanders the pennant was a case in point, but the warning was prescient as tragedy in 1920 would prove.

The only death ever recorded in the major leagues of a batter struck by a pitched ball occurred that season when Cleveland Indians shortstop Ray Chapman was struck in the temple by a ball thrown by Carl Mays of the Yankees. Chapman died the following morning. Fans and players who witnessed the event were horrified. Griffith's admonition that the spitball and emery ball could injure players did not anticipate fatalities, but the words took on new meaning and made the outlawing of the pitch stand with new merit.

Even as he helped usher in the new era, Clark Griffith was hamstrung by it. Not only had he mastered how to use every bump on the surface of the ball during his playing years, but he had created winning teams in a single mold. Speed, defense, and good pitching were what made a winner according to the tried and true prescription provided by Dr. Old Fox.

Although the 1920 Nationals could hit, and led the league in steals by a wide margin, they lacked the new weapon that was being used increasingly in the major leagues, the home run. In 1920 the Nationals were fifth in the league in home runs. Left fielder Braggo Roth led the Nationals with only nine homers and the team as a whole hit 36. Babe Ruth hit 54 and re-wrote every concept about the game that Clark Griffith had learned in 30 years at the big league level.

With their pitching decimated by Walter Johnson's illness and their lack of a long-ball threat, the Nationals fell off the pace. They were five games over .500 when Johnson no-hit the Boston Red Sox in July, but after the loss of Johnson they played 21 games under .500 and fell all the way to sixth place in the American League standings. The Cleveland Indians won the AL championship and the Yankees finished third.

As the 1920 season ended and World Series play began, a long-simmering issue finally exploded across the front pages as the fixing of the 1919 World Series by the "Black Sox" was confirmed. Gambling and the willingness of players to supplement their income by consorting with those who managed the betting process had been a concern in the game since the first professional teams played.

Spalding and Hulbert had tried to clean up the game, then Ban Johnson, but it all came unraveled in 1920 and a "fixer" was summoned in the form of Kenesaw Mountain Landis. As a juror Landis had a reputation as an ardent anti-trust judge, but his record was largely idiosyncratic, determined more by the situation than the law. In 1915 the Federal League issue had been put before him and he surprised those familiar with his background by refusing to rule in favor of the upstart league's "anti-trust" claim.[7]

In 1915 he had proven to be a friend to the owners, and in 1920 he took over the new position of Commissioner of Baseball after the Black Sox scandal. He quickly sided with the owners again, issuing lifetime bans on the players involved, while restoring the public's confidence in the game. Though the most famous players affected by the scandal were Joe Jackson and Eddie Cicotte, Chick Gandil, whom Griff had brought to the big leagues in 1912, also was among those banished.

The game was changing fast and Clark Griffith realized that he needed a new direction after the failures of the 1920 season. He had only one scout to augment his own eye for talent, Joe Engel. In 1920 Engel was busy searching for the new talent to allow Clark Griffith's Nationals to compete with the team that was re-defining baseball, the New York Yankees.

The most obvious alteration for the 1921 season was Griffith taking himself from the playing field and dugout. He could not guide the team both from the front office and on the field, and he sought a capable field general as a replacement. Setting a trend that would last for 35 years, Griffith looked close to home among his most trusted players. George McBride was an easy pick for Griffith. The shortstop for the best teams Griffith fielded in 1912 and 1913, McBride had functioned as the captain of the team during those years.

McBride was a popular figure in Washington and the *Washington Post* applauded the move and Griffith's choice, saying, "The fact that Griffith should recognize his (McBride's) loyalty and diligent work through years of association with the Nationals strikes a happy note."[8] It was a mold Griffith never broke as he never named a Nationals manager who had not been a trusted player.

The same newspaper article recognized the importance of the move from the larger perspective. "The passing of Griffith from the ranks of big league managers is another interesting point. He has been on the major league fighting front for years ... Griffith has developed the Nationals into a profitable proposition, and now that he has decided to give up the active work of leadership, he will devote the rest of his life to the direction of his club from the business office."[9]

Clark Griffith was 52 years of age when he stepped down as a field manager for good. He had been a fixture in major league dugouts without interruption for nearly three decades. It was no small feat and few could claim such consistency other than Connie Mack and John McGraw.

Griffith's life was taking a new direction in other ways as well. The average life expectancy at the time was little more than six decades, and it was easy for reporters and observers of the game to see a not-so-distant future when Griffith would fade from the baseball scene altogether. They were wrong. The Old Fox had just begun to fight.

The same *Washington Post* article announcing McBride as the manager pointed out that the Nationals had become a profitable enterprise. It was time for Griffith to use his sole control of the purse strings, and he purchased and discarded talent at a furious pace prior to the 1921 season. During the off-season Griffith made trips to Wisconsin and Chicago and continued to rummage the shelves of baseball talent wherever there were rumors of something special.

He was looking for that rough gem that he could polish and use to put his team on the same page as Colonel Ruppert's impressive Yankees sluggers. He was not just looking for sluggers. In 1921 he was also seeking a proven talent to add to the pitching staff. Walter Johnson had begun to show his age in 1920 and it was not certain what the lingering effects of his arm problems would be.

So, to begin the 1921 season Griffith acquired George Mogridge from the Yankees. Mogridge had pitched his own no-hitter in 1917. The feat was indicative of the success he had known dating to his rookie year in 1911. He had pitched for Chicago and New York in the American League, but it was as a Yankee that he threw the no-hitter. In the next season with New York, Mogridge had been among the league leaders with a 2.18 ERA and 16 wins.

Griffith's first attempt to move the team into the "lively ball" era was a contract offer to Home Run Baker. Considered a dangerous slugger during the height of his career, Griffith attempted to sign him for $35,000, but the deal fell through and Baker went to the Yankees who had more than enough power. It was smart money not spent as Baker never bumped his modest home run totals from their deadball level and $35,000 was serious money in 1921.

The season started with much the same Nationals team that had finished in sixth place in 1920, although the pitching was augmented by Mogridge. The biggest difference would be in the Big Train, who slowly was working back into form. On opening day against the Red Sox, the Big Train was there as dependable as ever. Umpiring that day, Tommy Connelly pronounced, "The smoke ball king is just as good as ever."[10]

With a renewed Walter Johnson, a proven number two in Mogridge and the developing talent of Tom Zachary, Griffith had the makings of a very good pitching staff. But he had holes all through the lineup. Griffith auditioned young players for the left side of the infield to complement his youngsters Joe Judge and Bucky Harris.

Griff still had Howie Shanks playing third base in 1921, the anchor of the infield since 1912. Shanks had a good season in 1921, leading the league in triples, but he was not getting any younger. At shortstop was Frankie O'Rourke, who was a good fielder but not the kind of offensive player the game demanded in 1921.

On July 14 he made the most important move he would make that season, when he went to Columbia, South Carolina, to sign Leon "Goose" Goslin. Goslin had been scouted initially by Engel. It was the young man's first year in professional ball and he was hitting well over .300 in the Sally League, but after Engel's first report there was little follow-up.

According to Shirley Povich, Griffith then heard about Goslin during a golfing match with one of the owners of the Baltimore International League team.[11] The offer on the table from Baltimore was $3,000 to play minor league ball. Griffith doubled that and got the power hitter for whom he had been searching. Goslin would have a brief call-up to the majors in 1921, but he did not stick with the Nationals at the major league level until the following year.

Goslin was the closest thing to a power hitter that Griffith would develop, and he fit in the mold of many of the great sluggers, "just a big old country boy having the time of his life."[12] His home run totals would always be limited by the immense expanse of outfield in Griffith Stadium, but his slugging numbers ranked him near the top of the league for years to come.

Even without the big home run hitter to compete with the Yankees, the Nationals were much improved in 1921. George McBride's team finished at 80 wins against 73 losses. The team was above .500 for the first time since the war-shortened 1918 season and the new players were starting to make a difference. Joe Judge had a fine season in 1921, as both he and Sam Rice hit over .300 and formed a solid core in the heart of the lineup.

They were no match for the offensive fire power of the Yankees. It was the first season that the Nationals pitching staff was led by someone other than Walter Johnson. George Mogridge won 18 games to Walter Johnson's 17 and his 3.01 ERA was by far the best on the staff in the year that saw ERAs shoot up generally. His 288 innings also lead the team as Walter Johnson formed the secondary part of a pitching tandem in Washington for the first time since 1908, when Tom Hughes was the ace.

It would be Clyde Milan's last season in center field for the Nationals. For the last weeks of the season, when Goslin was called up for the first time, the Nationals outfield consisted of Milan, Rice and Goslin. They were three of the greatest outfielders to play the position for the Nationals over the course of the team's 60-year history.

Clyde Milan and Walter Johnson had been the backbone of Washington baseball for 14 years. The two men were the closest of friends and in a game in August of 1921 Milan helped the Big Train one last time, making a great shoestring catch to save the win for Johnson. Though their families would continue to share social time for decades to come, it was their last season sharing the same field.

Although Clark Griffith was happy with the work of George McBride as manager, McBride resigned at the end of the season because of a freak accident. In August McBride was struck in the head by a ball thrown during practice by outfielder Earl Smith. It hit him in the face, and he suffered dizzy spells and never fully recovered as the season ended. Clyde Milan was named the acting manager during McBride's absence and was named the permanent replacement in the off-season.

The new star of the Nationals was Sam Rice. He hit .330 that year and led the club in almost every offensive category except stolen bases, where he was a close second to Bucky Harris. Contract negotiations with Rice before the 1922 season reflected Rice's new status with the club, and Griffith quickly had him on board as the cornerstone of his lineup along with Joe Judge and Bucky Harris. Griffith spent the money he saved on Home Run Baker to plug one of the holes on the left side of the infield.

For $50,000 Griffith secured the services of Roger Peckinpaugh to play shortstop. It was hardly as simple as plunking down the cash. He included in the deal two regulars, Frank O'Rourke and Joe Dugan — the latter of whom became an excellent infielder in coming years. The total price for Peckinpaugh included the three players Griffith sent — valued roughly at $15,000 at the time — as well as the cash. Harry Frazee, the increasingly unpopular owner of the Boston Red Sox, was at the other end of the deal. It was a high price, but Griffith always prized a smooth fielding shortstop and he paid to have one of the best.

Peckinpaugh played the 1921 season with the Yankees and had been an important cog in their pennant winning team. He was traded to Boston in another large Harry Frazee deal in December of that year. Griffith persuaded Connie Mack to trade Dugan for cash and Bing Miller, who became a stalwart for the Athletics.[13] Frazee to his credit got Joe Dugan and the cash in the complicated maneuvers.[14]

Griffith made the announcement of the trade with some pride at a Kiwanis luncheon. The deal was touted as the most expensive to date for the Nationals and estimated at $65,000 of total investment by Griffith. In fact the Nationals' biggest contribution to the deal was the money, although Bing Miller would be a fine addition to Connie Mack's team. The deal was noted in the press as running against the grain, since Griffith's reputation was "in some quarters of being a little tight-fisted."[15]

Peckinpaugh proved to be a championship caliber shortstop. He became an integral part of one of Washington's best double-play combinations, Peckinpaugh-to-Harris-to-Judge. Griffith said of the group, "when the ball is hit in their direction, everyone is out."[16] The trio set what was at the time a major league record for double plays at 168 for the season.[17]

"Peck," as he was known, represented the third piece in Griffith's infield, leaving the most pressing matter to find a quality third baseman to replace the aging Shanks. Catcher was also a position that Griffith prized, and he had Patsy Gharrity playing behind the plate in his first teams. Like Shanks, he was a solid player, but unlike Shanks in his prime, Gharrity was disappointing with the bat.

Although all of the pieces were not there yet, the 1922 Nationals team looked like a good one. Griffith added Bobby LaMotte to platoon with Donie Bush and Howie Shanks at third base. He brought in one of his young signings, Frank Brower, to play the outfield with Rice and Goslin.

Tragedy struck the team however, when Walter Johnson lost his little girl, Elinor, to influenza in December 1921. The Big Train had lost his father Frank during the summer before and it was more sadness than one person could be asked to shoulder at any point. Coming in such a short period of time, it was especially devastating to the entire family.

Less weighty considerations also seemed to go against Griffith and the Nationals in the spring of 1922. The new star of the infield, Peckinpaugh, showed up late for training. Clark Griffith set great store by his spring regimen and was not happy that the player for whom he had shelled out $65,000 was late. Goose Goslin also ran into problems with Griffith's stern management of spring training as he spent more time gambling and chasing good times than he did in conditioning. He was fined numerous times for his troubles.[17]

Johnson was still the emotional rock of the team and began the 1922 season very slowly, pitching only intermittently. Johnson's arm was getting stronger if his heart was heavy. The team behind him never got off the ground, however. Joe Judge had a great year, but Sam Rice began to show his one serious weakness — picking up ground balls hit into the outfield. Goose Goslin had problems with the glove as well as with curfew. Both men made repeated errors in 1922 and Rice was booed for the first time in his career.

The team fell to sixth place. Much of the blame came to rest at Clyde Milan's doorstep after the high expectations for the team in the spring. The truth of the matter was that the team neither hit nor pitched well. The team batting average was seventh-best in the American League and the pitching ERA was third-best.

Yet Clyde Milan became the scapegoat. The attacks in the press took a toll and Milan began to experience stomach ulcers. Late in the season rumors appeared in the *Post* and other papers that Griffith was trying to hire George Stallings to replace Milan. Though Griff denied the allegations, few believed

it. Griffith had decided to replace Milan and the attempts to bring in Stallings
were legitimate, but the price was too high.

Griffith, in his usual fashion, was gracious to Milan and allowed him time
to find another position.[18] He was concerned, however, that he was making
a mistake in hiring his managers. In each of his two selections Griffith had
sought out players who would be respected by the players, but accepted as a
leader in much the way Griffith had been.

After watching the 1922 team, Griffith came to believe that Milan had
too many ties to the players to be an effective manager, and he sought a sterner
hand on the tiller in 1923. Once again he turned to an aggressive player whose
strength in the infield made him seem like a natural leader.

Donie Bush was a back-up shortstop in 1922 for the Nationals but had
known success as the starting shortstop playing with Ty Cobb and the Detroit
Tigers for more than a decade. Griffith liked his background with the tough-
minded Detroit team and always loved the aggressive style of play of the
Tigers behind Cobb. Thinking Bush would instill the same spirit in the
Nationals, Griffith signed Bush to manage for the 1923 season.

The press generally concurred with Griffith's hiring of Bush, citing the
intelligence and feisty nature of the "scrappy new 'midget' manager."[19] Bush
stood 5 feet 6 inches, perhaps even shorter than Clark Griffith himself, and
was known for taking issue with umpires. During spring training Bush was
described as "a fighter from the word go, and if he can instill his fighting
spirit into his athletes, his success is assured."[20]

One of his least popular decisions early in the season was to replace Nick
Altrock as the third base coach. Bush wanted to coach from third himself and
believed the position too important to trust to others. Altrock was a popular
figure for Washingtonians since Griffith had installed him as a coach in 1912.
Though he took his job in the coach's box seriously, he was known for his
entertaining antics along the base line.

Washington fans as well as those in other cities loved Altrock and his
wit — usually directed at umpires. Milan and McBride had retained Altrock,
but Bush removed him. In noting the change, the *Washington Post* observed
of Bush, "The little pilot has asserted himself on two or three occasions when
slight infringements on the leadership position have been made."[21] Those
words would prove prophetic.

Clark Griffith was still building the roster of a championship team. He
added two of the final pieces to the puzzle to start the 1923 season. He admitted that he was looking for a catcher like Billy Sullivan that he had stolen
away from the Boston Beaneaters for his pennant winning White Sox team
in 1901.

Sullivan was adequate with the bat, but a great defensive catcher and a team leader who went on to manage the White Sox. In 1922 Griffith found a catcher even better than Billy Sullivan in Muddy Ruel.

Ruel was the smartest player ever to suit up for Clark Griffith. He graduated from the University of St. Louis Law School, was admitted to the bar and practiced as an attorney during the off-seasons. The former Billiken was much more than an able attorney; he was one of the best defensive catchers of his day and could handle a bat with remarkable skill.

Ruel was a natural fit for the Nationals — men of small build whose intensity and drive made up for whatever stature they lacked. His nickname came from his propensity to practice hitting even when the conditions were wet and muddy. Only 5 feet 9 inches tall and weighing only 150 pounds, he became one of Walter Johnson's favorite receivers and during the final years of the Big Train's career was almost always behind the plate when he pitched.

Ruel had grown up idolizing Johnson, making particular effort to catch any game in St. Louis when the star pitched against the Browns.[22] His biggest contribution may have been to convince Walter Johnson that he could get more out of his arm, even late in his career. Ruel encouraged Johnson to mix up his pitches and rely less on the hard fastball. It had limited impact on the Big Train in 1923, but helped him finish the 1923 season stronger than he had pitched in several years, a sign that there was still life in Walter Johnson's 35-year-old arm.

Ruel came over in a trade with Boston, but Griffith acquired the final part of his championship infield via good scouting alone. Joe Engel found Ossie Bluege in Chicago playing in the Three-Eye League (Illinois, Indiana and Iowa) for the Peoria team. He was sure-handed enough to play shortstop, which he did often in his career, but he developed a unique approach to playing third that would make him not only the best to play the position, but "the greatest infielder I ever saw," according to Clark Griffith.[24]

He played closer to the plate than any of his peers, trying to cut down the angle to the ball the way a hockey goalie would as a breakaway shooter came at him. As a result he could come in on the bunt remarkably well, and his lightning reflexes allowed him to play the line drives that made it the hot corner. When he signed in 1922, the only part of his game that was lacking was his bat.

It was uncertain whether Bluege would ever hit enough for the majors and he struggled initially, but came around in the first two seasons. By the end of 1923 he was showing signs that he could handle big league pitching well enough to stick.

Every year Clark Griffith had added that extra outfielder, looking for the final piece, and in 1923, the candidate was Nemo Liebold. He purchased Liebold in May of 1923 from his favorite trading partner, the Boston Red

Sox. The tip about Liebold came from Donie Bush, who was concerned about the health of Goose Goslin. The power hitter's lack of conditioning resulted in needless injuries in his first full year.

Injuries and bad feelings seemed to plague the 1923 Nationals from the beginning. Walter Johnson hurt his knee in July and was never the same for the rest of the season. Sam Rice collided with a wall and suffered a gaping wound from a nail in the wall. Then he ran into Bucky Harris and the two men became irate arguing about the collision.

Donie Bush heightened the tensions or may have been their source. He was the stern manager Clark Griffith believed might turn the team around, but for all the talent Griffith had amassed, Bush could not mold it into a contender. The fiery nature of the manager boiled over into his relationship with his players, and his most contentious relationship was with Sam Rice.

After Harris and Rice collided on the pop fly, Bush exploded at Rice in full view of his teammates. Rice's response was every bit as fiery, but ultimately Bush had the last word as he suspended Rice for five games for insubordination.[25] Clark Griffith supported his manager publicly, saying, "The chances are that the two will straighten things out ... I don't believe Donie will keep Sam on the bench long."[26]

Griffith always supported his players, and he had the last word with Bush when he fired him in October, almost as soon as the season ended. The press noted that Griffith had been through a different manager every season since buying the team. While the belief among fans and press alike was that Bush had done well with a young team, Griffith saw only a talented team that had failed to win. Its fourth-place finish masked a season of disappointment and tension.

Clark Griffith set out to remedy the turnover in managers by hiring a manager from among the current stars of the game. His first target was Eddie Collins, the 37-year-old second baseman playing for the White Sox in 1923. Collins wanted to manage and was being considered for the position with Chicago, but Charlie Comiskey hired Frank Chance for that job. Griffith knew these situations quite well.

He approached his old friend Comiskey about Collins, and the price was a steep one. Charlie Comiskey wanted Sam Rice and Bucky Harris for Collins.[27] Griffith weighed the offer quickly. Collins posted a .360 batting average along with a league-leading 48 stolen bases in 1923, so Griffith knew that Collins still had gas in the tank.

Griffith countered, offering Bucky Harris and cash. Collins had been one of the stars on Connie Mack's great Philadelphia Athletic teams in 1910 to 1914 that had won four American League pennants and three World Series championships. He was the prefect manager for a Clark Griffith team. He was only 5' 9", fast and great with his hands on the infield. He was an aggressive baserunner and a perfect fit for a deadball era team. Griffith teams were built more for that era than the one emerging in the early 1920s.

Comiskey was not willing to trade his star second baseman for Bucky Harris, and Clark Griffith was not willing to part with enough money to bridge the talent gap Comiskey perceived between the two players.

Griffith continued his search. He considered Roger Peckinpaugh, who seemed like the natural replacement. Peck had been the interim manager for the New York Yankees in 1914 when Frank Chance had quit in mid-season. The problem foreseen in the press was that Peckinpaugh could not hold the jobs as manager and starting shortstop concurrently.[28] That problem proved insurmountable and left Griffith in a quandary that he resolved with one of his greatest baseball decisions.

CHAPTER 12

When It Became
Griffith Stadium

The Washington Nationals had been a good draw at the box office since Clark Griffith took over as the majority share holder in the team in 1919. Baseball in general was doing well after gaining distance from the disaster of the war years, most notably 1918. Attendance around all leagues surged in 1920.

Fans were coming to see the more interesting players in the game that began grabbing more and more of the spotlight after the war. The chance to see Babe Ruth hit a long home run always drew large crowds to Griffith Stadium every time the Yankees were in town. In New York the Yankees were drawing a million fans per season, and John McGraw's fine Giants teams were close behind. The two New York teams sat atop the standings and were a major factor in the surge in attendance that almost doubled in the early 1920s from the lowest pre-war years.

Clark Griffith took advantage of the trend by investing in his park, making small improvements in the park in 1920 and 1921. Fans responded to Washington's new owner's popularity and his attentions to the stadium with a spike in attendance. Attendance rose to 360,000 in 1920, 456,000 in 1921 and 458,000 in 1922. Three losing seasons robbed some of the enthusiasm and fan attendance dropped to 357,000 in 1923, but one thing remained readily apparent. Clark Griffith the owner was part of the draw, and he was making money on his own popularity and the belief among fans that he could build not just a more attractive ballpark, but a better team.

Building a pennant winner was always front and center for Clark Griffith. It was always about the game — or at least everything that flowed from winning baseball, but there was a more concrete rebuilding plan in the mind of Clark Griffith. First Griffith changed the main entrance of Nationals Park from

Georgia Avenue to a refurbished one on the Florida Avenue side before opening day of the 1920 season. He spent $3,200 to provide himself an office suitable for a "magnate," the first such on-site command center at the park.[1]

It was in that office beneath the grandstand, but near the main gate, that he held forth in the mornings, playing cards — pinochle mostly — with his friends, most of whom came from the ranks of former players. The office was decorated with his treasures from the game, pictures from his time in Chicago, New York City and Cincinnati, and of course the old Winchester rifle from A. G. Spalding that occupied the most revered space. There were other small renovations made around the ballpark, but the biggest changes to his stadium were yet to come.

On August 21, 1923, Clark Griffith announced his plans to greatly expand the seating capacity and generally refurbish what was known as Nationals Park — originally American League Park.[2] The steel and concrete structure had served as home to the Nationals since the fire of 1911 destroyed the wooden grandstands constructed in 1901. The structure built in 1911 was a hastily finished project that provided only minimal seating and other accommodations even when compared to the other ballparks of its era.

Griffith's intention was to build on the burgeoning interest in his team with a modern baseball showcase. *The New York Times* described Griffith's plans on August 22, saying, "the improvements will cost $100,000 and the name of the field will be changed to Clark Griffith Stadium."[3] On the same day the *Washington Post* announced the improvements as well, and put the new seating capacity at 50,000. The *Times*, seemingly intent to diminish the accomplishments of the marquee Washington sports team, put the seating figure considerably lower at 35,000.

Unfortunately, the *Times* figure squared more accurately with the ultimate facts. Griffith's ambitious plans were only partially realized and the permanent seating capacity of the stadium peaked at something less than 32,000.[4] The maximum seating capacity cited by the *Post* was to be accomplished by adding temporary seating for football games. But even the temporary seats added for World Series games maxed out the capacity of Griffith Stadium at around 38,000.

The additional new seating of Griffith's grand design was added in a second tier to the existing grandstand along the left field foul line. Calling it an addition is misleading. The left field grandstand was rebuilt from the ground up to stand as a separate structure. It was made distinct by a separate roofline for the new structure that protruded well above that of the original grandstand behind home plate. There was a space between the new grandstand and the original that rendered the impression that the two were unconnected. For its imperfections, the renovation added 12,000 seats to the original capacity in 1920 estimated at approximately 20,000.[5]

One parameter in Griffith's vision and the architects' design was accommodating the Army-Marine Football Game, held on December 1 each year. The event drew large crowds and the temporary seating was aimed to serve that game's needs as well as other local football contests. Other planned uses for the renovated stadium would include Georgetown and Howard University athletic events slated for the field.

The numerous football events to be staged at Griffith Stadium presaged George Preston Marshall's move of the Washington Redskins to play their home games at Griffith Stadium in 1937. The sharing of a single turf field for both football and baseball would create conflicts in the future. In 1923 baseball was the preeminent sport, and the field that both would share was also a focus of Clark Griffith's attention.

To insure that the ball bounced true for his new infield anchored by Peckinpaugh and Harris, he had a new groundskeeper, Reddy O'Day, who was tending a newly installed sod field that was compared to that of the best golf courses.[6] Such grounds would have been in sharp contrast to the scruffy infield that can be seen in photographs of the stadium prior to 1923. Before the new sod was installed, the area around the dugouts was worn and little more than dried mud, but Griffith sought to greatly improve the quality of the playing field. Always concerned about his players, Griffith also renovated the clubhouse facilities.[7]

Although it would become increasingly a venue for other professional sporting events in the future, the new Griffith Stadium also served as a home to a wide array of community and non-professional sporting events, including public school contests and displays, church revivals, and military preparations. The Thanksgiving Day football game between Howard University and Lincoln University was one of the most well-attended events during the year, drawing thousands of African American alumnae and fans from the surrounding neighborhoods.[8] All of those events helped stitch Griffith Stadium into the community.

The area adjacent to Clark Griffith's new showcase was part of an important and historic neighborhood within the city of Washington, D.C. It was known as the Shaw Neighborhood, and Griffith Stadium had been a part of it almost from the beginning. The first ballpark was built on the Griffith Stadium site in 1891 and called Boundary Field. The location provided cheap and plentiful land in an area that was accessible by trolley along Georgia Avenue with a stop directly in front of the stadium.

The Shaw Neighborhood helped birth the Harlem Renaissance and was one of the most affluent and successful African-American communities in the country. The first black YMCA stood on 12th Street, and President Theodore Roosevelt laid its cornerstone in a ceremony held there in 1908.[9]

Langston Hughes lived at the 12th street "Y" and wrote his earliest poetry there.

Hughes described life along Seventh Street, heading north toward Griffith Stadium, as "teemingly alive with dark working people who hadn't yet acquired 'culture' and the manners of stage ambassadors."[10] The neighborhood was home to a wide range of working class people such as described by Hughes, but also to a professional class who were the elite African Americans in Washington. Early in the twentieth century the burgeoning Shaw population included many lawyers, doctors and professors from Howard University. They set an upbeat tone for the neighborhood, but it was the throng who shared it with them that brought it alive.

The heart of the Shaw Neighborhood was the U Street Corridor that ran west from the Stadium toward 16th Street — whose terminus was the White House. U Street was known as the Black Broadway and it featured famous nightclubs like the Club Crystal Caverns, the Old Rose Social Club and Café Deluxe. Famous theatres dotted the map including the Howard Theatre, the Republic, where Duke Ellington performed, and the most elegant of all — the Lincoln Theatre. Entertainers like Billie Holliday and Pearl Bailey were proud to play venues in Shaw and join great bandleaders like Ellington.

Duke Ellington and many other famous people worked in one capacity of another at Griffith Stadium during their lives, and thus were employed by Clark Griffith. Ellington sold hot dogs at Griffith Stadium as a youngster. Bowie Kuhn, the Commissioner from 1969 until 1984, grew up in Takoma Park, MD, and worked the scoreboard at Griffith Stadium as a young man. Ted Lerner, who would buy the Washington Nationals in 2006, worked that same scoreboard in the late 1930s.

The Shaw neighborhood dated to the Civil War, when freed slaves had flooded the town of the Great Emancipator, President Lincoln, seeking refuge. Many of those immigrants set up semi-permanent quarters along the northern edge of the city and then slowly constructed a neighborhood of modest wood homes after the war. Irish immigrants joined the aggregation in Shaw in the decades leading to the twentieth century, but after 1900 the area increasingly became a monolithic African-American community.

As an oasis of white privilege within an African-American community, Griffith Stadium was not officially a segregated place. Yet the unofficial policy observed at the stadium early after the completion of the renovations was that African-American patrons sat in the right field pavilion.[11] Calvin Griffith, Clark Griffith's nephew and adopted son, related years later that seating was for the most part segregated because of "colored preachers ... asking Mr. Griffith to put aside a section for the black people."[12] They occasionally sat in the box seats or in the new pavilion in left field, and there was no prohibition against their doing so. But that was the exception rather than the rule.

Considerable dispute has grown up in recent years as to how strictly enforced the practice of segregated seating was at Griffith Stadium. It was most in evidence during Nationals games and less strictly enforced for the wide variety of other contests hosted at the stadium.[13]

Segregation in the city of Washington, D.C. as a whole followed a complex social code that reflected the diverse pressures of the metropolitan region. Racial codes were relaxed in federal workplaces in the District of Columbia, but Jim Crow customs were observed in most private establishments, especially away from the core government office areas. However loose the restrictive codes may have been at time, the exceptions to segregation did not diminish the reality experienced by many African Americans who remained restricted to the right field bleachers and were uncomfortable breaching social codes, written or otherwise.

Mark Judge, the grandson of the famous first baseman, told a story about the dominating physical presence of Griffith Stadium in the Shaw neighborhood. In his book, *Damn Senators,* Judge recounts the time shortly after the end of World War I when soldiers returned home to learn that their jobs in the industrial heartland had been given to African-American workers brought in from the south.

Tensions between ethnic groups were fanned by the Ku Klux Klan and other groups until riots broke out in dozens of America's largest cities. Blacks were pulled from streetcars and beaten and their neighborhoods invaded by marauding gangs of angry whites who killed indiscriminately. According to Judge, the *Washington Post* fanned the flames in the District of Columbia with reports that several white women had been raped by a black man.

A large and unruly crowd of whites marched toward Shaw bent on revenge but were met by "a group of two thousand armed black men, carrying weapons distributed to them on the corner of Seventh and U, right next to the ballpark."[14] The confrontation was avoided for the most part because the black community was well-prepared and they chose as a gathering place Griffith Stadium because it was such an important landmark in the community, a meeting place that all could identify. It would play an increasingly important role in the African-American community in the decades to come.

Historic events were held at the stadium, including the heavyweight title fight between Joe Louis and Buddy Baer in 1941. Louis Armstrong, the legendary trumpeter, squared off against Charlie Barnett in a battle of the bands that ended in a riot and wrote that Griffith Stadium event into the lore of the neighborhood. "Blacks considered Griffith Stadium their ballpark," wrote

Brad Snyder many years later after interviewing many neighborhood patrons of the park.[15]

The relationship between the community and the ballpark dictated the dimensions of the field itself and the stadium around it. The location may have been chosen for the availability of cheap land, but not all of the land could be aggregated to support the original design. Several of the necessary landholders refused to sell and five townhouses occupied the area behind the center field wall. An elegant old oak tree in the back yard of one house spread to the top of the center field wall and was visible from the grandstands. That tree was a favorite meeting spot for fans, especially young ones, before games.[16] The tree occupied one lot still held by an original owner and the center field wall jutted in to accommodate another owner who would not sell.

Griffith Stadium's dimensions heavily favored the pitcher and the park was consistently the most difficult in the majors in which to hit a home run. It was 405 feet to the wall along the left field line, a dimension more common to dead center in most modern parks. The nook in right center extended to 457 feet, a cavernous expanse that required the athleticism and speed of great fielders like Clyde Milan to defend it. The right field wall was 326 feet from home plate, but right field was guarded by a 30-foot-high wall constructed to block the view of the surrounding buildings. The scoreboard was part of that wall.

For all of the history that swirled around the stadium, there are two things that fans always remembered about attending games there. When asked to recall their memories of that time long ago, those who can remember always note the smell of bread baking and the president's throwing out the first pitch. The Wonder Bread Bakery — originally known as the Broad Bakery — baked thousands of cakes and loaves of bread daily just a block from the stadium, and the smells permeated every game making them a delight for all of the senses. Many also remembered the National Bohemian Beer Bottle that stood 50 feet tall above the right center field wall.

Grand construction schemes and stadium building were part of the new Clark Griffith, the one who had sold his interests in cattle ranching to become a big city entrepreneur. When Griffith sold his ranch, it left a significant hole in the lifestyle of the former westerner. He replaced his love for riding and hunting for the most part with a new hobby, golf.

Like hunting, golf allowed Griffith to spend time out-of-doors where he had been most comfortable as a youth. He began playing shortly after he and William Richardson bought the Washington Nationals in 1919. It may have seemed to Griff that as an owner he should establish himself with the country club set and discuss matters of substance there. That notion proved out, as shortly after he began playing, a golfing partner provided crucial information that allowed him to sign Goose Goslin.

Griffith became an excellent golfer who could shoot in the high 70s—just a bit over par—on a good day. Golfing outings became an important part of his spring conditioning, and his game was good enough that he entered amateur championships in Florida in the spring.[17] His name came to be mentioned in the local press as much for his golf as his baseball. In the spring he played with Bucky Harris and sometimes other players, as well as in Washington, but he was frequently paired with Secretary of the Nationals' board, Eddie Eynon, on the local links.

As the game of golf gained a large following in the 1920s, many of his players took up the game as well. Baseball players found it a pleasant avocation that complemented their love for swinging the bat. Friendships among players developed around the game. Sam Rice was an avid and talented golfer as was Goose Goslin, though his form was not as smooth as Rice's.[18]

There was a concern among managers and others that the game was not good for players during the season. At the beginning of the 1923 season, Griffith joined John McGraw and Ty Cobb in forbidding players from playing during the baseball season.[19] Although McGraw would be slow to change, Griffith came around to seeing that the sport posed no threat to his players and relaxed the ban in July of that same year.

It was all coming together for Clark Griffith, but it flowed from the investment in the team and the renovations to the ballpark. The grand design for Griffith Stadium came to symbolize the stature of the man himself. His timing was the most amazing thing of all. He was expanding the seating capacity of old American League Park by 12,000 for the beginning of the 1924 season. The money for that expansion would be the best bet Clark Griffith would ever make. In 1924 his team would begin a run of success to take advantage of the added capacity of the stadium.

The golden age of baseball in Washington, D.C. would fill the stadium and the coffers of his team and bestow the magnate status on Clark Griffith in a way he had talked about for years, but only dreamed would come true. He would increasingly become an institution unto himself, important to all segments of the community in the "little southern town" known as Washington, D.C.

CHAPTER 13

Griffith's Folly

"I liked Harris from the first day that I saw him in Buffalo, where I scouted him personally," said Clark Griffith about Bucky Harris. "He knew I was in the stands watching him and he made eight hits in a doubleheader that afternoon, although he wasn't supposed to be much of a hitter."[1] Clark Griffith's admiration for Harris remained a constant for more than 30 years. "I liked his fight. He had showed me a lot of fire."[2]

For all the high praise, however, Clark Griffith had tried to trade Bucky Harris for Eddie Collins three months earlier. Griffith believed at the time that the answer to the revolving door of managers he had used since stepping down himself was Eddie Collins. But on February 9, perhaps convinced by his insistence that Harris was a fair trade for Collins, Clark Griffith announced Harris as the new manager for the Washington Nationals.

Griffith sent his young second baseman a letter as Harris readied for spring training in Tampa. The letter laid out the terms of an offer to Harris to take on the job of manager of the Nationals. According to Shirley Povich's account, the young man first tried to call and then sent a breathless telegram to Griffith: "I'll take that job and win Washington's first American League pennant."[3] Harris's own account contains no promises about a pennant, but the enthusiasm for the task was the same.

Harris was only 27 years of age, though he had been the starting second baseman for the Nationals since early in the 1920 season. Griffith said he had considered Harris managerial material for several years, but thought additional seasoning would help him. As with Peckinpaugh, Griff was concerned that playing and managing might affect their play in the field, but he decided that Harris was game enough to handle both jobs.

It is ironic that Griffith turned to Harris after failing to trade him for Eddie Collins. Harris had told Clark Griffith in his first spring training several years earlier, "I'd like to be able to eat those flies up the way Eddie Collins does," meaning infield pop-ups. Harris had marveled at the way Collins could go back on fly balls behind second base.[4] Griffith worked Harris out ceaselessly, hitting the young man flies in shallow right field to give his budding young star a chance to become a great major league player, then worked him at bat to give him the offensive spark that Collins had.

In press descriptions of the new manager, Harris was referred to as an "iron man," because he had played in 378 consecutive contests until July, 1923. That strong constitution would be needed in the season to come, but Griffith was confident in his pick. Griffith assured the media that Harris would be the only one making decisions about the team on the field and that he had provided Harris an open-ended contract that would allow the young man to retain the job as long as he was willing to do it.

Griffith said of Harris, "He has achieved a ranking as a player which has made nearly every team in the league look at him with longing eyes and try to get me to trade or sell him."[5] Griffith was hedging the truth a bit on that one since he had been willing to trade Harris for a proven player like Eddie Collins, but that was in the nature of the game.

Griffith's words of admiration for Harris were sincere enough. "Full of the type of fighting spirit that makes for success on the ball field, I believe Harris will instill the same spirit in his teammates" said Griffith.[6] Harris himself said that Griffith told him, "You've been hustling since you were knee-high to a duck ... you're willing to learn, you know how to use your head, you're a good ball player and you've got guts. If that won't make you a successful manager, I give up."[7]

Few in the press took as sanguine a view and described the selection of Harris as "Griffith's Folly."[8] The consensus was that the Old Fox had erred in bringing in a young man not ready for the challenges ahead. Griffith was undeterred and believed in his basic baseball intuition, going on his gut in effect, that Harris had a baseball pedigree equal to the task.

Bucky Harris had started his career in a Detroit Tigers training camp with Ty Cobb at the age of 19. He had first tried out with John McGraw in New York and had been working towards a big league career since a teenager. Harris left home for baseball much the way a young Clark Griffith once had. There was something else familiar to Clark Griffith about Bucky Harris. It was the fire and confidence that had marked Clark Griffith from his earliest playing days with Cap Anson.

As surprised as the press was at the selection of Harris, it was greater folly to see the Nationals as a competitor for the American League pennant. The odds were no longer quoted in the *Chicago Tribune* next to the racing sheet; Judge Landis would not stand for such. Yet for those so inclined, the Washington Nationals were a long-shot bet as the 1924 season began.

The failure to land Eddie Collins did not instill confidence in baseball scribes who made their living guessing those odds. Contributing to the perception of the Nationals as a team on the wane was the slow diminution of Walter Johnson's capabilities. As his career ebbed towards its end, so too the Nationals were seen as a team whose fortunes were at low tide.

Clark Griffith announced that all players had to report to the team's newest spring training camp in Tampa, FL, by March 10, but the pitchers and a few others were working back into shape in mid–February. Griffith gave Nick Altrock the left-handers to work into shape and he brought in his old stalwart, Jack Chesbro, who Griffith was asking "to teach the young right-handers ideas how to shoot."[9]

Bucky Harris was already in Tampa when he was announced as manager, so he was ready to go and anxious to begin getting his mates back into shape. The Nationals spring camp in Tampa that year did not suffer from the pessimism that affected the press. Bucky Harris set a different tone for the team. Clark Griffith always believed in a tough spring regimen to set the tone for the long season. Harris began a conditioning program that put a smile on the face of the Old Fox. One of the most avid participants was Walter Johnson, who Harris dubbed "the Mountain Goat" for the fast pace he set on their runs.[10] Harris noted the new physical sharpness of the Big Train as did others in the Nationals camp.

Harris and other players spent time in Hot Springs, AR, getting in shape even before the Florida camp opened. They had played golf and enjoyed the vacation atmosphere that had long been enjoyed by players there, but the time also helped teammates get to know one another in something other than the working grind of the long season.

From the start, Harris knew that to enforce Griffith's regimen he would need the support of the senior members of the team. He sought out Joe Judge and Walter Johnson for advice and counsel. Walter Johnson was completely in the young manager's corner and said, "The boys all like Harris and are going to work hard for him."[11]

Bucky Harris believed in hard work during the day, but sought support from his players by initiating a less rigorous after-hours regimen than Griffith had required during his years as manager and had continued under McBride, Milan and certainly under Donie Bush. As a contrast with the unpopular Bush, Harris allowed an "honor system" that encouraged a reasonable curfew but did not require bed checks and other training rules more common to the military.

Most of the players were able to live within the constraints of self-management, but Goose Goslin was still a young man whose reputation was that of a free spirit, and it set up Harris's first test. Goslin had tested the limits in spring trainings past and been disciplined by all of his prior managers. In 1924 push came to shove when the Goose failed to run out a ground ball in an early spring game. Harris benched him promptly, but talked to the emerging star as an equal and the tact worked.[12] Goslin reacted by hitting .522 for the spring to lead the team.[13]

The team had senior leadership like Johnson and Mogridge on the mound, Sam Rice in the outfield, and Joe Judge and Roger Peckinpaugh in the infield. But overall the Nationals profiled as young and hungry. There was an air of potential stardom in players like Goose Goslin — the youngest player among the starters at 23 years of age. In the preceding season he had led the league in triples and posted his second consecutive season hitting over .300. Ossie Bluege was only 23 and though Muddy Ruel was 28, it was only his second year as a starter.

There were young faces on the pitching staff as well. Tom Zachary was 28, but Clark Griffith had brought in a young pitcher named Fred Marberry who would be one of the crucial payers in the coming season. Sports writers had given him the nickname "Firpo," and while he was not fond of it, the moniker was his nonetheless.

Marberry had the temperament of a latter-day reliever, Al Hrabosky, who thrived during the 1970s for the St. Louis Cardinals as the "Mad Hungarian." Marberry's countenance on the mound was all angry determination. He relied almost exclusively on his fastball and used it to challenge hitters. Like Hrabosky, Marberry ran the whole way in from the bullpen to the mound as if he could not wait to get at opposing hitters. And from the moment he arrived, he would "paw the ground, fret and fume. Finally he would rear back with his leg high in the air, his shoe in the batter's face, and fire in a smoking fastball."[14]

Harris and Griffith would use Marberry primarily as a reliever, but he was effective as a starter as well. Griffith added "Rubber Arm" Allen Russell to the team purely as a reliever. The Old Fox's strategy was to use Marberry and Russell to lengthen the career of Walter Johnson and Modgridge, the two aces on his pitching staff. Griffith had been one of the first in baseball to extensively depend upon relief pitchers. John McGraw had picked up on the notion, but it was Griffith who believed in the concept from the beginning.

He had done it to extend his own playing career. He had expanded the number of starters he used for the 1901 White Sox beyond the traditional three starters who each piled up more than 300 innings. But with the Highlanders in 1904, Griffith had taken it a step further and relegated himself to the bullpen where he continued to make important contributions to the staff. He had used Bill Hogg and Jack Powell almost as much from the bullpen in 1905 as he had started them. In 1924 the Nationals would use the concept of bullpen stars to its best effect ever.

In the team photograph taken in 1924, Walter Johnson stands above the crowd, both in legend and in size. Most of the 1924 Nationals were cast more from the mold of the five-foot, six-inch Clark Griffith than Big Train as they fanned out from their diminutive owner who was at the center. There was a curious division among the players. The pitchers were to a man larger than the position players. Only Allen Russell among the pitchers was less than six feet in height, and he was taller than all of the starters taking the field behind them. Standing over six feet were the pitchers, Mogridge, Johnson and Zachary in that order. Oyster Joe Martina — a spot starter — was 6 feet in height.

Nemo Leibold was the newest starter on the team and may have been the smallest. He was 32 years of age, a veteran who had played for the Chicago Black Sox — though avoiding the scandal. He stood only five feet, six inches and may have been just a smidge taller than Muddy Ruel. Clark Griffith had picked up Leibold on waivers early in the 1923 season, hoping the veteran still had another good season in him. Leibold was cut from the same cloth as Dummy Hoy and Wee Willie Keeler, and it was Clark Griffith's hope that he would play to that level and cover the vast expanse of green in the Nationals Park outfield.

Bucky Harris believed that he had a team that could contend as they headed north, but there were few in his corner that shared the faith. N. W. Baxter, sports editor of the *Washington Post*, described the team as having "all of the essentials features of the 1923 team" that finished in fourth place.[15] The only notable area of improvement, according to the sports writers, was in the pitching. Despite the careful work to construct a pennant contender by Clark Griffith, there were still two holes in the team as the spring drew to a close.

Baxter of the *Post* pointed out the ongoing problem filling the shoes of Howie Shanks at third base. Doc Prothro had been given a look, but he was uncharacteristically large for a Clark Griffith team and the fault showed as he could not shed the necessary weight to play the position. Ossie Bluege was an excellent glove man at third base, but no one believed he would hit well enough to play as a regular.

Then there was the ongoing search for the third outfielder. Nemo Leibold had the position coming out of Florida, but as Baxter reported, "he is no longer a great player, but his asset is dependability."[16] Baxter believed he was being kind when he picked the home town nine to finish fourth.

Griffith no longer made bold predictions of playing against McGraw in the post-season, but he still cherished the dream of doing so. Aside from the two holes noted in the press, it was the consummate Griffith team relying on speed, defense and pitching. The Nationals played in the perfect park for such a team, where it was almost impossible to hit a home run, where speedy outfielders could make a difference.

The one thing that the 1924 Nationals seemed to lack was a Jack Chesbro at the front end of the staff. No one believed that Walter Johnson still had the stuff to dominate the league. The consensus at the end of the 1923 season was that Walter Johnson's career was drawing to a close, and the Big Train said as much, announcing in the spring that it would be his last season. He wanted to follow Clark Griffith and seek his fortune as a baseball owner starting in the Pacific Coast League, a prospect to which he would devote himself in the next off-season.[17]

Clark Griffith had tried to build a winner to take advantage of Walter Johnson, but it looked as though he had missed his chance, that the Big Train's career was slipping away just as the rest of the team caught up to the great man. Nonetheless, the *Washington Post* opined as opening day loomed, "as Walter Johnson goes, so goes the Washington American League baseball club."[18]

There was a near sellout crowd of 26,000 fans to hear the Navy Band play the anthem for the opening day game.[19] It was the largest park's crowd ever as fans filled the newly double-decked left field grandstand. After the colors had been saluted, Walter Johnson caught the opening day toss from President Calvin Coolidge, who would prove during the 1924 season to be one of the most faithful of presidential fans. The opponent on opening day was Philadelphia, and Connie Mack's Athletics were a second division club. They had added a young player named Al Simmons whose presence in the outfield would have ramifications for the Nationals in June.

That first game on April 15 provided a glimpse of a much stronger Walter Johnson, one who had been running hills all spring. He tossed a complete game shutout, one of six that he would post that season to lead the league. There had been those in the press that noted the Big Train looking strong and fit again during the spring: "The American League's greatest moundsman is the picture of health and looks better right now than he has at this time for any number of years back."[20] Though Johnson was giving off signals that it was his last spring, early indications were that it would be a grand finale.

The Nationals presented their skeptics with plenty to crow about in the opening series with the Athletics. The four runs in the opener were the most they could manage against a less than stellar collection of Athletic hurlers as they dropped the next two games after opening day. The Yankees followed Philadelphia to Washington for three games and the uninspiring start did not bode well with the World Champion Yankees coming to town.

New York's American League representatives were led by Babe Ruth, but also were thought to have the best pitching staff in the American League. Waite Hoyt, Herb Pennock, Bullet Joe Bush, Bob Shawkey and Sad Sam Jones were a talented aggregation that had beaten John McGraw's Giants in the World Series in 1923. Herb Pennock was the ace of the staff who won twice in the Series, including the deciding sixth game.

The games between New York and Washington over the course of the 1924 season would determine the American League pennant, but few would have guessed they would be crucial to the final outcome when the two teams squared off for their first meeting in April. The Nationals won two of the three games and in the second knocked around the vaunted Yankees pitching staff, scoring 12 runs in a 12–3 victory.

Despite playing well against the Yankees, the Washington Nationals began the 1924 season much as they had in 1923, quickly falling off the pace and sinking into the second division of the American League. It was not until June that the Nationals turned their fortunes around. It was then that the new spirit of the club began to assert itself.

The inconsistent offense emanated from the weak hitting of Leibold and Ossie Bluege. Doc Prothro was playing a lot of third base, but he had no range and committed far too many errors when he got to the ball. Clark Griffith and Bucky Harris were able to address the concerns about the third outfield position early in the 1924 season and it may be what turned that historic season around.

Neither Rice nor Leibold were natural center fielders, and Clark Griffith needed another speedy outfielder to run down flies in Griffith Stadium He tried two young players out, hoping either they would stick or would prod Nemo Leibold into better play in center field. None of the auditions went well, but Leibold caught fire in the second half of May. Still Griffith felt the need to add to the talent he had and he made two deals that helped change the course of the season.

In June Griff brought in Wid Matthews, who had played well for Connie Mack in 1923, but had angered his manger. Mack could afford to discipline Matthews because he had a fine young player in Al Simmons to man the outfield in his stead. Matthews began the 1924 season in Milwaukee after being waived by the Athletics at the end of 1923. He was hitting .350 in Milwaukee and playing a good center field. Griffith took a chance and paid the freight for another outfield prospect. Matthews became an immediate spark plug and catalyst that turned around the Nationals 1924 season.

Griffith also purchased a new pitcher named Curly Odgen. Odgen was the most unlikely of heroes. A graduate of Swarthmore College, which was known more for turning out suffragettes and intellectuals than athletes, Ogden altered the course of his career and that of the Nationals. He needed the help of Nationals trainer Mike Martin since Ogden's biggest problem was a perennially wounded wing that Martin was able to keep in shape well enough so that Ogden could start every few days.[21]

Ogden won the last game of May against the Red Sox who were tied for first place at the time, a complete game shutout, 12–0. Sam Rice was playing extremely well and went 11-for-15 in that Boston series. It was the first notice served by Washington that they were ready for something bigger and better.

After winning two of three from Boston, the Nationals moved up only a notch in the standings to fifth place. They had an uninspiring record of 17 wins and 19 losses. They had knocked the Red Sox out of first place, but were looking up at the Browns, Tigers, Red Sox and Yankees in that order.

Bucky Harris initiated the last important change in the team in June that greatly improved the fielding behind the much improved pitching staff. Doc Prothro made an egregious error in a game against Chicago in mid–June and Harris benched him for the final time. He handed the job to Ossie Bluege, who could play second, short or third and play them well. It was a slow process, but by the end of the season Bluege had proved he could hit by steadily raising his average until he finished at .275 by the end of the season.

The Boston series began a 21-game road trip that was the courtesy of the scheduling needs of the day. The trip continued on a sour note when the Nationals lost four straight to the Cleveland Indians. But at that point Wid Matthews caught fire.[22] Matthews and the rest of offense broke out on June 11 against the St. Louis Browns when they won by the lopsided margin of 12–1 behind a Goose Goslin home run and three hits by Roger Peckinpaugh.

Firpo Marberry was proving his vast worth, pitching both as a starter and reliever. On June 17 he relieved against the White Sox and went 6 innings to win, and came back the next day to shut down the White Sox in the ninth inning with the game on the line. Then two days later he finished off a game against Philadelphia that gave the team five wins in a row and pulled the Nationals record to 29–26. They were in third place behind the Tigers and the Yankees in that order.

Washington opened a crucial series against the Yankees in New York City on June 23. It was the city that had gotten the best of Clark Griffith in 1908 and sent him packing when he could not boost the new American League franchise to the top. Now he was more than happy to see that same club struggling after winning three straight pennants.

The series started with a doubleheader. Bucky Harris sent George Mogridge to the mound in the first game and he prevailed by a 5–3 score. Tom Zachary won the second game in equally impressive fashion, 4–2 and the "spark plug" was Matthews. He had three hits in the doubleheader and the press was describing him as the "big wow." The next day Matthews was again the hero as he had two hits, one an extremely rare bunt double, and he knocked in the game-winning run in the tenth inning with a sacrifice fly. "Rubber Arm" Russell pitched six innings for the win in the third game.

Firpo Marberry started and won the final game. It was a tight seven-inning contest and Marberry outpitched "Bullet Joe" Bush, though he gave up a home run to Babe Ruth. The final score was 3–2. All four games had been tight from beginning to end. But in many ways the Nationals outplayed the Yankees badly. New York errors accounted for several runs and the Yankees pitching staff that had looked to be the certain salvation of the team in the spring appeared shaky. Even Goose Gosslin sparkled in the field with a game-saving catch to record the final out that pushed the Nationals into first place for the first time so late in any American League season.

When the team returned from New York City, they found a "Tumultuous Welcome" awaiting them at Union Station. "Hurrah, Hurrah, Three Cheers for the Washington Baseball Club," proclaimed the crowd, "Hurrah for Manager Harris and the same for the president of the club, Clark Griffith."[23] The *Washington Post* heralded the victory of "the boy manager's pieced together team over the million dollar collection of athletes gathered together under the banner of Huggins and Ruppert."[24] The irony of Washington accomplishing this feat in New York City was not lost on the press either, as the *Post* began its piece, "The mountain has come to Mohammed. Washington is leading the American League."[25]

The second major shift in fortune that changed the direction of the 1924 season was the rejuvenation of Walter Johnson. The Big Train did not pitch in the New York series. He had won the final game at Philadelphia to move his record to 9–3 with an ERA of 3.03. He was near the top of the American League in both categories for the first time since 1919. He was about to start a remarkable run that would stand up well against almost any of his other pitching wonders, including his record-setting 1913 season.

With everything seemingly clicking, the Nationals began to strut like champions. They had beaten the World Champion Yankees four straight to take over first place and it gave the team a cockiness and swagger that emanated from their manager, Bucky Harris. Harris had roots in the Pennsylvania coal country and his early life bred in him a rugged competitiveness that led Clark Griffith to make him the "boy manager," as the *Washington Post* repeatedly called him in 1924.[26]

Harris and Griffith collaborated in 1924 the way few managers do with an owner. As he had sought the counsel of Judge and Walter Johnson early in the spring, Harris sought out Clark Griffith as the most experienced baseball manager from which to garner advice as the pennant race heated up and Washington dived into the thick of it.

"He met with Griffith each morning to go over personnel matters and discuss strategy."[27] Each man saw something they liked and needed in the other. Griffith liked the fiery competitor in Harris, but Harris appreciated the grandfatherly wisdom of Griffith. "Clark Griffith was the smartest baseball man I ever knew," Harris would say.[28]

Everyone was contributing to the effort as the team pulled ahead in June. Sam Rice, Joe Judge, Goose Goslin and Peckinpaugh were tearing the cover off the ball, each hitting over .300 for the month to complement the red-hot Matthews. Bucky Harris was a driven soul on the field, stealing bases — even home — when it meant a win.

The team took two long series against the Red Sox and Athletics at the end of June and going into the Fourth of July holiday Washington enjoyed a four-game lead over the New York Yankees and a three and one-half game lead over the Tigers. It looked like a three-way race for the American League pennant. Yet for all the swagger, the pressure of a summer drive for a championship was new to Harris and the Nationals, and the realization of what they were doing and had so far accomplished sank in. It took actions by the two oldest pros in their ranks to right the ship.

The Griffs had tough opposition as well. The Yankees were a strong team and they would not go easily. The Tigers still had an outfield of Ty Cobb, Harry Heilmann and Heinie Manush. While Cobb was in the autumn of his career, he was still a great player. It was a great outfield of future Hall of Fame talent and they were mashing the ball in July of 1924.

Washington played a return engagement against New York in Washington, including a Fourth of July doubleheader. The contests were again close and hard fought, but the Nationals lost them both. Then Walter Johnson lost by a 2–0 margin to Herb Pennock and the Nationals failed to score over 22 consecutive innings as the offense collapsed. When the series was over, Washington had lost four of five to the Yankees.

Detroit came to town and showed no greater respect for the Nationals than had the Yankees as they won three of four. They beat Walter Johnson in the final game and when the Tigers left town the Yankees were back in first place and the Tigers were only one game behind Washington in third.

The best news for the Nationals was the tightness of the race and the gameness of the Tigers, who repeatedly beat the Yankees at key points in the season. Just when the Yankees appeared ready to run away with the pennant in July, the Tigers won ten of 11 games and took three of four from the Yankees in New York City to take over first place with a half-game lead over both New York and Washington.

It was one of the best pennant races in the American League in years, perhaps since 1908. But as the scheduling had worked against the Nationals in June, it worked in their favor in July. Playing against the Cleveland, St. Louis and the cellar-dwelling White Sox, Washington was able to find its hitting shoes once again. They beat Cleveland on three successive days by scores of 9–2, 15–11, and 12–0.

Then the Indians turned the table on the Nationals in Cleveland and Washington managed to score only seven runs in losing three of four. As the Nationals headed for Detroit and a series there, they stood in third place behind the Tigers and the first-place Yankees.

The Yankees were a one-man team at this point in the season. It was a remarkable show of power by the Babe. Over the course of a 48-game spree from the end of June to the middle of August, Ruth hit .480 with 20 home runs and 49 RBI. He would hit for more power in 1927, but overall, there were few stretches where any batter matched Babe Ruth in the summer of 1924. He moved the Yankees back into first place almost single-handedly.

Another move by the Old Fox helped shift the balance of power back toward the Nationals. Wid Matthews had fallen off and though he was still hitting .300, Bucky Harris and Griffith decided that help was needed. Griff traded Matthews, two other players and $35,000 to Sacramento of the Pacific Coast League for Earl McNeely.[29] McNeely disclosed shortly after the trade that he was suffering from a dislocated shoulder.

Outraged, Clark Griffith filed papers with Judge Landis to have the trade annulled. It was a huge gamble by Griffith. He and Bucky Harris had been scouting players at every opportunity, traveling to Buffalo together to look over talent, but the trade of Wid Matthews involved a fan favorite. His departure and the injury to McNeely was stirring controversy when the newest outfielder began to hit. Trainer Mike Martin was given credit for getting McNeely back into shape much as he had done earlier with Curly Ogden, who was still pitching effectively.

McNeely focused not on his physical condition but on the tight pennant race into which he had been thrust. He began to make important contributions shortly after he arrived. He had two hits on the August 16 and his triple drove in the winning runs in the contest. He did it again on the August 24 as he got two hits that led to both Washington runs. The *Washington Post* recounted his "football dive" that snared a sinking liner to center field that would have robbed Mogridge of a narrow 2–1 win.[30]

McNeely's offense was in support of a good cause: Walter Johnson's greatest season since 1919. In the heat of a pennant race, a team turns to its true leader, and for Washington that was Walter Johnson. He was as good as he had ever been that August. He started the month with a key win against the Tigers and halted a losing streak on the 7th with a tough ten-inning complete game win against Chicago. He shut out the Indians to start the home stand on the 12th.

The most important win was on the 17th of the month against the Tigers, who had won the day before. Every game against the league leaders was crucial, and Johnson pitched the team to an 8–1 win. He finished the game by striking out his friend and nemesis, Ty Cobb.[31] Bucky Harris reported years later that Johnson came to him during August and told his manager, "If he could help Washington lead the league, he did not care what happened to his arm."[32]

Winning four of five from the Tigers during that series in mid–August moved them back into second place and closed the gap with the Yankees to two games. McNeely played a big part in the series as he had four hits to support Johnson and he, Joe Judge and Goose Goslin took apart the Detroit pitching staff.

Detroit recovered quickly and traveled to New York after leaving Washington where they beat the Yankees two of three. Again the schedule favored the Nationals, who won three against the White Sox with Walter Johnson again masterful in a 2–1 win. Then against the Browns, Johnson had a seven-inning no-hitter that was called due to rain. The wins moved the Nationals back on top of the American League for the first time since early July. They split the games with St. Louis before beginning a crucial series in New York that would do much to determine the pennant.

On August 28 Washington opened play in the Big Apple behind the Yankees by a half-game. Tom Zachary started the first game and Babe Ruth showed his affinity for Zachary's offerings with his 41st home run of the season to push the Yankees to an early 3–1 lead. But the motto of the Nationals had been asserted earlier in the year by Bucky Harris when he said the team had no quit in them, that they were "never beaten until the game is over."[33]

Harris's motto was at a severe test as they trailed 6–3 in the eighth inning, but Joe Dugan made two errors and Goose Goslin had a triple to start a rally that did not end until the Nationals had scored eight runs. Firpo Marberry came in to put down a late Yankees rally and the Nationals won the contest, 11–6. Much of the no-quit came from Rice, who collected five hits in the game, and Goslin, who drove in six runs.

Walter Johnson called that contest "the turning point."[34] One of the more curious points in the game — unthinkable in today's context — occurred when the Yankees fans cheered the underdog Nationals during the eighth-inning rally. They could not have been more enthusiastic than the Washington players who once again in New York City had taken the measure of the World Champions.

The following day the Nationals continued their mastery over the Yankees as Walter Johnson won, 5–1. Johnson's wife was in the crowd when he struck out Babe Ruth to end the first inning and she reported the roar of the crowd as akin to anything he would have received in Washington. Johnson was pulled from the contest in the eighth inning when he was winged by a line drive, the ball striking his pitching hand.

The crowd was numb with worry. Bucky Harris came out to examine his star and despite his assertions that he could continue, Harris took him out. A post-game examination revealed no damage to the big man's most valuable appendage.

On the third day the Yankees came back to save face and won a close contest against Curly Ogden, 2–1, behind the pitching of Waite Hoyt. Washington was in front by only a half-game with another game to play against the Yankees in the series. George Mogridge was the starter against Sad Sam Jones and Big George had the lead, 2–1, as the eighth inning began.

The Yankees tied the score in the eighth and Firpo Marberry was called on once again.[35] The Texan with the angry mound countenance got through the ninth and Sam Rice doubled with the bases loaded in the tenth inning to give Marberry the win. In passing Marberry on the field after the game, Miller Huggins, the Yankees manager, said, "If my hurlers had the guts you have, young fellow, we'd have beaten you today."[36]

Beating the Yankees in the last game of the series widened the Nationals' lead over the Yankees as the final month of the season began in earnest. In the crucial head-to-head match-ups with New York in 1924, Washington won the series convincingly by a 13–9 margin.

For the second time a huge crowd awaited the New York train that brought the team into Union Station, but this time there was even greater excitement. The *Washington Post* reported that the loudest cheer went up when the crowd caught sight of Walter Johnson. "No greater claim could have been given a president or a potentate returning as the leader of a victorious army than that extended to Walter."[37] Not to be outdone, President Coolidge invited the team to the White House. He shook the hand of every player and encouraged them to give him a chance to cheer for them in the World Series.[38]

The Philadelphia Athletics came to town and Tom Zachary beat the Athletics in the first game. The Nationals won four of five before going to Philadelphia to start a 20-game road trip that would end the season on September 30 in Boston.

With Washington ahead in the standings by only a single game, Walter Johnson took the hill in Detroit. It was not his best game, but with the help of Firpo Marberry he held on to win by a 6–4 margin. Detroit won the next two, but the road trip carried Washington to weak sister Cleveland, then St. Louis and Chicago where they won eight of nine. Walter Johnson won his 13th game in a row on September 22 against Chicago during the western swing. It was his 23rd win of the season and lowered his ERA to a league-leading 2.73.

The Nationals at the White House: Bucky Harris, President Coolidge, Walter Johnson with ball in hand, and Griffith (Library of Congress).

There were two great pennant races going on in 1924. Both New York teams — heavily favored to win — were being pushed hard. The Pittsburgh Pirates were giving John McGraw's Giants all they could handle behind the breakout season of Kiki Cuyler, and the Brooklyn Robins were even better with Dazzy Vance and Zack Wheat.

Close races are decided when one team cracks while the other continues to run hard, and in 1924, Bucky Harris made sure that the Nationals ran hard to the finish. Instead, it was the Yankees that showed the wear and tear of too many pennant races. They went to Detroit on September 19 for three games against the Tigers. They were dead even with Washington when play began. As in the big series against Washington, Joe Dugan made a crucial error that opened the floodgate and the Tigers came back to win the first game 6–5.

The Tigers swept all three games, although each was a hard-fought contest. In the end it was errors by the Yankees that were the deciding factor as Wally Pipp and the Yankees fumbled away the pennant.

Bucky Harris was showing similar strain in St. Louis where he committed an un-characteristic three errors, but his teammates bailed him out as the team won that game, 15–9, over the Browns. Goose Goslin's bat was as loud as a cannon down the stretch as he hit .388 for the final road trip with three home runs. Sam Rice had a 31-game hitting streak in August and September and hit .348 on the final road trip to add muscle to a lineup that was hot from top to bottom.

The Yankees righted themselves after the Tigers series and stayed on the heels of the Nationals, though a solid two games back in the standings. The season came down to Washington's final four games in Boston. Boston won the first game 2–1, and the Yankees won in Philadelphia to close the gap to a single game. The word "choke," the most dreaded in any athlete's vocabulary, appeared in the press the next day. Even worse, Walter Johnson took the loss against Boston and was again struck by a batted ball, this time on the elbow. Disaster was averted as he pronounced himself healthy to pitch the next morning, saying he would take the mound as often as was needed in the series.

The Yankees lost on the September 27 as the Nationals won, providing the Nationals a huge opening. They had only to win an additional game in Boston to close out the pennant, and with Firpo Marberry holding the Red Sox scoreless for the final six innings of the game on the September 29 the Nationals won their first pennant by a score of 4–2. Aptly enough, the game ended on a smooth double play turned by Bucky Harris, who fielded a tough grounder, ran to second and fired the ball to the waiting Joe Judge.

Jubilant Boston fans, who were cheering the underdog Nationals' attempt to beat the Yankees, tried to spirit the ball away from Judge, who clutched the final out at first base. He gave the ball to Walter Johnson, who then handed it to Clark Griffith, who had watched the game from a box seat next to the field.

"I would not take a million for it," said Griff to the onlooking fans as he held the ball high.[39] Clark Griffith's pride exceeded anything he had felt in almost a quarter century, more than when he finished his first championship season in 1901. He had been predicting success every spring for so long. There had been the close calls in New York and in Washington in 1912. So when asked, Griffith said from his box, "See, what did I tell you?"[40]

Griffith believed that the credit for victory did not belong to Walter Johnson or Firpo Marberry for their gutsy pitching down the stretch, or to Rice or Goslin. It belonged first to the team and then their manager, Bucky Harris. No one was talking about "Griffith's Folly" any longer. Clark Griffith said of the team the next day to reporters, "It has fought one of the most courageous fights in the history of baseball."[41]

But when asked, "What is the one big factor to which you attribute the success of your team?" Griffith replied, "Stanley Harris." Griffith said of Harris that day, "He is one of the hardest fighters and best leaders of men I have ever met ... I count the example that Harris has set his men and his general good fellowship with them as the single greatest asset to the team this season."[42]

Fans in Washington were delirious. They watched the pennant-clinching game in the rain on electric scoreboards set up in the downtown business district that displayed the inning-by-inning activities via a live feed from Boston. "When the flash of victory came at 4:42 P.M. a wild outburst of cheering and shouting erupted. Umbrellas flew into the air and traffic cops neglected their traffic."[43]

President Coolidge's press secretary sent a telegram to Bucky Harris and the team in Boston, "We are proud of you and behind you. On to the world's championship."[44] When the team returned to Washington, a parade was held down Pennsylvania Avenue and an estimated 100,000 gathered at the Ellipse behind the White House to hear the President's remarks congratulating the team. In the wild celebrations, the quietest presence was that of William Richardson, Clark Griffith's partner and owner of the Nationals, who left the stage with the Old Fox as the two men followed President Coolidge and his family from the dais.

In 1901 Ban Johnson tilted the board in Clark Griffith's favor as he put together a championship team, his first ever. Now, the 1924 Nationals were all his, the results of his scouting and keen eye for talent. More than anything else, the team was the result of his ability to put the money down when he saw the talent that he believed necessary for a winner. He had not had that ability since 1901, not until he owned the team and had a free reign to build a true champion.

The Nationals' pennant-winning aggregation was much the same team as the 1901 White Sox, built not around a home run hitter, but with excellent pitching, defense and of course speed — always speed. In that sense they were an anachronism, a team conceived around the notion of baseball during Clark Griffith's heyday as a player. He always had pitching, and the Nationals staff in 1924 was by far the best in the American League. The team ERA was 3.34 — a half-run better than the second-place Yankees and almost a full run better than the league average.

The Nationals lineup in 1924 was stronger than Griffith's championship White Sox. Bucky Harris had the lowest batting average at .268. The heart of the order, Joe Judge at .324, Sam Rice at .334 and Goose Goslin at .344 were good enough to beat the best offense in the game, the Yankees.

But the biggest difference between that White Sox team and the Senators was Walter Johnson. Clark Griffith, the ace of the White Sox in 1901, had a great year, good enough to snag a pennant, but Walter Johnson in 1924, even at the end of his career, was much better. Clark Griffith might have sold his soul for Walter Johnson's fastball, even the one that he had in 1924. The baseball scribes recognized Johnson with the Most Valuable Player of the Year award for his valiant run in 1924, a fitting tribute for the greatest player on the Senators that year or any year.

CHAPTER 14

Finally, a Championship Match Against John McGraw

Every spring in New York City when Clark Griffith managed the High-landers, he set the bar as high as he could, telling the press that he would meet John McGraw in the championship game against the Giants. It never happened. Clark Griffith's career as the manager of the Highlanders had ended in disappointment while McGraw went on to become the game's greatest manager. Clark Griffith always gave his old nemesis his due and waited for one last chance.

In an article in the *Washington Post* Bucky Harris, McGraw's counterpart in the coming World Series, acknowledged as much. "John McGraw is the game's greatest manager. This, of course, is no secret ... his ten pennants speak for themselves."[1] Harris also cited the presence of Frankie Frisch, the "Fordham Flash," and called him the best field captain in the game, "sure to bring out an extra bit of brilliancy."[2]

The only thing McGraw's team in 1924 did not have was Christy Mathewson, but McGraw had the game's most fearsome lineup, better top to bottom than the Yankees. McGraw's hitters dominated National League play as well as Griff's pitchers had dominated American League hitters. The Giants averaged 5.5 runs per game in a year when no other team averaged close to five runs. It set up the inevitable contest between an immovable object — the Giants hitters — and an unstoppable force, Walter Johnson's still formidable fastball.

Which is not to say that the Giants' pitching was inadequate. Hugh McQuillan was second to Dazzy Vance in ERA in the National League and Virgil Barnes was not far behind. McGraw had two fine lefties in Art Nehf and Jack Bentley, and like Griffith he used his bullpen extensively to keep his starters fresh. Taken as a whole, the Giants were an intimidating prospect for a team like the Nationals, untested in post-season combat.

William Richardson, Commissioner Landis, and Griffith inspect the field before the 1924 World Series (Library of Congress).

The Giants lineup was anchored by the power of hitters like first baseman George "High Pockets" Kelly, who had 21 home runs in 1924, a batting average of .324 to lead the team, and a league-leading 136 RBI. There were only two Giants hitters who failed to hit above .300, and the team led the Nationals League in home runs. One of the hitters who failed to crack the .300 mark was Hack Wilson who still hit a solid .295. He was in his rookie year and would become the most feared hitter in the National League.

Frankie Frisch and Travis Jackson were a fine double-play combination, and joining Wilson in the outfield were Ross Youngs and Irish Muesel, outstanding hitters and defenders. Bucky Harris compared Youngs to Ty Cobb as one of the game's great players, and it was a fair comparison.

The "Boy Manager," Bucky Harris, had to be intimidated looking across the diamond into the other dugout and seeing the greatest legend of the game—John McGraw—staring back at him. Although the Giants had the more powerful lineup, McGraw still relied on the old game of speed, hustle and bat control when required. Harris had one weapon to level the playing field: the vast knowledge of Clark Griffith. No one knew the wiles of Muggsy McGraw better than the Old Fox, and no one wanted to beat him more than Griff. Harris warmed the heart of his mentor Griffith when he said of the Nationals owner going into the Series that he knew as much baseball "as that old Buzzard" McGraw.[3]

The Giants presented the Nationals a daunting challenge, but a surprising development tilted in the Nationals favor. In the last days of the season, with the Brooklyn Dodgers winning an incredible 24 games in September, New York had been pushed to the limits to win the National League pennant. With the Giants leading the National League standings by only one and one-half games over the Dodgers and pressure building, Jimmy O'Connell — one of the Giants' bench players — offered a bribe to Philadelphia shortstop Heinie Sand to help the Giants during the last two games of the season.

The Giants alleged it was in jest, but the Philadelphia manager, Art Fletcher, learned of the matter and took it to Commissioner Landis.[4] With rumors that many of the Giants' best players were involved, Ban Johnson demanded that McGraw's team be banned from the World Series. No one in Washington wanted that to happen. They wanted to beat the best, and Landis called Jimmy O'Connell before a hastily convened hearing where he confessed and implicated Giants coach Cozy Dolan.

Landis expelled O'Connell and Dolan from the game for life, but with no further proof of wider participation, decided to allow the October contest to go forward without effect. Waiting for a verdict from the Hanging Judge may have drained some morale from the Giants, but they were still the best team on paper. After the decision was handed down, the press wondered "whether the Giants can shake off the shame."[5] Although the penalties accrued only to one player, the affair cast a pall over the entire team.

Commissioner Landis and National League President Heydler were also in Washington to inspect Griffith Stadium. Clark Griffith had engaged construction crews to add temporary seating to bring the capacity of the stadium to 37,000 for the World Series. The *Washington Post* opined that "temporary seats ... have been added at every available place in the park."[6] The two men toured the premises and were impressed with the physical plant.

Griffith pointed out that the additional seating would still allow "the actual playing field to be the largest on which a world's championship was ever fought out."[7] He told the press that the infield had been re-sodded and the playing field was in perfect shape. A reported crowd of 150,000 Washingtonians had sought tickets at Griffith Stadium in the days leading up to the series, and the *Washington Post* speculated that a standing room crowd of as many as 38,000 would cram Griffith Stadium for the first contest.

The World Series began in Washington with the Nationals sentimental, if not betting line, favorites. President Coolidge was true to his word and was there for the first game. Babe Ruth and Ty Cobb were on hand and were introduced to the President. Bucky Harris handed the President the game ball and he tossed it to Umpire Connolly to officially begin the proceedings. Clark Griffith sat just to Coolidge's left along a short wall that like everything else in the stadium was aglow with patriotic bunting.

Lawrence Phillips was the man who, in the days preceding a public address system, held a megaphone and announced the starting lineups to the crowd. The press box was modernized by wiring it for radio to start the 1924 World Series. The *Washington Post* said of the coverage, "Every move of the players was broadcast ... and rebroadcast in every direction of the country so that even in crossroads hamlets where the mail only arrives twice a week, the rural districts heard all that occurred."[8]

The fans wealthy enough and lucky enough to have landed tickets inside the stadium were dressed for the opera. "The fact that it was October gave them [women] sufficient provocation to sport everything that had been in mothballs since the last snow."[9] The must-have item, based upon its popularity with women in the stands, was a small shoulder-length white fur that was worn despite temperatures in the 70s at game-time.

Amid all the festivities and celebration, Walter Johnson waited in the clubhouse for the biggest moment in his long and much acclaimed career. For 18 years he had toiled without ever pitching in a championship game. Johnson was the natural selection to start the series for Washington and he gave the Nationals an immediate edge as the Giants sent Art Nehf to the mound. As Bucky Harris stated, "Like all great athletes, he (Johnson) had always done his best when most depended upon his efforts."[10] The Big Train was nervous in anticipation of the biggest game of his life, however, telling Babe Ruth, who was covering the game for the New York papers, "I am doggone fidgety about the game this afternoon."[11]

Walter Johnson had good control over his best — and some said his only — pitch, the whooshing sidearm fastball. His only problem was the temporary seating that crowded the outfield. In the second inning George Kelly lifted a fly ball into left field that would have been routine on an ordinary day in Griffith Stadium, but found its way into the temporary seats for a home run to give the Giants a 1–0 lead. In the fourth inning, Bill Terry found the same set of seats for the Giants' second run. After Earl McNeely doubled and scored for Washington in the sixth, the Nationals were looking up at a 2–1 deficit to start the ninth inning.

In matching Walter Johnson that afternoon, Art Nehf made fools of those who dismissed the Giants pitching staff and said they were a one-dimensional team. He used a curve ball to keep Sam Rice, Joe Judge and Goose

Goslin stymied throughout the game. In the Giants' ninth inning, John McGraw faced a key decision. He had Hack Wilson on second base with two out and Art Nehf due to bat. He could have pinch-hit and counted on his bullpen to put down the Nationals in the bottom of the ninth — the modern move without hesitation. But Nehf was holding the Nationals in check and he was a good-hitting pitcher with five home runs during the 1924 season. McGraw gambled that the down side of having Nehf facing the Nationals with only a one-run lead in the bottom of the frame was sustainable.

Nehf made his manager look all-knowing as he laced his second hit off Johnson, a single to right field. Sam Rice deftly fielded it and using the arm that had once been his ticket to the majors, fired a strike to Muddy Ruel, who was waiting at the plate with the ball for the heavy-footed Hack Wilson. The umpire signaled him out, and play moved into the bottom of the ninth and the Nationals' last chance.

Ossie Bluege got a one-out hit off Nehf and Roger Peckinpaugh doubled him in, and the Washington fans finally had something to cheer about as the score was tied 2–2. It would not last. Walter Johnson and Art Nehf continued to duel into the 12th inning when the Big Train walked Giants catcher Hank Gowdy and Art Nehf got another hit. Then Earl McNeely lost a ball in the sun, and that hit coupled with a sacrifice fly gave the Giants two more tainted runs off Walter Johnson for a 4–2 lead. Bucky Harris pinch-hit for Walter Johnson in the bottom of the inning. He went with one of his most dependable bats off the bench, Mule Shirley. Shirley got to second on a poorly played fly ball. Harris singled him home to cut the margin to 4–3. Sam Rice got another hit, and it should have put men on first and third, but Rice was aggressive when Billy Southworth — the Giants centerfielder — bobbled the ball. Rice was thrown out at second base for the second out of the inning.

Goose Goslin was Washington's last hope and though he would go on to have a great series with the bat, he failed to get Harris in with the tying run. Walter Johnson was saddled with a loss despite pitching 12 innings in which he struck out 12 but was touched for 14 hits. He threw 165 pitches during the course of the game, an amazing effort, but it was not enough.

The second game went to the Nationals by an identical 4–3 score. With considerable pressure placed on him by the opening game loss, Tom Zachary pitched one of the best games of his career. He held the Giants hitters in check with the assistance of three double plays. Despite registering not a single strikeout, he had the lead going into the top of the ninth by a 3–1 margin. He weakened and allowed the tying runs to score, but Firpo Marberry came in and struck out Travis Jackson swinging to extinguish the Giants rally.

John McGraw made one of his few bad decisions when electing to pitch to Roger Peckinpaugh with the game on the line in the bottom of the ninth.

Peck doubled in Joe Judge from second base with the winning run. McGraw was criticized for pitching to the Washington shortstop rather than Muddy Ruel who was struggling with the bat and waiting in the on-deck circle. McGraw went with his instincts. Bentley had been sharp in the eighth inning and McGraw was confident in his pitcher and his team. But Griffith's shortstop won the wager and left Little Napoleon with only his desire to fight another day.

For Washington fans the highlights of Game Two were home runs by both Goose Goslin and Bucky Harris. Clark Griffith was especially proud of his young second baseman's cool resolve. Griffith said of Harris, "He did not ask his team to go out and win, he showed them how. Here's the kind of competitor Harris was: he had hit only one home run all season, because he wasn't a home run hitter. Yet in the World Series he clouted two home runs that won ball games for us."[12]

The Series switched to the Polo Grounds in New York for Game Three, and the larger arena provided seating for 47,000 fans. The *Washington Post* reported a remarkable percentage of the fans came from Washington for the game. Bucky Harris decided to start Firpo Marberry in game three although the reliever had pitched to a single batter in the ninth inning the day before. Some in the press questioned the decision of the young manager when things went awry.

Marberry was uncharacteristically wild. He walked two batters in a long second inning and hit a batter. He allowed a run to score on a wild pitch and before Harris removed him to start the fourth inning, he had allowed three runs over the first three innings.

Making matters worse, Roger Peckinpaugh had hurt his leg rounding first base after getting the game-winning hit in the second game. He tried to play in the third game, but could not manage it. When he came out of the game at the end of the second inning, Harris was forced to shift Ossie Bluege to short, where he played comfortably. The substitute for Bluege at third base was Ralph Miller. His experience at third was limited, and in the intense pressure of the World Series he posed a real danger for the Nationals at the hot corner.

The best defensive play in the game was made by Frankie Frisch on a beautiful over-the-shoulder grab of a pop fly in short right — exactly the kind that Clark Griffith had once drilled Bucky Harris on. The Giants won the game, 6–4, and seemed to have things the way they wanted, a two-games-to-one lead and two more games in New York City.

The next day George Mogridge was chosen by Harris and Griffith to start Game Four. The left-hander was a good match-up against the Giants, who did not hit southpaws as well as right-handers. Modgridge pitched a good game, giving up only three hits into the eighth inning. Firpo Marberry made his third appearance in the series in the eighth and put down a threatening rally, allowing a run to score but escaping with the lead intact.

The hero in the convincing 7–4 win was Goose Goslin, who continued to be a one-man offensive showcase. Babe Ruth was seen talking to Goslin during the pre-game festivities, and something the great home run hitter said to the "Goose of the Potomac" must have enlightened the New Jersey slugger. The Goose hit a long three-run home run into right field and went four-for-four for the day. He also made a fine running catch of a Hack Wilson shot to cap off a "star of the game" showing.

With Washington's win in the fourth game, the momentum shifted back to the Nationals. They had Walter Johnson taking the hill for the fifth game. Despite pitching on three days' rest after his grueling 12-inning affair in Game One, Johnson was unaffected and had his best stuff. Johnson later said he "was more concerned about his infield than his arm."[13] Miller was still at third base and Bluege at shortstop, and Miller already had committed two errors in two games.

Walter Johnson personally sought out Peckinpaugh, imploring the regular shortstop to play in the fifth game. It was not physically feasible, and Ralph Miller was the only option. He was not up to the challenge at third base. In the third inning he failed to make a routine play on a grounder that was scored a hit. Then he failed again on a slow-hit ball to third by Freddy Lindstrom with a runner on third. His throw to first was late and the first run of the inning scored. Miller's third miscue of the inning loaded the bases when he failed to hold the ball after Bluege threw to him at third for the force out on what should have been the second out.

With only one out ant the bases loaded, Sam Rice caught a line drive and uncorked a rifle shot that Walter Johnson relayed to a waiting Muddy Ruel to catch the less-than-fleet-footed Jack Bentley at the plate, keeping the damage to a single run. Johnson's stuff did not hold up, as the Giants collected 13 base hits, including three long extra-base hits — one a home run by Jack Bentley, the pitcher.

Washington remained in the contest, however, as Goose Goslin collected his third home run of the series in the eighth inning to bring Washington within a run, down 3–2 going to the bottom of the eighth. Of the nearly 50,000 fans at the Polo Grounds the press estimated as many as 40,000 were cheering for Walter Johnson. But the great man was beaten. Walter Johnson let in three runs in the bottom of the eighth inning. The Giants won by a 6–2 score and the Big Train had to live with the realization that he now had two World Series losses to his name.

A saddened Johnson shouldered the blame for the loss. Every baseball writer was critical of Bucky Harris for leaving Johnson in the game in the eighth inning when the Nationals had such a good bullpen. They were dumping the blame for the loss at the Boy Manager's doorstep, but the Big Train said it was his fault. "I couldn't hold 'em," he offered in the clubhouse after the game.[14] On the way back to Washington on the train, Clark Griffith told Johnson, "Don't think about it any more, Walter. You're a great pitcher. We all know it."[15]

The Giants were up by a game, but the Series shifted back to Washington for the final two games after the Nationals won a coin toss to decide the site of a Game Seven if needed. The omen of the coin toss made Bucky Harris the picture of certainty in the run up to Game Six. Roger Peckinpaugh said he would play even "if I break the leg."[16] Harris gave the starting mound assignment again to a lefty, this time Tom Zachary.

Zachary was shaky in the first inning, giving up a single run before being bailed out by a great catch by Sam Rice. Then Zachary settled in and used his slow curve to frustrate the big swingers, Youngs, Kelly and Meusel, in the middle of the lineup. He kept the Giants scoreless until the Nationals rallied in the sixth inning for two runs.

Roger Peckinpaugh led off the sixth with a single. He came around to third on two ground ball outs. Earl McNeely walked and stole second base. That put him in scoring position for the man Clark Griffith considered the hero of the 1924 World Series, Bucky Harris. Harris was the weakest hitter in the lineup, but throughout the series he got clutch hits, and this was his biggest. His single scored both McNeely and Peckinpaugh and gave the Nationals a 2–1 lead.

In the ninth inning, the Giants mounted a final rally. With one out George Kelly singled and Billy Southworth was sent in to pinch-run. Irish Meusel hit a hot smash up the middle but Peckinpaugh dived for the ball and corralled it. He was sprawled on the infield behind second base, and would not be able to walk from the field, but he was able to shovel the ball to Harris for a force out. Peckinpaugh had to be helped from the field, but Zachary struck out Hack Wilson to seal the victory.

Again, there were many contributions to the victory, but it was Zachary's masterpiece that made it possible, and it could not have been more well-timed. It set up a final Game Seven, but Washington would have to play again without its star shortstop whose bat and glove had been a big factor in the Series.

Bucky Harris was stuck with the troops he had. He decided against Ralph Miller and went with Tommy Taylor — a rookie — at third. To level the playing field the Boy Manager improvised a surprise for the Giants and John McGraw for Game Seven. The idea stunned even Clark Griffith for its daring when the two men discussed it before the game. "Bill Terry is murdering us," Harris told Griff.[17] Terry was having a great series, batting a cool .500 on 6-for-12 hitting.

Bucky Harris knew McGraw would start Terry against a righty, so he decided to start the game with Curly Odgen. Then after the game began and lineups were set, he would switch to the lefty Mogridge, who would warm up out of sight and be ready to go. Mogridge was the best pitcher for the crucial seventh game, but if he started him, McGraw would shift to George Kelly who was having a great Series as well.

Harris was betting that he could keep George Kelly on the bench and have Terry at the disadvantage of hitting against a lefty early in the game. McGraw was unlikely to switch out his first basemen as soon as the Nationals changed pitchers and limit his options later in the game. "I liked the idea. If he (Harris) had the nerve enough to try it, I was going along with him," said Clark Griffith.[18] Harris announced Curly Ogden as the starter on the day of the game.

John McGraw may have been warned that something was afoot. He warmed up three pitchers himself— Nehf, Virgil Barnes and Jack Bentley. But when the first pitch was thrown Curly Ogden faced Fred Lindstrom to start the top of the first inning. Ogden struck him out and Harris left him in to face Frankie Frisch. Frisch coaxed a walk and Harris promptly sent the signal for Mogridge, who had been warming beneath the stands.

John McGraw had George Kelly batting fourth and Terry batting fifth. For Game Seven he benched outfielder Irish Meusel, who was not hitting during the Series, and had been 0-for-4 in Game Six. Mogridge faced third-place hitter Ross Youngs with Frisch on first base. He struck out the dangerous Youngs and got Kelly—starting in center field—to ground out. McGraw ended the suspense about the pitching matchup by bringing Virgil Barnes in to start the game.

Barnes was sharp in the bottom of the inning, getting three quick outs. It was in the second inning that McGraw faced his dilemma with Terry due to lead off. McGraw refused to lose one of his best hitters so early in the game and left him in. He made the first out.

Ossie Bluege made a great play at shortstop to end the top half of the fourth inning with the score still tied at 0–0. In the bottom of the fourth, Bucky Harris hit his second home run of the Series. Clark Griffith was astonished that the weak-hitting Harris could muster even one homer, but two left him speechless. The Giants did not counter until the sixth inning. With men on first and third, Terry was due up. McGraw gave up the pretense that his rookie could hit lefties like Mogridge.

He substituted Irish Meusel into the game, and Bucky Harris countered by bringing in Firpo Marberry. Meusel managed a long sacrifice fly to score the Giants' first run. Then two errors, one by Joe Judge and another by Ossie Bluege, let in two more runs on grounders, either of which could have been an inning-ending double play.

McGraw left Virgil Barnes in the game and he stayed sharp until the eighth inning. With the score still 3–1 Giants, the Nationals rallied in the bottom of the eighth. With one out Nemo Leibold got a pinch-hit double. Muddy Ruel was due up and he was in a tough slump, going 0–19 for the Series. He managed an infield single in this clutch situation to put men at the corners. Marberry had pitched amazingly well since the sixth, keeping the Giants in check, but Harris pinch-hit for him with young backup catcher Bennie Tate. Despite the pressure of the situation, the rookie Tate worked a walk.

Henry Thomas's account lays the blame for Virgil Barnes's sudden inability to find the plate against Tate on the crowd's cheers for Walter Johnson, who had run down to warm up after Marberry was lifted from the game. The chant from the Washington crowd grew louder with the repetition of "We Want Johnson!"[19] Bucky Harris had decided to warm up Johnson for this vital point in the game saying, "You're the best we got."[20]

Barnes found his control and got Earl McNeely to pop to short center, and suddenly the rally was fizzling. The bases were still loaded and McGraw left Barnes in to face Bucky Harris. McGraw would say later it was a huge mistake on his part, but Harris managed only a darting grounder to third. The path of the ball was the first of three providential occurrences in the last few innings of the game. Like Dickens' Christmas Carol, John McGraw was visited by three different ghosts, the first of which was Bucky Harris's ground ball.

It was a well struck ball, but Freddy Lindstrom was a capable infielder and when the ball struck a pebble and bounded high over his head and into left field, it was no fault of Lindstrom's. He was subbing for Heinie Groh, the regular third sacker, but no one could have gloved the errant ball.

Since two were out, both Ruel and Leibold were running on contact. Both men raced around third base as the ball bounded into the corner. The crowd erupted and even President Coolidge and his wife jumped from their seats to cheer the two men home. Leibold beat the throw easily and when he touched the plate, it tied the score at three runs apiece. McGraw brought in Art Nehf to finish the inning, and he quieted the Nationals to send the game into the ninth inning tied.

Walter Johnson had been depressed, certain that he would be remembered as the reason his team had lost its first World Series. But Clark Griffith had called Johnson on the phone the night before the final game. Griffith had told him to get some rest, "we may need you tomorrow."[21] Now the chance for redemption was laid at his feet, and he would not disappoint.

Bucky Harris brought Johnson into the game in the most important situation in the history of Washington baseball. "If I didn't make good in that crisis, then the (Nationals) would lose their last chance to win a world championship."[22] Harris brought Johnson in to pitch the ninth because "I knew he would pitch his arm off, if necessary to win the game," Harris later wrote in his biography.[23]

Clark Griffith was so overcome by the unfolding drama that he left his box seat along the left field foul line, left the President and the First Lady to fend for themselves as he hurried to the dugout where he stationed himself on the top step. "I never saw such a grim face as Johnson's when Harris gave him the ball," said Griffith years later, recalling that unique afternoon.[24] He "grabbed the ball so hard the white showed through the knuckles."[25] With luck running so clearly in his favor, Griff said that he stood still on the dugout steps "too superstitious to move."[26]

Walter Johnson retired the first batter in the ninth, but the crowd was quieted when Frankie Frisch poled a line drive into the gap that center fielder McNeely could not run down. Frisch made it all the way to third where he stood with the go-ahead run and with only one out. Then Johnson walked Ross Youngs. He recounted later that he walked Youngs because "I knew I had George Kelly's number."[27]

It was late in the afternoon and the sun was sinking. Harris had thought the fading evening light would help add a few feet to Johnson's fastball. Whether it was that advantage or pure will, Johnson smoked three fastballs past George Kelly, who seemed helplessly overmatched. Now there were two outs.

Harris said that at that point he knew "Walter was himself."[28] But another of Harris's strategic changes came into play at this point. Had Harris not changed out the pitchers, left-handed hitting Bill Terry would have been available to hit against Johnson at this crucial point in the game. But he was firmly fixed on the bench as Irish Meusel came to bat. He was a dangerous hitter as well, but not having a good Series, and the righty-righty match-up favored the Big Train. He got a weak grounder from Meusel to end the threat.

McGraw countered with Hugh McQuillan after Nehf allowed a hit in the bottom of the ninth. "Handsome Hugh" set the Nationals down in order in the ninth and tenth innings. The Giants were able to get base runners on against Walter Johnson, but when he needed it he reached back for something extra and struck out Frisch and Kelly in key spots.

Griffith Stadium had been a sea of bedlam since Harris's ball bounded over Lindstrom's head, and each time Johnson struck out another Giants hitter they erupted afresh with wild exhortations for their champion. President Coolidge and his wife were both transfixed by every pitch, and even the President had been seen losing his cigar when Harris's ball bounced into left field.

In the bottom of the 12th, the light had become so poor that the umpire behind the plate was having trouble seeing the ball. But play continued with Jack Bentley on the mound for the Giants. Then the second providential happening occurred, and this time the ghost came in the form of Hank Gowdy's catcher's mask.

With one out, Muddy Ruel was the batter. He hit a harmless pop fly behind the plate that would ordinarily have been the second out. Hank Gowdy, the Giants' well-respected catcher and a great defensive player, tossed his mask away as he had done thousands of times, but the fly drifted back just enough that Gowdy stepped on the mask and stumbled haplessly while the ball bounced off his glove and onto the ground.

"A sinner forgiven," Ruel hit the next pitch into left on a vicious line. [29] It fell for a hit and even the slow-footed Ruel got two bases. Walter Johnson batted for himself. Always a good hitting pitcher, he was aided by fate. He stroked a grounder to the usually sure-handed shortstop, Travis Jackson, who bobbled the ball, and Johnson was safe. Runners stood on first and second when the third and final providential act played out. The third ghost was again a pebble in front of Freddy Lindstrom.

With Ruel at second and Johnson on first with one out, Bentley pitched to Earl McNeely, hoping to get a grounder for an inning-ending double play. McNeely obliged with a grounder to Lindstrom. Just as in the bottom of the eighth inning, the routine grounder hit something in the infield dirt and "took a 10-feet leap" over Lindstrom's head, bounding crazily into left field toward Irish Meusel.

Muddy Ruel was running on contact, determined to make something happen at third base as Lindstrom moved to tag the base. When he saw Lindstrom jump and the ball sail past, he barreled past the third baseman and headed for the plate. Griffith described the tension of watching Ruel's journey to the plate as "an eternity of running ... the 180 feet between second base to the plate which Ruel covered, seemed to me like 180 miles." [30] By the time Meusel fielded the ball, the strong-armed outfielder concluded he had no chance to throw out the Nationals catcher at the plate. He pocketed the ball and in so doing handed the World Championship to the Washington Nationals and their screaming fans.

The celebration erupted immediately from the stadium as the fevered body of fans held back by the railings spilled onto the field. Earl McNeely was set upon by joyous fans who ripped his jersey from his back. Walter Johnson was standing on second base, tears in his eyes until he was brought back to reality by the swarm of fans.[31] President Coolidge required the Secret Service to escort him to a point of safety, but he insisted on stopping so that he could watch as Walter Johnson made his way from the field to the dugout, as though he wanted to savor every moment that the great man had given him that day.

Clark Griffith completely neglected his most privileged guest. "I was so all-fired excited, I forgot," he said, and he never returned to the box seats after the game to help the President of the United States leave the stadium. Griff welcomed the players as they made their way to the dugout and then accompanied them into the clubhouse while the riot of joy went on above them in the stadium for hours. "A kaleidoscopic cross section of joy-frenzied men and women stormed the players' dressing rooms," reported the *Washington Post* the next day, but they were soon locked out.[32]

The gaiety was at its zenith in the Washington clubhouse. As a breathless Bucky Harris strode about totally nude smacking his teammates on the back and exclaiming to anyone who would listen, Clark Griffith lit a victory cigar and pulled on it continuously as he strolled through the crowd of his players. He shook hands all around, but gave his biggest hug to Bucky Harris, saying, "I am certainly proud of you, Bucky Boy."[33]

Harris deserved the singular praise. He had taken on the greatest manager in the game and beaten him. Every beat writer and all the great writers of the day including Grantland Rice acknowledged that Harris had won the tactical battles of the series. He is still the only manager under the age of 30 to win the World Series, and he did it in his first year, when he had been labeled "Griffith's Folly."

The press described Griffith as "speechless" after the game. Griffith had shed the image of an outspoken youth. No longer did he jump on tables or stages for a chance to address the crowd and plead his case. Now the media described his Old Fox persona as "taciturn, expressionless and enigmatic."[34] Even in the hours after the World Championship win, Clark Griffith was a more reserved and deferential individual who let his players express the joy that he felt inside. He said only to a gathering of players, "It happened the way I wanted, with Walter winning for us."[35]

Although *The Washington Post* claimed that Griffith made no speech to his team, in his book on his grandfather, Mark Judge claims that he addressed the players, saying, "This is the happiest moment in my life ... I am the only fellow in the world who was certain that Washington was a baseball town. For twelve years it's been a long haul."[36] Griffith had said, "Washington is my home," when he convinced William Richardson to back his purchase of the team. But now it was more than just his home, it was the home of which he had always dreamed, where championship baseball had found a home beside him.

Hank Gowdy and Frankie Frisch made their way to the Nationals club-house to give their congratulations to Walter Johnson. John McGraw joined them and was generally gracious to his youthful adversary, Bucky Harris. Yet in his official remarks to the press later, he was a somewhat less gracious loser, remarking that "they got the breaks ... I don't see how Washington can be called a better ball club than the Giants."[37]

Clark Griffith never said he took any special pleasure in beating McGraw, who had turned down the intra-city series many years before rather than play the Highlanders.

There was no room for remembering New York as Clark Griffith savored what he would call the highlight of his long and storied baseball career. "Of all the 10,000 afternoons I have spent in a ball park ... as a player, manager, and club owner, that afternoon is my pet."[38] That sentiment was shared by every baseball fan in the nation's capital.

Washington, D.C. is home to celebrations of dignified political victories and to joyous and animated celebrations of wars brought to grateful conclusion and peace restored. It is a statement on the cultural pinnacle that baseball had achieved in the United States in the 1920s that the festivities following a World Series victory could approach the level of such emotional moments in the nation's history. Yet the press reported it that way, ranking it with almost any other celebration held in the city.

Fans "kept up an all-night carnival of cheers," as they rambled back and forth across Pennsylvania Avenue and the streets along it on either side.[39] There were thousands of them, "drunk with happiness."[40] They maintained a parade of jubilation across the busiest intersections in the city, many wearing Clark Griffith's slogan, "I told you so," on white ribbons.[41] At 13th and F Streets young men dressed in women's garish hats rolled up their pants legs and directed traffic as thousands of cars crushed into the central city to participate in the chaos.[42]

It lasted until the wee hours of the morning, when the historic moment of October 10, 1924, faded, and the city that was too small to support a championship team finally slept, with their team's great accomplishment a treasured memory forever.

Commissioner Landis, who had worried that the game would sink into controversy with the threat of another betting scandal just a week before, called Game Seven of the 1924 Series the "greatest game ever played."[43] For Washington baseball fans it would so remain for the rest of the century.

CHAPTER 15

All the Eggs,
One Elegant Basket

The players fared well for their World Championship win in 1924. Each National received a bonus check of nearly $6,000, about the average salary level of major league players at the time.[1] Mike Martin, the trainer, got a full share, and others who played lesser roles in the season, such as Wid Matthews, got smaller shares. But the biggest bonus went to Clark Griffith. The total gate for the 1924 World Series was $1,093,104.[2]

Clark Griffith had expanded the stadium that now bore his name just a year earlier and added 12,000 seats, plus temporary seating to accommodate another 4,000 fans for each World Series game played in Washington. The return on that investment was something that Griffith had been waiting for his entire baseball career, since he had first seen Charlie Comiskey step off the playing field and into the owner's suite in Chicago.

For the long-shot bet that Washington, D.C. could become a competitive force in the game and make economic sense of investment therein, he reaped the majority share of the return that accrued to the Nationals as a corporate entity. It was a fair return on a risky investment that he brought home through hard work and application of his unique baseball intelligence.

Attendance was up at Griffith Stadium for the entire 1924 season and reached almost 585,000. That record figure would be topped with an unheard-of 817,000 in 1925. Washington was one of the smaller cities to host a major league team, but Clark Griffith was proving that a winner could make money in the nation's capital.

World Series Championships and record-breaking attendance translated into big profits that Clark Griffith as the president of the operation decided to invest in a more gracious lifestyle. It was the culmination of what Shirley Povich rightly termed a Horatio Alger story. Clark Griffith was 54 years of age, entering what he could reasonably assume was the twilight of his career and perhaps his life. His origins in a frontier cabin, even the more urbane existence of Normal, Illinois, were a fading memory.

Yet in Washington, Griffith maintained a relatively humble existence until 1924. When he and Anne had moved from Cincinnati in 1912, they had rented an apartment in an eight-story apartment building immediately adjacent to the National Memorial Baptist Church and across Columbia Road from All Souls Unitarian Church. The building was part of the thriving Mt. Pleasant neighborhood that was relatively close to the stadium and the life-blood of Clark Griffith.

The Griffiths shared the modern apartment with his mother-in-law, Jeanne Robertson, and his sister-in law, Jane. Clark Griffith and his wife Addie had no children. The company of three spirited Scottish women at home was enough for the Old Fox, who was often out of town on baseball business.

His family situation changed dramatically at the end of the 1922 season when Addie Griffith visited her brother, James Robertson, in Montreal. Her brother had a burgeoning family and his wife had just given birth to twin boys. What Addie found on her visit shocked her. Her brother and his wife could barely take care of the existing children, and the two babies were more than they could manage. She set out to remedy the situation, and her solution would irrevocably change the life that Clark Griffith had known.

The Robertson family into which Clark Griffith married immigrated to the United States from Scotland in the late nineteenth century. They eventually settled in Chicago, where mother Jeanne cared for son James and his two sisters, Ann and Jane.[3] Clark Griffith met his future bride, Ann Robertson, in 1900 at a party attended by several ballplayers in Chicago where they were introduced by a mutual friend. She worked at the Marshall Field's Department Store in downtown Chicago. Clark Griffith said, "It was a case of love at first sight."[4] After a six-month courtship, the Griffiths were married on December 3, 1900.

Though the new bride knew nothing about the game of baseball, she was a quick study and her admiring husband was willing to wait while she learned. "Aunt Addie," as she would forever be called, went with her husband to every spring training camp. "She always arrived there with him and stayed until the season opened."[5] Her mother Jeanne became one of Washington's most ardent baseball fans who spent almost every day at the ballpark in the same grandstand seat.

Calvin Griffith was one of the best witnesses to the relationship between Clark and Addie Griffith. "He idolized her and she idolized her husband," he later said of the household into which he moved as a boy, one he described as a model of "domestic bliss," especially after the one he left in Montreal.[6]

Clark and Addie Griffith (Library of Congress).

Clark Griffith III, the grandson, would recall his great-aunt Addie as a woman of uncommon character who exerted tremendous influence in her household and on Clark Griffith senior.

Addie Griffith's brother, James Robertson, had played minor league baseball in Montana in the years before she met Clark Griffith. He may have met Clark Griffith there, and some accounts indicate he was the one responsible for introducing his sister to the Old Fox. James still nursed a dream of playing big league ball like his new brother-in-law, Clark Griffith. The well-connected Griffith arranged a tryout, but Robertson did not have major league talent and came back to Chicago where he moved back in with his mother and sisters while working at Marshall Field's like his sister.

Perhaps to put distance between himself, his failed baseball ambitions, and his successful brother-in-law, James Robertson moved to Montreal where he married Jane Davies and started a family in 1908. James Robertson's wife brought forth five sons and two daughters over the next 14 years. The oldest child was Mildred, followed by son Calvin and the only other daughter, Thelma.

James Robertson's life was a troubled and short one. He was an alcoholic and an abusive parent, and the oldest of the children bore the brunt of their father's worsening problems. The more he drank, the greater the abuse he targeted most frequently at eldest son, Calvin. Mildred was the strength of the family as she helped her mother, Jane Robertson, cope with the financial stress of an often unemployed father. Her mother worked as a seamstress and left much of the child-rearing to Mildred when she was out of the house.

When Aunt Addie came to visit the family in 1922, she witnessed the desperate situation in which the children existed and realized that the recently arrived twin boys were aggravating an already untenable household. The Robertsons' life in Montreal was marginal and all of the children worked to help make ends meet. Addie Griffith was appalled at the conditions.

Most alarming was the condition of her brother James. He was in a sickened condition when she arrived in Montreal, gripped by alcohol that had him in a downward spiral that saw his health worsening with each passing day.

Addie was especially concerned about the effects of James Robertson's poverty and abuse upon the oldest children. Speaking of that visit to Montreal by Aunt Addie, Calvin later recalled, "She (Addie) did a lot of talking with my mother."[7] The long conversations between the Jane and Addie sought a means for the Griffiths to help in whatever way made the most sense, and with Jane and Mildred overwhelmed with care for the twins she proposed that she take Calvin Griffith back to Washington for what was termed a "visit" at the time.

Calvin was reluctant to leave alone and insisted that his sister Thelma go with him. That was quickly arranged with Addie escorting the two children back to Washington. When they arrived in Washington, the first stop was at Griffith Stadium to meet their uncle, Clark Griffith, and Calvin later said they made it just in time for the last game of the 1922 season.[8]

Shortly after the two children arrived in Washington, the Griffiths sought to formally adopt them. But the courts in Washington ruled that Calvin was beyond the legal age for adoption, and Clark and Addie refused to adopt one child and not the other. The Griffiths settled for a name change instead. Where Calvin had been named Calvin Griffith Robertson, the last two names were switched so that he became Calvin Robertson Griffith, and his sister Thelma was formally renamed as well.[9]

Left behind initially in the care of their mother Jane Robertson and eldest daughter Mildred were brothers: Bruce, Sherrod, and small twins named Jimmy and Billy. The relocation of two of the oldest children did not change the circumstances for James Robertson, the father. Complications from alcoholism led to his death in 1923.

Jane Robertson struggled to support the remaining children alone in Montreal after her husband's death. In 1925 Griffith arranged to have the rest of the family moved to Washington, where they re-joined their siblings Calvin and Thelma. Griffith purchased them all a home in a suburban — almost rural area — between Washington and Silver Spring, Maryland, near the Walter Reed Army Hospital. The house was only a short distance from the Griffith mansion on 16th Street, and soon all of the children had as their focal point the lifeblood of the entire brood, Griffith Stadium.

The Robertson children became part of an extended family that Clark Griffith had not known since he moved from the Normal-Bloomington, Illinois, area. The press reported on the new arrivals at the end of the 1925 season and depicted Clark and Addie Griffith at the head of the extended family, "almost besides themselves with joy over the little brood. The Old Fox seems years younger as he played with the twins, and it seemed as if the kiddies were just as happy as he."[10]

When the two children first arrived from Montreal in 1922, the old apartment could not accommodate the new family. A new apartment in the building next door was quickly found. While the apartment was in one of the nicest areas of the city, it was adequate neither as a place to raise children nor as a showcase for an emerging magnate and owner of one of the most successful franchises in the American League.

Using the wealth drawn largely from his championship season, Clark Griffith bought a lot further up 16th Street. The lot was on the southwest corner of Decatur and 16th Streets, near Rock Creek Park and the recreational fields the park offered. The *Washington Post* reported that the house Griffith planned to build on the lot would be an "imposing" one.[11] It would become the new home for his two children and his wife's sister and mother.

Officially the address was 4720 16th Street, but the house was large enough to command two addresses, one on Decatur Street as well. The lot cost Griffith approximately $200,000 — an amount that would command a present value of nearly $2.5 million.

The home Griffith built on the property was — and remains — an elegant red brick structure with Tudor-styled appointments including large bay windows across the front of the structure and turreted windows at several corners. Clark Griffith III, said the design of the house was Scottish and the inspiration of Addie Griffith. The tile flooring of the imposing foyer, the heavy beamed ceilings, the sweeping elegance of the stairs that led to the upstairs, all of it were fashioned from the memories of Scotland brought forth by Addie Griffith.[12]

There was a grand entrance off Decatur Street, with a circular drive, though it was clearly not the front of the house. There was a two-car garage at the rear of the house at a time when few families owned a single car, much less two. There was room for two servants to attend to the mansion, and a couple was employed by the Griffiths to manage the house.

Calvin Griffith described his new home as "palatial," and after the tough circumstances in which he and Thelma had lived, it must have seemed quite a change. "It was so damn beautiful it was unbelievable," he recounted in later years.[13] Calvin Griffith described the interior architectural detailing as more impressive than the exterior, noting ornate lighting, and detailed brick-work and woodworking throughout the structure. He recalled that the downstairs rooms featured light posts, each adorned with baseballs, scattered throughout.

Clark Griffith III, remembers the house warmly for the huge family cel-ebrations that occurred there with regularity. Thanksgiving and Christmas were large gatherings that saw all of the children and grandchildren gathered around an expansive dining room table that seated 24. "Joe Cronin would bring his family down from Boston for those gatherings," remembers Clark Griffith III.[14] The kids would play in the basement and often would stage plays for the grownups before the meal.

"The climax of the meal was when dessert was served. It was always plum pudding," recalls Griffith, III.[15] The traditional Scottish desert was served flaming and was carried into the dining room by a servant with great ceremony to the delight of the assembled children. Griffith continues to make the dessert. "It had one-and-one-half cups of Old Grand-Dad whiskey," he remembers, and that is the way he makes it still.[16]

Until adoption of the larger Robertson clan, Clark Griffith had main-tained contact with his mother and the larger Griffith family back in Illinois, especially when playing in the Midwest. After 1902, when he homesteaded the ranch in Montana, he brought his oldest brother Earl out frequently to hunt until he sold that property to buy his first stake in the Nationals in 1912. Griffith's brother named a son for the most famous descendant of Isaiah Griffith as a measure of their closeness. Though Griffith was especially fond of his namesake, that boy died before he reached his 21st birthday.

In 1921, shortly before assuming parental responsibility for the Robertson children, Griffith was in Normal, Illinois, visiting his mother and her family. While there he addressed the local boys club. "It's good to be back in one's home town," he said just months after he had proclaimed that his new team in Washington was his home.[17] He said he was always glad to get back and praised the local youth, one of whom — Eddie Johnson — was playing for the Nationals' minor league team in Chattanooga. But those trips became less frequent after he was subsumed by the Robertson family, and contact with that side of the family almost completely disappeared.

In assessing the accounts Clark Griffith provided of his life, he invested as much personal energy in his teammates and they seemed at times to fill in for any shortage of family he knew during large parts of his life. That situation changed abruptly when the Robertson children came to Washington to stay. Clark Griffith confronted his new family responsibilities the only way he knew to do anything, by incorporating them into the baseball team.

He had tried to help the children's father, James Robertson, to find a life in baseball, but that effort failed. Now he took the man's surviving children and set them up in life, exposing them to the best thing in life he had ever known, the game of baseball. Mildred Robertson was only 16 when the family moved to Washington, but shortly thereafter she began to work in the team offices at Griffith Stadium and quickly became Clark Griffith's personal secretary. She was an attractive girl and warmed up the office for the ballplayers, members of the press and management from other teams that always dropped by the office of the Old Fox when they were in town.

Jane Robertson's task of raising the remaining children was considerably improved by the move to Washington. They were often at the Griffith mansion and played in the park nearby with their brother Calvin or among themselves. What bound them all together was baseball and Clark Griffith.

Thelma said of the experience of the family in Washington, "while we've been a family that was reared in two different households, we've stayed very, very close, and that is nice."[18] All of the boys would become accomplished athletes. Bruce Robertson died in 1926 of rheumatic fever, but Calvin, Sherrod and the twins would all go on to play baseball at various levels, with Sherrod making the majors as a utility player in 1940. After World War II, Sherry Robertson was again with the Nationals where he played ten professional seasons, although with modest results.

"We were always together at the ballpark, year around," Jimmy Robertson would recall years later of his family's closeness to the Griffith family business.[19] When the children weren't playing the game, they were often at Griffith Stadium which served not only as a place of employment for Mildred and eventually others, but also as a gathering place for all of them. It was a family and there were three places were they could be found over the years: Griffith Stadium, the house on 16th Street, and with increasing frequency as the younger children came of age, the playing fields nearby.

Calvin was the first to get his feet wet with his adopted father's team. Beginning from the first visit in 1922, Calvin Griffith became the bat boy for the team. He described his job as retrieving bats and balls during the game and at its end. He performed these chores during the 1924 championship season and watched the World Series from the dugout according to his later accounts.

Clark Griffith sought to expose Calvin not just to baseball, but to the educational opportunities that Griffith had never had time to pursue. Clark Griffith had always believed in education, and even as the owner of the Washington Nationals Griffith was studying law at Northwestern University through an extension in Washington. He enrolled Calvin at age 17 in Staunton Military Academy in Virginia to finish a high school career that had lapsed too long with the boy working for the Nationals every day after school.

As Shirley Povich said of the family, "they were privileged, but there was a sense that there was work to do."[20] Calvin described his uncle as stern when necessary, but exceptionally "kind-hearted" and with a generous spirit. The work was baseball and Griffith instilled a knowledge and appreciation of the game that was second to none. One of the twins, Jimmy Robertson, recalled, "you really had to know your baseball inside out."[21]

Life at a boarding school was a difficult adjustment for Calvin Griffith, and the military regimen was as well. Calvin Griffith had suffered from the rough existence he had known in Montreal.[22] He described himself as "a mean son-of-a-bitch" during his formative years in Montreal, when he was in frequent fights that he attributed to life with a father who seemed uncaring and pugilistic.

At boarding school he had to adjust not only to military discipline that Clark Griffith assumed would help the boy, but also to socializing with the sons of wealthy parents whose early lives had been less challenging. One of his classmates was Barry Goldwater, who went on to become a United States Senator and presidential candidate.[23]

Calvin Griffith valued the educational opportunities given him, but not surprisingly sports proved to be the leveling influence that helped socialize Clark Griffith's adopted son. It also helped that his sister Thelma was sent to a girl's academy nearby within several months of Calvin's enrolling at the military school. Both kids were in Staunton, Virginia, about two hours from Washington, D.C. in the Shenandoah Valley, and the physical proximity of the two children was indicative of an enduring friendship that lasted through their adult lives.

Calvin Griffith played baseball for the Staunton Academy, but he was a big, lanky kid standing six feet tall. Basketball proved to be his best sport in high school. Academics were more of a challenge. Calvin Griffith would never be known for his intellectual gifts and while he graduated from Staunton, his marks were less than stellar.

He enrolled after graduation at George Washington University in Washington, D.C. where he would have even less academic success, but continue to play a good brand of baseball. The Colonials — as the GW team is still known — played for a baseball championship at Griffith Stadium in Calvin's last year at the school in 1934, and Calvin pitched and caught for the team.

Clark Griffith was grooming Calvin as an heir from the moment that he invested in the young man's private school education. But Calvin Griffith was never secure in his place within the family. Clark Griffith had no other male descendants from his mother's family. His brother's child, Clark, was a favorite, but he died when he was 21 from a tonsillectomy operation.

Clark Griffith's adopted son was his choice to carry on the family business and name. Yet Calvin Griffith was clearly a rough-cut commodity. He would always be known more for malapropisms than articulate communication. Clark Griffith provided his nephew a first-rate education, but the effects were superficial at best if the biography in which he collaborated is any guide.

The wealth generated by the 1924 and 1925 baseball seasons supplied Clark and Addie Griffith with the means to provide comfortably for their new family. It is a testament to the largesse of the man that he took on the children of another and cared so unflinchingly for them. The 1920s were the best of times for the Griffith clan. The team won a World Series Championship, Clark Griffith was recognized finally as one of the pillars of the baseball community, and he had a family gathered about him with which to share it.

Yet even at the height of Clark Griffith's fame and accomplishment, the smallest signs of decline could be seen. The biggest problem was the game of baseball itself. The brand of baseball that Clark Griffith learned from Cap Anson and perfected in 1901 with the Chicago Whites Sox has been called "inside baseball" by many and other names as well.[24] It depended upon bat control and the ability to hit the ball where it placed the greatest pressure on the defense.

To win, Clark Griffith's teams had speedy outfielders, accomplished defenders at every position and above all else, the best pitching. No baseball park was more conducive to Clark Griffith's style than his stadium with its large and expansive outfield areas, and no outfielders were better fitted for it than Clyde Milan and Sam Rice.

The third outfielder in the best Washington outfield of all time, Goose Goslin was notable for exactly the opposite reasons. He was a talented defensive player but it was his ability to hit that made him special. Goslin could hardly get the ball over the fence in Griffith Stadium, but had the power to do so in every other major league park. It is testament to how difficult a park Griffith Stadium was for home run hitters that Goslin hit only one home run in Griffith Stadium in 1924 and 11 on the road. In 1926 he would hit all 17 on the road. Only when he moved out of Washington to play for the Tigers would his power be fully grasped, as he hit 37 home runs for the Tigers in 1930.

Babe Ruth had decided that it was easier to hit the ball over the fence than to spend time moving baserunners around the diamond like chess pieces.

He revolutionized the game and for a moment in time John McGraw adapted better than Clark Griffith. But John McGraw was on his own decline in 1924 and it would be a far more precipitous one than his rival Clark Griffith's.

For the most part McGraw's great teams had looked remarkably like Griff's and Connie Mack's because the formula was much the same for all the great teams through the 1910s. Bill James has said that the game of baseball changed the most suddenly and dramatically as at any time during the twentieth century between the decade of 1910 and 1920.[25] It did not happen in a year, but slowly and steadily over the course of the decade, the game was largely remade.

Clark Griffith was following dated blueprints in other ways as well. He had emulated or tried to follow in the footsteps of Charlie Comiskey, who was the first of the former players to make a fortune as an owner of a major league team. Comiskey and Ban Johnson had made their names in the game by cleaning up its image, taking it out of the ethnic melting pot and the rough house environs in which it grew to national prominence. The game became a respectable "national pastime," to be enjoyed by women and families and men in suits and ties who were in the professional world.

Clark Griffith had played a role in that transition as a player and a manager. Then he had stamped it personally by making it the game of presidents. But the ability of men like Comiskey to rule the game by dint of will was at an end as well.

It has been said that Clark Griffith served as his own General Manager in an era that saw owners and managers wearing many hats. But the game was beginning to specialize. Player-managers were beginning to disappear and front office staff was being hired by wealthy industrialists who did not know the game but could afford to buy a team and pay handsome sums of money to men who knew the game well and could put together winning teams.

Mark Armour names the three most prominent of the emerging professional baseball management staff in his wonderful book on Joe Cronin: "Branch Rickey of the Cardinals, Bill Veeck, Sr. with the Cubs, and Ed Barrow with the Yankees."[26] They were taking the game in a very different direction from what Clark Griffith knew. It was a path that Griffith and his family-owned business was not well-suited to travel.

Branch Rickey's name is synonymous with the establishment of the minor league farm systems that would funnel talent to the majors. This kind of diversification and specialization began to increasingly mark the game of baseball as it became more and more both a part of the culture and a money-making enterprise. But the old shibboleth that "it takes money to make money" became increasingly true in the game of baseball. To run a minor league organization was especially capital intensive.

Clark Griffith had helped baseball overcome the ban on Sunday games. In New York and other locales he had shown the tact and diplomacy needed to gain the acceptance of power brokers who could help that process. He did no less in Washington, D.C. by enlisting the well-connected and powerful preachers of the day to become partners with the Nationals. Then he reached out to the black ministers in the Shaw neighborhood to bring that group into the stadium as an institutional presence.

The new era in the game that confronted Clark Griffith after his championship season would require more than tact and intelligence. He would fight the changes because he could not afford to accommodate them. The family business that the Washington Nationals became as they won pennants and World Championships in the 1920s would face new challenges in the years to come. Increasingly Clark Griffith would be seen as a grand old man of the game who, along with Connie Mack in Philadelphia, could not keep up with the times.

Shirley Povich said it as well as anyone when he said that Griffith was trying to "be a corner grocery store in a supermarket world."[27] The world of baseball was showing the first signs of a new direction, new specialization and diversification. But in the middle of the 1920s Clark Griffith was in his element. He was running one of the best baseball operations in the business, even if it was a family enterprise.

As Clark Griffith moved off the playing field and advanced in age, his persona as a rebellious leader of labor uprisings mellowed into that of a reserved senior citizen of the game. Already 43 when he arrived in Washington, his days as an angry youth taking the mound for Cap Anson were largely forgotten. When he bought the mansion on 16th Street, he was 55 and he had put that lifestyle in a closet. He only brought it out to entertain baseball writers who were taken with the contrasts between the man they saw and the poor but determined lad from the frontier whose wits and athleticism had helped him scuffle his way to the top.

CHAPTER 16

The Big Train in the Big Rain

Clark Griffith did not rest on his laurels after the accomplishments of the 1924 season. Again concerned that his greatest asset, Walter Johnson, was nearing the end of his career, he sought to bolster his pitching staff almost immediately. In December he brought in one of the best spitball pitchers still allowed to use the pitch, Stan Coveleski, who had pitched for Cleveland for nine seasons, including four in which he won 20 or more games. Coveleski, known as the "Big Pole," had a down year in 1924 and at the age of 34, Cleveland management was willing to part with him for the paltry sum of $10,000 and young pitcher Byron Speece.

For even less — $8,000 — Clark Griffith landed another established pitching star, Dutch Ruether. Ruether was 32 and the left-hander was less accomplished than Coveleski, but the press began to notice a change in the tenor of the acquisitions by Griffith going into the 1925 season. Along with the 37-year old Walter Johnson, the Nationals pitching staff took on a particularly veteran appearance.

Across the board the Nationals were not really a young club any more. Sam Rice was 35 and Joe Judge 31. Roger Peckinpaugh — whose age had showed in the '24 World Series — was 35 to start the 1925 season. It was clear that Clark Griffith was no longer looking to the future, but was investing in the here and now. He had a mansion on 16th Street and a mortgage to pay, and he needed more paydays like that in 1924 to afford his new family and lifestyle.

By adding Coveleski he had one of the most successful pitchers in the American League over the past decade. Ruether and Zachary gave him two very good left-handers. Clark Griffith outmaneuvered his competitors during the off-season as the Yankees added Urban Shocker, who had been a consistent winner but would not have the kind of bounce-back season that Coveleski would produce.

The Nationals still had young players like Ossie Bluege and Firpo Marberry coming into their own along with Goose Goslin and Curly Odgen, but as the *Washington Post* noted, "the president and manager of the Washington Nationals have overlooked no opportunity to place on the payroll a veteran … for another slice of the World Series profits."[1]

The biggest investment of all was Walter Johnson, who gave up once and for all his attempts to gain a financial foothold as an owner of a Pacific Coast League team. Clark Griffith had supported these efforts in every way and offered counsel to his star pitcher as he explored the ownership opportunities.[2] Johnson still had connections on the West Coast from his days living and playing there, and his wife Hazel was still influential in Reno, Nevada. But his chance to buy into a team proved ephemeral in the end, and after a winter in the sunny southern California vacation lands, Walter Johnson headed for Hot Springs, Arkansas, to join his teammates as they readied for another spring and another season.

Johnson said before he left, "My own welfare alone would never be sufficient to tear me away from the Washington club. I am strongly attached to my teammates, to Clark Griffith and to the Washington fans."[3]

As spring training began in earnest in Florida, Walter Johnson expressed concern that he could not travel around the state of Florida doing barnstorming games and still have time to condition the body of an aging champion. Bucky Harris and Clark Griffith had always emphasized the latter, but Griff was pressed that spring to take his championship team on tours of the state.[4] The popularity of the underdog victors of the 1924 World Series did not diminish over the course of that spring or the long season, and Clark Griffith could only be delighted as sellout crowds awaited his team wherever they went.

On April 22, the home opener for the Nationals was played at Griffith Stadium before a crowd of 32,000 that filled out the newly added second tier in the right field grandstand.[5] Though smaller than its counterpart in left field, it added additional seating at a time when the Nationals were drawing as well as they ever would.

Walter Johnson caught the ceremonial pre-game toss from now-perennial fan, President Calvin Coolidge, who was surrounded by almost his entire cabinet. The crowd voiced its most vociferous "roar of appreciation" as the name of Walter Johnson issued forth from the announcer's megaphone, their vote of concurrence for the Big Train's decision to return for one more season.[6]

The gathered aggregation, though suited and stocked with dignitaries, seemed determined to pick up where the clamorous mob had left off the previous October with loud celebrations. They were delighted by the offensive showing for the team's return to Washington as the Nationals scored ten runs against the Yankees' newly acquired pitching legend, Urban Shocker.

"The crowd came to see the champions of the world and they left satisfied that the trust had not been displaced, for by contrast with the New York Yankees, the Nationals looked good enough to win any pennant."[7] The Yankees showed the effects of playing without their star, Babe Ruth, who failed to start the season because of a stomach abscess that resulted in surgery. Yankees manager Miller Huggins would be without his star slugger for nearly three months as he recuperated from surgery during an era when any surgical intervention was life-threatening and required significant recuperation.

The Washington Nationals got off to a roaring start and their competition was not the Yankees, but Connie Mack's Athletics, who had three young players named Mickey Cochrane, Al Simmons, and Lefty Grove. Together they would spell trouble for the Nationals for years to come. But Washington as a team was having a collective career season.

Though already 35, Sam Rice put together his best season, one in which he would hit .350 and stay near the top of the American League in numerous batting categories. He was followed closely by Goose Goslin, who had established himself as a star in the 1924 World Series, but his display of raw power during the 1925 season was awesome. He led the league with 20 triples that year, batted .334 with 18 home runs, and led the team in steals with 27.

By the beginning of June the American League was a two-team race with the Athletics and National pacing the field in a virtual tie for the lead. Then, during a 30-day stretch from June 4 to July 4, the Nationals went on a tear and won 22 games to move ahead of the A's into first place with a two-game margin.

One of the most exciting moments in the early part of the season came on June 11 when Clark Griffith and Bucky Harris raised an American League pennant above Griffith Stadium for the first time. Commissioner Landis and Nationals League president Heydler were on hand for the ceremonies, and both teams stood watching in center field as Griffith and Harris hoisted the flag, each taking a turn as hand-over-hand they hoisted the pennant to its position with 15,000 fans cheering.[10]

Walter Johnson was having another surprising season and was again one of the best in the American League, even at age 37. At the mid-point in the season he led the league with a 2.68 ERA and 12 wins. The "Big Pole," Coveleski, was almost as good as the "Big Train." He had 11 wins and an ERA of 2.76 at the mid-point in the season.

Reverting to the form that had made him the toast of New York City in 1904 and strutting like a bantam rooster, Clark Griffith asked of the rest of the American League, "Who is going to beat it?" meaning his Nationals baseball team. "There is no secret why we will win again," he said. "We have the best all-around team in the league. It was the best in both leagues last year, so why shouldn't it be this year?"[8]

The occasion for the remarks was a query from a reporter about the effects of Walter Johnson's brief absence from the team at mid-season. Griffith assured the press, "A glance at the records, I think, will convince almost anybody that our pitchers have done pretty well so far."[9]

Washington pitching in 1925 was once again the best in the league, and except for the Philadelphia Athletics staff it wasn't even close. Yet the difference between the 1924 and 1925 Nationals was the hitting. Whereas in '24 the Nationals attack had been in the middle of the pack, in '25 it was among the best. Clark Griffith's analysis was right on target. The '25 Nationals were the best all-around team in the American League.

Griffith left nothing to chance, however, as he added several key pieces in mid-season. Griffith was determined to win it all again and not be at a loss down the stretch — or in the World Series. He did not want to have a key player go down and not have the right pieces to win. Shortly after the season began, Griff traded for greater bench strength, sending Paul Zahnhiser to Boston for Joe "Moon" Harris, who could play numerous positions. A colorful player to say the least, Harris lost two years of his career to a suspension for playing in an outlaw league, but he was a capable bat. In June Griffith traded George Mogridge to the St. Louis Browns for a reserve catcher named Hank Severeid.

The moves were intended to add depth rather than to address any players that were struggling. Moon Harris would play first base primarily, but it was not because Joe Judge was slipping. The elder statesman of the Washington infield was having another fine season, hitting .314. Muddy Ruel was having his best season to date with the stick, hitting over .300 as well.

The Nationals had a fight on their hands with Connie Mack's Athletics throughout July and into August, during the hottest summer months of 1925. The problem for Mack's team was that they could not beat the Nationals in head-to-head match-ups. With the lead in dispute at the end of June the two teams played a five-game series that started with two games in Philly and then moved to Washington for three more. The Nationals won four of those contests to re-establish themselves in first place for the first time since early May.

Coveleski and Walter Johnson were both brilliant during the series with the Big Train pitching a masterful game in the deciding contest, a 7–0 shutout in which he allowed only two scratch hits.[11]

George Sisler's St. Louis Browns were also a factor in the race in July. The Browns had no pitching but did have the best offense in the league with Sisler leading the way. He had plenty of help. Ken Williams and Baby Doll Jacobson were the corner outfielders and Harry Rice — no relation to Sam — hit .359 for the season. With Babe Ruth out for the Yankees until June, the

Browns were able to tie the Bronx Bombers for the league lead in home runs with 110.

The 1925 season saw the emergence of a new star in New York City. Lou Gehrig first appeared in the Yankees lineup subbing for Ruth in the outfield for several games, but it was not long before he got a start at first base, where he proved he could hit and play the game with the best. He would not be moved from first base until May 2, 1939, and only stepped aside for Babe Dahlgren when sickness overcame him.

Connie Mack wrestled the lead away from the Nationals in the middle of July again and hung on to first place for the rest of the month and into August. Then the Browns swept Philadelphia in the middle of August to put Washington back on top. Connie Mack's team lost 12 games in a row, which helped the Nationals put a growing space between themselves and the Athletics, building a ten-game lead in early September and then coasting home.

The last major transaction came in August when Griffith added Alex Ferguson to the pitching rotation to give his regulars a rest. Though only intermittently successful with Boston, Ferguson was brilliant down the stretch for Washington, winning five key games starting in late August.

Ferguson won his first game on August 23 and pitched as well as anyone on the staff down the stretch. Tonsillitis laid up Walter Johnson in July and he only got his full strength back in August as he battled back to form. He won four games in August and set himself up for another great finish. Shirley Povich claimed later that Griffith told Bucky Harris that if Washington could keep their pitchers fresh, Connie Mack would be the first to blink and would over-work Slim Harriss and Eddie Rommel.[12] Ferguson's contribution was more important than just winning five games. His biggest contribution was taking the pressure off Walter Johnson so that Griffith would have a rested rotation down the stretch and in the World Series.

Griffith was not the only one making all the right moves. Bucky Harris was being acclaimed as a genius for his moves on the field as the Nationals steamed away from the fleet.[13] Philadelphia had one last chance in September to get back in the race. The two teams met for seven games in the first two weeks of September. Griffith and Harris had Walter Johnson and Coveleski ready for the two key contests with Philadelphia in the nation's capital.

Johnson was at his best and won the first game by a 7–3 score going three-for-four at the bat. There were 25,000 fans in the stadium and the atmosphere was described as "reminiscent of last October's World Series."[14] Another star of the game was Roger Peckinpaugh, who drove in two runs in the third inning with a double and then stole home, "toppling over a sleeping Mickey Cochrane at the plate."[15]

In the second game of the series, with numerous Philadelphia fans in attendance who had made the trip down by train, Coveleski was sharp until the late innings. He was ahead 7–1 on hitting up and down the batting order as well as a few errors by the Athletics. Coveleski let in three runs in the eighth, but still won, 8–5. The win put the Nationals up by five and one-half games.

Washington went to Philadelphia five days later for four games. When play started in Philadelphia on September 7 the Nationals had a commanding seven-game lead over the Athletics. Philadelphia had lost nine in a row and was failing fast. Again, the Nationals had Walter Johnson pitching the key contest and he won the "morning" game, pitching eight scoreless innings, hanging on for a 2–1 win after Joe Harris hit an early two-run homer.

Walter Johnson had three hits himself in that contest, part of a surprising offensive explosion for the pitcher that saw him used numerous times as a pinch-hitter. Johnson hit .433 for the year, which remains the batting average record for a pitcher.[16] It began in April when Johnson was recalled from the clubhouse to hit when he thought he was finished for the day. After an inordinate delay to put his uniform back on, Johnson "drilled Pennock's first pitch" for a two-run single.[17] He had a pinch-hit home run in May and finished the season with a robust .577 slugging average.

The second game of the doubleheader against the Athletics that day was won by Washington, 7–6. Though Philadelphia won the last two games of the series, Washington left town up by seven games. There were huge turnouts for the games in Philadelphia, and the Nationals had lost the veneer of lovable losers that had followed them in 1924. Now they were the favorites and the fans in Philly "booed, jeered, and cursed every one of the champs in the field in both games."[18] Only Walter Johnson retained the fans' affection as he "was cheered when his name was announced," even by the rabid fans in the City of Brotherly Love.

The Nationals went on to clinch the pennant on the September 24 on a Dutch Ruether win in Cleveland. The old southpaw wound up the season with 18 wins and was part of the best and oldest rotation in baseball that year. Coveleski led the league in ERA with a 2.84 mark and had 20 wins against only 5 losses. Clark Griffith had an uncanny ability to bring out the best in spitballers dating to the 1904 season when he had tutored Jack Chesbro.

Walter Johnson was fourth in the league with a 3.07 ERA to go with 20 wins. The Nationals led the league by an amazing ten games at the end of September, but lost the final three games of the season when it was all over but the shouting. The day before the season ended, Roger Peckinpaugh was voted the Most Valuable Player in the American League, a year after Walter Johnson had received the same award.

In neither league did the pennant races match those tightly fought contests of 1924. Pittsburgh won the National League as John McGraw's Giants finished eight-and-one-half games back. It was the beginning of a slow decline for Clark Griffith's most cherished competitor. McGraw would finish further off the pace in 1926 and only once more, in 1928, would he contend for the National League pennant. In that season he lost in the last week to the Cardinals.

McGraw's health began to fail. He outlived his most hated enemy, Ban Johnson, who was forced out of the American League in 1927 and died four years later. McGraw continued to curse umpires and his own players, but he was unable to field a winner. In a legal imbroglio in which McGraw sided with Giants owner Charles Stoneham against other stockholders in the team, the judge ruled in 1931 against McGraw and Stoneham, saying that "they were all drinking men, all cursing men, all fighting men."[19] McGraw handed the keys to the Polo Grounds to Bill Terry as manager of the Giants in 1932. McGraw's last hurrah was managing the first All-Star Game in 1933 against Connie Mack, and he died the following February at age 61.

The 1925 World Series promised as much drama as any before it. The Washington Nationals were still considered the underdog team from the underdog city, but now they were taken seriously based on their World Series win in 1924. The Pittsburgh Pirates were seen as a fitting successor to McGraw's Giants. Much like the Giants, they featured a lusty-hitting lineup from top to bottom. They had a team batting average in 1925 of .307; among the regulars only second baseman Earl Moore failed to top the .300 mark, and he hit .298.

Any one of their players could win a ball game with a clutch hit, but they had three future Hall of Fame stars. Kiki Cuyler and Max "Scoops" Carey were the anchors of an outstanding outfield. Cuyler was only 26 and at the beginning of a career that would carry him to Cooperstown. Cuyler's mark of 369 total bases in 1925 is still the single-season best for the Pirates franchise.[20] Carey was the kind of player that Clark Griffith coveted. He was fast and perennially in the league lead in stolen bases. He had 738 steals over his career, a figure that still ranks among the all-time leaders.

Third baseman Pie Traynor was one of the best ever to play the position, and while arguments rage to this day as to who is the best, few exclude Traynor in the discussion. With Glenn Wright at shortstop the Pirates had one of the strongest infields ever. Wright had 18 home runs in 1925 and his power and defensive abilities helped Pittsburgh fans forget one of their favorites, Rabbit Maranville, whose arrest for drinking led to his ouster after the 1924 season.

Wright, along with Cuyler and Goslin, were the sluggers going into the Series. Sam Rice and Max Carey were the rabbits. But on the mound there

Clark Griffith and Bucky Harris leaving for the 1925 World Series in Pittsburgh (Library of Congress).

was no comparison between the two teams. Pittsburgh had capable pitching from Lee Meadows, who was the team leader in 1925, although Ray Kremer was the better pitcher over the course of his career. But they had nothing to compare with Walter Johnson and Stan Coveleski, or Firpo Marberry for that matter.

The Pirates were still owned by Barney Dreyfuss, from whom Clark Griffith had pilfered the players on his 1904 Yankees team that had contended for the pennant. Jack Chesbro had pitched for the Pirates in 1902 before the Highlanders were formed in 1903. Dreyfuss had been the owner of the Pirates when Clark Griffith and Ban Johnson had conspired to create the American League and had been one of those with the vision to see the value of having two leagues.

Dreyfuss had one of the better field generals in the game in Bill McKechnie, who had turned the Pirates into contenders in 1922, and like Bucky Harris was headed to the Hall of Fame for his ability both on the field as a player and in the dugout as a manager. Like Harris, McKechnie had the ear of ownership and worked closely with Dreyfuss to put together the pieces of a winning team.

Dreyfuss was sitting in the owner's box across from Clark Griffith for the first time as the 1925 World Series began play in Pittsburgh, Pennsylvania. Though the two men were almost a quarter century removed from the crime, it was unlikely Dreyfuss had forgotten the names of the players Griffith culled from his roster at the end of the 1902 season.

Dreyfuss had been there before as his 1909 team had played in one of the great World Series matches, between Ty Cobb's Detroit Tigers and Honus Wagner's Pirates. The Pirates won that Series in seven games and the crowd of 42,000 on hand in the "Iron City" were hoping to see a repeat as Wagner and Cobb stood at home plate in the pre-game festivities, shaking hands and grinning for the cameras.

Grantland Rice revisited the issue of age among the Nationals and opined that McKechnie might consider starting Wagner in the lineup to provide the Pirates with the same senior leadership as Walter Johnson, Peckinpaugh and Sam Rice offered Washington.[21]

Walter Johnson took the mound for the Nationals against Lee Meadows for the Pirates in Game One. Bucky Harris put Joe "Moon" Harris in right field and slid Sam Rice into center field, benching Earl McNeely for the stronger hitting Harris, who had been so good down the stretch. It proved a smart play as Moon Harris got the Nationals an early lead with a second-inning home run.

The press noted that Walter Johnson's 19 years in Washington exceeded the term of even the longest serving U.S. Senator, but the Big Train looked as good as he had in 1913.[22] He struck out ten of the best hitters in the game in a complete game victory and had one of the best curveballs in his career. All of the Pirates hitters were waiting on the big "whoosh" of Johnson's fastball, but he got them swinging at the curve.

Babe Ruth, a fair critic of pitching and hitting, said of Johnson that afternoon, "I don't believe I ever saw him when he was better."[23] Sam Rice and Ossie Bluege supplied the offense along with Joe Harris as the Nationals scored four runs behind the Big Train and won the first game in Pittsburgh by a comfortable 4–1 margin. Pittsburgh's lone run came on a Pie Traynor home run in the fifth inning, but the Pirates managed only four other hits, and Johnson walked but a single batter.

Walter Johnson admitted that he had been nervous in the 1924 Series, his first. He was more comfortable in his second fall classic and the difference was clear for all to see. Max Carey said after the game that he couldn't even see Johnson's fastball that afternoon and the sun was bright all day long. Muddy Ruel's throw to second had plenty of stuff on it as well. The Washington catcher threw the speedy Max Carey out in the first inning trying to steal second and limited the Pirates' running game throughout the Series.

The second game of the Series was a deeply saddened affair as the news of Cristy Mathewson's death was announced early in the day. The players wore black armbands as a show of sympathy, as did many of the fans who gathered for the game. Many of the press corps and players in both dugouts had seen the one of the game's greatest pitchers at one time or another. They had known him as one of the smartest and ablest to wear a uniform. John McGraw was the hardest hit of any in attendance and he rushed off early in the day, accompanied by his wife, to serve as a pallbearer at the funeral.

Stan Coveleski pitched the second game for Washington and Vic Aldridge matched him with a fine performance as the two men battled into the eighth inning with a 1–1 tie. In the bottom of the eighth inning Kiki Cuyler gave the Pirates fans something to cheer finally as he hit a long home run into right field with Eddie Moore on base to give Pittsburgh a 3–1 lead. Moore had reached on a Peckinpaugh error, one of eight costly blunders he would commit during the Series.

The Nationals came back in the top of the ninth inning. Joe Judge's home run in the second had been their only scoring until then, and Sam Rice had been the only other National able to solve Aldridge. In the ninth inning the Nationals pushed across a single run. Down by one, with two runners on base, Rice came up with the game on the line and everyone in Washington confident the right man was at the plate. But Sam grounded out weakly to end the game.

Ossie Bluege was struck in the head by Aldridge in Game Two and had to be taken from the game. Hospital x-rays revealed no concussion, but a young player named Buddy Myer took his place at third. Myer was much heralded by Clark Griffith as his next big prospect and he would play a key role in Washington baseball in years to come. Bluege was cleared to play when the two teams returned to Washington, but the players were given extra rest when rain forced a postponement of the third game.

For all of the unexplained wrinkles that had worked to the favor of the

Nationals in 1924, the baseball gods did not seem to favor Washington in 1925. The weather would prove the worst enemy as the temperatures plunged and the rain continued to fall. Yet the consensus was that the extra day favored the Nationals as it gave Walter Johnson much-needed rest that would allow his greater availability in the series.

The third game was in Griffith Stadium and the weather was windy and cold, though Griffith's new bleachers in right field swelled attendance to 35,500 including President Coolidge and members of the cabinet. Starting on the mound was Alex Ferguson.

It was a fitting call given Ferguson's contribution to the pennant drive in August and September. Also figuring in Bucky Harris's decision was the strength of the Pirates lineup against left-handers like Dutch Ruether and Tom Zachary. Only Max Carey and the catchers batted lefty among the Pittsburgh regulars and he was just as strong against lefties.

Starting Ferguson was just the first of several strategic choices that Bucky Harris would make in Game Three. Hugh Jennings, writing in the *New York Times,* said that "Harris anticipated everything that came to pass."[24] Harris deftly employed his bench, but it was shifting his outfielders that saved the day.

Nerves were clearly getting to Alex Ferguson in the first inning. A regular for only four seasons, he had never pitched in a post-season game before. He walked Eddie Moore to start the game and then plunked the next batter, Max Carey, to put two runners on base in quick order. He got out of trouble with the great double-play combination of Peckinpaugh-to-Harris-to-Judge bailing him out. But in the second inning a Pie Traynor triple led to the first run of the game, and Pittsburgh took a 1–0 lead to the third.

Leading off the third, Sam Rice singled, and Joe Judge brought him in with a double to tie the score. Ferguson gave up single runs in the fourth and sixth innings, but Goose Goslin hit a solo home run and brought Washington back to within a run going into the seventh inning, the Nationals trailing, 3–2.

It was here that Harris's strategic moves won the day. To start off the seventh inning he pinch-hit for Ferguson, who had been game against the best lineup in baseball, but was tiring. He sent to the plate Nemo Liebold, who led off with a walk. Harris inserted Earl McNeely to run for Liebold. After Rice flied out, Bucky Harris then bunted and Pittsburgh catcher Earl Smith watched it roll along the foul line. Then, in what Hugh Jennings called the biggest mistake of the day, Smith pounced on the ball before it could roll foul. The speedy Harris beat out an infield hit.

Another bunt, this time by Goose Goslin — Washington's only true power hitter — caught the Pirates by surprise, and he reached safely to load the bases.

Joe Judge knocked in his second run of the day with a sacrifice fly and Joe Harris continued to perform, getting a two-out single to put Washington ahead, 4–3.

Harris now set out to protect his shaky lead. He brought in Firpo Marberry and shifted Rice to right field. The Boy Manager now had his best defensive outfield in place with Earl McNeely at his natural spot in center field and Rice in right for Joe Harris, who exited the game. Marberry was excellent and got two quick outs to bring up Pirates catcher Earl Smith, who wanted to atone for his fielding mistake.

He caught a Firpo Marberry pitch and drove it deep to right field. Sam Rice ran the ball down and, according to his own account — released in a letter opened after his death — caught the ball several feet in front of the low outfield wall, but was unable to prevent his momentum from carrying him over the wall and into the crowd. Second base umpire Charley Rigler saw the catch and watched the outfielder disappear into the stands. He saw nothing to indicate that Smith was anything but out, especially when Rice reappeared with the ball in hand after Earl McNeely helped the right fielder climb back into the field of play.[25]

Pirates manager Bill McKechnie ran out to protest immediately to umpire Rigler. McKechnie claimed that Rice had dropped the ball in the stands and had to be handed it by a sympathetic Washingtonian. McKechnie protested long and loud, even taking his case to Commissioner Landis, watching from the box seats. But all attempts to overturn the umpire's ruling failed. Marberry pitched a spotless ninth inning to hang on to the win and put Washington ahead in the Series, two games to one.

The controversy over Rice's catch continued to roil the press coverage, but the next day was all about Walter Johnson. The largest crowd yet for a World Series game in Washington, over 38,000, was on hand to watch what everyone knew might be one of the last and most memorable moments in the famous pitcher's career.

Johnson was better than in the opener, getting a 4–0 win and shutting out the best offense in the game that year. The truly remarkable part of the performance was not fully understood until the next day. Johnson was pitching on a bad leg that he re-injured trying to stretch a single into a double in the third inning. He pitched from the stretch from that point until the end of the game to lessen the pain.[26]

The pain was such that he could not put his full weight on the leg without feeling it, and N.W. Baxter called him a "virtual cripple" the next day in the *Washington Post*, one whose "heart, courageous to the very core, made the fourth game of the 1925 World Series the greatest."[27]

Washington trainer Mike Martin performed many a miracle with injured players, but getting Walter Johnson through that game was perhaps his best. Johnson was spurred by the big bats of Goose Goslin and Joe Harris, both of whom homered in the third inning as Washington scored four runs and took a commanding 4–0 lead. Harris's shot was notable for its length, going 30 rows up into the left field stands, estimated to be at least 425 feet. After getting the lead, Johnson told Mike Martin, "I've got a four-run lead and I'm not going to lose credit for this game. I'll pitch."[28]

The win gave the Nationals a 3–1 lead, and no team had ever lost the World Series after taking gaining such a commanding margin. But at this point, Bucky Harris made a decision that would call into question those that had worked so well in game three. He chose not to pitch either Ruether or Zachary in Game Five because of the strength of the Pirates lineup from the right side. He decided to bring Coveleski back on three days' rest for the next game.

Coveleski started in trouble and was wild for much of the game, giving up nine hits and walking four over 6 tough innings. He was helped by three doubleplays and wonderful fielding plays by Joe Judge, but when Coveleski left in the seventh inning Washington was down, 4–3, and Pittsburgh went on to win by a final score of 6–3. Joe Harris had another long home run, but there was little to cheer about for the big crowd of 36,000, as Washington was behind almost the entire game.

The Series moved back to Pittsburgh, and Harris again refused to use Ruether as he went with Alex Ferguson on two days' rest against Ray Kremer, a rematch of Game Three. This time the Nationals could find no clutch hit to bring them from behind despite another Goose Goslin home run. Though Ferguson and reliever Win Ballou kept it close, Washington lost the sixth game, 3–2.

The Series was tied, and that had seemed improbable enough after Game Four. Now Bucky Harris sought to shift some of the momentum back to Washington when he announced that he was starting Walter Johnson for Game Seven. Events seemed to favor Washington when it rained heavily, forcing another postponement amidst the worst October weather to plague any World Series since 1911. The extra day gave Johnson's aching leg more rest and his aged arm an extra day as well.

The rain persisted the next day and the temperatures dipped even further. The field was sodden and the conditions were atrocious. A fog hung over the field, but still Commissioner Landis did not want another postponement. He ruled the game would go ahead despite the conditions. The weather did not dampen the spirits of baseball fans in Pittsburgh as 50,000 showed up at the stadium in hopes of gaining admittance to the deciding Game Seven.[29]

When the players took the field they moved about as "vague and shadowy figures."[30] Goose Goslin said that he could barely make out what was going on in the infield, much less measure the flight of the ball.[31]

Walter Johnson was up against the Pirates' Vic Aldridge, who had won the fifth game. Neither man could be said to have much advantage in the conditions that immediately came into play in the first inning. Aldridge walked three batters after Sam Rice led the game off with a single. Catcher's interference was called to put another runner aboard and the Nationals had three runs in. Johnny Morrison relieved Aldridge, who could not find the plate with the slippery ball. Muddy Ruel brought in the fourth run on an error.

Walter Johnson was hardly in better shape to deal with the muddy mound. His leg hurt but he still was able to strike out Kiki Cuyler in the bottom of the first inning as well as fourth-place hitter Clyde Barnhart. Bucky Harris bailed Johnson out of a jam in the second on a nice double play given the conditions. But in the third the Pirates pulled to within a run on four hits and three runs.

Joe Harris was the hero again in the fourth inning as his clutch double brought in Rice and Goslin to give the Nationals some breathing room at 6–4. In the sixth inning, Johnson got three quick outs and, with the game far enough along to be official, and with the rain beginning to come down even harder, Commissioner Landis said he had seen enough. Clark Griffith was sitting next to him in the stands, and Landis turned to him and said, "I'm calling this game. You're the World Champions."[32]

Clark Griffith was too game a competitor to win something that would forever seem tainted. He had the lead and Walter Johnson on the mound, so he told Landis that he wanted to play out the game. He wanted to take home a real championship for a second year in a row and it seemed that the odds were in his favor, so he rolled the dice in the name of doing the honorable thing.

The Old Fox's game optimism was ill-served. In the seventh inning the Pirates scored twice to even the score at six runs apiece. In the seventh Roger Peckinpaugh's home run to give the Nationals the lead at 7–6. As Shirley Povich wrote 30 years later, all of Peck's errors would have been forgiven if the Series had ended there, but there were still two innings to play.

In the eighth Walter Johnson got two outs and it was oh so close when the Pirates got back-to-back doubles to tie the score. After a walk to Eddie Moore, Max Carey hit a routine grounder to Peckinpaugh. Peck's throw was off the mark at second base trying to get Moore, and his last error of the series — his eighth — loaded the bases with still two outs.

With the score still tied, Kiki Cuyler, batting third, hit a ball that Goose Goslin said landed two feet foul down the right field line, though it was ruled fair. "I know it was foul because it hit in the mud and stuck there. The umpires couldn't see it. It was too dark and muddy."[33] On the strength of Cuyler's hit, two runs scored and the Pirates had a 9–7 lead.

Bill McKechnie brought in a fresh pitcher, Red Oldham, who set Washington down in order in the top of the ninth inning to give Pittsburgh the victory in the game and the Series, making them World Champions. It was increasingly dark in the ninth inning as the Nationals batted, but both teams faced the same adverse conditions. In the end Max Carey and the Pirates — who fought from behind three times in the final game and from a three-game deficit as well — deserved credit for their gameness.

Stuffy McInnis, a part-time player for the Pirates that year after a long career with Connie Mack, wrote a special feature for the *Washington Post* about the Series. He praised the never-say-die composure of his teammates, but saved his kindest words for Walter Johnson, saying he likewise continued to pitch without relenting "when in the hole or the hottest kind of water. His name will go down in baseball history as one of the greatest pitchers of all time."[34]

There were no parades or crowds to greet the Nationals upon their return. There was some recrimination, but mostly from afar. Much of the blame was saddled on Bucky Harris. He was accused of not taking risks that would have won one of the final three games, but most often of letting Walter Johnson continue to pitch in the eighth inning. Ban Johnson asked whether "sentiment" had been the reason Harris stuck with Johnson, saying there was no room for it in baseball and that Harris was wrong to let it affect his decisions.[35]

Harris made no apologies to Ban Johnson or anyone else. He had gone with Washington's best pitcher in a situation that any baseball man would have gladly given his World Series loot to have. Circumstances may have conspired against him, but Walter Johnson was not diminished by losing the game, nor was Harris in the end. The loyal fans knew that it was a matter of the very same "breaks" that had gone the way of the Nationals in 1924, only to mysteriously move for Pittsburgh in 1925.[36] Nor were there any lasting recriminations against Peckinpaugh for the errors after the two pennant-winning seasons he had provided Washington fans.

In that atmosphere Clark Griffith did not immediately recount his conversation with Landis in the sixth inning. He was loud in praise of his players when the World Series loot was split among the team. The loser's share was less, but still a payday of nearly $4,000 for the regulars, and there was less complaining about the minor shares to other players than had been the case in 1924. Clark Griffith gave Stan Coveleski and Firpo Marberry an extra $1,000 on top of their shares as compensation for their extraordinary efforts during the season and the Series.[37] No one second-guessed that decision either.

There were rumors shortly after the series that Goose Goslin might be on the trading block, but Clark Griffith said, "I wouldn't trade the Goose for Yankee Stadium."[38] And Clark Griffith did not need Yankee Stadium. He had made a handsome profit of nearly $150,000 over the course of the 1925 World Series.[39] Clark Griffith was on top of the world and had enough money to pay for the new house on 16th Street.

CHAPTER 17

While the Hunting
Is Still Good

After winning his first World Championship in 1924, the 57-year-old Clark Griffith had significantly retooled his pitching staff to begin the 1925 season, and it was a significant reason for his back-to-back American League titles. Yet for the 1926 season he believed in his existing lineup and was playing a mostly pat hand as the season began. He did complete one important deal shortly before spring training camp, acquiring veteran pitcher Bullet Joe Bush for Tom Zachary and Win Ballou.[1] Zachary was one of the few Washington starting pitchers under 30 and by trading for the older Joe Bush, Griffith moved the average age of the pitching staff higher.

Firpo Marberry, still under 30, was now the youngest among the proven pitchers on the staff. Bush was already 33 on opening day and gave the Nationals a rotation that counted Dutch Ruether as its youngest member at 32.

Griffith was still scouting with Joe Engel for the next generation, but having limited success. He was much impressed with a young infielder named Buddy Myer. Myer was being groomed by the Old Fox to replace Roger Peckinpaugh. Griffith announced early in 1926 that Myer would be his regular shortstop and that Peck would have to sit for the young player that he called better than Cleveland wunderkind, Joe Sewell.[2]

Sewell was perhaps the best overall shortstop in the American League at the time and it was testament to Griffith's confidence in Myer that he would put him in such elite company. "I think in Myer we have a better player than Peck," he stated flatly, although Bucky Harris was reluctant to agree.[3]

Another promising prospect according to Griffith was young catcher Bennie Tate. The Old Fox promised the press the youngster would push for playing time. He had signed Hank Severeid to back up Muddy Ruel, but urged Bucky Harris to find more time for Tate. Keeping everyone happy in a crowded dugout would be one of the Boy Manager's biggest challenges in 1926.

Harris was to be paid handsomely for trying to keep the best players on the field for the American League Champions. Before the season started, Harris inked a contract for three years that was estimated at close to $100,000 total. The new deal also gave him an office in Griffith Stadium for his personal use.[4]

More daunting than finding playing time for all of the talent in the infield was finding a winning pitching combination. In the regular column "In the Press Box with Baxter," *The Washington Post* editorialist noted that "Washington has no individual whose sole duty is to handle the young pitchers."[5] Griffith had brought in Jack Chesbro early in 1924, but since then there had been no pitching coach for young talent. It was a measure of the times that columnists were noting the Nationals' lack of coaching compared to other teams. Griffith was counting on pitchers who knew how to throw and needed no training.

When the season started on April 13 at Griffith Stadium, the spirit of the two pennant winning teams was still palpable. The home opener was against the Philadelphia Athletics, and once more Connie Mack and Clark Griffith teed it up together to start the season. Walter Johnson looked undimmed by the disappointments of the prior October in Pittsburgh, though there were "sullen skies, arctic temperatures, and a crowd of 23,000 persons including Vice-President Dawes" to cheer the beginning of the Big Train's 20th professional season. As the presiding officer of the Senate, Dawes adjourned that body so that they could be on hand for baseball's opening day. President Calvin Coolidge — the most loyal of Washington fans — was absent because of the death of his father.[6]

In the opener Walter Johnson faced 54 batters over 15 innings and not one scored. It was an amazing show of stamina for the 38-year-old veteran. He pitched a six-hit shutout and bested an equally game Eddie Rommel, 1–0. Johnson was good throughout May and Stan Coveleski pitched in fine form again, but Dutch Ruether could not find his way. Bullet Joe Bush was bothered by a bad knee almost from the day he arrived in spring training and he was hit hard any time he tried his turn. There was neither enough pitching nor hitting to overcome the Yankees, who had a healthy Babe Ruth again in the middle of their order.

The outfield of Rice, Goslin and McNeely was excellent again, but the missing link was Roger Peckinpaugh. Buddy Myer played a good shortstop and hit with some authority, but he was neither the most valuable player in the league, nor an adequate substitute for one. The Nationals were good enough to climb back into the first division in the second half of the season, finishing fourth. But they were never a factor in the pennant race.

The Yankees had a young lion named Lou Gehrig batting in front of the Babe. The American League became the two men's personal game room. They also had Tony Lazzeri, Bob Meusel and Earle Combs to complement the super duo and a credible pitching staff led by Herb Pennock, Waite Hoyt and Urban Shocker. Nonetheless, the Yankees won the pennant by a scant three games over the Cleveland Indians and lost a tightly contested World Series against Rogers Hornsby's and Jim Bottomley's St. Louis Cardinals.

Clark Griffith committed himself to rebuilding during the 1926 season, realizing that he needed new talent to compete in the American League of Gehrig and Ruth. He announced to the press on the eve of a long scouting trip with Joe Engel to the west and south, "no matter how we fare in this year's race, we have decided to dismantle our present team and start all over on an extensive rebuilding program."[7] Finding talent with the limited scouting that Griffith employed had been difficult enough in the past. Now the question moving forward was not just the minimalist scouting, but whether the Nationals had the coaching and teaching personnel in its organization to develop talent as well.

The scouting trip was not fruitless. Griffith purchased the contract for General Crowder — known initially as Alvin Floyd Crowder. The press noted the similarities to Griffith's earlier trips when he rode the train back to Washington with Chick Gandil to assure that the talented first baseman arrived safely in Washington. He did the same again in July of 1926, personally escorting Crowder north after the signing.

Clark Griffith was also high on Georgia Tech shortstop Bobby Reeves and he signed the young captain of the Tech squad happily on the same southern swing. His comments sounded somewhat familiar when he described Reeves: "To my mind he is the best prospect I have ever seen."[8]

Alvin Crowder took the name "General" from the head of the World War One army draft board. Crowder had become serious about baseball during a stint in the army at the end of World War One, so the nickname was a natural. When Clark Griffith saw him, he was the best pitcher in the Southern Association, winning 17 games in only 20 starts. He featured a trick pitch named the "Filipino Ball," and was touted for his flexibility as either a starter or reliever — modeled after none other than Firpo Marberry.[9]

Griffith spent the kind of money on new talent in 1926 that he had once hoped to get as a manager. The press speculated that as much as $115,000 had gone for "Rookie Mound Talent" alone after the season was concluded.[10] Clark Griffith continued to dismantle his pennant-winning team by trading Roger Peckinpaugh, in January 1927, to the White Sox. He got Sloppy Thurston and Roger Mangum, two pitchers of no great pedigree. Thurston would throw 205 innings for the Nationals in 1927, but it was more a statement on the team's pitching talent than on Thurston turning a page on his lackluster career.

Another veteran talent found his way to Washington in February as Griff announced that Tris Speaker would begin the 1927 season with Washington. Speaker was 39 and his MVP days with the championship Boston Red Sox teams of 1912 and 1915 were behind him. He had been player-manager for the Cleveland Indians for a decade when he came over to the Nationals in February 1927.

In 1926 Speaker and Ty Cobb had been accused by Dutch Leonard of fixing a game in 1919, and the charge had caused both Cobb and Speaker to resign their respective managing positions, though they were cleared of any wrongdoing and made "free agents" after the decision by Landis.[11] Speaker said he had signed with Washington in part out of respect for Clark Griffith, but he revealed nothing about the price that Griffith paid to bring him to town.[12]

Speaker had hit .304 in more than 500 at-bats in 1926, so he filled the center field hole in the Nationals lineup ably despite his age. But there was ominous news within the first weeks of the spring. Walter Johnson was the same age as Speaker and he looked just as good when the two men arrived in Tampa for the beginning of spring training in 1927.

The Big Train's early showings in the spring provided hope that he might have another solid season in his long right arm. Then a freak accident felled the pitcher on March 9 as he threw batting practice to Joe Judge.[13] The first baseman knocked a pitch back through the box that caught Johnson on the ankle and broke it.

Nothing worse could have happened in Washington than such a calamitous injury to the Nationals' most famous player. The broken ankle was set in a plaster cast and the prognosis was for Johnson to be out at least three to four weeks.[14] The scouting of new talent, the arrival of shortstop Reeves, and the addition of Speaker were all cast into a secondary position as the negative news trickled out about the condition of the Big Train each day. The final blow was a picture of Johnson being taken to a waiting train in a wheel chair and returned to Washington weeks before the beginning of the season.

For the first time in 16 years, the opening day festivities in Washington did not feature Walter Johnson. Tris Speaker took the throw from Calvin Coolidge and Stan Coveleski pitched the first game of the 1927 season. Griffith handed the starting shortstop position to Bobby Reeves in May when he traded Buddy Myer to Boston. It was indicative of the uncertainty with which the Nationals were moving forward. Myer had played well in 1926, but after only a month of the new season, was deemed expendable. The Old Fox got almost nothing in return.

Clark Griffith might well have been asking himself who he would add to the roster to take advantage of Goose Goslin's prime playing years. In 1927 Goslin was only 26 years of age and already in his fifth season anchoring the middle of the Washington batting order. He was in the top ten in total bases, steals, hits and home runs, though he continued to be hampered by playing in the broad expanse of Griffith Stadium and registered only 13 round-trippers.

Joe Judge, Sam Rice, and Muddy Ruel all had good seasons with the bat as the team was in the top half offensively. Judge, more than any other Nationals player, may have been trying to make up for the absence of Walter Johnson.

The Big Train was not giving up without a fight, however. He worked his way back from his injury and made his debut on Memorial Day with a 3–0 win against the Red Sox. It was a spectacular recovery from a serious injury, but the rest of the season went inconsistently. He showed signs of the old "whooshing" fastball, but only occasionally. Hitters like Gehrig got the best of him too often, though he was good enough to win his fifth and last major league game in July, giving him 417 total major league victories.

As in 1926, the '27 Nationals slipped into the second division in the first half of the year, but slowly fought their way back into the first division. Clark Griffith and Bucky Harris sorted out the pieces and after the July 4th holiday the team caught fire, vaulting into third place behind the Yankees and Athletics. The young pitchers in whom Clark Griffith had invested money the previous year were making a fair showing. Hod Lisenbee and Bump Hadley began the season trying to take the place of Walter Johnson. They showed remarkable promise, much as Buddy Myer had done in 1926.

Lisenbee led the team with 18 wins and Hadley led in ERA with a 2.85 mark. It was a good return on investment for the Old Fox. The Nationals cooled after their early July spurt, but the highlight of the season came on August 2 when the American League and the Washington Nationals both honored Walter Johnson with a personal day to celebrate his career. The "Walter Johnson Day" committee in Washington was chaired by Herbert Hoover, then Secretary of Commerce, and Clark Griffith brought out every dignitary that he could find to mark the career of the Big Train.

"I wouldn't trade him for ten times his value as a player," said Griffith, who had aggressively asserted in years past that he would trade any player in his quest to build a winner in Washington.[15] "This is one time where I will rate sentiment higher than the money or material anyone has to offer."[16] Secretary of State Frank Kellogg was the emcee, and team comedians Nick Altrock and Al Schacht were at their best entertaining a sellout crowd.

Both comedians had both played alongside Johnson and coached many of the games of his career. Perhaps one of the best tributes to Johnson came

Walter Johnson Day, 1927: Aunton Stephan, Secretary of State Kellogg, Johnson and Griffith (Library of Congress).

from his new teammate, Trip Speaker, who was seriously hurt at this point in the season, but had himself taped so that he could play in Johnson's tribute game. Walter Johnson started the game that day against the Tigers and though he acquitted himself well, the team lost by a 7–6 score. The Big Train appeared in a few more games as the 1927 season ran out, but his career ended for all intents and purposes on that memorable day with the stadium decked out in the same red, white and blue bunting that it featured on all those remarkable opening days he had pitched.

Clark Griffith and Walter Johnson had become the two icons of baseball in Washington, D.C. Johnson was the most beloved figure in the game during his two decades as a player, and no one had more respect or affection for him than Clark Griffith. Griffith had not been able to reconcile himself with someone as talented as Johnson when he first arrived in Washington in 1912. "You've' got to learn some trick deliveries," the Old Fox had opined, drawing on his own experience "in the box."[17]

Walter Johnson had resisted Griffith's tips on how to pitch, but he respected his manager's commitment to winning, and more than that, he respected his commitment to his players. "No matter what the argument, Griffith stood behind his players," Johnson said of the manager and team owner. "In a row with an umpire, Griffith was the first man in a Washington uniform to come to his player's support."[18] But it was during the Federal League dispute that the two men moved beyond respect to real affection.

They realized at that juncture how much one needed the other to succeed within the game, to reach the highest level of play. Johnson could have been a great pitcher anywhere, without a doubt. But like Griffith he was committed to his teammates and he knew the only man that could shape a winner in Washington was the Old Fox. They had made it work, though it took longer than they had each hoped, but they had climbed the hill together and that bond would unite them throughout their lives in the city they had each adopted as home.

"Griffith and I are the best of friends and there is no manager in baseball I would rather work for," he had said in 1915.[19] The words were no less true in 1927. Clark Griffith remained as true a friend to Walter Johnson as an owner and magnate as when he had managed him every day from the dugout.

The 1927 season was Stan Coveleski's final year in Washington as well. He tried another season with the Yankees before calling it quits. Although his tenure pitching with Walter Johnson was brief, they may have been the best tandem ever to pitch for the Nationals.

With the departure of Walter Johnson and Stan Coveleski, the youth movement became a matter of dire importance. The early results were mixed. The Nationals played out the 1927 season much as in 1926. In September they regained their July form and played their best ball of the season to end the year a distant third to the Yankees.

Clark Griffith continued to look for replacement pitching wherever he could find it and brought Tom Zachary back to Washington in a waiver deal with the Browns in July. It assured Zachary's date with destiny as on October 1, 1927, he threw the pitch to Babe Ruth that resulted in "the Bambino's" 60th home run of the season and set a record that would stand for 34 years.

As good as Ruth and Gehrig had been in 1926, they had their greatest season together in 1927 as the Yankees won the league by a 19-game margin. In total the 1927 Yankees hit 158 home runs, a feat unmatched in baseball history to that point. Gehrig had 47, and no player other than Ruth had hit as many in a single season previously. Having two hitters of such unique talent on one team compounded the impressive numbers each man was able to post almost daily.

Bucky Harris and Clark Griffith were spectators in October as the 1927

World Series pitted the Pittsburgh Pirates, who had beaten the Nationals in 1925, against the New York Yankees. The Pirates had two new outfielders named Paul and Lloyd Waner—"Big Poison" and "Little Poison" respectively. They were both bound for the National Baseball Hall of Fame, but in 1927, they could do nothing with the Yankees pitching staff. The '27 Yankees crushed the Pirates in four straight games.

Despite the difficulty Griffith had in fielding a competitive team in 1926 and 1927, he kept his turnstiles spinning. Attendance did not reach the record levels of 1925, but held steady at well over 500,000 fans each year. The team was prosperous and part of the attraction was seeing the Yankees when they came to town, as Ruth and Gehrig were solid attractions wherever they went. The American League had two weak sisters, the Boston Braves and St. Louis Browns, teams that were calling into question whether those cities could support two teams.

The 1928 season continued the slow slide of the Nationals. Tris Speaker was gone and to replace him, Clark Griffith brought in George Sisler. Trading one future Hall of Fame hitter for another did not work out. Griffith signed Sisler for a relatively modest sum of $15,000 but the 35-year-old Sisler was complaining of chronic sinus infections that had limited his playing time for Cleveland and would end his career. He proved no great bargain for the Old Fox as the 1928 season got under way.

Griffith did find a gem in the bargain bin for his pitching staff. For only a $7,500 waiver price, he obtained Sad Sam Jones from the St. Louis Browns. Jones had been a stalwart for the Yankees during the 1920s but had slipped badly during their down years when Ruth was hurt and the Nationals had ruled the roost. He found his old form in 1928 and became the ace of a young staff that other than Firpo Marberry and Tom Zachary was composed of players doing short stints as they tried out with the Nationals.

For all of the season's myriad frustrations, it was the beginning of a turnaround that was once again initiated by Joe Engel's tireless scouting of talent for the Old Fox. Engel was scouting a young infielder named Joe Cronin. He had seen him play for the Pirates during spring training and later that year when he was shipped out as a minor leaguer to Kansas City. He was considered a "good-field, no-hit" prospect, but Engel liked him and got an irascible Clark Griffith to wire the $7,500 to sign him.

Griffith was not much impressed, noting Cronin's batting average of only .245. He told the press after the signing that he would be likely to use Cronin as "trading material."[20] It is understandable that Griffith was not enthusiastic about signing another middle infielder. He had waxed eloquent about Buddy Myer only to trade him when he struggled in his second year in favor of the middle infielder of the day, Bobby Reeves from Georgia Tech.

All of these varied attempts were modeled on Bucky Harris. He was the consummate spirited middle infielder with natural leadership skills. Clark Griffith had thought he had the same talent in first Myers and then Reeves, but neither had played up to his promise. It was Harris who first saw that same potential in Cronin. He was sold on the talent and drive of the young Cronin by his exposure to the young man on a day-to-day basis playing alongside him on the baseball diamond. Clark Griffith no longer had the advantage of seeing the players as often.

Harris would stake his reputation on Joe Cronin's ability in 1928 and eventually prove his mentor wrong. Griffith was seeing the game more and more as a business venture and it clouded his best instincts. That approach came into play with regards to Bucky Harris, who was in the third year of one of the largest contracts Clark Griffith had ever given anyone. It had come as a reward for back-to-back pennants but in 1928 Harris and Griffith were three seasons removed from those memorable wins. While their apparent differences may have been about the starting shortstop, the money may have been the more important issue for Griffith, who was usually operating on a shoestring.

Harris liked Bobby Reeves at shortstop, but the young man made too many errors for the likes of a smooth infielder like Bucky Harris. Cronin's reputation was as a fielder, and when Harris began to insert him into the lineup in July 1928, the young man responded well. The timing was right. By July, Washington had played itself out of any thoughts of contention, and whether Reeves or Cronin played short, the team wasn't going to beat the Yankees or Athletics.

The team had once again started slowly, but this time there was no spurt to reach the first division. In the middle of July the team was 14 games below .500 and headed nowhere when Harris decided to give Cronin a prolonged chance to shine. The team was on a road trip and maybe Harris thought that the distance from Clark Griffith's office at the stadium would allow him some room to maneuver. He was wrong.

No sooner had Reeves been benched for Cronin than the wires arrived inquiring why Harris had benched Reeves. "Reeves will never be a ball player if you don't play him," was the instruction from Griffith.[21] Harris's retort, according to Shirley Povich, was "Neither will Cronin."[22] In response Harris gave his own position at second base to Reeves and allowed Cronin to continue playing.

Cronin responded well initially, but he was not yet as accomplished a hitter as Reeves. He was better with the glove, and Harris believed that having the better glove at shortstop was helping the team. The Nationals played out the season with Cronin getting significant playing time as well as Reeves.

Whether it was Cronin's glove or not, the team began to win and climbed back into the first division, finishing with a 75–79 record, good enough for fourth place in the American League.

The main reason that the Nationals were competitive was Goose Goslin, who had his career year. He hit .379 to lead the league. He was locked in a tight race with Heinie Manush in the final week of the season, but the Goose went 12-for-24 over the final six games to edge Manush on the last weekend of the season.

Being the American League batting champion was a crowning achievement for Goslin, but it only tells part of the story. His OPS of 1.056 was third in the American League, just behind Gehrig and Ruth. The Goose was more than just a singles hitter; he was a slugger of note during the era when great home run hitters ruled the game.

From 1922 to 1928 Goslin established himself as the best offensive player ever to put on a Washington uniform. He carried the team throughout the long summer of 1928 and while debates raged between Bucky Harris and Clark Griffith about who was the shortstop, Goose Goslin did the same thing day in and day out, piling up extra-base hits at every stop in the American League.

Bucky Harris had the worst year of his life at the plate. As good as Goslin was, Harris was bad. He hit only .204 for the season, and one reason he was willing to give playing time to Reeves at second base was the realization that the player-manager could not justify writing his own name into the lineup as poorly as he was hitting.

At the end of the season the money, the poor performance of the team and the disagreement about Cronin all came together to spell the end of the Bucky Harris era in Washington. Under the heading "Deposed," the picture of Harris in *The Washington Post* might have been wreathed in black crepe. The article noted the atmosphere at the announcement by Clark Griffith and Treasurer Edward Eynon as "cheerful as a morgue," noting that both men considered Harris "a close personal friend."[23]

The follow-up articles were not as sanguine in their assessment of Clark Griffith's motives, and Frank Young of the *Post* asked if Griffith was playing a "deep, dark game" with the firing.[24] Griffith's loyalty to his players and his desire to craft a winner were at loggerheads, but he eased his own conscience by finding Harris a job managing the Detroit Tigers for Griffith's old friend Frank Navin — the same man who had once been mystified whether the Old Fox was serious when Griffith wrote him a $100,000 check for Ty Cobb.

The hunt for a new manager began immediately, but Griffith was a homebody and did not look far from the comfort of his trusted colleagues in Washington. Walter Johnson had spent the 1928 season managing the Newark

Bears, but he had maintained close contact with Clark Griffith after his retirement. For a man of such imposing physical presence and strength, Walter Johnson was prone to illness. During one bout in the spring of 1928, Griffith and his wife brought Walter Johnson to Washington for treatment at a local hospital where the local press noted how grateful Johnson was for their attentions, none of which could be attributed to a concern that he would be ready to pitch on opening day.[25]

Griffith came to Newark on scouting trips during the 1928 season and maintained his contact with the Big Train during those visits. Two weeks after "deposing" Bucky Harris, Clark Griffith got Walter Johnson's signature on a three-year contract to manage the Nationals. The salary was less than what Bucky Harris had made for three seasons, so Griff was saving money, but the important thing was keeping management of the team all in the Griffith family.

Addressing the concern that Harris could no longer fill the second base slot in the lineup, Griffith traded for Buddy Myer, whom he regretted having given to Boston for almost nothing. Now he paid a handsome price to get him back. He parted with five of the young players he had groomed during the previous seasons, including Bobby Reeves, the shortstop, plus pitchers Horace Lisenbee and Milt Gaston, who had all experienced a level of success with Washington during the 1926–28 seasons.

According to Shirley Povich, the five players appraised for $125,000.[26] The trade was made only because Griffith came around to Bucky Harris's assessment of Joe Cronin. He chose to keep Cronin rather than Reeves, as Boston asked for both players in the deal. But Griffith balked at adding both, holding onto Cronin instead of Reeves. Cronin became one of the few bright spots on Walter Johnson's first team.

Griffith was spending considerable sums of money on developing his team. The *Washington Post* itemized the acquisition prices of all the rookie talent acquired in 1928 and came up with a princely sum exceeding $200,000.[27] However, when offered the chance to acquire the Hagerstown minor league franchise in the Blue Ridge League, Griffith balked. At the time he preferred his position as a "spot" trader, acquiring talent when and where he could find it, rather than developing his own farm teams.

One problem that made Clark Griffith's operations somewhat tenuous was the fall-off in attendance at Griffith Stadium. It had declined each season since 1925, but in 1928 it bottomed out at its lowest figure, under 400,000 for the first time since 1923. Yet the Old Fox continued to spend on talent in the only way he knew how. He was pushing all of his chips into the middle of the table and betting that he could find another winning combination.

Many believed that the 1929 Nationals could contend if they could find a pitching staff. Much of that confidence was based on Clark Griffith's selection of Walter Johnson to manage, but Johnson could not work magic with the pitching talent. Sad Sam Jones was back and while his 1928 season had been his best in several years, he was 36. The young pitchers Garland Braxton and Bump Hadley had shown promise, and Firpo Marberry wanted to convert to a full-time starter. That was the starting rotation, and there was no Walter Johnson in the lot.

"The Big Train Comes Home" was the headline as another presidential opening day neared in April of 1929.[28] Saying that no man knew Walter Johnson better than Clark Griffith, the *Post* credited the Old Fox with the foresight to bring the most popular figure in Washington back to Griffith Stadium. Johnson was re-united with his old friend Clyde Milan, who came back to coach.

The team had a fine spring training, winning 27 of their 29 exhibition contests. For all of the positive momentum coming out of the spring, Walter Johnson's team did not look good on their first opening day. It was cold and overcast and only 25,000 braved the conditions to watch the Philadelphia Athletics beat the Nationals. A new president was on hand for the game as Herbert Hoover followed the faithful Calvin Coolidge in the White House and in the presidential box at Griffith Stadium.[29] Hoover stayed for the entire contest and showed a strong arm.

Connie Mack's team had been the only real competition to the Yankees in 1928 when they finished a scant two and one-half games back in the final standings. To start the new season the Athletics were without Al Simmons, but they had a new 21-year-old first baseman named Jimmie Foxx who had shown star potential at the end of the 1928 season.

Foxx picked up where he had left off in 1928, going three-for-three to start the new season in Washington with a home run and a double. It sparked an attack that chased Sam Jones after four innings. Then Garland Braxton tried his luck, but with little to show for it. The final score was 13–4 and the only bright spot for the Nationals was the relief pitching of side-armer Ad Liska. Walter Johnson was philosophical about the loss of his first game as manager, saying, "the defeat won't hurt us any, in fact, I think it will help as the boys had gotten a little chesty after their fine exhibition season."[30]

There was another new name on opening day, Shirley Povich. It was his first home opener as the "Sports Editor" for the *Washington Post*. Frank Young covered the game as well and it was the beginning of an era when at least two sports writers at each of the dailies covered the team.

Walter Johnson's prediction that the Nationals would return to their exhibition season form was wrong. The season went poorly from the outset as the team fell off the pace, and by the end of May they were ten games below .500 and 14 games behind the Athletics. Worse yet, Walter Johnson was hospitalized with a kidney infection. "Clark Griffith personally rushed him (Johnson) back to Washington staying up all night in Johnson's stateroom applying ice packs to his sweating brow."[31]

After his return to the field the team slowly re-emerged from its funk. Johnson initiated early morning practices that would have been appropriate only in the spring. But he believed them necessary and they had a huge impact as players like Cronin began to make the routine plays they had been booting before. They began playing better as a team in the second half of the season and showed the promise of things to come.

Connie Mack's Athletics were on their way to a World Championship behind the pitching of Lefty Grove and the hitting of Al Simmons and Jimmie Foxx. The only counter the Nationals had shown in 1928, Goose Goslin, fell off sharply in 1929. Sam Rice, now 39 years old, showed amazing resilience, hitting .323 and playing a strong right field again. Goslin and Rice were joined by a center fielder, Sam West, who had logged more than 300 at-bats in 1928, but became the full-time center fielder.

Buddy Myer showed all of the reasons why Clark Griffith had been so aggressive in pursuit of his new second baseman as he played a solid second base and hit over .300.

Although Walter Johnson started the season with an infield of Ossie Bluege at shortstop, Myer at third and Jackie Hayes at second base, Joe Cronin played his way into the starting lineup when Hayes failed to hit.

Cronin's bat showed the first hint of what was to come in 1929, but he made uncharacteristic blunders in the field, committing a whopping 62 errors to lead the league in that category, although also leading the league in assists.[32] However, it was the eight home runs and the .281 batting average that made Clark Griffith take notice.

Washington finished with its lowest mark since the 1925 pennant, finishing fifth in the league with a record of 71–81, but they had a winning record in the second half of the season and finished ahead of Bucky Harris's Tigers. The pitching was worse than the hitting, though neither was particularly good. Firpo Marberry was the best starter that Walter Johnson could send out during the season. The former reliever posted 19 wins and had the kind of season that made Johnson proud as Marberry finished second to Lefty Grove in ERA with a 3.06 mark.

After the season Walter Johnson said, "I may have had my bumps this year, but I have learned something."[33] Clark Griffith remained committed to his manager. He said that he was as certain that Walter Johnson would manage again in 1930, "as I am they will not move the Washington Monument."[34] He cited the value of the experience that Johnson had gotten in 1929, saying that it was like any other business, experience was vital to success. He quieted the concern that Walter Johnson had been soft on players he knew too well, saying, "Walter can be hard as iron and cold as stone when it is necessary."[35]

Clark Griffith was embarking in other new directions with the management of his organization. In June he purchased the Atlanta minor league team that was playing in the Southern Association. The price was $650,000. Although he denied that the team would be a "farm" team operated as an "adjunct" to the Nationals, it was clear from having Joe Engel as well as Edward Eynon there at the announcement, that it would be a source of talent for the major league team.[36]

Washington had trained in Atlanta prior to 1919, when they switched to Tampa, but it was speculated that with their commitment to Tampa up at the end of the 1929 season, the team would move its spring training to Atlanta as well. In assessments of the team after the purchase, most concluded that the Atlanta Crackers club was not ready to contribute talent to Washington in the near future, yet Griffith said, "I am committed to putting a winning ball club out there."[37]

No sooner had the sale been announced than it was annulled because of charter restrictions that prohibited the team's operation by a major league team. Engel and Griffith were determined, however, to get into the business of minor league ownership. The St. Louis Cardinals owned no less than nine minor league teams and it was estimated that approximately 60 percent of all minor league franchises were owned by major league organizations in 1929.[38] Commissioner Landis was opposed to "chain store" operations but was not prohibiting teams like the Cardinals from seeking a horizontal monopoly on talent.

Joe Engel had voiced enough concern about the developments in the minor leagues to move Griffith to action, saying that he was being thwarted in his attempts to sign talent because so many players were being locked up early with commitments to other organizations. The charter prohibition in the Southern Association did allow the Nationals to maintain strong ties to teams — as they had with Birmingham — but these situations were quickly disappearing.

Griffith had been offered a chance to buy the Hagerstown team in the Blue Ridge League earlier in the year and had demurred. Now he and Engel settled on the team in Chattanooga, Tennessee, the "Lookouts," who played in the Southern Association with Atlanta. However, the owner of the Atlanta team vetoed Clark Griffith's purchase of the Chattanooga team on the same grounds as had been used to prohibit Griffith's purchase of his team. The Old Fox got around this issue by having Joe Engel named as the purchaser of the team.

Clark Griffith provided the financial backing for Engel, but as team president Engel was allowed to purchase the team despite opposition from Atlanta. Engel was only too happy to create an organization in Tennessee that was a subsidiary to the one in Washington. He modeled his team completely after the one Clark Griffith had built. Engel built a new stadium in the city bordering three states and named it, fittingly enough, Engel Stadium.

The league officials refused to allow Engel a spot on the governing board of the league, citing his ties to Griffith and Washington. The team became an economic success as Engel followed the lead of his mentor, the Old Fox, focusing on keeping the fans entertained with a wide variety of gimmicks. He gave away cars and chickens to the point that he was losing money even while filling the stadium with happy fans. Chattanooga became a frequent stop for comedians Nick Altrock and Al Schacht. Schacht perfected his routines as the "Clown Prince of Baseball" in Chattanooga. In later years minor league venues like Chattanooga became his bread and butter.

CHAPTER 18

Shopping a New Market for Talent

The Old Fox was 60 years old as the 1930 season approached. But he was still in great shape as his golf game attested. He was sharp enough to break 80 for 18 holes, and still well enough attuned to the game to know he was falling behind as new trends emerged and his talented core from Washington's championship seasons continued to age. Sam Rice was 40 and Joe Judge 36. Both men hit over .300 in 1929 but they were no more immune to the march of years than Griffith himself.

There were solid youngsters like Myer, Tate and Cronin, but the roster for 1930 was almost identical to that of 1929 and few believed the outcome would be much improved. Clark Griffith continued to hunt for what sports writers in the day called "ivory," those highly talented, though often raw players. But ivory hunting was a game for the wealthy and Clark Griffith was spending liberally on expeditions that were returning with less booty each year.

To make matters worse, the team had lost money in 1929 and no dividend was declared for stockholders.[1] Clark Griffith was buying talent the way he always had, on the open market, but it was a market that was being cornered by new baseball executives exemplified by Branch Rickey, then the business manager for the St. Louis Cardinals. Rickey was in much the situation that Griffith was, trying to compete against larger cities like New York and Chicago that had more money to buy talent. Beginning in 1919 Rickey did something about it, even as prices were going up and the pool of available talent shrank in quantity and quality.

Griffith was part of an internal debate in baseball about the future of basic player development. Now part of the baseball establishment, Griffith sided with Commissioner Landis, who was opposed to Rickey's new system on two grounds.[2] When major league teams took control of a minor league franchise, they eroded its local control and flavor. Landis believed that local ownership was key to the survival of baseball in sites far from the big cities of the northeast. Equally important, Landis believed that Rickey's system was unfair to both its competitors and to the players themselves, who could be stuck inside the Cardinals organization for years.

Charles Alexander's book on baseball during the Great Depression states that the average age for players in the Cardinals minor league organization was several years older than the overall average because of the additional time it took them to reach the major league club.[3]

Clark Griffith sided with Landis, completely discarding his persona as the labor radical siding with the players against an unfair system. He was being squeezed in his search for talent like a pitcher squeezed by an umpire with a stingy strike zone. Each season Frank Young detailed the amount of money that Griffith had paid the prior year in acquiring young talent. The price was going up, and Young asserted that the take was thinner than it had been in Griffith's heyday when he was building his 1924 Championship team.

There were other more pressing economic issues clouding the horizon. The stock market had crashed the previous fall. A few of the more high-profile ballplayers and many of the owners lost much of their savings, but the full impact of that market collapse had not yet begun to spread through the rest of the economy.[4] Though the Nationals experienced an economic down-turn at the end of the 1929 season, it was unrelated to the stock market crash. The game of baseball as an economic enterprise was in excellent condition at the beginning of the 1930 season, and its champions believed it "impregnable."[5]

The biggest downturn for the Nationals came from injuries, age, and a depleted pitching corps. Ossie Bluege had been lost for much of the 1929 season to surgery. That loss had given more playing time to Joe Cronin, who took ownership of the shortstop position. It was a crucial cornerstone in the championship Washington teams in '24 and '25.

Cronin convinced Clark Griffith of his bona fides in 1929 and the young shortstop came into the 1930 season with a starting position securely his. Nothing spoke louder than the Old Fox's checkbook as Griffith gave Cronin a $2,000 raise in his contract over the winter. Cronin reacted to the new confidence in his abilities by working out in the off-season to add strength, putting an additional 30 pounds of muscle on his frame over the three off-seasons since he had come over from Pittsburgh.[6]

The team had another excellent exhibition season, this time in Biloxi, Mississippi, their new training camp. They finished their camp with a week of games in Chattanooga. The team was without Goose Goslin in the spring.

He was in a stubborn dispute with Clark Griffith over his contract. Goslin had made $17,000 in 1929 but his numbers had fallen off sharply after his remarkable 1928 season.

Griffith had given his shortstop a raise, but the team's economic concerns may have played into the notably low offer of $10,000 made to Goslin over the winter.[7] The star left fielder claimed to be insulted by the offer and held out until early April, when he reluctantly signed and reported to the team.

In the end the Nationals roster for the 1930 season was much the same as had finished fifth the year before. No one gave them any chance to contend against the strength of the Athletics as they took the field against the Red Sox in the Presidential Opener on April 14. President Herbert Hoover, presiding over the worst economic calamity in the history of the union, was accused of a "wild pitch" in his opening toss.[8]

The game was played in the first sunny, warm conditions that opening day had seen in years, and it may have been a portent. Washington players wore numbered uniforms for the first time and Firpo Marberry was given the opening day start in recognition of the fine season he had in 1929. He pitched well enough to win, but Garland Braxton blew the lead in relief and the team lost a tough 4–3 decision.

Besides numbered uniforms, another modern contrivance was introduced in 1930—electric illumination of the playing field that allowed evening games to be played. It started in the minor leagues where it was used to help prop up struggling teams who could not draw paying fans for afternoon games. "Flood Lighting," as it was initially dubbed, was marketed as the next big thing in baseball.[9] But it was a big expenditure of upfront capital and as with farm system baseball, Clark Griffith could no longer afford to keep up with the changing trends in the game.

Although President Hoover was largely ineffective in addressing the economic chaos that spread through the economy as 1930 wore on, Clark Griffith's spending plan for the Nationals began to take hold as the spring baseball season unfolded. The Nationals lineup on opening day featured only three position players who had not started in 1925, and Firpo Marberry was on the mound. It was in the middle of the field where the players were all new and remarkably talented—Buddy Myer at second, Joe Cronin at short, and Sam West in center. Bigger changes were brewing.

Walter Johnson's Nationals won eight in a row to end April and the team climbed into first place on May 16. The team batting average was .319 and the manager had to warn the team of over confidence.[10] The team slumped badly in late May and June and dropped off the pace set by the Athletics, as the pitching was not nearly as good as the hitting.

Griffith's staff consisted of Sad Sam Jones again, Firpo Marberry and young pitchers Bump Hadley and Lloyd Brown. As usual he had a good bullpen. The emergence of young side-arming Ad Liska had allowed Marberry to move into the starting rotation, but overall it was not an aggregation that could compete with the Athletics. Marberry was not having the same season as in 1929 and Sam Jones was 38.

Clark Griffith set out to remedy the situation. Goose Goslin was in a batting slump and many attributed it to his failure to get into shape while he argued with the Old Fox over money in March rather than report to camp. Griffith was a loyal backer of his players, but money was the name of the game in 1930. His margin of error was a thin one. Joe Cronin was leading the team in all of the categories once the sole proprietorship of the "Potomac Goose." Goslin was making $10,000 and Cronin $6,000.

In mid–June Clark Griffith pulled off one of his best trades in a sign that the Old Fox could still find room to maneuver in the changing baseball landscape. He traded Goslin to the St. Louis Browns, where his power would play much better in the modest confines of Sportsman's Park. Over the remainder of the 1930 season, Goslin would hit 30 home runs as the shorter expanses of Sportsman's Park showcased his talents far better than Griffith Stadium. For Goslin Griffith got two players, Heinie Manush and Alvin Crowder.

"Washington fans are pinching themselves all day to shoo away a feeling that it wasn't true," wrote Shirley Povich of the trade after the final dimensions were announced.[11] The owner of the Browns, Philip de Catesby Ball, had the money to own the team, but not enough to make it a contender. The team had never won a pennant in all of its years in the American League. They drew poorly and the idea of having a slugger of Goslin's reputation may have convinced the Browns owner that Goslin would draw more fans.

Manush's best season had been 1926, when he had teamed with Ty Cobb near the end of the Georgia Peach's career and with Harry Heilmann near the peak of his. They had formed a fine outfield. Manush hit .378 that year to lead the American League, but dropped off the following season and was traded to St. Louis. He was in the middle of a bounce-back campaign and his slashing hitting style would play well in Griffith Stadium. Defensively, Povich rated the two men a draw as modestly talented defensive "fly-chasers."

Coming with him was the pitcher that Griffith had originally scouted and signed in 1926, "General" Alvin Crowder. Crowder had gone on from Washington to become one of the best pitchers in the American League, winning 21 games for the Browns in 1928. As with Buddy Myer, Griff was bringing home another one that he had let slip away.

Manush was hitting .328 on the day of the trade, 57 points higher than the slumping Goslin. He was excited to be playing for a potential contender, saying, "I am tickled to death to get with a club that has a chance to cop the old rag."[12] He provided the offense an immediate boost, but it was the addition of Crowder that helped fuel a second-half run by the Nationals. One of Crowder's first games was against his old teammates the Browns, whom he beat, 5–3.

Clark Griffith was not done dealing. Several days later in June he announced a trade for Art Shires, one of the most colorful players in the game at that time. He called himself "The Great Shires" and had punched out his manager early in his career before deciding that boxing might be his best sport.[13] When that career proved a dead end, he came back to baseball.

Povich called him the "freshest busher in the game," one who believed himself to be the best fielding, hitting first baseman in the game, and the one with the biggest wad of chew in his mouth at any major league park where he played.[14] Griffith gave up Garland Braxton and Bennie Tate to get Shires. The assumption was that Shires would replace Joe Judge, but the latter was hitting well and playing his best ball since the championship seasons. Griffith explained his thinking, saying "Joe Judge is the greatest first baseman in the game, but when he is out of the game, we need a man like Shires."[15]

Shires would see only limited action, but hit lustily when in the lineup much as Mule Shirley had done for the 1924 team and Joe Harris had done in 1925. The trade seemed to affirm that Griffith believed he was constructing that kind of team once again.

The trades also sparked new fan interest. The New York Yankees came to town for a July 4 doubleheader and a sell-out crowd of 35,000 was there for the games, both of which were won by Washington with Sam Jones pitching a shutout in the opener and Fred Marberry throwing a complete game winner in the late afternoon. The Nationals took over undisputed possession of first place several days later, the first time that claim had been made in July since 1925. Heinie Manush, Joe Cronin, Sam Rice and Buddy Myer were the offensive charge that allowed Marberry and Washington to overcome Babe Ruth's 32nd home run of the season.

The team sagged after beating the Yankees, but got traction again in August and played .700 ball for the month. They could not catch the best team Connie Mack may have ever fielded. Griffith made the last big move of the season when he purchased Joe Kuhel from Kansas City for the princely sum of $65,000. It put the trade for Shires in a curious light since Kuhel was a young and very talented first baseman. Joe Engel pronounced Kuhel the best prospect he had seen in many a year, and Griffith gushed as well. This time the hyperbole would prove out as Kuhel became an important cog for Washington in coming years.

Player potential and the team's position in the American League pennant race were soon overshadowed by a devastating sadness. Walter Johnson's wife,

Hazel, who had been a quiet, constant presence beside the Big Train, took ill in July and declined rapidly during the heat of an historic summer that ushered in the Dust Bowl across the southwest. Johnson's son had been struck by a car earlier in the year, and Hazel Johnson was with him and the other children as they traveled to be with Walter on the road. She stayed for a while in Coffeyville, Kansas, where the Johnson family still lived.

After driving back to Washington with her children from Kansas in the stifling heat, she was hospitalized with heat exhaustion. She was given the best care, but she never recovered her strength and died on July 31.[16] Walter Johnson was inconsolable and never truly recovered from the loss of his wife. The entire team mourned with Walter Johnson, and as the patriarch of that family, Griffith was as affected as any.

The Big Train was left with five children to raise. Hazel Johnson's family from Nevada came east to help. Walter Johnson had close friendships with Clyde Milan and others from the team and they all pitched in. Long time coach and player, Al Schacht, summarized the feelings of the team when he spoke of the love they all felt toward the couple, "We all love Walter and realize what this means to him ... nothing I can remember has affected me this way."[17] Clark Griffith gave his manager as long as he needed away from the team.

The mournful team without a manager managed to hang onto second place and finished ahead of the Yankees, though eight games behind the Athletics. Joe Cronin's 1930 season established him as a star, as he hit .346 and drove in 126 runs. Attendance jumped for the year as Washington fans reacted favorably to the new faces and the new competitiveness that Griffith was exhibiting. Over 600,000 fans came to Griffith Stadium in 1930 after only 350,000 in 1929. Baseball attendance overall climbed above the 10 million mark for the first time.

Part of the new popularity of the game was the offensive explosion of 1930. The average runs per game leapt to its highest total in the history of the American League at 5.41 runs. Only after the rule change that moved the pitching box in 1893 was there a more pronounced surge in batting marks. The National League of the nineteenth century saw average run production at over 6 runs per game numerous times, but it was a different brand of baseball.[17] The pitching marks for the Nationals in 1930 that seemed so out of whack with the trends of the mid–1920s reflected the jump of the league average to 4.65 runs.[19]

Connie Mack's Athletics were too much for Branch Rickey's St. Louis Cardinals team in the 1930 World Series as they won four games to two. Lefty Grove beat Burleigh Grimes twice, once in relief. Al Simmons hit .364 for the Series and hit two home runs as did Mickey Cochrane. There were omens, however, even for the World Champions. Attendance at Shibe Park to see the World Champions play in Philadelphia was less than at Griffith Stadium in their championship seasons.

Connie Mack's personal fortune was rocked by the Stock Market crash.[20] Despite having put together one of the greatest teams in baseball history, the Philadelphia Athletics may have been the leading edge of a downward trend just starting to spread across the sport.

On January 7, 1931, Frank Young provided the market report for the Washington Nationals as they approached yet another season. Again the money spent by Clark Griffith in search of another winning combination totaled well in excess of $200,000. The young talent that was evaluated in Chattanooga, Birmingham and elsewhere did not fall off in quantity, but Griffith and Engel could not find the young pitching talent to support one of the better offensive teams Washington ever had.

Young did not mention whether the Nationals made money on the 1930 season or declared dividends, but the attendance figures that increased by 75,000 overall in both 1929 and 1930 had to have added some value to Clark Griffith's precarious bottom line.

The writers and everyone else tiptoed around the name of Hazel Johnson and tried to treat the 1931 season as just another for the Big Train, his third as the manager of the Nationals. As Johnson knew, there was a big hill to climb in the American League. The Athletics and Yankees were awesome teams, each lineup filled with future Hall of Fame icons. The Nationals were swimming in treacherous waters.

Clark Griffith had to be encouraged by the sell-out crowd that showed up for opening day in 1931 to see President Hoover throw out the first pitch. There were sunny skies for the first game of the season against the World Champion Athletics. Lefty Grove matched up against General Crowder and Connie Mack's nine won, but the Nationals came back to win the next three games and got the season off to an auspicious beginning.

Joe Kuhel, whom Frank Young described as the most expensive investment Griffith made prior to the 1931 season, supplanted Joe Judge as the everyday first baseman after Judge was forced out in May to have his appendix removed. Judge had hit over .300 in 1930 and Kuhel was not yet ready to take on Judge's senior role on the team.

Roy Spencer became the everyday catcher and only Ossie Bluege at third base remained from the 1925 Nationals infield once Judge was sidelined. But the outfield had the ever-present Sam Rice, now playing beside Sam West and Manush. Sam West had a breakout season in 1931, hitting .333 and knocking in 91 runs. Buddy Myer and Manush had big years with the bat, but it was Joe Cronin's year. Although he hit only .306, he drove in 126 runs for the second straight year, and led the team in home runs and extra-base hits. It is important to note, however, that Lou Gehrig drove in 184 runs during the same season as the might of the Yankees continued to overwhelm everyone.

The Nationals no longer stole bases with the reckless abandon of Clark Griffith teams during the deadball era. One reason was that perennial leadoff batter Sam Rice no longer had the juice in his legs to steal bases. The other was that the brand of baseball was changing dramatically, and the slugging game Babe Ruth and Lou Gehrig had established in New York City was being emulated around the league.

It was a brand of ball that sold extremely well at the box office in 1930. But in 1931 the first fall-off in attendance occurred as the effects of the deepening economic crisis spread throughout the nation as a whole. Even with the Nationals playing competitive baseball for consecutive seasons in 1930 and 1931, attendance dipped again and fell below 500,000 fans. It was a very noticeable fall-off of 125,000 paying customers in a year when Clark Griffith continued to outlay capital to build one more winner.

For his money Griffith got remarkably better pitching in 1931. General Crowder was the ace of the staff and the young pitchers who had struggled in prior years, Bump Hadley and Lloyd Brown, both had good seasons. But there was no relief corps to support them. Firpo Marberry was one of the best starters Clark Griffith had after Crowder. Ad Liska was gone, replaced by no one of note.

Walter Johnson was criticized for his handling of the pitching staff and blame was laid at his door for the failure of the team to beat the Yankees and Athletics. Despite playing solid baseball and staying in contention for most of the season, there were critics of Johnson who again said he was too friendly with his team and exhibited poor judgment in handling the pitchers.

Clark Griffith gave him a valuable new piece to add to that staff in July of 1931 when he purchased Monte Weaver from the Baltimore Orioles minor league team. Griffith gave the Orioles Harry Rice, who had been a promising young outfielder but was playing in a reserve capacity for Washington in 1931. Weaver was a professor of mathematics at the University of Virginia, but he was hardly the bespectacled academic. He was described as a "strong husky lad" who much impressed Walter Johnson, and was worth "the large slice of cash" that Griffith parted with for the young hurler.[21]

Griffith watched over the development of Weaver during that summer as he pitched out the season for Baltimore, with the Old Fox protesting any time the Baltimore manager allowed him to throw too many pitches in the off-chance that he could lead the Orioles to a pennant in the International

League. The Old Fox was building a relationship with the team up the road as he shunted outfielders and pitchers back and forth to the Orioles.

Connie Mack had secured the services of Lefty Grove and George Earnshaw, two of his big three pitchers, from Baltimore. The loyalties of Baltimore baseball fans were thought to lie with Philadelphia as a result, but Griffith was making a conscious play for them by adding players from Baltimore and shipping players like Ad Liska to Baltimore when they failed to pitch to expectations in Washington. Although it was no "farm" team for the Nationals, the relationship was a profitable one for both cities in 1931.

Another signature development in 1931 was Clark Griffith featuring a popular Negro Leagues game at Griffith Stadium in August. The game spotlighted the Baltimore Black Sox and Philadelphia Hilldales, who played in the Eastern League of black professional baseball. The home run king of the Negro Leagues, Jim Beckwith, belted one out of Griffith Stadium during the game, a portent of things to come.[22]

From May to September the Nationals were in second place consistently and did not fall off the pace to the Yankees until the final week of the season, when they slipped to third. One problem was the loss of Joe Judge and the failure of Kuhel to hit as lustily. In the end the team finished with a record of 92 wins and 62 losses — exactly the same as that of the 1924 World Championship team.

The post-season provided a rematch of the Cardinals against the Athletics. Shirley Povich wrote a compelling article about the Series, detailing the iron control of Commissioner Landis over the proceedings and how the umpires waited for Landis's arrival before the games could begin, regardless of what the posted start time might be. Landis's word was law regarding the World Series as the Nationals had learned with the rain-soaked affair that had decided the 1925 Series.

In the 1931 World Series Landis was up against his most consistent and artful opponent, Branch Rickey. Rickey had raised a new player down on the farm and introduced him for the 1931 season. His name was Pepper Martin and he played center field for the Cardinals, providing depth and energy to a lineup that still featured Jim Bottomley and Frankie Frisch at its heart.

Martin put his signature on the series, however, playing in all seven games and batting a cool .500. He was the epitome of a Depression era player and a hero to those feeling its effects most deeply. Martin was from such meager surroundings that he had hopped freights to reach his first spring training with the Cardinals in 1931.[23] The Cardinals fan base extended into the Ozarks and to Oklahoma, where Martin grew of age. Those areas of the country were in the grips of a worsening drought, and a perpetually disheveled Martin, who talked and looked like them, provided a natural hero. As a player Martin appealed to Clark Griffith, who had always sought fast center fielders to patrol behind him when he was on the mound and later when he was in the dugout.

Martin had help in winning the 1931 World Series from Burleigh Grimes, whose spitball was extremely effective that fall. He got the best of Lefty Grove in the '31 Series and the Cardinals won a tightly contested series, four games to three. They were a force to be reckoned with in the thirties and Branch Rickey was just getting started building World Champion teams in new ways that would continue to bedevil Commissioner Landis.

CHAPTER 19

Last Hurrah

The 1932 season brought new names to the Nationals that hastened the departure of several of Washington's finest veterans. Clark Griffith traded Bump Hadley, Sam Jones and Jack Hayes to the Chicago White Sox for outfielder Carl Reynolds. Reynolds had hit 22 home runs during the offensive explosion of 1930 with an average of .359. His numbers had dropped off in 1931 due to injuries, which made him available to Griffith.[1] Reynold's powerful bat would take the place of 42-year-old Sam Rice in 1932, but Rice was deemed good insurance if Reynolds proved fragile again.

Rice had collected 207 hits in 1930 and made himself the only player in the major leagues ever to reach that milestone after his 40th birthday. He was closing in on 3,000 hits for his long and impressive career, but he would fall just short. In 1931 Rice had split time with Dave Harris, but still logged 120 games.

Joe Kuhel continued to wrestle the first base job away from Joe Judge, though Judge would log almost 300 at-bats in 1932. The most enigmatic player in baseball history, Moe Berg, joined the Nationals in 1932 when he served as a backup catcher to Roy Spencer. As with Monte Weaver, Berg was an intellect of considerable acclaim, having starred as a linguist at Princeton. But "Berg's happiest moments at Princeton were on the baseball field," and he deferred his academic pursuits in favor of baseball after he left the Ivy League.[2] When Weaver was pitching to Berg, it was probably one of the most talented intellectual duos ever to connect over the game of baseball.

When the Nationals' 1932 season opened on April 11 against the Red Sox, two even more notable figures were on the field at Griffith Stadium for the last time. President Hoover was in his last year as president when he tossed out the first pitch of the season. In the Nationals' dugout, Walter Johnson was in his last year as manager.

In 1932 the Nationals played another year of competitive baseball hampered only by the all-star lineups in New York and Philadelphia. However, early in the season — until May 19 — Washington sat atop the league in first place. They could not keep up that pace and by mid-season were mired in fourth. Despite a credible finish they could again rise no higher than third.

The Yankees continued adding the best talent with players like catcher Bill Dickey — whom Clark Griffith and Joe Engel had fought mightily to sign — and a young shortstop named Frankie Crosetti. The Yankees outspent Griffith for Dickey. The New York team had deeper pockets in the market place for new talent. Even in the early years of the Great Depression, Colonel Ruppert of the Yankees was spending in excess of $400,000 in acquiring minor league free agent talent — almost twice as much as Clark Griffith was stretching to afford. In 1931 the wealthiest team, in the wealthiest city, would begin to develop a farm system as well.[3]

Yankees pitching equaled that of the Athletics in 1932 as they featured two aces in Red Ruffing and Lefty Gomez. Gomez had premiered in 1931, winning 21 games, and came back to win 24 in 1932 with the powerful Yankees lineup behind him. Red Ruffing was his partner and the better pitcher of the two in many ways in 1932, but the two pitchers allowed the Yankees to match up better against the Athletics in 1932 as Earnshaw and Rube Wahlberg dropped off in performance.

Jimmie Foxx hit 58 home runs to lead the league in that category and both the Yankees and Athletics scored runs at the prodigious pace of 6.4 per game. It was a race of two powerful offensive machines won by the Yankees, who sported a final record of 107 wins against 47 losses, a remarkable 60 games above .500. They crushed the Chicago Cubs in the World Series, winning four straight, scoring 12 runs in the first game of the Series and 13 in Game Four of what was never really a contest in doubt.

Joe McCarthy, who would be the winningest manager in Yankees history, had been fired by the Cubs ownership the previous year, and his victory over them in the World Series was especially sweet. McCarthy had said when he was hired by the Yankees, "If I could beat the Cubs with my new club, I would be willing to jump off the Brooklyn Bridge."[4] McCarthy went on to manage the Yankees for 15 years, with more wins than any other Yankees manager, though Casey Stengel would win more pennants.

There were notable off-the-field occurrences in 1932, as the leagues decided to curb the offensive explosion of 1930 by raising the seams on the ball and providing a thicker horsehide cover than had previously been employed. That change was given greater impact when the owners, feeling the economic pinch of the Depression, ruled that fewer balls would be supplied for games. Players noticed that change more than any other as balls got soft during the course of play much as they had in the Dead Ball era.[5]

The owners met before the 1932 season and the most pressing order of business was the economic crisis now affecting even the baseball industry. Both leagues passed a resolution to reduce salaries, and in the baseball press's coverage of the event there was no sympathy for players whose salaries were seen as outsized in relation to bread lines and other symptoms of the economic crisis visible in every American city. Team rosters were diminished from 25 players to 23 and umpiring crews reduced.[6]

Clark Griffith had been unusually brusque in dealing with his own hold-out in 1932, Heinie Manush. Manush had fallen off during the first half of the 1931 season and only a protracted binge of hitting in September had raised his average above .300. Griffith cut his salary in his first contract offer. When spring training began and Manush refused to sign that offer, Griffith barked in the press that the outfielder would do well to sign that one because he would rescind the offer and send a new one for less. He was more willing to do without his star outfielder than pay more money to players.

The only player to get a raise after the 1931 season — Joe Cronin — was clearly a favorite of Clark Griffith. Early in the 1932 pre-season evaluation of the team, Griffith gave his assessment of the team to Frank Young in concert with Joe Cronin. "Griffith, Cronin Bemoan Lack of Pitchers by Nats," was the headline.[7] No mention was made in the article of manager Walter Johnson. In the article the young shortstop provided player evaluations of Washington veterans such as Joe Judge alongside those of Griffith.

The article reflected a growing reality as the 1932 season wore down that Walter Johnson was on his way out. When the season was over and the fans' attention turned to the looming World Series between the Yankees and Cubs, Clark Griffith announced the firing of Walter Johnson. It was not his record as manager that undermined his position, but his salary. Johnson had taken a team that was finishing in the second division and brought the first contender back to Washington after 1925. Two third-place finishes and one second-place finish in three years behind the juggernauts the Yankees and Athletics had built was a fine record.

Although Walter Johnson's salary was not known, Clark Griffith had always paid his most famous player well. Joe Cronin, in stark contrast, was a player who was making far less. Making him the manager in fact eliminated whatever money Johnson was making at the time from the team's balance sheet. The move was not solely dictated by team financing. The press had been critical of Johnson and his handling of pitchers, and while Shirley Povich said the move was a surprise, Frank Young — the other *Washington Post* sports-writer — had almost predicted as much late in the season.[8]

In the immediate aftermath there was speculation that Sam Rice, Joe Judge or maybe even Bucky Harris would manage the Nationals. Clark Giffith quieted the rumors quickly by naming Cronin four days after the announcement about Johnson. Cronin was 26 when he took over the job, a year younger than the Boy Manager, Bucky Harris. had been in 1924. The move was eerily reminiscent of '24 when Roger Peckinpaugh had been thought the logical choice as the older, more experienced player on the field. Had Griffith not done much the same move earlier, the economic foundations of the move would have been more front and center in the analysis of the day.

Griffith was more than comfortable with the comparisons to Harris. "I like these scrappy youngsters as leaders," he said to the press after the announcement. "Cronin is one of those fellows who is interested in nothing else but baseball," he added, a comment that would be proven untrue when Cronin married the boss's niece.[9]

By moving quickly, Griffith prevented other favorites from gathering momentum and provided the Old Fox with someone whose counsel he clearly trusted as the team approached the off-season. Cronin attended the owner meetings that December with Griffith, and the first order of business was to look again for ways to confront the worsening economic situation for baseball.

The eight season openers played to begin the 1932 season had drawn only 121,000 fans — barely 15,000 fans per contest.[10] It was a huge retrenchment from the prior year when fans had celebrated the beginning of that season as a release from the bad news buffeting the nation. To address the situation, the owners immediately voted to cut salaries by a target of no less than 20 percent.[11]

The biggest news coming out of the meetings may have been the cut in Commissioner Landis's salary from its outsized $65,000, reduced by the same amount as the players, allegedly to $50,000.[12] The meetings also banned the use of radio broadcasting for anything but the World Series. Since 1930 the Series had been a favorite radio broadcast across the country and the owners were not so shortsighted as to curb that. But their moves did seem curious in some regards. They cut the duration of spring training which was a clear savings, but restricting broadcast of games was meant to dampen any motivation of fans to listen quietly at home rather than paying to see the game in person. Baseball owners were years away from making money on broadcast rights to major league baseball games.

The Yankees and Dodgers, as the two richest organizations, opposed the monetary restrictions, but they were quickly outvoted. The mood of the owners against player salaries marked a complete about-face for the former labor radical, Clark Griffith. Said Griffith at the meetings, "The ballplayer alone has not felt the Great Depression. I believe he will be fair enough to realize he must take a 20 percent reduction."[13]

Cronin was sharing a suite with Griffith during the meetings, and while the Old Fox was there to cut his costs, the two men spent more time talking about how to augment the Nationals' pitching staff. They were willing to trade almost anyone if they could get a pitcher of quality to pitch alongside Crowder. They were especially interested in Lefty Stewart and Earl Whitehill and wanted to bring Goose Goslin back to play in Washington.[14]

The biggest trade may have been the first, when they traded the St. Louis Browns Sam West, Lloyd Brown, and Carl Reynolds for outfielders Goose Goslin and Fred Schulte, and pitcher Lefty Stewart. The biggest loss for Washington might have been Sam West and Reynolds, both outfielders, but during the 1932 season, Bill Dickey, the Yankees catcher, had sucker-punched Reynolds after a collision at the plate and broke his jaw in two places. Reynolds' season had been a disappointment as a result.

St. Louis could hope that Reynolds would hit like Goslin had at Sportsman's Park, but nothing had slowed the Goose. He had adapted well to the new offensive surge in 1930 with 37 home runs and then hit 24 more in 1931 while batting .328. He remained one of the best bats in the American League and now he was teamed with Heinie Manush and Schulte in the Washington outfield. Schulte was termed an able replacement for West, Shirley Povich noting the day after the trade that he had stolen more bases than West in 1932.

The middle of the Washington lineup in 1933 would feature Cronin, Goslin and Manush. It was the most formidable threesome Washington would ever see in the same year and the heart of the second-best offense in the American League.

Griffith and Cronin seemed more focused on the trading than on the finances during those meetings, and Griffith was clearly taking his shot at another winner for the 1933 season with his newest boy manager at his side. They completed a second trade the very next day, sending Firpo Marberry and Carl Fischer to Detroit for Earl Whitehill. Marberry had been a star in Washington for a decade, but he was well along on the back nine of his career.

Earl Whitehill had been around longer than Marberry. He had been a Detroit stalwart for ten years, but he was still only 32. Like any pitcher, he and Stewart must have been excited about pitching in Griffith Stadium, especially Stewart who had been pitching in the hitter's paradise of Sportsman's Park. Washington picked up Jack Russell from Cleveland for Harley Boss, who was the best farm player that Griffith had in Chattanooga. When Cronin and Griffith left the meetings they had a pitching staff of General Crowder, Whitehill, Stewart and Monte Weaver, with Jack Russell in the bullpen. It would prove the best pitching staff in the American League in 1933.

The last acquisition was Luke Sewell as catcher. Roy Spencer had contracted malaria during spring training and never fully recovered during the 1932 season. Griffith traded Spencer for Sewell in early January to finish out his lineup for 1933. It was a remarkable accomplishment as Cronin and the Old Fox constructed a remarkably strong team in little more than a month of trading.

Griffith built his new team despite the worst economic circumstances in the history of the game. Cleveland business manager Jack Evans estimated that to break even a team needed to draw 500,000 fans at home.[15] Only four teams had broken that barrier in 1932 as attendance plummeted to under seven million, a figure not seen since the World War One resurgence in 1919. Only the Yankees and Cubs made money in 1932.[16]

Clark Griffith may not have made money in 1932, but he was not letting it bother him. He was the most active member of his elite fraternity of baseball moguls in the off-season and was confident going into the spring of 1933. There were no holdouts when the team reported to Biloxi, Mississippi, for spring training. Heinie Manush had been the last to send in a signed contract, but Clark Griffith was bullish on baseball in the spring of 1933.

To instill the old spirit of the 1924 and '25 champions in the fans, Clark Griffith challenged the fans of Washington, D.C. to a contest whereby they named the best players ever to play in the nation's capital. After hearing from the fans, Clark Griffith took up his pen to write an article about his lifetime passion for the *Washington Post*.[17] Although Griffith was knowledgeable only about the past two decades of baseball lore in D.C., that time frame represented a large chunk of the best teams that had played there, since the old Senators from the nineteenth century had rarely been competitive.

Griffith's pitching staff consisted of Stan Coveleski and Walter Johnson, predictably, but then he went with General Crowder and Firpo Marberry for the rest of his staff. His lineup included Muddy Ruel, Joe Judge, Bucky Harris, Joe Cronin, Eddie Foster, Heinie Manush, Goose Goslin and Sam Rice. Clyde Milan was left out of the elite outfield and Roger Peckingpaugh the infield, though many fans had included them in their picks.

The contest was intended to pump interest into the fan base that Griffith knew would fall in love with the team that was headed north. But first they had to find the money to get there. President Roosevelt had declared a bank holiday early in March as a way to stanch the concern about a nationwide run on banks fed by numerous bank closures. There was concern that more dire circumstances were in the offing for the nation's banking system, and the press opined that the team could well be stranded in Mississippi. In response Griffith suggested the players might have to pay their own way to Washington to open the season.[18]

The banks were not the only institution teetering on the edge. Clark

Griffith's team was operating on thin margins, and bank loans were not easy to manage during the worst years of the Depression. Griffith was betting on a pennant winner to put him back in the black again, but it was a risky venture taken by one of the grittiest competitors to ever play it.

The Old Fox continued to opine on baseball matters in the press more than he had in all of the prior years combined. He shared his opinions on the effects of the Great Depression as it affected the purchase of young talent, saying it was going to depress prices for a "deuce of a time to come."[19] He admitted the highest price he had ever paid was $65,000 for Joe Kuhel, but that the best deal he ever got was Goose Goslin for $7,000. He still wished he had gotten Ty Cobb for $100,000.

His outfield to start the season was on a par with the best of the Tigers and included one of Ty Cobb's better pupils in Manush. Griffith extended an invitation to the newly installed President, Franklin Delano Roosevelt, to throw out the first pitch of the 1933 season. Griffith and John Heydler, President of the National League, were invited in turn to the White House to meet with the President. Roosevelt enthusiastically accepted the offer to throw out the first pitch and Griffith identified Joe Cronin as the one who would catch the presidential toss.[20]

Prohibition was officially ended, and National League President Heydler used the occasion to announce that alcohol sales — 3.2 beer was all that was allowed — would be back in ballparks around the country. Clark Griffith announced that he would continue with his own practice of banning the sale at his own stadium. With or without beer, the Associated Press writer concluded that opening day in Washington with the president and associated national dignitaries was "the most glamorous in the industry."[21]

Griffith's attempts to increase interest in the new season bore fruit on April 12 as the 1933 season began against Connie Mack's Philadelphia Athletics. A year after opening day crowds had been so anemic, there were 33,359 fans at Griffith Stadium to see the new president throw out the first pitch. The weather was cool and windy, not uncommon for Washington in April, but the crowd warmed to the contest at hand.

"President Roosevelt dealt the baseball industry a hand of cards in the New Deal," opined the *Washington Post* after opening day, but it was not coming soon enough for Connie Mack. He had sold off Al Simmons in the off-season to stay afloat after signing Simmons to a three-year deal worth $100,000 following the success of the 1931 World Series.[22] The economic climate had still seemed flush then, but now Mack could not afford the contract and had packaged Simmons with "Mule" Haas and Jimmy Dykes and sent them to the White Sox for $100,000 in cash.[23]

Connie Mack and Griffith were two baseball dinosaurs doing battle once again. They were the last of the owners who had risen through the ranks as players and managers to hold a significant ownership stake in their teams. It was a last stand by players against what Griffith had once called "bushwackers," the industrialists who knew the game only from the grandstands. Both Griffith and Connie Mack were perilously close to the edge as the Great Depression roared on in 1933.

The loss of three important players was evident in the first game of the season as Philadelphia could muster only a single run off General Crowder and the Nationals won, 4–1. President Roosevelt stayed until the end of the game "and saluted the people in a prize fighter's duke, both hands clasped above the hat and waggled vigorously."[24] It seemed a good omen.

Earl Whitehill won the second contest as the Nationals hitters exhibited their new muscle, scoring 11 times against George Earnshaw and two other Philadelphia pitchers. Goose Goslin hit his first home run of the season to show the faithful that he was happy to be back in Washington.

The Nationals won two of three against the unbeaten Yankees in Washington and then two more in New York City to capture second place late in April. The wins against one of the best teams in the game were further reason to believe that the Nationals had turned a corner. The Yankees embarrassed the Nationals in the last game of the Washington series, 16–0, just to keep the upstarts in their place.

There had been ill will between the two teams since Bill Dickey's unrepentant posture following his breaking of Carl Reynolds' jaw in 1932. During the third game in Washington, Buddy Myer and Yankee outfielder Ben Chapman came to blows around the second base bag. Both men were tossed by the umpires and things simmered until after the game when Earl Whitehill caught up with Chapman under the stands and the two exchanged blows. That confrontation turned into a riot with players, umpires and fans all engaged thoroughly until police dispersed the mob.[25]

The Nationals settled into an uneasy peace with the Yankees, occupying second place behind the New Yorkers throughout May. The Yankees took two of the three games at the end of May in Washington, and most assumed the powerful New York team was headed to another pennant. Then on June 8, in Boston, the Nationals started a torrid streak. Joe Kuhel got hot and the rest of the team followed suit. They beat Boston three in a row, then St. Louis and Philadelphia two apiece, scoring double-digit runs in four straight games before old friend Bump Hadley cooled them off as the Browns won a tight contest, 3–2.

Washington was on a western trip and after losing to St. Louis on June 18, they reeled off eight more wins to take over first place from the Yankees on June 23. They held the lead throughout the long road trip until they went into New York for the last two games of the trip at Yankee Stadium on July 4. Joe Cronin was proud of his team's hitting and believed that New York was floundering because they could not get their pitchers going. Ever cautious, however, Cronin warned Shirley Povich before the first game, "They're liable to swing into stride any day."[26]

A crowd of 77,365 jammed Yankee Stadium to watch Lefty Gomez try to put meaning into Cronin's words, but he could not manage it as the Nationals won, 6–5 in the first game and Earl Whitehill hurled a gem in the second game to win, 3–2. Winning both games put the Nationals up by two and a half games in the American League pennant race following a 15–3 road trip.

For the first time since 1925 there was a big crowd when the team came into Union Station. Five thousand fans greeted the team on their return from New York and the team responded with a doubleheader sweep over Cleveland to go up by four and a half games over the Yankees. There were 25,000 fans on hand, and even in the midst of the Great Depression, excitement about American League baseball was building again in Washington.

General Crowder, Jack Russell, Lefty Stewart and Earl Whitehill were pitching as well as Clark Griffith and Joe Cronin had foreseen in December when they put the staff together. It was the best staff in the American League as the Yankees pitchers continued to waver in the midsummer heat. But the Nationals' hitting was even better. There were those that gave the credit for the resurgence to Cronin, but the team had Clark Griffith written all over it.

New York and Philadelphia hit more than twice as many home runs as the scrappy crew Griff had patched together with his meager budget. But the Nationals were out-hitting them in every other category and scoring nearly as many runs with the old "inside baseball" that Clark Griffith had been preaching for more than three decades. Joe Cronin was merely the Old Fox's latest convert to learn that the old formula could still win championships.

The league lead jockeyed back and forth through July until the Yankees and Nationals played a four-game series at the end of July in Washington. Nursing a single game lead over the Yankees, the Nationals won the first two games behind the pitching of Jack Russell and the bat of Joe Kuhel, who knocked in four runs in an 11–5 win. New York won the next two to keep the race close. The Nationals won three in a row against Boston and when the two teams teed the ball up again a week later in New York, Washington was up by three games.

Feeling the pressure, the Yankees won the first two games to pull to within a game of the lead. It seemed to many as if the Nationals would wilt and turn the pennant over to the stronger club, but Earl Whitehill would not be bested as he pitched one of his best games of the season on August 8. He went the distance against the Bombers, giving up only five hits for his 14th win, 5–1. Monte Weaver won the next day and Washington extended its lead again to three games.

Clark Griffith was drawing crowds, and the speculation in the press was that Griffith was going to make money again with his 1933 team. Westbrook Pegler said as much in a column where he questioned whether Clark Griffith was the baseball romantic he held himself out to be, or just another business-man trying to manage his bottom line.[27]

Pegler did not understand the Old Fox's love for the game. As if to prove his point, Griff went out and bought the pitcher that he believed he needed to stay out in front as the teams came down the stretch. He purchased the contract of Butch Chapman from Rochester where he was 9–5, with his most impressive win coming over Baltimore with Griffith in attendance. Griffith was unspecific about how much he paid for Chapman, but said, "He cost plenty with extra money thrown in for early delivery."[28]

Chapman was not an issue as the race went into the make-or-break weeks of August. Whitehill, Weaver, and Crowder provided adequate pitching as the Nationals starters began a thirteen-game winning streak starting with the two wins over the Yankees on August 8 and 9. Whitehill held the Bronx Bombers to five hits in a 5–1 win and then Weaver came back and beat Lefty Gomez by a tighter score of 4–1.

The Nationals beat Boston three in a row and went on to extend their lead over the Yankees to eight and a half games. Heinie Manush had a 33-game hitting streak and along with Kuhel, Goslin and Cronin, the Nationals had the best attack in the American League in the final months.

Washington clinched the pennant on "Women's Day," September 21, which delighted Clark Griffith, whose mother-in-law Jeanne Robertson had been one of the most faithful fans at Griffith Stadium until she died in 1932. On that day Lefty Stewart beat the St. Louis Browns and Bump Hadley, 2–1, to assure a third American League pennant for the Nationals. The only thing Washington failed to do was win 100 games. But their record of 99 wins and 53 losses was the best ever posted by a Clark Griffith team or a Washington team.

Shirley Povich gave the credit for putting the team together to Joe Cronin. "It was he who conceived the pennant-winning lineup," wrote Povich the day after the Nationals beat the Browns to win it all. Cronin and Griffith had little time for deciding who deserved the credit as they sat on a trunk in the locker room being interviewed for radio and outdoing one another in crediting each other for the fine season.

The players had much to do with it and especially the pitchers. Crowder (24) and Whitehill (22) both won over 20 games. Crowder threw almost 300 innings, but Whitehill was the staff ace with 22 wins and an ERA of 3.33.

Jack Russell's impression of Firpo Marberry was the most convincing in years as he won both as a starter and reliever and led the team with a 2.69 ERA. Monty Weaver was good when he was healthy, but he was hurt several times during the season.

Joe Kuhel and Heinie Manush led the attack with batting averages of .322 and .336 respectively. Cronin led with 118 RBI and Kuhel, whose 11 home runs led the team, had 107. To the heart of the order was added Goose Goslin, who had a fine season as well. He was not quite the great "Goose of the Potomac" any more, though he managed to hit .297 with ten home runs.

The National League pennant race was not much closer than the AL as the New York Giants beat out the Pittsburgh Pirates by six games. John McGraw had stepped aside as the manager of the Giants after the 1932 season and watched the '33 season from the stands.

McGraw had been called back onto the field to manage the National League team in the very first All-Star Game played in Chicago's Comiskey Park. The game was the brain child of sports writer Arch Ward of the *Chicago Tribune*, who proposed the game be part of the Chicago Exposition and benefit the pension fund for old ball players. Connie Mack was in the American League dugout as manager, and two of the greatest men ever to guide baseball teams were fitting opponents for the first All-Star contest.

The game was a huge success, drawing a crowd of almost 50,000 and many more gathered around radios as the game was broadcast by both NBC and CBS radio.[29] With Crowder and Cronin representing the Nationals, the American League won, 4–2. Somehow Clark Griffith should have been part of the fun.

Bill Terry had taken over from McGraw as the manager of the Giants and had the best pitcher in the game in Carl Hubbell. John McGraw was dying in 1933. He did not yet know it, but he had suffered for years with what would become in later years a treatable prostate cancer. McGraw, Connie Mack and Clark Griffith were the three most recognizable faces left in the game from an era when baseball had been played much differently. All three men adapted and prospered as the game changed in the 1920s, but by 1933 they were in danger of running aground.

John McGraw died the following winter and never saw the game move beyond what the three great stars had known from the prior era. "To the end McGraw saw putting together a winning team as mainly a matter of spotting and buying the best talent in the higher minors and buying and trading for what was available in the majors."[30] It was the formula Clark Griffith and Connie Mack still employed. Griff had made it work for one more time in 1933, spending his last buffalo nickel to build a pennant-winning team, and he was going up against the Giants in the World Series again. His only regret may have been that his oldest nemesis and one of the greatest competitors ever involved with the game, Muggsy McGraw, was not there trying to beat the Old Fox at his best.

The Giants' Bill Terry was one of the many player-managers employed during 1933 to help baseball owners get the most out of their payroll. He was still one of the best players in the game, but he was overshadowed by two unique talents. In 1933 the Giants' Carl Hubbell had one of the most dominating seasons of any pitcher since Walter Johnson retired. He led the National League with a remarkable 1.66 ERA and his 23 wins led the league as well. Hall of Fame slugger Mel Ott backed Bill Terry in the lineup and was the key to the Giants' attack.

The most notable statistic for 1933 was the difference between the two leagues. The National League had become a pitcher's league with the different baseball in use with the thicker cover. The average runs per game in the National League in 1933 was less than four, while in the American League it was exactly five runs per game. Jimmie Foxx's 48 home runs led the American League while the best the National League could show was Chuck Klein's 28. Mel Ott was still only 24 years old, but managed 23 home runs and was third in the league.

Carl Hubbell's fine performance has to be seen through the prism of that league differential, but it is not intended to diminish his performance any more than pointing out the advantage Walter Johnson had pitching in Griffith Stadium. Carl Hubbell was the Most Valuable Player in the National League in 1933 and almost single-handedly put the Washington Nationals at a disadvantage going into the World Series.

The series started in New York at the Polo Grounds. Clark Griffith had once fought for ink against games played at the crosstown park, spurring the local press to provide equal space to the Highlanders, but that had been before there was even a fall baseball championship between the two leagues. Now he was assured a chance to play against his old rivals in the fall classic and there was no doubt about his equal billing in 1933. Now the focus was all about the Old Fox and who his starting pitcher would be in Game One.

"Cronin runs the team without any advice or suggestions from me," Griffith told the press.[31] Joe Cronin respected Clark Griffith too much to rely on his own counsel, however, and the two men debated who should start for Washington against Hubbell. Cronin decided late that Lefty Stewart was the best choice against Ott and Terry, who both batted from the left side. The odds makers favored the Nationals based on their superior offensive profile.[32]

It was the depths of the Depression, and the owners worried that attendance would be down during the two games in New York. Pre-game sales lagged behind their levels from 1924, so to make matters more affordable tickets were put on sale the day of the first World Series game at $1.10. When the box office opened in the morning a crush of fans created a mob scene that resulted in numerous injuries before police on horseback restored order.[33]

The first game was sold out and Carl "King Carl" Hubbell and the bargain ticket holders were there to see whether he could be the great leveling influence between the two teams. He had ten shutouts in 1933 and he looked just as dominant against Washington as he struck out ten Nationals hitters during a complete-game win. Ossie Bluege went down swinging three times, but he had plenty of company as the Nationals were unable to solve the Hubbell screwball. Cronin and Griffith had imported Garland Braxton to pitch batting practice, using his screwball to help the Nationals hitters anticipate Hubbell's offerings, but it did little good.[34]

The Nationals were able to score, but were too far in the hole to matter. Mel Ott was unimpressed with Lefty Stewart and his home run in the first inning to right field gave New York a two-run lead it would not relinquish. Jack Russell relieved Stewart in the third inning and shut down the Giants the rest of the way, but the damage had been done.

Mel Ott went four-for-four during the game and drove in the third and decisive run in the third inning before Russell was summoned by Joe Cronin. Washington did not quit. They loaded the bases in the ninth and closed the margin to two runs, but Hubbell's screwball still had enough swerve to set the uprising down and win the game, 4–2.

In the second game, Giants pitcher Hal Schumacher was not as baffling as Hubbell, but had greater effect, winning 6–1. General Crowder was ineffective for Washington. The Nationals could manage only five hits, ending the speculation that the American League's offense was better than the senior circuit's.

Thousands of Nationals fans made the trip to New York and they were not willing to concede defeat as the two teams arrived in Union Station for three games in Washington. No one knew better than Washington fans how easily momentum could swing in the World Series. They had watched Pittsburgh come from behind in 1925, so there they were, several thousand strong at the train station to greet the two teams who disembarked together, the Giants led by none other than John McGraw, who was traveling with the team.

Cronin held a team meeting at Griffith Stadium before the third game to pump life back into the deflated spirits of his team. President Roosevelt recreated his opening day toss before a disappointing crowd of only 25,000 fans. Earl Whitehill, ace of the Washington staff, gave the faithful reason for hope by tossing his own complete game gem to rival Hubbell. Though he struck out only two batters, he gave up only five hits and shut out the Giants,

4–0. Mel Ott and Bill Terry were held hitless by Whitehill's left-handed offerings. Buddy Myer was the other hero of the game, going three-for-four and driving in two runs from the leadoff spot.

Many had speculated that Monte Weaver would pitch in Game One against Hubbell, but Cronin went back to the pitching lineup he had used against the Yankees so successfully: Stewart, Crowder and Whitehill. In Game Four, however, it was Weaver's turn and he matched Hubbell through ten innings. Neither team was able to break through for more than a single run. Bill Terry's home run in the fourth inning was the only offense the Giants could muster against Weaver.

Joe Kuhel was having a tough Series going into Game Four and tried to bunt against Hubbell in the seventh inning. King Carl fumbled the ball, allowing Kuhel to reach. Bluege bunted Kuhel to second and Luke Sewell brought him in with a single to center to tie the score.

Monte Weaver gave the Nationals three more chances to win the game as he blanked the Giants in the eighth, ninth and tenth innings. Joe Cronin had a chance to win it in the bottom of the tenth inning with two men on base and two out, but he grounded out. In the 11th inning, Monte Weaver allowed a leadoff single to Travis Jackson. After a sacrifice bunt, he came around to score when eighth-place hitter Blondy Ryan singled him in. Cronin brought in Jack Russell to close out the inning, but the damage was done.

The Nationals had the bases loaded against Hubbell in the bottom of the eleventh inning and Cronin had to make a choice as to his pinch-hitter. His best choices were 43-year-old veteran Sam Rice, who had hit .294 in limited action during the season, and Cliff Bolton, a rookie with a .410 average in a partial season with the Nationals that year. In the top half of the inning, Bill Terry had been unable to pinch-run for the injured Travis Jackson because the rookie he asked to go in had been shaking so badly he decided it unwise to use him.[35]

Nonetheless, Cronin went with the rookie Bolton in one of the most high-pressure situations imaginable. To complicate matters, the rookie was up against the best pitcher in the game with a pitch he had never seen before. The Giants got the double-play ball they needed and put the Nationals into a deep World Series hole — down three games to one.

A highlight of the game came when fans were treated to an outburst of temper from Heinie Manush, who argued a close call at first base with umpire Charlie Moran. Manush claimed he was safe on a close call at the bag, and his vitriol was undiminished as he was joined by Joe Cronin and Luke Sewell, the three men circling Moran and heaping abuse upon him. Then head umpire George Moriarty walked over to the group quietly. Moriarty was known for fighting the entire Chicago White Sox team during a dust-up the previous season. The contest had been rated a draw.[36] "The arrival of Mr. Moriarty with his large physique and his impressive reputation as a useful man in a riot, seemed to cool off all of the boys."[37]

Bad calls were quickly forgotten by the Nationals, who now had their backs to the wall. Rain had dampened spirits before the first game and for the fifth game of the 1933 World Series. A little more than 28,000 fans were on hand. It was far less than the sellouts that had watched in 1924 and '25, yet those who were in attendance saw another tense and well-played game.

General Crowder was in a rematch against Hal Schumacher. Schumacher got the best of it early again, but the Nationals broke through finally in the bottom of the sixth inning to tie the score by scoring three times. Fred Schulte and Joe Cronin had the best Series of any Washington hitters. Schulte hit a home run to deep left field with Cronin and Manush aboard that knotted the game, 3–3.

The game remained a tie until the top of the tenth inning, when Jack Russell allowed a two-out fly ball to Mel Ott that carried to the wall. Fred Schulte leapt to the top of the temporary wall and got his glove on the ball, but his forward motion carried him into the crowd without the ball. It was unclear whether the call was a home run or a double.

Mel Ott stood on second while Washington favorites, Umpires Moran and Moriarty, debated the decision. Finally, Moriarty signaled a home run. After another protracted argument, the Nationals got their chance in the bottom of the tenth against Cuban pitcher Dolph Luque, who had shut them down since the 6th inning. With the heart of the order up, Goslin grounded out and Manush lined out. Cronin got a single and Schulte a walk to keep the fans in suspense, but Joe Kuhel fanned on three straight pitches, and the second straight World Series loss for Clark Griffith's Nationals went into the books.

Great pitching beat the superior offensive lineup that Washington threw at Carl Hubbell, Hal Schumacher and Freddie Fitzsimmons. Clark Griffith said as much after the final game. "We were out-hit, out-pitched, and even out-bunted."[38] Griffith was convinced that his team was the better of the two and said as much — sounding every bit as poor a loser as John McGraw in 1924. He criticized the Series, but left the exact nature of concern unspoken. Many believed Schulte had caught Mel Ott's fly ball. Griffith said, "It was the best World Series I ever saw and but for one bad decision would have been the best in history."[39]

Griffith never elaborated beyond that vague critique. It was most likely a reference to the umpire's decision, but it just as easily could have been a reference to the use of National League rules for the Series or his manager's selection of pinch-hitters. If the criticisms were about his manager, they were muted when Griffith gave Cronin a three-year contract to manage the Nationals going forward at $23,000 per year.[40]

Shirley Povich noted the irony of Griffith signing his second boy manager to a three-year deal just as he had done with Bucky Harris after the 1925 World Series. That contract had included one of the worst runs by the Nationals during Clark Griffith's tenure. Povich had considerable confidence in Joe Cronin, however, and voiced it consistently during the second half of the season, giving Cronin much of the credit for the moves that created the team and its winning drive to a pennant. He closed the column with a portentous note: "Some day, however, Griffith will step down. Methinks Cronin will move in upstairs."[41]

CHAPTER 20

Finding the Road Tilts Upward

The Old Fox dug deep to put together the championship run in 1933 and as he headed into the 1934 season he did not rest on his laurels. Yet there was a disappointing bounty to feed the beast. The World Series purse in 1933 was diminished by the much smaller crowds in Washington. The shortened series did less to generate funds as well. Neither team sold out its stadium for a single game except the opener, when ticket prices were lowered. Nor did Griffith's pennant-winning team draw well during the regular season. The attendance in 1925 of 817,199 was nearly double the 437,533 who came out to see the last Washington pennant winner in 1933.

Griffith had realized large profits after his two championship seasons in the 1920s. After four years when he lost money — from 1929 to 1932 — he had bet that by spending heavily to build a winner he could reach profitability again. Like Roosevelt and his New Deal, the Old Fox attempted his own version of deficit spending to claw his way back to economic health. But what would eventually work for the country was not working at Griffith Stadium in 1933, and Clark Griffith approached the December baseball meetings after the season as if he needed to shed a few pounds after a hearty Thanksgiving dinner.

Joe Cronin wanted to stand pat and said as much. "All we want to do is hold what we got."[1] Cronin admitted that talks had been held about Goose Goslin but seemed skeptical that any team would give Washington enough to make trading one of their best hitters worthwhile. Clark Griffith was driven by other considerations, and only days after the owners meetings commenced, the "Goose of the Potomac" was headed to Detroit for outfielder John Stone.

Stone was not the offensive force that Goslin was in his prime, but the Goose no longer produced those numbers either, while still getting paid as an established star. Joe Kuhel, Heinie Manush and Joe Cronin all out-hit Goslin during the 1933 season. Griffith and Goslin had squared off over con-

243

tract demands in years past, so John Stone was a cheap knock-off brand that played better in a tough market. Cronin was not anxious to part with Goslin, but it was Cronin's own new three-year salary that may have necessitated the trade.

Griffith was looking for help as always from young players. When Ossie Bluege was hurt in 1933, Cecil Travis had filled in capably, hitting .302 in 43 at-bats. He was the best prospect that Joe Engel had in Chattanooga and Bluege had continued his struggles into the post-season, hitting only .125 in the World Series. Both Cronin and Griffith had put the blame on the hitters for their October loss. So there was an opening for the youngster if he could hit.

Griffith opened the door when he said at the December meetings, "I am not satisfied with the work of Ossie Bluege and Luke Sewell."[2] Sewell had hit well during the 1933 season and was considered one of the best defensive receivers in the American League, but Griffith wanted to give young Cliff Bolton a look as catcher.

Griffith's dissatisfaction with his veterans like Goslin continued as he gave Sam Rice his release in January. His letter to Rice was "near heart-rending."[3] The letter read, "It is with deep regret that your time of service with the Washington club has ended, but I hope that our personal friendship will carry on for all time." Griffith's letter included a long salute to Rice's service with the team. "You were ever willing to give your best and oh what that best was. I consider you one of the best ball players of all time and the Washington fans and myself will miss you."[4]

Griffith was searching for young talent much as he always had. He had a new scout working for him in 1934, an Italian named Joe Cambria who owned a laundry business in Baltimore and numerous minor league teams, including the one in Albany, New York. Cambria became increasingly important to Griffith over time, supplanting Joe Engel, who became tethered to his venture in Chattanooga and less capable of scouting trips.

Cambria and Griffith had first encountered each other sitting in the stands in Washington watching sandlot baseball, the way Griff always had, hoping to find unlikely talent playing for teams like the Old Heurich Brewers. Griffith was looking for pitching and it was getting hard to find talent that had not already signed with the Cardinals, the Yankees or someone else well before Griffith could find them.

Griffith needed young talent because he knew that pitchers like Earl Whitehill did not have much left. But he and Cronin talked confidently during the off-season about the pitching staff as it stood. Despite Earl Whitehill's age, when he teamed with Crowder, Stewart and Weaver it seemed a solid rotation, especially with Jack Russell filling in behind them. Griffith was hoping that Monte Weaver would be healthier in 1934 and that the young Virginian would step to the front of the pitching rotation. "I figure our pitching will be better with Monte Weaver returning to top form."[5]

Although Griffith and Cronin argued publicly that they had added punch to the lineup, they were playing a pat hand and hoping they were less weakened than their chief competitors, the Athletics and Yankees. They hoped to get much the same performance from their team in 1934 as in '33 and if the opportunity presented itself Griffith would add talent like he always did. Even with the dustbowl raging and attendance falling, Cronin hoped the 1934 season would follow on 1933 like 1925 had followed 1924.

Shirley Povich was the only one who seemed to understand what the future held. In a column in late March he recalled a cartoon about the 1925 Nationals pitching staff that lampooned the age of the staff and showed their arms separated at the shoulder and still attached to the ball as both came toward the plate. He recalled when the 1925 team had been called the "Old Man's Home" of the American League and noted that Griffith had been told then that he needed to begin to rebuild around younger talent.[6] He saw the '34 pitching staff more along those lines — in need of new talent.

The 1934 season got off to the worst kind of start when the presidential opener was called by a persistent rain. The game had not been a sell-out, but Griffith was forced to provide all in attendance with rain checks and he lost one of the best crowds of the year. Washington was forced to open the season two days later in Boston, with the president's official toss pushed back to April 24.

The Nationals won the first two games in Boston with General Crowder winning the opener in 11 innings. Earl Whitehill started the first game but was knocked out in the sixth innings. Jack Russell and Crowder pitched in relief. Griffith and Cronin were looking for Crowder to be the kind of pitcher Walter Johnson once had been — a valuable starter who could pitch whenever he was needed.

In Whitehill's first game in 1933 he had beaten Earnshaw and the Athletics with a complete-game effort. The 35-year-old left-hander was game, but his results would ultimately match the prior season's. Still, Cronin and Griffith heralded their opening day win as evidence that the season was on track.

In the early going the Nationals stayed in the middle of the pack, playing just above .500 baseball. By Memorial Day the Nationals were in fourth, just behind Detroit, with Walter Johnson's Cleveland team leading the league by a half-game over the Yankees. The pitching was holding up and Cecil Travis had staked a claim on third base, hitting well over .300. Heinie Manush was near the league lead in hitting and John Stone was producing, though perhaps not as well as Goose Goslin.

At the end of June the team was in third place with a 36–32 record, and a two-game series in New York against the Yankees offering a chance to get back into the race. The press gave the series all of the play they had in the prior year when the Nationals had returned to Washington in a dead heat with the Yankees, looking to win the American League title.

There was no repeat performance. Washington lost both of the games in New York and began a steep, unending descent that saw the team win only eight times during the month of July. They rallied briefly in August, but by the end of the season the Nationals had sunk to seventh place, the worst finish for a Clark Griffith team since 1919.

Povich's March analysis of the pitching proved prescient. Whitehill, Weaver and Steward, who had been so good in 1933, all had ERAs of over 4. General Crowder, whose 50 wins in the prior two years had been the best on the staff, was waived in August after a sore arm rendered him increasingly ineffective. He had appeared in over 100 games in the prior two seasons as well, and also 35, he was done two years later, probably the victim of over-use.

The only positive light cast was that of Joe Cronin managing the American League All-Star team with Walter Johnson and Al Schacht coaching in the dugout alongside the younger man. The star of the All-Star Game was Carl Hubbell, who struck out Babe Ruth, Lou Gehrig, Jimmie Foxx, Al Simmons and Joe Cronin in succession, but the American League rallied to win, 9–7.[7]

Cronin's star was ascendant. He was the best shortstop in the league and his reputation as an on-the-field leader was second to none. Headed in the opposite direction was the financial situation for the Washington Nationals. Attendance dropped to 330,000 fans in 1934, the lowest figure since 1919. With gate receipts as the biggest source of revenue for major league teams, Griffith was in the worst financial situation since acquiring majority ownership of the team in 1919.

Griffith knew that even if he could find the way to win another pennant, it would not be enough. The payback for the 1933 season had only allowed him to break even. There was no ready answer for recovering from the disastrous finish of his 1934 Nationals. The failures of 1934 left him with the as many creditors as a Depression-era widow surrounded by a starving brood.

He did not throw in the towel, however, and continued to shop for talent, cementing his relationship with Joe Cambia as his newest chief scout. In September, with the season lost because of a disintegrating pitching staff, he bought players from Cambia's Albany team.[8] He spent only $5,000 for four players, but the return Griffith was getting for his money was dropping off dramatically. It was a pittance compared to the money he had spent each season to put together his three pennant-winning teams, but it was all he had as the disastrous 1934 season limped to its conclusion.

Clark Griffith was forced to confront the same reality that Connie Mack faced every year after his championship season in 1931. Balancing his accounting ledger at the end of the season had forced Mack to sell off the pieces of that '31 team. His 1934 team was almost as bad as Griff's after he sold Lefty Grove and Rube Walberg to Tom Yawkey for $100,000 and $35,000, respectively, to start the '34 season.[9]

Griffith had once bought the bargain pieces that the St. Louis Browns were offering and had crafted them into his 1933 AL pennant winners. But the shoe was on the other foot now. Joe Cronin was the best player Griffith had, and Cronin's new contract for $23,000 made him the highest paid player on the team. It was two salaries — both player and manager. By comparison, however, Heinie Manush, the next-best player on the team, made little more than $10,000 in 1934.

One reason the Washington season had finished so poorly was a bit of bad luck, a freak accident when Cronin broke his arm on September 3 in a collision at first base. He sat out the final four weeks of the season during which the Nationals sank from sixth to seventh. Although Cronin was disheartened by the end of his season, he had good things happening in his life off the field. He secretly had become engaged to Mildred Robertson, Clark Griffith's niece and executive secretary, in the spring of 1934 after a covert but determined courtship.

When Cronin's season ended, Clark Griffith encouraged his manager to proceed with his wedding plans and not to wait for the end of the season. It was unlike the Old Fox to concede anything, much less to allow his player manager to abdicate, but Griffith said only to go.

Shirley Povich was one of the few to speculate openly that the closeness of the two men marked Cronin as a possible heir to the Old Fox's team, and he said so on several occasions. Povich had the ear of Clark Giffith, however, and in September after the marriage was announced, Povich speculated, "Joe was in the family now and would succeed Griffith as President of the Washington Club in some year not too distant."[10]

Clark Griffith saw the situation differently or at least maintained in public that he did. "I loved the boy as if he were my own son," Griffith admitted, but he believed that having Cronin part of the family opened him to charges of nepotism.[11] "There was a lot of in-law talk around the league that year," Griffith asserted, believing that the talk about his favoring his new son-in-law would only get worse.[12]

In August of 1934, Eddie Collins, who had first helped his old friend Tom Yawkey buy the Boston Red Sox before the '33 season, stated in the

Boston press that Joe Cronin would look better in a Boston uniform than a Washington one. Griffith was angered by the piece and wrote to Collins to squash any further rumors. But it was only weeks later that Griffith allowed his injured manager Cronin to depart with a month left in the season.

According to all accounts, however, it was in October, at the World Series, when Yawkey sought Griffith out and made his first explicit offer to purchase Cronin for $250,000. Griffith was in serious debt, owing one Washington bank $124,000 at the end of the 1934 season.[13] Attendance was down and did not show signs of bouncing back after the worst season in memory.

Although the Great Depression was abating, there were no economic certainties in 1934 and with banks continued to fail at alarming rates, few could afford to keep outstanding debts for long. There was no privilege for baseball magnates whose books looked shaky.

On October 27 the news was announced officially on the front page of the *Washington Post*: "Joe Cronin is Sold to Red Sox in Game's Biggest Cash Deal."[14] The article cited the $30,000 in annual salary that Cronin would make, the great opportunities opening up for the young man, and Clark Griffith's sanguine appraisal of the situation, but it was front page news because it was the death knell for the team. The same bells that had tolled for Connie Mack's Athletics rang out across the front page of the Washington press.

Clark Griffith was in a very difficult position and it is doubtful he had any other option. The 1934 season made it more than evident that the team needed serious re-building, but he had not a penny to contemplate the task.

According to Griffith's accounts that surfaced over the years, he only reluctantly replied to Yawkey and he claimed that he did so with all the grit with which he always approached the game. As proof of his gameness, he offered his demand to Yawkey for Lyn Lary to replace Cronin.

In truth Lary had just completed a very disappointing season for the Red Sox. Yawkey was asking for the best shortstop in the American League, so letting Lary go was an easy decision and the only value it had was as a face-saving device for Griffith. To Griffith's credit he did secure a promise that his son-in-law would get a five-year contract, one that provided the kind of financial security Griff believed Cronin deserved.

After completing the deal, Griffith contacted the honeymooning couple in California and asked Cronin whether he was comfortable with the sale. After explaining the parameters of the agreement for both men, Cronin concurred. "Mr. Griffith was like a father to me," Cronin said, but he understood the career implications.[15]

Yawkey had paid large money for Lefty Grove and was clearly intent on building a winner for the Fenway faithful, whatever it took. Although the emotional connection with Griffith may have tugged at Cronin, he was putting himself at the head of Yawkey's very ambitious enterprise as player-manager. He had a contract for the next five years and a chance to compete against the Yankees at the head of one of the few organizations that had the money to do so. Clark Griffith was catapulting Cronin to stardom, offering him an exit from a sinking ship.

Cronin requested to take Al Schacht along to Boston as a coach. "I said it was all right with me if Schacht wanted to go," said Griff.[16] Schacht got on the same train with Cronin and took his act to Boston after 15 years in Washington. Cronin was taking Clark Griffith's executive secretary and his third base coach. When Yawkey threw in Lyn Lary for Griffith, he was just being polite.

Even with the additional funds from Yawkey, the Nationals still did little better than break even in 1934.[17] The bank note for $124,000 was just part of the debt Clark Griffith confronted when he sold Cronin, and most of the money went to get the team back on solid financial footing.

Griffith hired Bucky Harris to replace Cronin as manager in November. He offered Harris a salary of only $11,000.[18] Harris's record with Detroit had been disappointing. Nonetheless Yawkey had hired him to manage the Red Sox in 1934 and he brought the team home in fourth place, its highest finish since 1918.

Harris no longer commanded the formidable money he once had gotten from Clark Griffith. He was a loyal and trusted co-conspirator, however, and both men were genuinely happy to be reunited. Whether either had the faith or burning fire that once existed in 1924 was another matter. "I think I know what Griff wants and I think I can give it to him," said Harris when his hiring was announced.[19] It was not a promise to put the team in the World Series again, more an admission that he was filling an empty niche as well as could be expected.

The two men set out to build a contender, but were aware that their problems exceeded anything that could be solved quickly. To counter the growing grip of teams like the Cardinals on minor league talent, Griffith used the funds left from the sale of Cronin to purchase two franchises, one in Selma, Alabama, and another in Panama City, Florida.[20] They played at the C and D levels and were unlikely to produce talent in the near future, which Griffith was the first to acknowledge. The Southeastern League in which they played folded and the purchase was voided.

In March he bought two more minor league teams, this time in Pennsylvania, one in Harrisburg and the other in Lancaster. Harrisburg played in the New York-Penn League and Lancaster in the Pennsylvania State League.[21] Joe Cambria, who owned the Albany, New York, team playing in the International League, facilitated the deals. The two teams expanded Griffith's farm system to encompass Chattanooga, Albany, Panama City, Harrisburg and Lancaster. Griffith was endorsing the "Chain-Store" battle that Commissioner Landis had fought gamely. Branch Rickey's initiative to build farm systems was catching on with even the Old Fox.

Other teams had successfully outflanked Rickey by constructing their own extensive minor league systems, each with showcase venues for their best talent. The Yankees owned the Newark Bears and the Cubs owned the Los Angeles Angels — two of the best minor league franchises of the decade.[22] Two of the richest teams in baseball, the Cubs and Yankees, were able to compete on a level playing field with Rickey.

Clark Griffith's purchase of small teams in the rural south and in the Northeast was not enough to bring him into serious competition with the richer teams. He was starting late and the key ingredient was still capital with which to fill the rosters of these farm teams.

Another move that would have far more consequences in the long term occurred when he added his nephew Calvin to the organization in 1935. As Cronin emptied his locker at Griffith Stadium at the end of 1934, Calvin Griffith stepped into the larger niche that Shirley Povich had seen for Cronin as the heir to the Old Fox's executive office at Griffith Stadium. At the end of spring training in 1935 Clark Griffith dispatched his nephew Calvin Griffith to Chattanooga to apprentice in baseball management with the Old Fox's best talent, Joe Engel.[23]

Calvin was studying at George Washington University in 1934 and playing baseball for the Colonials. He was more talented as a ball player than as a student, but not likely to achieve stardom in either endeavor. Calvin was exposed during his adolescence to every great mind in the game. He sat in on discussions between his uncle and Connie Mack and Joe McCarthy as they discussed the trends in the game and the business of baseball. He listened as his uncle and Joe Cronin talked strategy for the 1933 World Series, and how to deal with Carl Hubbell.

There was a world-class education in baseball there for the taking and Calvin Griffith was a willing student. He began a graduate course of study as the Secretary-Treasurer of the Chattanooga Lookouts for the 1935 season.

Confronting a new season in Washington, Clark Griffith knew Lyn Lary could not fill Joe Cronin's shoes at shortstop. Bucky Harris moved Ossie Bluege to short and put Cecil Travis at third. Travis became part of a talented infield that also included Joe Kuhel and Buddy Myer. Heinie Manush provide help in the outfield, but the team hit only 32 home runs, the lowest by far in the major leagues in 1935. Although Buddy Myer excelled with a league-leading .349 average, nobody on the team hit more than six home runs. Their batting average of .285 was second only to the pennant-winning Tigers, but

Detroit had Hank Greenberg, who hit 36 home runs to eclipse the total by the entire Nationals team.

Griffith could not compete for that kind of talent any longer, and the lack of star power was hurting attendance. Crowds in 1935 fell off even more than in 1934, as attendance at Griffith Stadium dropped to 255,000 fans. Only the lowly St. Louis Browns were in more serious trouble when they brought only 81,000 fans to Sportsman's Park. The lack of paying fans was diminishing Griffith's ability to afford player development and support for his new farm teams.

Cecil Travis was one of the last players Griffith would develop during the pre-war years. He bought players on the periphery of the market when they were not sought by the top teams. He brought Carl Reynolds and Earl Whitehill back in 1936 and the team finished third. It was the best finish for the team after the 1934 disaster until the outbreak of war in 1941.

The 1936 season made it seem that Griffith could still field a competitive team the way he once had, buying spot talent on the open market and bringing along the core talent he scouted and developed close to home. In mid-season he traded for outfielder Ben Chapman of the Yankees, who was made expendable by the arrival of Joe DiMaggio. Chapman joined John Stone in the Washington outfield and the two men provided the kind of speed and power that Goslin and Rice once had.

Joe Kuhel had a big year in 1936 and along with Cecil Travers and rookie Buddy Lewis they provided a solid infield. But team captain Buddy Myer was out most of the season with a stomach ailment that never seemed to give way. Missing the American League batting champ in 1935, the most important cog in the Nationals lineup, may have hampered a higher finish for one of Griffith's last competitive teams.

Several of the better players on that 1936 team were developed by Griffith and Joe Engel, but they were never able to find a pitching staff that could compete. In a decade when Branch Rickey found and signed talent like Dizzy and Paul Dean in obscure pockets of the Ozarks, Griffith came to rely increasingly on Joe Cambria, whose links to Cuban baseball intrigued the Old Fox.

Clark Griffith had been the first in major league baseball to sign Cuban ball players when in 1911 he had inked third baseman Rafael Almeida and outfielder Armando Marsans for the Cincinnati Reds.[24] Marsans had greater success than Almeida, and both played in the majors after 1911. In 1936 Cambria brought up his first and most controversial contribution to the Washington baseball club in Bobby Estalella. Estalella was born in Cardenas, Cuba, and was dark-skinned enough to raise immediate suspicion about his racial heritage.[25]

Cambria spent so much time scouting in Cuba that in later years he would claim to have scouted Fidel Castro.[26] The claim grew in Washington legend, but got little credibility from historians. Cambria was known more for his "exploitation of Cuban players — signing them to blank contracts and then burying them on his minor league teams," which raised questions about Cambria's moral compass.[27]

Estalella was the first significant Cuban talent Cambria brought through his system to the majors. Estalella was the test case for Cambria's theory that Cuban talent could compete equally in the majors. Estelella was of mulatto background and Griffith had been careful to avoid that issue in Cincinnati in 1911. He had verified that both Marsans and Almeida were of Hispanic heritage. Estalella was less so, but was light-skinned and spoke Spanish, so there was little concern that he would be challenged on racial grounds. Even in the market for Hispanic players, Griffith was behind the curve. In 1936 Tom Yawkey boasted Mel Almada, born in Mexico but raised in Los Angeles, who had a breakout season in '35 for the Red Sox.

Estalella was the first Washington foray by Griffith and Cambria into Cuban baseball. There would be others, and Cambria would be a conduit for Clark Griffith to get involved in Negro Leagues baseball. Cambria had owned the Baltimore Black Sox in 1932. He had little money to support the team and his ownership was neither successful nor long term.[28] Cambria moved on to the Albany team.

In 1936 Cambria became the manager of the Salisbury, Maryland, Indians, a Class D team, in 1937. They were one of the more successful minor league teams that year, and Clark Griffith bought five players from Cambria, though none ever played more than a handful of games.[29]

Despite casting a wide net for talent in the middle of the decade, by the 1936 season it became increasingly clear to baseball experts that the sport was becoming a bigger business than Clark Griffith had resources to sustain. Connie Mack was addressing similar concerns in Philadelphia with no greater success. Increasingly Griffith and Mack were becoming grand old men of the game who were tied to a past that was being left behind by radio, night games and other innovations and technologies being employed to expand the reach of the game and the riches of the owners.

In an article for the *Washington Post*, one of the owners of the original American League team in Washington, William Dwyer, lamented the changes that baseball had experienced since the days when home runs were hit into the queue of horse-drawn carriages outside the stadium. His final lament was for the departure of former players from the ranks of ownership. "At this writing, Clark Griffith is the only former player with controlling interest in a big league team."[30] The other teams were all owned by wealthy individuals with excess capital to devote to an expensive hobby, and Dwyer saw the game as diminished by losing the last connections between the front office and the playing field.

Clark Griffith fought a game battle to save Dwyer's vision. He held on to his small family-run operation by looking beyond the traditional boundaries for talent and an aggressive campaign to use Griffith Stadium for external events. Professional football was his most successful effort. Griffith had brought in football teams to play at Griffith Stadium from his first expansion of the stadium in 1923. He lured George Preston Marshall from Boston in 1936 when he brought his professional team to play in Griffith Stadium during the off-season. Griffith would find other lucrative uses for the stadium, but none that matched that of the Redskins, as they came to be called.

Griffith used the funds he was generating from outside sources to purchase major league talent whenever the opportunity arose. He bought Bobo Newsom in the middle of the 1935 campaign for $50,000 in hopes of spurring a run, but the team finished a distant sixth. With veterans like Newsom he was often buying little more than a headache for contract negotiations the following winter.

Searching the college ranks in Virginia and Maryland was another effort that the Old Fox tried repeatedly in the 1930s, hoping to find that diamond in the rough like Walter Johnson around whom to build a pitching staff. Though sandlot baseball was not the sport it once had been, Clark Griffith continued to attend those games as well. He had found Carl Cashion on Washington sandlots in 1912 and he was still watching the best of the Heurich Brewery team in 1936 with Joe Engel, hoping to find a big league talent in their star pitcher, Archie Scrivener.[31]

In 1934 NBC radio began airing Washington games, and Arch McDonald was the broadcaster. He was known as "The Old Pine Tree," for his musical introduction, a song of the same name by Ralph Stanley.[32] He began broadcasting for Joe Engel in Chattanooga, and like other talent made his way to Washington to work for Clark Griffith. McDonald interviewed Griffith and Harris for a special pre-season show broadcast in the city, but was limited to broadcasting only away games.[33] McDonald, like George P. Marshall, was a southerner and would become known as much for his ugly racial views as for his colorful broadcasts.

Griffith did not allow local games in Washington to be broadcast. He believed as others did that it kept paying customers at home listening on the radio. Griffith was among the last to relent, however, prohibiting home game broadcasts starting in 1938 as he continued to struggle to come to grips with new developments in the game.

Another innovation that Griffith opposed from its inception was night baseball. Night games spread through the minor leagues as a way to keep

these struggling ventures afloat in the worst-hit rural areas of the Depression. Night baseball came to the majors in 1935 when the Cincinnati Reds played their first games under the lights. Like every other team, the Reds were hurt by lagging attendance and, after watching minor league teams achieve success with it, Larry McPhail — the general manager — decided it made sense for Crosley Field.

Griffith was opposed to night games on the same grounds as anything else: it posed a threat to his bottom line. He did not have the capital to invest in new lighting for Griffith Stadium. As with most things, Griffith came around to see the wisdom of playing under the lights, but he sought help to subsidize their installation. Once he found the money for lighting, subsidized by an interest-free loan from the league, he would become a proponent of more night games in the run up to World War II. But the league was not providing subsidies for small-market teams in the 1930s.

Clark Griffith III, Griffith's grandson, came to know the financial aspects of the old Nationals as well as anyone. He cited the shortcomings of Griffith Stadium as one of the enduring hardships faced by his grandfather as time passed. The costs of maintaining it ate at the Old Fox, but it did not have the seating capacity to take advantage of the good years. "It was never a hugely profitable business," he said of the Nationals in his grandfather's day. "He was late into broadcasting, late into advertising, and just did not have the same resources as the large market teams like the Yankees."[34]

For the remainder of the 1930s, Griffith continued to search unsuccessfully for a pitching staff. His lineup — anchored by Cecil Travis, Buddy Myer, John Stone and Joe Kuhel — was respectable enough, but without pitching the team remained mired in the second division. In 1940 the team finished an abysmal seventh.

The highlight of Clark Griffith's tenure during the late 1930s was the 1937 All-Star Game. After the success of the first game in Chicago, the popularity of the concept took a hit in 1936 when it was played in Boston before 17,000 empty seats. The next year the All-Star Game was due to be played in a western city, but Clark Griffith proposed that Washington could provide the pomp and splendor to bring the game back to popular support. The other owners were well aware of Griffith's ability to stage a successful show, so they agreed.[35]

On July 7 Griffith staged what was probably his last great show at Griffith Stadium. With a sold-out crowd of 32,000 in the stands, President Roosevelt was paraded onto the field by a phalanx of Boy Scouts. He was seated in the Presidential Box, surrounded by cabinet members and Congressmen, Com-

Opposite: **1937 All Star Game at Griffith Stadium: Lou Gehrig, Joe Cronin, Bill Dickey, Joe DiMaggio, Charlie Gehringer, Jimmie Foxx, and Hank Greenberg (Library of Congress).**

missioner Landis and National League President Ford Frick. All of the players were led to the box to shake hands with the dignitaries before the game would begin, and Walter Johnson was in the broadcast booth to describe the game to a huge national radio crowd.[36]

To start the game, Lefty Grove was matched against the newest pitching star and a great showman in his own right, Dizzy Dean. Ironically the game would mark the beginning of the end of Old Diz's career after a line shot off the bat of Earl Averill hit Dean in the toe. He was never able to recover from the ensuing arm injuries. After 1937 Dean would never hum his "Old Number One" by the best hitters in the game with the great aplomb he once had. The home run he gave up to Lou Gehrig before Averill's shot was the highlight of the game. The event went down in the books as a great success, as the American League won, 8–3.[37]

It was Clark Griffith's last triumph after the 1933 American League pennant. During the regular season games at Griffith Stadium, he continued to be plagued by poor attendance and the inability to compete in the American League. He abandoned his minor league farm system within years of starting it. He sold the Chattanooga team to Joe Engel and abandoned his other teams. Before the war started in 1941 he still maintained a relationship with Chattanooga, an A-1 team in the Southern Association. He controlled only Charlotte in the Class B Piedmont League and Orlando in the Florida East Coast League.

Calvin Griffith was at Charlotte, where he continued to be groomed to take over control of his Uncle's declining empire. He married and assured that the family name would endure as his wife gave birth to a son, Clark Griffith III, on October 15, 1941. But the potential empire he might be heir to was diminishing in size and value as war approached.

The Old Fox was not going down without a fight, however, and in the owners meetings in 1939 Griffith pushed through a resolution that forbade the winner of the pennant from making any deals to improve their championship team. *The New York Times* described it saying it established Clark Griffith as the "No 1 Yankee Baiter in the Land." Griffith denied that the rule was aimed at the Yankees, saying he knew they were "about at an end."[38]

Despite his protests, the gambit was aimed clearly at the New York Yankees, and owner Ed Barrow fought it without success. Will Harridge, the president of the American League, and Walter Briggs, the Detroit owner, backed Griffith. The only move that the Yankees — or other pennant winner could make — was to add a player only after every other team.[39]

The move was all show, of course, and the only thing to slow down the Yankees would be the war. But show was such an important part of the Old Fox. It was when he was at his best, when he was the cock of the walk, still strutting out on the mound baiting the opposition batter into swinging at whatever the next pitch might be. He was as oppositional as ever and not willing to give in without a fight.

There was a bigger fight coming, though. The unique combination of toughness and grace that was Clark Griffith would excel as the nation set off into one of its longest and most costly tragedies — the Second World War.

CHAPTER 21

The War Years

The baseball owners were attending their annual December meeting at Chicago's Palmer House when the Japanese attacked Pearl Harbor and United States participation in the Second World War began. In the first article after Pearl Harbor, Shirley Povich speculated that the Japanese bombs "may have scored a direct hit on Chicago's Palmer House," implying that baseball would be shut down by the war.[1] He dismissed any chance that Clark Griffith might have to re-enact his efforts from 1918 to gain a continuance for baseball, saying his chances were "flimsy at best." He granted that there might be a need for diversions during a time of war, but hypothesized that war would be the death knell for Griffith's proposal to increase the number of night baseball games.

Clark Griffith, who had opposed night baseball, was now its most ardent champion. He had spent much of the December 1941 ownership meetings lobbying for an increase in the number of night games included on the master major league schedule. He was entertaining offers for Cecil Travis, whom Shirley Povich was speculating might be the next player the Old Fox would sell for a price of $250,000.

Blackouts would preclude any night games if there were to be baseball of any kind, Bob Considine observed in an article in which he coined the phrase "game called on account of blackout."[2] Clark Griffith hurried back to Washington from Chicago in December 1941. He concluded several trades that he had been discussing in Chicago by phone, but he knew better than any other owner or figure in the game the danger baseball was facing. Griffith met with Ford Frick to begin an effort to collect baseball equipment for the soldiers in a replay of the World War I effort that Griffith had led. The attack on Pearl Harbor had been on American soil and the peril that Germany posed in Europe made the new war less an affair that was "over there," and more one that was going to be fought with an all-out effort at home.

Griffith was not only organizing another bat and ball effort, he was lobbying President Roosevelt directly to allow the games to continue, much as he had done in World War One. Commissioner Landis sent a letter to Roosevelt requesting the 1942 season be allowed to move forward. Landis, however, had stridently opposed the President's New Deal programs and had made his opposition public, using his profile as Baseball Commissioner to add weight to his political opinions. Roosevelt was no friend of Landis.

Yet on January 15, 1942, little more than a month after Pearl Harbor, the president wrote to Commissioner Landis allowing the games to continue. "I honestly feel it would be best for the country to keep baseball going," Roosevelt wrote. "Americans will need to take their minds off work even more than before."[3] Roosevelt's memo came to be known as the "Green Light" memo. Its words could have and may have been penned by Clark Griffith. Whether he was the direct source of the words or not, Griffith took credit for the president's writing of them.

Griffith described Roosevelt's negative opinion of Landis, saying he was "not much more welcome at the White House than the Japanese ambassador."[4] Griffith's role as the wordsmith behind the "Green Light" letter is not certain, but it is difficult to believe that Roosevelt responded positively to a letter from Landis without prodding from his friend Clark Griffith, who had been supporting Roosevelt's trips to Griffith Stadium since the origins of the New Deal in 1933.

The first Washington players to be drafted into the service were probably the best, Cecil Travis and Buddy Lewis, who were drafted even before the war began and were lost for the 1942 season. Griffith was able to gain temporary exemptions from the war for many of his other players. He lobbied the draft director, General Hershey, and gained them deferments to finish the 1942 season.

After war was declared Griffith lost the ability to sell Cecil Travis or any other player, as they had no obligation to baseball that outstripped their obligation to country in the face of all-out war. Shirley Povich highlighted the young shortstop Travis, touting his brave heart and speedy legs as assets for any army facing down the Germans. Patriotic fervor gripped the country and everyone was looking for ways to contribute.

Some players were able to continue playing who were married or had some other family exemption from the draft, and many played under the President's limited deferment under his initial ruling that the game was essential to maintaining war-time morale.[5] Griffith also lobbied President Roosevelt heavily to allow night baseball. He dispatched an official letter to the president and got a favorable response, although the number of night games remained fixed at pre-war levels.

There is no doubt that the war spared the Old Fox its worst tragedies.

His adopted family survived intact and his team suffered less than some others did. His team benefited from the huge financial upsurge in Washington as the center of the war economy. He played his own unique role as ambassador for the game of baseball and its owners in the nation's capital, and the heightened visibility for the 73-year-old Griffith lent him a role as a patriarch of the game.

During the darkest hours in 1943 when every able-bodied man was caught up in the war, Griffith remained committed to playing the season. Baseball will continue, he said, "as long as each team can place nine men on the field, even if they are very old men."[6]

Although several of the Nationals' best players were eventually drafted and served extended tours of duty, several remained playing throughout the war. Bucky Harris remained the manager through the first two years of the war and many regulars made it through the first year of the war with him. George Case played every season during the war and led the league in steals from 1940–43. Yet the Nationals continued to haunt the nether regions of the American League, finishing sixth in 1941 and seventh in 1942.

Joe Engel contributed one of the best talents to surface during the prewar years. Early Winn was like Cecil Travis, another rural southerner lacking in sophistication, but full of a love for the game and a talent to match. He was signed by Engel for almost nothing when, according to Shirley Povich, Wynn "walked into the Sanford, Florida, training camp of the Senator's Chattanooga farm team ... wearing jeans, barefooted, with a glove dangling from his belt."[7] Clyde Milan was the manager for Engel's Lookouts team that year and Wynn impressed Milan enough to get a regular turn in the rotation. Wynn worked his way to Washington in 1941 and became one of Clark Griffith's last home-grown pitching talents.

Joe Cambria was still the most important talent scout for Griffith during the war years, and his role was enhanced by the desperate need for talent to fill war-depleted rosters. He filled in the holes the draft created, sometimes with remarkable new talent. Cambria had brought George Case to Washington where the track star became the regular left fielder and one of the showcase talents on the Nationals for nine seasons. One of Cambria's best finds was Mickey Vernon, who became the starting first baseman in 1941, the last season before the war.

Zeke Bonura had been the Nationals first baseman in 1940, taking his name for his "phys-zeke." His strong-man act played better with the ladies than with the opposing pitchers. Bonura's power translated into only 22 extrabase hits and it opened the door for Vernon to take over at first base in 1941.

Cambria discovered Vernon through his connections in the Maryland Eastern Shore League, where he maintained an ownership interest in the Salisbury team. Vernon played college ball for Villanova and had been signed by the St. Louis Browns, but Cambria lured him away to his Springfield, Massachusetts, team where he hit well over .300 for two seasons. Vernon's play made an impression on Clark Griffith, who saw in Vernon another Joe Judge. Vernon's tenure would last almost as long.

Cambria was more well-known for his Cuban connection, however, and Latin players filled important roster positions for the Nationals during the war. Since the Cuban and South American players were exempt from the draft, they were a key resource for Griffith. Bobby Estalella rejoined the Nationals during the war and was the regular third baseman in 1942. Then Griffith traded Estalella to Connie Mack for outfielder Bob Johnson, who was asking more money than Mack could afford.

In 1943 Griffith replaced Bucky Harris with Ossie Bluege as manager. Griffith said that he wanted more "fire" from his manager than Harris felt was warranted by the talent he was given.[8] It was the seventh time that Griffith had changed manager and every time he had sought out one of his family of former players. Those who played long years with the Old Fox maintained his greatest confidence, and Griffith invariably turned to one of them to manage his teams.

Griffith's relationship with Harris was merely taking another sabbatical. They would be reunited after the war and Harris would go on to manage the Yankees in the post-war era, taking them to a World Series Championship in 1947. Harris achieved as much fame managing teams like the Yankees and Nationals as he did during his playing days and he would always be indebted to Griffith for giving him that first vote of confidence, for making him the first of the Nationals' "boy managers" to make good.

Bluege took over a strong team given the circumstances of the war. Johnson, Case and Stanley Spence — who had hit .325 in 1942 — provided the Nationals a respectable outfield. Mickey Vernon had his second strong season with the bat, but it was the pitching that carried the Nationals to their strongest showing after 1933. Early Wynn anchored the rotation and Washington veteran Dutch Leonard had a good season pitching to the less impressive American League lineups depleted by war. Wynn won 18 games and Leonard 11 and both threw more than two hundred innings.

An important part of the 1943 pitching staff was Alex Carrasquel, a Venezuelan whom Cambria had signed. He was a part of the Nationals staff throughout the war years, but 1943 was his best year when he won 11 games. Behind the deep pitching staff the Nationals won 84 games and lost only 69 to finish second in the American League. Attendance was up substantially to levels that Washington had not seem since 1930, the last year before the Great Depression took its toll on teams like the Nationals.

In 1944 Joe Kuhel returned to Washington, but he was well past his prime and the team was more known for the Cuban contingent that played an even more prominent role as more players were compelled to leave the major leagues to comply with the newest "Work or Fight" order that was promulgated in 1943. The Cuban players, who included Roberto Ortiz, Mike Guerra and Carrasquel, were routinely subjected to racial harassment around the league.

The tensions between white and Hispanic players reached its apex in St. Louis when an altercation between George Case and Browns pitcher Nelson Potter spilled over into the Washington dugout. Mike Guerra had been taking insulting harangues from the Browns all day. Roberto Ortiz went to the aid of his friend Guerra, taking a bat after Browns catcher Tom Turner. He did not use the bat, but won a unanimous decision against Turner in a fight that was allowed to go several minutes before it was broken up.

Clark Griffith expanded the uses of Griffith Stadium to break even financially, and regular boxing cards were featured, including historic matches like that between Joe Louis and Buddy Baer. The Redskins, who played their home games at the stadium, were another big draw during the war years. Griffith Stadium was rented for a wide variety of entertainment that allowed Clark Griffith to maintain his only real passion, the Nationals.

He put Calvin Griffith in charge of concessions in 1941, and his nephew played an increasingly prominent role in managing the non-baseball side of the business. Calvin had mentored with Joe Engel in Chattanooga on how to run stadium operations, then moved on to running the Charlotte farm club where he served as president, treasurer and manager of the highest-level farm team the Nationals claimed.[9] When he came to Washington to manage his uncle's concessions, he oversaw boxing and wrestling as well. More importantly, he took a large role in the games played by the Homestead Grays.

In April of 1945 there was one last season to be played before the full contingent of players returned from the front lines. The war in Germany was won after soldiers like Cecil Travis fought across the western part of that country, defeating the once powerful German army decisively, grinding it to nothing in the process. But the peace was yet to be made with the Germans, and the war with Japan, while going well, still was taking a heavy toll in American lives.

On April 12 one of Clark Griffith's staunchest allies in the White House, Franklin Roosevelt, died. The country was grief-stricken by the passing of the President who had seen the nation through two of its greatest tragedies, the death and destruction of World War II and the deeply affecting economic malaise of the Great Depression. His death occurred with opening day just a week hence.

Harry Truman, a diminutive Missourian much like Clark Griffith, was sworn in as the President. When the baseball season began in Washington on April 21, the tone was a somber one as Roosevelt was remembered by the crowd of 25,000. "A minute of absolute silence broken only by the sound of a soldier's last tribute, "Taps," that was almost a prayer, made the picture more fitting a church than Griffith Stadium."[10] The Speaker of the House, the Texan Sam Rayburn, threw out the first pitch and in typical Texas style, over-threw the waiting throng of players considerably.

There was a new Baseball Commissioner as well. Landis had died in November after the 1944 season. Clark Griffith had been one of his staunchest allies and had been well served by that loyalty, but now Kentucky's former governor, "Happy" Chandler, took Landis's place. He announced that he would lobby for an All-Star Game in the summer although the game was suspended in 1944 until the war was concluded.

Chandler had a history in the game before he became a successful politician. He had played baseball in college and as a semi-pro, hoping to be spotted by one of those talent scouts like Joe Cambria. It never happened, but now he headed the game and had one thing Landis did not: connections in Washington. Chandler was an elected official with deep party ties to the Democrats, who looked like they would hold power forever. It was as if baseball was moving to replace its best spokesman in the nation's capital: the 75-year-old, white-haired, bushy eye-browed Clark Griffith.

The Washington lineup in 1945 continued its Cuban flavor as Gil Torres started at shortstop, Mike Guerra was the backup catcher, and Alex Carrasquel was a key member of the pitching staff. The staff relied heavily on knuckle-ballers, as four of the starters featured the pitch — Dutch Leonard, Roger Wolff, Johnny Niggeling, and Mickey Haefner.[11] Joe Kuhel at first base anchored the infield with a pesky second baseman named George Myatt who would have his best season in the game. George Binks and George Case started the season in the outfield, joined by Jake Powell.

Griffith's decision to acquire Powell from the Yankees in 1943 rankled the African-American community, where the Old Fox was winning fewer and fewer friends in 1945. Powell was well known for his baiting of Hispanic and Jewish players that had led to fights and other ugly confrontations. He was one of the most disliked players in the game and Griffith's willingness to continue playing him in Washington at this juncture was further evidence that increasingly he was preoccupied only by the need to keep his struggling business afloat and was largely insensitive to racial perceptions.

It was the effectiveness of the pitching staff that made the Nationals a threat in '45. Roger Wolff won twenty games and posted a fine 2.12 ERA. Dutch Leonard was just a step behind with 17 wins and a 2.12 ERA. It was the best staff in the league and Griffith was able to stretch his usually anemic offense in the last year of the war and make the runs count. In the middle of June the team was in its usual spot in the second division, holding down the sixth spot, when the team caught fire. Buddy Lewis came back from the war in early July and the team started to score runs, making Powell expendable.

The Nationals climbed to second place behind the Tigers and stayed there, trailing by only a game or two consistently through August and early September. It looked like they might win their first championship since 1933. But as a final measure of how far Clark Griffith had drifted from his roots, he had rented Griffith Stadium to the Redskins for the last few weeks of September to maximize their home games and the rent they paid. As a result the Nationals played a condensed schedule that included nine doubleheaders in September so that they could end their season on the 23rd of the month.

The fine pitching of Hal Newhouser, who led the league in about every category that year, was the most obvious reason that the Nationals lost out to the Tigers. The return of Hank Greenberg from the war was another as he hit a key home run in September to ice the pennant. Yet the knuckleballing pitchers of the Nationals were most effective during night games, and so many day-night doubleheaders down the stretch handicapped the team. Clark Griffith had dismissed any chance to win the season even before it began, an unheard-of admission by one of the game's grittiest competitors.

The war with Japan ended in August after the bombing of its major cities by all incendiary means possible. Their agreement to an unconditional surrender on August 14 ended one of the greatest human tragedies of all time and effectively began the post-war atomic era. Americans celebrated the end of the conflict and waved farewell to the Depression as any memory of tough times vanished in the jubilation of victory and spreading prosperity.

CHAPTER 22

Clark Griffith and
the Homestead Grays

Just weeks after the war's conclusion in August 1945, Branch Rickey announced his intention to integrate baseball the following season. Rickey scouted Jackie Robinson in Chicago with an eye toward the integration of baseball less than two weeks after peace with Japan was declared.[1] Rickey's announcement that he would breach the color barrier in baseball was the culmination of a long historical process that began well before World War II began, one in which Clark Griffith played a significant role.

Blacks in Washington, D.C., had long considered Clark Griffith a friend. The favorable impression Griffith enjoyed in the black community was based on his contrast to more openly racist figures such as George Preston Marshall. "Blacks almost never attended Redskins games because of Marshall, but enjoyed attending Griffith stadium for Nationals games," according to Brad Snyder, whose book *Beyond the Shadow of the Senators* examined the issue of Griffith's relationship with the African-American community in depth.[2]

Despite his positive image in the African-American community, Griffith's Stadium was largely segregated according to race when the Nationals played. But those racial strictures were not entirely rigid and there were so many other events hosted at the stadium for African-American patrons — for colleges, high schools and other institutions of the Shaw neighborhood — that the idea that Griffith Stadium was racially restricted was somewhat diminished.

The earliest game at Griffith Stadium that saw blacks and whites playing on the same field was an interracial exhibition between the Nationals and the Brooklyn Royal Giants in 1920. But in that game Washington's Frank Brower punched a black umpire. Subsequently, African-American fans who attended Nationals games hounded Brower from their bleacher seats. Griffith traded Brower in 1923.[3]

Griffith again began hosting black teams in exhibition contests in 1931 and did so regularly after the start of the 1932 season, black teams playing on Thursday nights when the Nationals were on the road.[4] In comparison to loud and virulent racists like George P. Marshall — who refused to integrate his Redskins team into the 1960s — and Arch McDonald, Griffith was seen as a positive force for change and his ballpark remained an important institution within the most elite neighborhood of the Washington African-American community.

In 1937 Clark Griffith was interviewed by African-American reporter Sam Lacy for the black newspaper, the *Washington Tribune*. Lacy who had worked at Griffith Stadium as a vendor in his teens, obtained the interview by way of a letter in which he told Griffith that if he considered signing Negro League players, he would "be sure of the endorsement of 162,000 Washingtonians."[5]

Griffith had been asked to meet with Lacy after he showed the letter from Lacy to Commissioner Landis. In the interview, Griffith told Sam Lacy that "the time is not far off when colored players will take their place beside those of other races in the major leagues."[6] Griffith's views in the article were hailed within the black community as more progressive than many of those associated with sports in Washington.

The solution he proposed in the interview was for the Negro Leagues to form a more professional organization modeled on the white major leagues. Griffith foresaw a day when those leagues would compete equally and opined that such competition would lead to a relaxing of racial restrictions. Griffith assured Lacy that he would assist with getting such an organization started. Griffith's words were measured and may have well been cleared through the Commissioner's Office. In the end they were completely consistent with the "separate but equal" strictures of the day.

The interview was one of several interactions that led Griffith and Homestead Grays president Cum Posey to formalize a relationship between Washington and the Negro League team from Pittsburgh, the Homestead Grays. Starting in 1940 Posey's Homestead Grays made Washington their base for home games.[7] The Grays had been one of the teams to play exhibitions at Griffith Stadium, but in the '40s they began their formal run as what many pundits believed would be one of the more popular attractions in Washington's U Street Corridor.

It did not happen, at least not initially. African-American fans remained committed to the Nationals during the Grays' first two seasons in Washington. One reason for the Grays' lack of popularity was the absence on their roster of Josh Gibson, the popular slugger many African Americans believed to be the equal of Ruth. In 1940 and '41 he was playing in South America for fatter paychecks.[8]

When the war began many of the players for the Grays were too old to be actively sought by the military. Buck Leonard was 32 and Josh Gibson 30 by the time the war was fully underway in 1942. Though young enough to serve, Gibson was beginning to show signs of the physical decline that would end in his death five years later. As the war economy sprang to life, Washington became one of the first places to feel the effects of its defense industry spending. Jobs were plentiful and they were good-paying jobs, some of which went to African Americans who swelled the ranks of those living in and strolling through the U Street neighborhoods.

Attendance for the Grays improved for the 1942 season because of appearances by Satchel Paige, one in an exhibition against a white team led by Dizzy Dean, who was always a big fan of Paige's. Joining Dean on the white all-star team was Cecil Travis — one of the most popular Nationals players after his 1941 season when he finished second to Ted Williams' .406 batting average with his own .359 mark. Travis was another southerner like Dean who reveled in playing against the best black players. The presence of a well-known local player pumped further interest into the game in Washington and was impetus for a near sell-out. The game even managed to get billing in the Washington white press that seldom provided space to black baseball of any kind.[9]

Dean's team had been beaten numerous times by Paige and the best of the Negro Leaguers, who made more money barnstorming than from regular season play. The game at Griffith Stadium featured Josh Gibson and Buck Leonard from the Grays as well as Paige. Dizzy Dean was not the player who had been a 30-game winner in 1934, and his team of barnstormers was not truly an All-Star aggregation. Cecil Travis was one of the best players in the starting lineup. Paige struck out seven in five innings and the black all-stars — playing in Grays uniforms — won by a final score of 8–1.[10]

In 1943 the Grays played so many games in Washington that there was uncertainty whether Griffith owned the team or Cum Posey. The Grays won the Negro National League in 1943 and played in the Negro World Series against the Birmingham Barons. Clark Griffith re-worked the schedule of the Washington Nationals that September to accommodate the Negro World Series which was won in seven games by the Grays. He hosted a "Cavalcade of Negro Music" at the end of the Series that featured musical acts such as Billy Eckstein and Art Tatum.

The Grays helped to create new popularity for the Nationals as well, who drew extremely well in the African-American community in 1943, contributing to the upsurge in attendance for the Nationals.[11] Events like the Negro World Series helped make the Grays into a source of important revenue to Clark Griffith during the war years. Although attendance improved at Griffith Stadium from Depression lows, Griffith needed the Redskins and Grays, and all the other attractions, to dig out of the hole that the lean Great

Depression years created. He was not alone in looking to the Negro Leagues for revenue. William Benswanger, owner of the Pittsburgh Pirates, was also receiving significant revenues by renting out his stadium for Negro Leagues games.[12] Griffith was making an estimated $700 in net revenue for each game the Grays played, and that increased to as much as $1,000 per game as the attendance improved.[13] For exhibitions where the attendance was often higher, the gate receipts were even better.[14] Josh Gibson hitting home runs out of the cavernous Griffith Stadium helped create fan enthusiasm, and while the Grays played only 26 times in Washington that year, many of those appearances were Sunday afternoon doubleheaders and total attendance for Grays games approached 225,000 fans.[15]

As World War II wore on, many in the African-American community wanted more than the Grays and exhibition games. Sam Lacy questioned Clark Griffith's position for separate but equal leagues in an article in the *Washington Post* where regular sports columnist Bob Considine turned over much of the column to comments directly from Lacy.[16]

Satchel Paige was backing a proposal for improved Negro Leagues, much the way Landis and Griffith proposed. Lacy first directed his scorn at Paige and then moved on to question Griffith's proposal, saying, "No one asks the Norwegians, Cubans or French to organize themselves into formidable groups before being admitted to major competition."[17]

Lacy's words reflected the growing frustration of the black community, members of which had begun to ask why Griffith was unwilling to move more aggressively toward the reality of blacks and whites playing on the same field, something his 1937 remarks had suggested. Again, Lacy urged Griffith directly in the press to integrate his major league roster.

Griffith said in later interviews on the subject that he considered Buck Leonard and Josh Gibson for tryouts in 1943. Griffith was concerned that signing Leonard and Gibson would rob the Negro Leagues of two of their most powerful draws and play havoc with the already tenuous bottom line of Negro League teams. As he contemplated tryouts for the two men he reportedly said, "If we get you boys, we are going to get the best ones. It's going to break up your leagues. Now what do you think of all that?"[18]

Snyder consistently argues that Griffith's concern for the fate of the Negro Leagues is motivated by his economic self–interest and his substantial need for the income that the Grays generated for the struggling Nationals. That motivation is a very real one, yet the tone of Griffith's remarks suggests a sincere concern for the Negro League players and their teams. His later arguments with Branch Rickey as the Brooklyn Dodger leader raided those leagues without compensating them with a single nickel, takes on greater meaning when considering the tone of those original comments.

The tryouts for Leonard and Gibson never happened as Griff succumbed to pressure from the American League ownership group who were opposed to even tryouts for African-American players.[19] Other owners were under similar pressure as brought to Griffith, and one of the most persistent voices for integration of baseball came from Wendell Smith of the *Pittsburgh Courier*. His advocacy resulted in a tryout scheduled by Pittsburgh Pirates owner William Benswanger for Negro League stars Roy Campanella and Dave Barnhill in the same year Griffith was to evaluate Leonard and Gibson. The result was exactly the same. Pressure from other owners convinced the Pittsburgh owner that only trouble would come from such tryouts.[20]

Concerns being raised by prominent journalists like Smith and Lacy brought the discussion to a head at the December owners meetings after the 1943 season, when three prominent black journalists were invited to address the owners. Commissioner Landis was at the meeting and invited the acclaimed singer and activist, Paul Robeson. Robeson succeeded in alienating many of the owners, who were wary of his communist sympathies, although some like Branch Rickey were moved by his presentation.[21] Yet Sam Lacy and others believed Robeson was invited by Landis solely to cast doubt on the issue of integration by associating it with Communism. Landis offered the owners the shield of subversion and Clark Griffith and others were comfortable hiding behind it.

Landis told the owners' group that they were free to make their own deals, that they could sign African-Americans to play in the major leagues if they desired. There were no takers. After the meeting Clark Griffith announced in the press that he was maintaining his position that the black teams should improve their leagues to the point that they could compete on an equal footing with their white counterparts. His position did not waiver in the coming years and remained largely unaffected by events even in the years immediately following Jackie Robinson's breakthrough into the majors.

Griffith's argument lost support in the coming years in the Shaw community. The contention that citizens who died equally in war should have equal opportunity in the peace gained traction. African-American citizens were not concerned about subversives and increasingly they saw Griffith's stance as little more than an attempt to maintain existing discrimination.

There were those like Shirley Povich who portrayed Griffith's actions more positively. In later years Povich highlighted Griffith's willingness to contemplate trading for Lary Doby, whom Griffith called "the fellow who would do us more good than any left-handed hitter in the league."[22] Yet later writers like Brad Snyder saw the same trade proposal very differently. Snyder saw Griffith's ultimate failure to make that trade as further evidence that the owner had succumbed to pressures from those opposed to the integration of his team.

There was no trade and no action of any kind, and it is exactly the lack of any positive move by Griffith that is his most critical failure. Bill Veeck broke the color barrier in the American League in 1947 when he brought Larry Doby to play in Cleveland. But Clark Griffith remained among the American League ownership who continued to field white-only teams. He bowed to a southern fan base that listened faithfully to the broadcasts of Arch McDonald and attended Redskin games without regard to the views of their owner.

Clark Griffith was no longer the crusading pioneer in the game that he had been earlier in his life. When he was interviewed, Griffith talked baseball because it was all he knew. He did not like to delve into his motivations. But in 1952 he gave one of his few lengthy interviews to *The Sporting News*. He attacked his critics on race saying, "I will not sign a Negro for the Washington club merely to satisfy subversives."[23]

The interview occurred at the height of the McCarthy era and Griffith used what became a popular ruse among segregationists who questioned the patriotism of Martin Luther King, Jr., and other giants of the civil rights movement. In 1952 Griffith seems a shadow of the man who once spoke convincingly of racial equality in his 1937 interview with Sam Lacy, who championed the rights of players early in his career. The eighty-three year old patriarch of the American League had no grasp of the historic moment or the times in which he was living.

In the same *Sporting News* interview Griffith provides nothing but empty promises to those who had lost patience with his actions. "To those who persist in speaking of me harshly on the Negro player issue, let me say that I would welcome the addition of players like Robinson, Campanella, Harry Simpson, Don Newcombe, Larry Doby and Orestes Minosos."[24] He continued, saying he "would be only too happy to give the black clientele [of the Nationals] a chance to root for players of their own race."

It was already late in the game and Griffith still did not follow through on those words in any meaningful way. He stood on the sidelines and let the American League owners openly opposed to integration have their way. Clark Griffith failed to act aggressively when the historic moment presented itself. Snyder is correct in saying that the sum of Griffith's actions calls his personal motives into question.[25]

As regrettable as his actions are, however, even Sam Lacy concedes that Griffith was no racist. Griffith suffered from a bankruptcy of courage, but much of it can be attributed to the post-war era economic reality he created himself by refusing every entreaty to modernize his organization. At the time that demands escalated for Griffith to give his loyal African American clientele a champion, his ability to hang onto the family business was becoming increasingly precarious.

His status as the majority stock-holder in the team was challenged in 1949 by John Jachym who bought the forty percent share that the death of William Richardson had made available. Griffith withstood that challenge, but it underscores the tenuous economic milieu in which he was operating, one that was vastly different than that of Branch Rickey, and one that undercut the elderly and increasingly cautious Griffith.

Branch Rickey's historic move to integrate baseball had the asset of a more conducive environment than did Griffith in Washington. During the war the Dodgers drew over a million fans twice, and as soon as the war ended the gate for every New York team reached two million fans annually, almost three times the relatively successful attendance marks set at Griffith Stadium. Rickey had the financial reserves to weather any storm his raid of the Negro Leagues created. More importantly, he had a fan base that was more likely to support the idea.

Washington was perceived, rightly or wrongly, as a distinctly southern town, and it still maintained segregated facilities in too many parts of the city. Brad Snyder echoed Lacy's belief that the same opportunities as existed for Rickey were there for Griffith. "By finding a few black players of his own, Griffith could have cultivated sellout crowds every night."[26] Yet even Branch Rickey questioned whether Gibson and Leonard as African-American stars had the unique character that would be required from the person who would have to carry the weight of an entire race when stepping onto the white-only ball fields of Major League Baseball.[27]

Branch Rickey's assertion that the Negro Leagues had no right to compensation for their players is as equally self-serving as Clark Griffith's that the Negro Leagues should be preserved. In the business of baseball, self-interest has been proven to be just as powerful as in the economy at large. Rickey and Griffith traded charges of hypocrisy against each other in the press.[28] In the end, however, their actions look much like those of businessmen, each seeking to maximize his competitive advantage in a Darwinian fight to the death that ultimately Clark Griffith lost convincingly.

It is compelling to imagine Buck Leonard and Josh Gibson playing in uniforms with a "W" across their chest and the difference they might have made for Washington baseball. Yet even Sam Lacy anticipated the problems when he had said in this interview with Griffith in 1937 that "the bulk of the trouble will come from the stands and the southern blood which flows through the anatomy of professional baseball."[29] Racial tensions that escalated around Jake Powell and others dating back to confrontations in 1920 made it questionable whether the emotional anatomy of Griffith's fan base was ready to be tested.

In 1949 Griffith admitted he had made a mistake in not seeking out black players. He told Joe Engel to scout African-American talent, but even then Griffith shied away from the issue. He would not integrate his team until 1954, when he brought up Carlos Paula, a 26-year-old Cuban of African descent. By then, however, his teams were the worst in baseball not because he lacked African-American talent, but because he lacked sufficient talent of any kind.

The tragedy for the elderly Griffith was how poorly he understood the way in which his actions on the issue of race would diminish his reputation in later years. But nothing hurt Griffith's reputation more than the words of his nephew Calvin, who was being groomed to take over the team. Never well-spoken or possessing the urbane air of the man whose name he bore, Calvin's racial views were always disappointing. Over the years he made numerous regrettable statements in public, and those comments created a prism through which the public perceptions of his uncle were seen.

Calvin resented when his uncle made him responsible for negotiating with promoters of Negro Leagues baseball, black boxing and wrestling matches. He said in 1978 that "black people don't go to ball games, but they will fill up a rasslin' ring and put up such a chant it will scare you to death."[30] The publication of his remarks came at a time when the sport was re-examining its role within the broader integration struggle. Such remarks by Calvin Griffith lent credence to those who looked back and questioned his uncle's role as a racial obstructionist.

Most came to believe that when Jackie Robinson broke the color barrier, the gritty competitor known in his best days as the Old Fox had lost that fiery edge that had made him a legend within the game. After the end of World War II, Clark Griffith was barely hanging on as his moment in history passed him by.

CHAPTER 23

Peace

The new Baseball Commissioner, Happy Chandler, convened a summit of the baseball brain trust to set the course for the game. He acknowledged the looming issue of race and appointed a four-person panel including journalist Sam Lacy and the Brooklyn Dodgers' Branch Rickey to bring back recommendations on the possible integration of the game.[1] Chandler also wanted umpires to be more circumspect in their dealings with players, and less chest-to-chest in their confrontations that still occasionally marked disputes between players and umpires. Baseball was back and would return to its throne as the king of American culture, more popular than opera, football or Hollywood, though in the latter instance there was plenty of argument.

In an editorial at the end of the season, Shirley Povich compared the efforts of Walter Briggs, whose team had just wrestled the American League pennant from Washington, with those of Clark Griffith.[2] Briggs, a wealthy industrialist, was renovating Tiger Stadium, making it more a showcase to rival ballparks like Yankee Stadium and other pristine venues that increasingly stood in marked contrast to old Griffith Stadium.

Povich noted that the Detroit stadium was "completely double-decked, seated 55,000, and featured three electric scoreboards."[3] He admitted that Griffith Stadium was not going to measure up to that, nor was its owner ever going to have the money to spend on players that Briggs did, but Povich was betting that after watching the Old Fox craft a winner from the scrap heap in 1945, Washington baseball would prosper in the post-war era from the savvy owner with the mile-long baseball pedigree. "To him what's important is the ball team he puts in the park."[4]

In one of the great ironies of his career, early in 1946 charges were filed against Griffith for "Unfair Labor Practices." He was cited for counseling his players against joining a fledgling baseball players association. The American Baseball Guild's labor relations director, Robert Murphy, filed the charges with the National Labor Relations Board in April.[5] It was front page news as were Griffith's denials. "I have never talked to my players about joining a baseball union," Griffith asserted.[6]

Griffith argued that he was only defending the reserve clause, but he did admit that he believed a union would destroy the reserve clause and on those grounds he was opposed to the union. Although he was stating a position that was conventional wisdom within the game and would remain so for another 15 years, it was a remarkable turnaround. Clark Griffith had made his name fighting the reserve clause as articulated by National League ownership in 1901. More than anyone in the game, his career had been built on labor organizing and rabble rousing.

Griffith was the vice-president of the players association in 1899 because of his long record of activism on behalf of the players. He had fought the ability of the owners to tie players to a single team because his first mentor in the game, Hoss Radbourn, had led that fight more than 60 years prior to 1946, teaching the young Clark Griffith how narrow the interests of baseball's ownership group could be. Clark Griffith was an owner arguing his narrow self-interests to the players exactly the way Radbourn had warned the young rebellious Griffith they always would.

The anti-labor charges came on the heels of one of Clark Griffith's greatest triumphs, election to the National Baseball Hall of Fame in Cooperstown, New York. The Hall of Fame had elected its first class in 1936, one that included Walter Johnson, Babe Ruth, Ty Cobb, Christy Mathewson and Honus Wagner. Ten years later, in January 1946, the Baseball Writers' Association of American announced its annual vote for the Hall. There were no winners.[7]

The top vote-getters in 1946 were Frank Chance, Johnny Evers, Miller Huggins, Ed Walsh, Rube Waddell and Clark Griffith. There were too many deserving candidates for the writers to choose from and votes were so badly split that it became impossible for anyone to make the 75 percent threshold to gain induction.

With no inductees selected by the BBWAA, the Veterans Committee elected the 11 new members to the Hall of Fame. Griffith joined the Baseball Hall of Fame and the celebrated group of 49 players and officials, including his old friends Connie Mack, Cap Anson and Hoss Radbourn. He came in with a class that included Jack Chesbro and Iron Man McGinnity, who had been such instrumental parts of Griff's great seasons in New York in 1903 and 1904.

In May the Touchdown Club of Washington honored Griffith for his selection, and the actor Charles Coburn was the guest speaker at the banquet recognizing the Old Fox's election.[8] Several months later, June 13, 1946, to be exact, the induction ceremony was held in Cooperstown, the highlight of which was the dedication of a special plaque for the first commissioner of the game, Kenesaw Mountain Landis.[9]

Election to the Hall of Fame was a fitting tribute for the formative efforts that Griffith had played in the founding of the American League, even if the man himself seemed to have lost touch with the youthful figure he once had been. The elderly Old Fox was still responsible for keeping baseball going throughout the war, and now the game was in a great position to prosper as the peace-time economy came roaring back to life.

The war years themselves had been relatively good to baseball. Attendance did not sink to levels that made precarious the economics of the game in World War I. Although attendance was off slightly in the worst of the war years, it quickly shot up in 1945 as the war came to and end, and by 1946 the budding prosperity that had formed during the war took off like a jet.

Clark Griffith had hitched his wagon to the post-war recovery in 1919 and built a winning baseball team and a personal fortune. Yet in 1945 he was handcuffed by new realities. He was shackled not just by burgeoning racial tensions. They were just a symptom of Griffith's retrenchment within the game. Less and less was he the gritty warrior and increasingly he was perceived as a throw back to a time passed.

Shirley Povich called Griffith's family-run team a "mom-and-pop" operation, and it was an apt description. After the World War I, Griffith was slowly able to amass a winning team the same way that Connie Mack and others were doing it, with slow culling through prospects bought and sold in the off-season, and through shrewd trades. Griffith was still trying to make that work in an era dominated by teams who had followed Branch Rickey's lead and developed extensive minor league farm systems that funneled talent to the big league club.

Griffith's ability to find talent like Goose Goslin while playing on the golf course was gone. Sports writers like Povich and the fans themselves remained confident about the Nationals' future and Clark Griffith was still looking for ways to make it work. He was mining the Cuban baseball scene for talent in hopes that the Latin countries to the south would prove a bounty of major league talent.

In February the Nationals and the Red Sox announced a seven-game exhibition series in Havana, Cuba. Griffith had the help of one of his best friends in the game, Joe Cronin, to pull off the event and it worked. Advance ticket sales for the games totaled 32,000—more than Griffith could lure to his opening day festivities when the president was on hand for the first game.[10] The Red Sox beat the Nationals in Havana, 7–3, behind Tex Hughson, and the score would be almost identical two months later when the 1946 season opened in Washington, D.C.[11]

Cambria convinced Griffith to buy into the Havana Cubans, who played
in the Florida International League, as a way to increase the Nationals' presence
on the island. Griffith was presented a gold medal in Havana for his contribution to expanding the game of baseball in Cuba and the Caribbean. But
with Griffith's concern about dark-skinned Cubans, almost all of the best
talent from Cuba evaded Griffith and the Nationals.

Spring training began after the exhibition series and all around Florida
excitement built for the first season after the war with a full contingent of
players returned from duty in the armed services. Opening day in Washington
was particularly cheerful as the Boston Red Sox came to town, showcasing
one of the most popular figures in the game, Ted Williams.

Everyone — including the Nationals players themselves — watched batting
practice as Ted Williams launched shots into the right field bleachers.[12] Joe
Cronin's sons, one aptly named Clark Calvin for Cronin's friend and mentor,
watched the game from two rows behind President Truman, who was on hand
for his first presidential toss.

The Nationals lost the opener as Williams had a solo home run to delight
the fans. They lost the next two games as Boston's impressive lineup over-
powered the Nationals. Ted Williams left town hitting a lusty .500 with a
home run, two doubles and a triple to show for his first three games. Williams
had a partner in the spotlight, Joe DiMaggio, and the two stars took up where
they had left off in 1941— great players who fit well within the long history
of the game, playing on two remarkably talent-laden teams, the Red Sox and
Yankees.

The post-war seasons were lent their immutable flavor by Joe Cronin's
Boston teams who locked in pennant fights with New York to bring the old
excitement back to the game. Washington baseball was neither competitive
nor quick to seize its part of the emerging economic dynamic. Clark Griffith
was losing his touch, but not his intrinsic sense of decency and commitment
to his baseball family.

The somber news that Walter Johnson had cancer of the brain was
revealed in the spring of the 1946 season. Clark Griffith was once again the
father figure in an extended family of famous players who rallied around the
lion of the game. During the war, Walter Johnson had joined Griffith at the
stadium several times for benefit events to support the War Bond effort. The
Big Train had never strayed far from the crowd at Griffith Stadium for very
long. He was still the heart and soul of baseball in the nation's capital.

No one played a greater role in rallying the city of Washington to the
side of the Big Train than Griffith. In September, with Johnson's health in
clear decline, Clark Griffith organized a "testimonial evening" for Walter Johnson at Griffith Stadium. When it was his turn to speak, Griffith was too

wrought with emotion to get beyond a few words and turned the microphone over to Arch McDonald. The purpose of the evening was to raise money to help the family pay for Johnson's hospitalization. The event was successful as donations large and small were forthcoming from every corner of the city and baseball's faithful fans everywhere.

When Walter Johnson finally gave up the fight in December, a ceremony was held at the Washington Cathedral where a thousand people gathered beneath the great vaulted arches of that sanctuary, the most imposing and serene spot in Washington. All of Walther Johnson's and Clark Griffith's baseball family were there. The men who played on the most memorable teams at Griffith Stadium — Joe Judge, Sam Rice, Ossie Bluege, Muddy Ruel, Roger Peckinpaugh, and Tom Zachary — carried the casket along with trainer Mike Martin and third base coach Nick Altrock. Jack Bentley, the pitcher he had beaten in the seventh game of the 1924 World Series, was there in a brave display of friendship.[13] Bucky Harris, Eddie Ainsmith, Clyde Milan and Clark Griffith walked beside them.[14] They carried Walter Johnson to Union Cemetery in Rockville, Maryland, where the Big Train was buried next to his wife Hazel.

With him went the best of Washington baseball history. Clark Griffith tried vainly to bring it back after the war ended. In 1946, in the season that concluded before Walter Johnson's death, Mickey Vernon, Buddy Lewis and Cecil Travis were back from the war. Travis would never be the same after suffering frostbite on two toes during the war. Although he would never admit to suffering any ill effects from the war, he never regained any of the speed or mobility that had been his forte before the war. After the Battle of the Bulge, Travis fought with the army into Germany during that same harsh winter and his feet were subjected to tough conditions that diminished his mobility.[16]

Bobo Newsom, in his fourth visit to town, had his best season with the Nationals, anchoring a capable staff that consisted of Mickey Haefner, Early Wynn and Dutch Leonard. Mickey Vernon had the best year of his career, winning the American League batting title with an average of .353 and leading the league with 51 doubles. He beat out Ted Williams in a remarkable finish that saw Williams' average dip to .342. The "Splendid Splinter" was at the top of nearly every other category, hitting 38 home runs behind Hank Greenberg's 44, and Williams was voted the Most Valuable Player as Joe Cronin's Red Sox took the pennant.

Washington managed a respectable fourth-place finish in the American League. It was the last time a Clark Griffith team would grace the first division. The expectations the team raised were dashed the following year when the team lost 90 games and finished a dismal seventh in the AL. After Ossie Bluege had seemed like the perfect post-war manager in 1946, he was done in 1947. Griff brought in Joe Kuhel to manage the team in 1948. He lasted only two seasons, unable to improve on Bluege's finish, and did worse in 1949 when the Nationals finally hit bottom, finishing in last place and winning only 50 games.

Bucky Harris, who had won the World Series with the Yankees in 1947, returned to Washington in 1950. There were two new stars in the Nationals firmament, Eddie Yost and Irv Noren. Playing opposite Mickey Vernon at third base, Yost gave Harris a second bat in the infield, but it was Noren who moved into the cleanup spot and filled it as well as anyone had since Griffith had traded for Heinie Manush.

Noren was the most valuable player in the Pacific Coast League in 1949 and Clark Griffith spent heavily to get him. He led the team in home runs in 1950 with 14. Vernon was the only one to hit over .300, but Noren and Yost were close behind at .295. Harris and Griffith could not find similar answers for the pitching staff. Sid Hudson, who would become a fixture in Washington for years as a player and coach, led the rotation. He was joined by two of Joe Cambria's Cuban talents, Sandy Consuegra and Connie Marrero.

They were not the worst pitching staff, but there was no offensive thunder to match the better teams in the league. The Yankees and Red Sox both hit twice as many home runs as Washington and outscored them by wide margins.

Clark Griffith finally found a slugger in 1952 when he traded for Jackie Jensen, getting him from the Yankees. A new talent in the Bronx named Mickey Mantle, who was replacing DiMaggio in center field, made Jensen expendable for the talent-laden Yankees. With Gene Woodling and Hank Bauer the Yankees had enough power to let the Nationals see what Jensen could do.

It was perhaps the Old Fox's biggest deal of the post-war era and it seemed to belie any rumor that he was no longer sharp as an 83-year-old. Washington traded outfielder Sam Mele to the White Sox and Irv Noren to the Yankees. In return they got the pitcher they desperately needed in Frank Shea and two outfielders, Jackie Jensen and Jim Busby.

Both Busby and Jensen would have long major league careers, but it was Jensen and Shea that were the heart of the deal. Jensen was the slugger Griffith's lineup had been without for so long. Griffith found a shortstop in Pete Runnels, but he was a lefty and better suited to first base where he moved quickly.

Although the trade was a good one for the Nationals, it did as much to illustrate how far the team had to go. The conventional methods that had worked for Clark Griffith for so long were no longer enough to build a pennant winner. Jensen was not an appreciable upgrade over Noren in 1952 and Busby proved to be a light-hitting outfielder in a league where the Yankees had three sluggers manning the outfield.

Frank "Spec" Shea had an excellent season in 1952, and it was the pitching that helped the Nationals win 78 games. They lifted the team to its best postwar record. Shea, Bob Porterfield, and Connie Marrero all had ERAs under three runs and though they did not get outstanding support from the offense, the staff was deep enough that they were never overworked. Bucky Harris was accorded the genius behind the improved Nationals. The team finished a respectable fifth in the American League and the optimists saw hope that the Old Fox still had the capacity to build a winning team as he had two decades previously.

There was a new and very popular president sworn in before the beginning of the 1953 season, Dwight Eisenhower. He dispatched his somewhat less popular Vice-President, Richard Nixon, to throw out the first pitch of the season. Both Eisenhower and Nixon would prove long and faithful fans of baseball in Washington. Eisenhower would be instrumental in keeping a team in the capital in 1961 and Nixon would remain a loyal fan as long as the game was played in the city.

There was additional room for optimism in 1953 as the Nationals again were able to reach .500 and finished in fifth place. Mickey Vernon found his timing again for the first time since 1946 and led the American League in hitting with a .337 average.

Bob Porterfield won 22 games to establish himself as a potential ace, and he had help. Spec Shea and Walt Masterson carried much of the load as well, but there wasn't enough depth behind Porterfield.

Washington continued to be a favorite baseball port of entry for Latin players, but as in all things baseball, the best of the talent went elsewhere. The Chicago White Sox were building the pennant winner Griffith foresaw with the Cuban talent he did not, or would not sign. Minnie Minoso, known as the "Cuban Comet," was a Cuban of clear African descent and had come from the Negro Leagues. He became one of the best players in the league.

Along with the Cuban Comet, the White Sox in 1953 had second baseman Chico Carrasquel, Jungle Jim Rivera and Willy Miranda to give that team a noticeable Hispanic flavor. Minoso would be the best Cuban player of the decade and one of the best players of African descent in the American League after Larry Doby. Charles Comiskey's daughter Dorothy controlled the team and had none of the concerns about black ball players that many other American League owners still nursed.

The Browns relocated to Baltimore at the end of the 1953 season. Clark Griffith did not oppose the move and more than anyone he knew the story of baseball's long absence from Baltimore after Ban Johnson moved the team to New York to start the 1903 season. Griffith served as part of the ownership committee that inspected construction of the new Baltimore stadium to house the team in 1954.[16] Ironically it was the Yankees who opposed the move, but Del Webb was voted down and the move went forward.

Clark Griffith announced that he was making his nephew, Calvin, the new Executive Vice President of the team after those meetings, taking singular control of operations under the 83-year-old owner.[17] Calvin's influence had been substantial in the 1950s, serving as General Manager in many regards, active especially in player trades and media relations. He was credited with signing the most lucrative radio-television contract in the American League, a three-year deal for $900,000 beginning in 1952.[18]

The new wealth began to show around the edges in Washington. In 1954 Clark Griffith brought Roy Sievers to Washington from the St. Louis Browns in a trade for Gil Coan. Roy Sievers had been Rookie of the Year in 1949 with the Browns, but injuries had limited his play until 1953 when he worked his way back to the majors as a regular for the first time. He hit 24 home runs in 1954, taking advantage of the outfield walls that had been moved in at Griffith Stadium to help the hitters. He was the most prodigious slugger at Griffith Stadium over his six-year career in Washington, leading the league in home runs in 1957 with 42.

Sievers had help in 1954 from Mickey Vernon, who hit 20 home runs himself to celebrate the new dimensions of the park. The walls in left field were pulled in for the 1950 season to provide a Beer Garden that marked an end to Clark Griffith's prohibition against the sale of beer by the club. It provided a natural complement to the tall and imposing National Bohemian Bottle that rose 56 feet above the center field wall. It was that bottle that was nicked by Mickey Mantle's mammoth home run in 1953 that measured 565 feet. It was the longest ever hit at the park and was courtesy of Senators pitcher Chuck Stobbs.[19]

The team finished a dismal sixth and the results were aided by the fledgling Baltimore team that struggled to compete in its first full season. The only bright spot was the emergence of a new face on the pitching staff, Camilo Pascual. Pascual would be the best of the Cubans that Clark Griffith brought to Washington and would go on to anchor the Washington rotation, winning 17 games for a last-place Washington team, then playing as the Senators, in 1959.

In November of 1954 Clark Griffith celebrated his 85th birthday. He celebrated with his 11 grandchildren in tow at his 16th Street home. His family had established a tradition of large birthday celebrations for Griffith and they were usually made public in the press. At his celebration in 1952, 300 persons had attended and the press was on hand to hear his complaints about unfair practices within the game that were limiting his team's competitiveness.

In particular he protested the ability of the Brooklyn Dodgers to maintain three Triple-A farm teams, saying, "There isn't enough talent to go around as there is."[20] He was protesting Branch Rickey's ability to shift players between those teams to avoid the draft that had been instituted to level the playing field between teams. Rickey was shifting his best players to one team so that only one of his best players would be eligible for the draft. "It's restraint of trade ... it's unfair to hold a young player back like that," Griffith said, repeating Kenesaw Mountain Landis' argument from the 1930s.[21]

At spring training to begin the 1955 season, Clark Griffith gave several interviews to journalists who quizzed him on topics wide and far. He was still a baseball man, and talking to James T. Farrell near Orlando and the Nationals spring training site, it was obvious how clear-headed he still was, how focused on the game he remained as Farrell sat with Griffith watching young players from Sid Hudson's baseball school play those from the Nationals' complex. Joe Engel and scout Zinn Beck were there with Griffith as the three men evaluated talent. They talked of teams from bygone eras and when the 1912 Washington team — Griffith's first in Washington — came up, he sadly noted that almost all of those players were dead.

It was also the last year that the Old Fox took the mound, and he recalled pitching to Hal Chase, who had played for him as a rookie in New York. There were so many names from such a long history stretching back to almost the very beginnings of the game. He still remembered getting a game-winning hit — a ninth-inning bloop single — in a 1–0 victory he pitched for Chicago in 1901. He always told the same stories to writers, about the string ball they used in Nevada County, Missouri, about the hangin' and the huntin'. Farrell was most impressed, however, with Griffith's recall of so many games from so long ago, as though "he has never forgotten one that he has played in or watched."[22]

He said of his longevity, "I never drank, smoked or kept late hours."[23] It was, on its face, a questionable statement from a man who was known for constantly having a cigar in his mouth, and who had negotiated the founding of the American League in a New York City barroom. But his stadium still did not serve beer until late in its history, despite the boon to concessions such sales would have meant. He had fought every modernization of the game only to give in when it became clear how beneficial they would be to his bottom line, but there were some compromises to time that Griffith would not make.

He gave away one of his most closely guarded secrets that year to Bob Addie when he told him how he had made Franklin Roosevelt a good friend by helping him win baseball bets with the members of his cabinet. "Franklin Roosevelt was like a kid when he went to opening day," Griff remembered.[24] He loved the game and would call Griffith to get the lowdown on the day's game so that he could bet on the score and the winner.

Clark Griffith and grandchildren (National Baseball Hall of Fame Library).

He was closest to Truman, however, who was from Missouri. It was Truman's dedication of the portrait of Walter Johnson at Griffith Stadium that made them friends. The picture stood just inside the front gate of the stadium and complemented the brass and concrete memorial that was outside the main entrance to the first base grandstands. Truman called to accept the ceremonial honor of dedicating both memorials the morning after his big win over Dewey in 1948. That had impressed the Old Fox and made him respect the man as much as any of the other Presidents he had hosted.

The 1955 season was not a memorable one for the Nationals as they spent another year in the cellar of the American League. Clark Griffith was out of ideas, but he was still sharp-minded and hopeful. At the end of the 1955 season, Clark Griffith attended Eddie Eynon's 50th wedding anniversary celebration. He had been Griffith's most faithful golfing partner and the longest serving official on the board of the Washington Nationals, serving as secretary-treasurer. Eynon would be dead by the first of November.

The day after attending the Eynon anniversary event, Griffith was hospitalized with neuritis—"an inflammation of the nerves."[25] Three days later the news was worse and he was listed as critically ill from a gastric hemorrhage. He rallied from the gastrointestinal problems but then was struck with pneumonia. Clark Griffith died on October 27.

The attending physician gave the greatest complement to Griffith, saying that even on his last day the doctor found him "looking at me with eyes that were glinting beneath those bushy brows."[26] The doctor said Griffith's face was "one of fight and determination."[27] He fought his final illness with the same grit that he had fought every baseball campaign for 68 years; with the same grit that Hoss Radbourn taught him was essential to success so many years before.

His death was reported in every major newspaper in the country, and every figure in the baseball community noted the passing of someone many considered a personal friend. Hank Greenberg said of Griffith that he was a close friend and noted that the game was losing its most treasured figures, "one by one and they are not being replaced." Will Harridge, the president of the American League, the institution Griffith helped found and of which he was a integral part for more than 50 years, said, "a great player and manager on the field, he was even more outstanding as a league executive whose ability over the years helped build develop the American League and added to baseball's stature everywhere."[28]

One notable quote came from Clarence Miles of the Baltimore Orioles. Calvin Griffith would acknowledge in the coming years that the relocation of the Browns to Baltimore hurt the Washington baseball club's chances economically. But Miles said of the senior Griffith, "Baltimore has lost a friend without whose counsel and assistance, we would never have gained re-entry into the American League."[29] Griffith believed that giving Baltimore its team was the right thing to do and in the best interest of the game. That had overridden his self-interest.

Almost every article included in it the line, "Griffith numbered eight presidents among his friends."[30] He had married the presidency to opening day and in finding that spark of a young baseball fan in every president, had linked the game in some small way to the affairs of state. It was one of his enduring legacies and the press was right to note it.

The mark of the man, however, was not his link to those of power and prestige but to his friends and family whom he supported without condition when need arose. Clark Griffith was a friend when it counted. Povich noted his magnanimous financial assistance to John Stone, his outfielder who was diagnosed with tuberculosis in the middle of the 1938 season. Griffith paid the rest of Stone's annual salary to the outfielder though he knew that Stone would not play another game that season. Other stories such as the one about the widow whose rent he had paid anonymously circulated in the eulogies that paid tribute to his large heart and willingness to help others from all stations in life.

His commitment to working men and women was best described by George P. Marshall. Marshall said of Griffith, "His is an organization in which the president is one with the lowliest employee."[31] Marshall complained that Griffith's old-timers — ballplayers who always could find work at the stadium — did not move fans into the stadium fast enough for the owner of the Redskins. Marshall demanded that Griffith replace them with younger staff. "Those old friends of mine will have to stay on their jobs," Griffith said, "Nobody is going to tell them they are through. Don't you see, it would break their hearts."[32]

Among those old friends was Connie Mack, who was 92 when his oldest baseball friend died. Mack had sold his team to new ownership in 1954. Mack's doctors would not tell the game's eldest statesman that his old friend had died, because they knew he would insist on attending the funeral and was not up to the trip. Neither Mack nor Griffith had been able to field competitive teams after the Depression. Neither had been able to compete in a game increasingly dominated by those who had never played it. Baseball came to be dominated by wealthy individuals and corporate interests that sought to benefit from the status and wealth endowed it by the lifetime endeavors of men like Clark Griffith and Connie Mack.

The Old Fox was laid to rest by George Case, Ossie Bluege and Sam Rice, who served as pallbearers along with less well-known players who had settled into the Washington business community and become close with Griffith, men like Bill Werber and Bill Jurges. Joe Cronin and his family were there along with Bucky Harris and Muddy Ruel. Jack Bentley, the losing pitcher in the 1924 World Series seventh game, was there as he had been for Walter Johnson. Walter O'Malley and Horace Stoneham were among dozens of dignitaries from the game there to pay tribute to one of the game's most notable treasures.

Of the hundreds in attendance there were simple fans, senators and congressman, and famous actors like Bruce Beemer, who played the "Lone Ranger" in one of television's first popular series. Griffith had been taken by the show and struck up a friendship with Beemer. The minister, looking out over the huge throng and the colorful flowers that filled the church, said, "It is Opening Day again for Clark Griffith."[33] He noted the presence of Branch Rickey, who had caught the last game Griffith had pitched for the Highlanders. The minister cited the exemplary nature of Griffith's honesty and integrity that he made part of the game. Baseball comedian Nick Altrock, coach and long-time friend of Griffith, admitted that at the funeral, "he cried like a baby."[34]

The Old Fox was buried in the family crypt at Fort Lincoln Cemetery in Bladensburg, Maryland. Griffith's will passed the ownership of his team to his adopted children, Thelma and Calvin. Calvin and Thelma gained control of approximately 60 percent of the shares in the team. The minority ownership rights of William Richardson had been bought by John Jachym of Jamestown, New York, in 1949 with the backing of Hugh Grant, a Pennsylvania oil man.[35] Jachym fancied himself a baseball man and had served as a scout for the St. Louis Cardinals. He had an impeccable reputation. He had graduated from the University of Missouri School of Journalism — one of the nation's best — and had won the Silver Star for bravery fighting with the Marines on Guadalcanal. He had purchased the Jamestown Jammers minor league team, but had sold it to work in the Detroit organization.

He presented himself to Clark Griffith at his office in the stadium shortly after the purchase, hoping to become an officer in the team and to play a role in its direction. It may have been the last chance for Griffith to provide new eyes and energy to a dying organization, to get a fresh take on issues of the day such as race. Clark Griffith froze him out completely and after Jachym realized he would never succeed in gaining a voice in the affairs of the team, he sold to Gabe Murphy, who promised never to meddle in the team's affairs, but requested a purchase option on the team if the family decided to sell.

Jachym sold his shares in the team for $615,000 in 1950. Although Povich reported a higher figure, Jachym's sale was comparable, resulting in an estimated value for all shares of the team's stock at $1.5 million. In a column after Griffith's death, Shirley Povich put the value of the team at $4 million. Taking the Jachym sale as comparable, Povich's figures seem high, but even so, the estimated value of Griffith's holdings in the team should have had a value close to $2 million.

The Griffith mansion was valued at almost $1 million, yet when the estate was settled, the net proceeds were estimated at only $250,000 according to newspaper articles after his death. Clark Griffith's most public and highest valued assets had a face value of nearly $3 million, along with whatever cash assets the family may have possessed. The difference can only be attributed to the debt that Clark Griffith carried in his last years, what his wife described as the sum of his efforts to keep the team playing in Washington.

That debt is a testament to the attempts that the Old Fox continued to make as he invested his last penny in a never-ending effort to craft one last winning season as his final legacy. It never happened but he left Washington, D.C. richer for its tradition as the place where presidents came to watch the national pastime, richer for the winning tradition he built over his first two decades in the city. He gave his adopted son Calvin the best tutors in the game and left him as his champion to carry on the hope that the old traditions would continue and that its greatest glories would yet return again.

Epilogue

When the press asked Cal Griffith about Gabriel Murphy's — the minority partner's — interest in the Nationals, he told them he would never sell the team. Calvin had been named the Executive Vice President and heir apparent. After his uncle's death he took over control of the team's affairs. He quickly assured the local press that the operation of the team would continue much as it had during his uncle's lifetime. Yet Calvin was far more aware of the troubled nature of the organization than Clark Griffith had ever been willing to articulate. And the two men saw the salvation in quite different terms.

Griffith was alarmed by the surrounding neighborhood that Clark Griffith treasured for its grittiness. The nascent civil rights movement was providing African-American families of means the ability to move to the suburbs with their white counterparts, and slowly Shaw was watching its best citizens depart. Calvin Griffith was concerned about the deterioration of the neighborhood and its impact on the stadium.

Two years after the death of Clark Griffith, Anne "Aunt Addie" Robertson Griffith died at the age of 82. Joe Cronin and his family and other Nationals players attended the funeral. She was known for her strong defense of her husband and his team when questioned by writers. In his tribute to her, Bob Considine told of her fondness for the handsome Zeke Bonura.

Sitting next to her husband one day, Aunt Addie watched as Bonura made an error on a ball that bounded between his legs into right field. The runner rounded the bag too ambitiously and the right fielder attempted to catch the runner, firing in to Bonura standing on the bag. When he caught the throw and applied the tag, Aunt Addie jumped to her feet cheering. Griffith asked her, "Addie, have you lost your mind? What is to applaud about that plumber (Bonura) out there messing things up?"[1]

She replied calmly, "Now, now, Clark, don't be critical, after all, Zeke caught the ball coming back." She reserved a special spot for Considine, saying, "I've never believed all those terrible things they say about you."[2]

Aunt Addie's death freed Calvin Griffith to run the team without fear of recrimination from those who had raised him in Washington and provided him a unique chance at fame and fortune. When the first rumors of her nephew's desire to move the team surfaced, only a month before she died she said of her husband's commitment to Washington, "He would never have moved. He put every dollar he had into the club. He mortgaged and he borrowed, but he kept major league baseball in Washington."[3] The young owner was having no luck with the team now being called the Washington "Senators," and he saw no way out of the troubled team's situation.

In many ways he saw more trouble than existed. All of the problems had been there before his uncle's death: the team did not have the financial backing to field contending teams. Neither Calvin nor the Old Fox could get the Senators out of the American League cellar. They finished in seventh in 1956 and fell back into eighth place in 1957, 1958 and 1959.

He admitted that he was worried about Griffith Stadium "getting to be all colored."[4] The racial issue cloaked the more serious concern about the stadium physically. The seating capacity was lower than any other major league stadium by 1960 and had not been adequate to support the team for decades. The stadium was old and needed to be upgraded to modern standards or replaced, but Calvin did not have the money to contemplate such a venture.

Instead, he cloaked his stretched financial situation in racial teams. Years later he would say, "The problem that we had run into in Washington was that our ballpark was in a very black district."[5] He blamed the problems on the surrounding neighborhood rather than team ownership that did not have the financial resources to get the worst team in the American League out of the cellar or renovate an aged stadium that could not support the team.

The heart of the problem was attendance that diminished as the team got worse. Fewer fans wanted to watch the Senators finish last every year. Calvin Griffith could not afford to address that problem. His uncle had left him the same financial equation he could not solve prior to his death. Calvin was proving even less adept.

He aped his uncle's great speech from 1920 when Clark Griffith had first bought the team and said, "This is my home." Now Calvin Griffith reassured Washington, D.C., saying, "I intend that it shall remain my home for the rest of my life."[6] Calvin knew that he needed to upgrade the team and the stadium in order to extricate himself and the organization from the economic spiral in which he found himself. He sought help from the friendships Clark Griffith had built over the years with the most powerful men in the nation.

Congress had control over the affairs in the District of Columbia until they ceded them to a mayoral form of governance in the late 1960s. In 1958 they controlled the purse strings and allocated $5 million to build a new stadium to replace the decaying landmark that Clark Griffith had inherited in 1920 and renovated in 1923 and thereafter. The measure did not pass, however, and Calvin Griffith continued to twist in the wind with the worst team and the lowest attendance in baseball.

The other baseball owners offered assistance as well as Congress, but Calvin Griffith had none of the connection with the ownership that his uncle once had. When Congress wanted to build a stadium in the District in a location that would continue the tradition of baseball in the capital, Calvin wanted to move to the western suburbs where the white population was to his liking. The impasse was resolved when the City of Minneapolis began courting the younger Griffith.

Though the rest of the family — Mildred Cronin, Thelma, the twins and Sherry Robertson — were all opposed to any move, Calvin Griffith saw a financial boon from a move that would resolve his most obstinate problems. He would get a new stadium in a white community and cash to operate. They were the magic ingredients, the same promise that William Richardson had given his uncle 40 years earlier.

In 1960, over the objections of the Congress, President Eisenhower and his family, Calvin Griffith betrayed every promise his uncle had made, as well as a few of his own, and moved the Washington Senators to Minneapolis, Minnesota, where they would play as the Minnesota Twins.

Eleven years later he would drive a stake through the heart of his father's chosen home. Calvin Griffith was a ringleader among the American League owners when the issue of relocating the expansion Washington Senators came to a head in 1971. The same team that President Eisenhower and others insisted play in Washington before Calvin Griffith could move to Minnesota, he helped uproot.

Bob Short was another Minnesotan, and his purchase of the expansion team in 1969 was intended from the start to scuttle the team so he could sell it. It is likely he had the backing of Calvin Griffith from the outset, but whether or not that is the case, he had it at the end when Calvin worked within the American League ownership group that his uncle had founded to move the last vestige of one of the founding franchises from the city.

Nothing could have betrayed his uncle's legacy more thoroughly.

Calvin Griffith's actions were worse for the guilt by association they extended to Clark Griffith from the adopted son's actions. Although Clark Griffith was not party to Calvin Griffith's actions, his racial insensitivity about his former hometown buttressed the analysis of Clark Griffith's refusal to integrate the Nationals. What could be seen as the failures of an old man to blaze a frontier when his peers were holding back, was colored by the racism of statements made by Calvin in Minneapolis at a time when such statements left little cover. In 1978 he said the conditions for moving to Minnesota had ripened "when I found that you only had 15,000 black people here ... we came up here because you got good hard-working white people."[7] It was an inarticulate statement that made many who heard it cringe.

Griffith was censured for making the statements and defended himself, although with little effect. The worst of the defense was to shift attention to the record of his uncle in his 1990 biography that devoted an entire chapter to the affair. The best defense was presented by his son, Clark Calvin Griffith, III, who plainly stated his own belief in his father's better nature.

That healing atmosphere was reinforced when baseball finally returned to Washington in 2005 and Clark Calvin Griffith, III — namesake for the Old Fox — spoke well of the chances for the new team relocated from Montreal. The Montreal press sought him out, believing that he would undermine the rationale for the move to Washington. Montreal was the city in which Calvin Griffith had been born and it was Clark Griffith III's father who had left Washington 45 years earlier. But the Old Fox's grandson said he favored the move and cited as evidence of Washington's fitness its modern subway system that could deliver fans to the stadium.

When the Expos were renamed the Nationals in 2005 it closed a loop that began in 1901. Washington once again had a team bearing the name under which Clark Griffith won the 1924 World Series. The first venue for the new baseball team was RFK Stadium, where the Clark Griffith memorial had been moved after the demolition of Griffith Stadium in 1961. Hundreds of thousands of hungry fans dreaming those old dreams of baseball glory streamed past the memorial statue of Griffith on their way to the games that year. It would have made the Old Fox proud.

APPENDIX I

Career Player Stats

Year	Team	League	Games	Won–Loss	ERA
1888	Bloomington Reds	Central Interstate League	14	10–4	na
1888	Milwaukee Brewers	Western Association	23	12–10	2.45
1889	Milwaukee Brewers	Western Association	31	18–13	na
1890	Milwaukee Brewers	Western Association	34	27–7	na
1891	St. Louis Browns	American Association	27	11–8	3.33
1891	Boston Reds	American Association	7	3–1	5.63
1892	Tacoma Daisies	Pacific Northwest League	24	13–7	na
1893	Oakland Colonels	California League	48	30–18	na
1893	Chicago Colts	National League	4	1–2	5.03
1894	Chicago Colts	National League	36	21–14	4.92
1895	Chicago Colts	National League	42	26–14	3.93
1896	Chicago Colts	National League	36	23–11	3.54
1897	Chicago Orphans	National League	41	21–18	3.72
1898	Chicago Orphans	National League	38	24–10	1.88*
1899	Chicago Orphans	National League	38	22–14	2.79
1900	Chicago Orphans	National League	30	14–13	3.05
1901	Chicago White Sox	American League	35	24–7	2.67
1902	Chicago White Sox	American League	28	15–9	4.18
1903	New York Highlanders	American League	25	14–11	2.70
1904	New York Highlanders	American League	16	7–5	2.87
1905	New York Highlanders	American League	25	9–6	1.68
1906	New York Highlanders	American League	17	2–2	3.02
1907	New York Highlanders	American League	4	0–0	8.64
1909	Cincinnati Reds	National League	1	0–1	6.00
1912	Washington Nationals	American League	1	0–0	inf
1913	Washington Nationals	American League	1	0–0	0.00
1914	Washington Nationals	American League	1	0–0	0.00
Major League Totals Only			453	237–146	3.31

*Led League

Career Managerial Record

Year	Team	League	Wins	Losses	Win Pct.	Rank
1901	Chicago White Stockings	American	83	53	.613	1
1902	Chicago White Stockings	American	74	60	.552	4
1903	New York Highlanders	American	72	62	.537	4
1904	New York Highlanders	American	92	59	.609	2
1905	New York Highlanders	American	71	78	.477	3
1906	New York Highlanders	American	90	61	.596	2
1907	New York Highlanders	American	70	78	.470	6
1908	New York Highlanders	American	24	32	.429	6
1909	Cincinnati Reds	National	77	76	.503	4
1910	Cincinnati Reds	National	75	79	.487	5
1911	Cincinnati Reds	National	70	83	.465	6
1912	Washington Nationals	American	91	61	.599	2
1913	Washington Nationals	American	90	64	.584	2
1914	Washington Nationals	American	81	73	.526	3
1915	Washington Nationals	American	85	68	.556	4
1916	Washington Nationals	American	76	77	.497	7
1917	Washington Nationals	American	74	79	.484	5
1918	Washington Nationals	American	72	56	.563	3
1919	Washington Nationals	American	56	84	.400	7
1920	Washington Nationals	American	68	84	.447	6
Totals:	Twenty Seasons		1491*	1367*	.522	

*These totals reflect only games he managed before quitting Highlanders in 1908.

Notes

Introduction

1. Clark Griffith III, telephone interview with the author, September 24, 2010, Chevy Chase, MD.
2. Bill James, *The New Bill James Historical Baseball Abstract* (New York: Free Press, 2001), 9.
3. Mark Armour, *Joe Cronin* (Lincoln: University of Nebraska, 2010), 32.

Chapter 1

1. Henry W. Thomas, *Walter Johnson* (Lincoln: University of Nebraska, 1995), 344.
2. *Ibid.*
3. J. G. Taylor Spink, "50 Golden Years in the American League," *The Sporting News*, July 30, 1952, 11.
4. Joel A. Rippel, *The National Pastime*, January 1, 2009, 1.
5. James T. Farrell, "Clark Griffith Watches a Ball Game," *The Redwood Sportsman*, May 1963, 16.
6. Shirley Povich, "50 Years in Baseball," *Washington Post*, January 16, 1938, X1.
7. *Ibid.*
8. Bob Considine and Shirley Povich, "Old Fox, Baseball's Red-Eyed Radical and Archconservative, Clark Griffith," *The Saturday Evening Post*, August 15, 1940, 15.
9. *Ibid.*
10. *Ibid.*
11. David Condon, *Chicago Tribune*, Jan. 16 , 1897, 2.
12. *The Pantagraph*, August 17, 1921, 11.
13. *The Pantagraph*, April 16, 2006, B3.
14. J. G. Taylor Spink, "50 Golden Years

in the American League," *The Sporting News*, July 30, 1952, 11.
15. Edward Achorn, *Fifty-nine in '84* (New York: Harper Collins, 2010), vi.
16. *Ibid.*, 235.
17. *Ibid.*, 13.
18. *Ibid.*, viii.
19. *Ibid.*, vii.
20. *Ibid.*, 14.
21. Fred Young, *The Pantagraph*, May 5, 1940.
22. David Condon, *Chicago Tribune*, Jan. 16, 1897, 2.
23. Fred Young, *The Pantagraph*, May 5, 1940, 14.
24. Although ERA was not officially recorded until 1912, *Baseball Reference.com* indicates Silver King's ERA for the 1888 season as 1.63 and further indicates it was the leading figure for that year.
25. *The Pantagraph*, April 16, 2006, B3.
26. Henry W. Thomas, *Walter Johnson*, 34.

Chapter 2

1. David L. Fleitz, *Cap Anson* (Jefferson NC: McFarland, 2008), 49–51.
2. *Ibid.*, 111.
3. *Ibid.*, 215
4. Bill Felber, *A Game of Brawl* (Lincoln: University of Nebraska, 2007), 56.
5. Achorn, 235.
6. Shirley Povich, "50 Years in Baseball," *Washington Post*, January 21, 1938, 19.
7. As previously noted, ERA was not officially recorded until 1912 and during the 1890s the value of ERA as an indicator of

performance was undermined by the large number of un-earned runs — roughly 35–40 percent — cataloged in official scoring.

8. Clark Griffith, "Twenty-Five Years of Big League Baseball," *Outing Magazine*, June 1914, 38.

9. Felber, in *Game of Brawl*, cites Griffith as "the trouble-making Colts ace whose attempts to stir labor unrest enlivened the league atmosphere," 152.

10. "Schriver's Feat," *Sporting Life*, September 1, 1894, 1. Many Washington baseball fans attribute the first toss from the monument to Gabby Street because of Morris Beale's account in his book on the Senators. He is contradicted by press accounts from 1894, however, which quite clearly describe the event and leave no room for equivocation.

11. Shirley Povich, *The Washington Nationals* (New York: Putnam's, 1954), 74.

12. *Ibid.*

13. Henry W. Thomas, *Walter Johnson*, 24.

14. Fleitz, 237.

15. *Ibid.*, 246.

16. *Ibid.*, 250.

17. *Ibid.*, 253.

18. Bob Considine and Shirley Povich, "Old Fox," 32.

Chapter 3

1. Michael Lynch, *Harry Frazee, Ban Johnson and the Feud that Nearly Destroyed the American League* (Jefferson, NC: McFarland, 2008), 11.

2. Norman L. Macht, *Connie Mack*, 21.

3. Lynch, 10.

4. *Ibid.*, 9.

5. Macht, 180.

6. Povich and Considine, "Old Fox, Baseball's Red-Eyed Radical and Archconservative, Clark Griffith," *Saturday Evening Post*, April 13, 1940, 30.

7. Lynch, 13.

8. Mark Gavreau Judge, *Damn Nationals* (San Francisco: Encounter Books, 2003), 14.

9. Povich, 131.

10. Lynch, 14.

11. Macht, 232.

12. *Ibid.*, 187.

13. *Ibid.*, 184.

14. *Ibid.*, 209.

15. Frank Deford, *The Old Ball Game* (New York: Atlantic Monthly Press, 2005), 99.

16. Griffith, "Twenty-Five Years of Big

League Baseball," *Outing Magazine*, May 1914, 171.

Chapter 4

1. Arthur R. Arens, "The Chicago White Sox of 1900," *Baseball Research Journal* (1978), 88.

2. *Ibid.*

3. Frank Deford, *The Old Ball Game*, 70.

4. *Chicago Tribune*, April 14, 1901, 24.

5. Macht, 234.

6. *Chicago Tribune*, April 29, 1901, 17.

7. Bill James, *The New Bill James Historical Baseball Abstract*, 72.

8. *Ibid.*, 75.

9. *Ibid.*

10. *Chicago Tribune*, April 27, 1901, 18.

11. *Chicago Tribune*, July 14, 1901, 14.

12. *Chicago Tribune*, August 25, 1901, 16.

13. *Ibid.*

14. *Ibid.*

15. *Chicago Tribune*, September 8, 1901, 8.

16. *Ibid.*

Chapter 5

1. Macht, 270.

2. *Chicago Tribune*, August 28, 1902, 12.

3. Charles Alexander, *John McGraw* (Lincoln: University of Nebraska, 1988), 89.

4. *Ibid.*, 88.

5. *New York Evening World*, October 14, 1902, 7.

6. Macht, 261.

7. *Ibid.*, 308.

8. Glenn Stout, *Yankees Century* (New York: Houghton Mifflin, 2002), 10

9. Lynch, 25.

10. Macht, 306.

Chapter 6

1. Deford, 40.

2. Macht, 326.

3. Clark Griffith, "Twenty-Five Years of Big-League Baseball," *Outing Magazine*, May 1914, 168.

4. *New York Globe*, March 26, 1904, 8.

5. Allen Sangree, *New York Globe*, July 20, 1904, 5.

6. *Ibid.*

7. Glenn Stout, *Yankees Century*, 32.

8. *Ibid.*, 36.

Chapter 7

1. W. F. H. Koelsch, "New York Nuggets," *Sporting Life*, Jan. 21, 1905, 3.
2. *Ibid.*
3. *New York Globe*, March 21, 1905, 8.
4. W. F. H. Koelsch, *Sporting Life*, June 2, 1906, 8.
5. Stout, 40.
6. *Sporting Life*, June 9, 1906, 8.
7. W. F. H. Koelsch, *Sporting Life*, July 11, 1908, 6.
8. W. F. H. Koelsch, *Sporting Life*, June 28, 1980, 8.
9. Baseball Hall of Fame Player File indicates date of poem as October 20, 1906, no source given.
10. Ren A. Mulford, *Sporting Life*, November 21, 1908, 8.
11. Ren A. Mulford, *Sporting Life*, March 13, 1909, 14.

Chapter 8

1. Henry W. Thomas, *Walter Johnson*, 90.
2. *Sporting Life*, November 14, 1903, 7.
3. www.ballparktour.com, 2.
4. Philip J. Lowry, *Green Cathedrals* (Reading, MA: Addison-Wesley, 1992), 243.
5. Judge, 32.
6. Clark Griffith, "Building a Winning Team," *The Outing Magazine*, May 1913, 131.
7. *Sporting Life*, Nov. 4, 1911, 3.
8. Bureau of Land Management web site.
9. Clark Griffith, "Building a Winning Baseball Team," *Outing Magazine*, May 1913, 132.
10. *Ibid.*
11. The phrase is commonly attributed to Charles Dryden, sports editor of the *San Francisco Chronicle*.
12. Griffith, 132.
13. *Ibid.*
14. Henry W. Thomas, *Walter Johnson*, 25, from Povich as noted.
15. *Sporting Life*, June 8, 1912, 7.
16. Griffith, 33.
17. Thomas, *Walter Johnson*, 90.
18. *Ibid.*, 91.
19. Griffith, 39.
20. *Ibid.*138
21. *Ibid.*, 136.
22. Shirley Povich, *The Washington Nationals*, 86.

23. Griffith, 139.
24. *Sporting Life*, June 22, 1912, 4.
25. *Ibid.*
26. Griffith, 140.
27. *Sporting Life*, September 7, 1912, 23.
28. Thomas, 102.
29. Povich and Considine, *Saturday Evening Post*, 19.
30. *Sporting Life*, November 2, 1912, 5.
31. Thomas, 110.
32. *Ibid.*, 116–117.

Chapter 9

1. Paul Eaton, *Sporting Life Magazine*, August 20, 1913,15.
2. Clark Griffith, "Twenty-Five Years of Big-League Baseball," *Outing Magazine*, June 1914, 163.
3. *Ibid.*
4. Judge, 24.
5. Macht, 259.
6. Thomas, 145.
7. Judge, 24.
8. James Gilmore, *Sporting Life*, June 20, 1914, 2.
9. Griffith, *Outing Magazine*, June 1914, 37.
10. Thomas, 124.
11. *Ibid.*, 131.
12. *Ibid.*, 132.
13. *Ibid.*, 131.
14. *Baseball Magazine*, December 1914, 54.
15. Walter Johnson, "Why I Signed With the Federal League," *Baseball Magazine*, April 1915, 56.
16. *Ibid.*
17. *Ibid.*, 55.
18. *Ibid.*, 57.
19. *Ibid.*, 60.
20. *Baseball Magazine*, April 1915, 11.
21. Thomas, 136.
22. *Baseball Magazine*, March 1915, 12.
23. *Baseball Magazine*, April 1915, 11.
24. Thomas, 137.
25. Clark Griffith, *Outing Magazine*, May 1914, 169.
26. *Baseball Magazine*, April 1915, 11.
27. Thomas, 137.
28. Clark Griffith, *Outing Magazine*, May 1914, 170
29. Thomas, 144.
30. Macht, 620.
31. Judge, 39.

Chapter 10

1. Jeff Carroll, *Sam Rice* (Jefferson, NC: McFarland, 2008), 34.
2. Thomas, 142.
3. *Ibid.*, 148.
4. Povich, *The Washington Senators*, 96.
5. *Ibid.*, 96.
6. From Clark Griffith's letter to President Woodrow Wilson, as quoted in *Baseball Magazine*, April 1918, 372.
7. Carroll, 40.
8. Povich, 99.
9. Judge, 45.
10. Thomas, 160.
11. *Ibid.*
12. *Ibid.*
13. *Washington Post*, December 14, 1919, 22.
14. Lee Lowenfish, *Branch Rickey* (Lincoln: University of Nebraska, 2007), 84–85.
15. *Sporting Life*, March 3, 1917, 7.
16. Macht, 203.
17. Povich, 98.
18. *Washington Post*, December 14, 1919, 14.
19. *Ibid.*
20. *Ibid.*

Chapter 11

1. Thomas, 162.
2. Thomas, 172.
3. Clark Griffith, "Why the Spit Ball Should Be Abolished," *Baseball Magazine*, March 1917, 371.
4. *Ibid.*, 372.
5. *Ibid.*
6. *Ibid.*
7. Brad Snyder, *A Well-Paid Slave* (New York: Viking, 2006), 99.
8. *Washington Post*, January 14, 1921, 9.
9. *Washington Post*, April 23, 1921, 10.
10. Judge, 67.
11. Thomas, 185.
12. Tom Deveaux, *The Washington Senators, 1901–1971* (Jefferson, NC: McFarland, 2001), 57.
13. *Washington Post*, January 27, 1922, 14.
14. *Ibid.*
15. Thomas, 185.
16. Deveaux, 58.
17. *Ibid.*, 57.
18. Carroll, 75.
19. *Washington Post*, March 19, 1923, 12.
20. *Ibid.*

21. John A. Dugan, *Washington Post*, March 21, 1923, 20.
22. Deveaux, 58.
23. Judge, 68.
24. Carroll, 77.
25. *Ibid.*
26. *Washington Post*, January 25, 1923, 17.
27. Frank H. Young, "Griffith Fails to Deny Rumor Regarding Peck," *Washington Post*, October 26, 1923, 19.

Chapter 12

1. *Washington Post*, Jan. 23, 1921, 40.
2. *New York Times*, August 22, 1923, 22.
3. *Ibid.*
4. Philip J. Lowry, *Green Cathedrals*, 244; and Brad Snyder, *Beyond the Shadow of the Senators*, 4.
5. *Washington Post*, April 23, 1921, 10.
6. Frank H. Young, *Washington Post*, April 9, 1924, S1.
7. Thomas, p. 188.
8. Brad Snyder, *Beyond the Shadow of the Senators*, 11
9. Paul K. Williams, *Greater U Street* (Charleston, SC: Arcadia, 2002), 34.
10. Brad Snyder, *Beyond the Shadow of the Senators*, 6.
11. *Ibid.*, 2.
12. *Ibid.*
13. *Ibid.* Snyder's interview of Bill Gilbert is one source of Snyder's contention that blacks were occasionally seen in other parts of the stadium, 2. The other is a footnote on page 303 referencing comments made by black historian Constance McLaughlin Green.
14. Judge, *Damn Senators*, 59.
15. Snyder, 12.
16. Ken Denlinger, "There Used to Be a Tree, and a Ballpark, and a Team," *Washington Post*, July 10, 1985, B1.
17. *New York Times*, January 29, 1926, 26.
18. Carroll, 84.
19. *Ibid.*

Chapter 13

1. Clark Griffith, as told to Shirley Povich, "My Biggest Baseball Day," *Washington Post*, 1944, 15–17.
2. *Ibid.*
3. Shirley Povich, *The Washington Senators*, 107.
4. Stanley Harris, *Playing the Game*, 138.

5. Frank H. Young, "Bucky Offered Pilot Birth," *Washington Post*, February 10, 1924, S1.
6. *Ibid.*
7. Harris, 180.
8. Shirley Povich, "50 Years in Baseball," *Washington Post*, February 10, 1938, 19.
9. *Washington Post*, February 18, 1924, S1.
10. Harris, 183.
11. Thomas, 193.
12. *Ibid.*, 193.
13. Carroll, 85.
14. Thomas, 188.
15. *Washington Post*, April 1, 1924, S1.
16. *Ibid.*
17. Thomas, 192.
18. *Washington Post*, April 14, 1924, s1.
19. Thomas, 196.
20. Thomas, 195, from *Washington Post*.
21. *Ibid.*, 201.
22. Reed Browning, *Baseball's Greatest Season 1924* (Amherst: University of Massachusetts, 2003), 51.
23. Arthur L. Knapp, *Washington Post*, June 26th, 1924, S1.
24. *Washington Post*, June 25, 1924, S1.
25. *Ibid.*
26. Judge, 45.
27. Thomas, 200.
28. *Ibid.*
29. Carroll, 87.
30. Frank H. Young, "Earl McNeely Stars as Griffs Win, 2 to 1," *Washington Post*, August, 24, 1924.
31. Thomas, 202.
32. *Ibid.*
33. Judge, 80.
34. Reed Browning, 81, from an article in *Baseball Magazine*, F.C. Lane "If I Were Only Young Once More," 531.
35. Browning, 81.
36. *Washington Post*, September 15, 1924, S3.
37. *Washington Post*, September 1, 1924, S1.
38. Thomas, 207.
39. Frank H. Young, "Griffmen Defeat Red Sox 4–2 as Rain Routs Yanks," *Washington Post*, September 30, 1924, 1.
40. *Ibid.*
41. *Ibid.*
42. *Ibid.*
43. Thomas, 213.
44. Harris, 201.

Chapter 14

1. Stanley Harris, "Breaks of the Game Will Decide Series," *Washington Post*, October 3, 1924, S1.
2. *Ibid.*
3. Clark Griffith, as told to Shirley Povich, "My Biggest Baseball Day," circa. 1942, Griffith clippings file, National Baseball Hall of Fame Library, Cooperstown, N.Y., 15–17.
4. Carroll, 92, and Thomas, 215.
5. N. W. Baxter, "38,000 Fans to Jam Stadium," *Washington Post*, October 4, 1925, S1.
6. "Capital on Edge as Day Nears for Opening Game," *Washington Post*, October 3, 1924, 1.
7. *Ibid.*
8. Francis P. Daily, "President Blends Into Yelling Mob," *Washington Post*, October 5, 1924, 4.
9. *Ibid.*
10. Harris, 207.
11. Thomas, 222.
12. Griffith, as told to Povich, "My Biggest Baseball Day," 16.
13. Thomas, 229.
14. *New York Times*, October 9, 1924, 1.
15. Judge, 118.
16. Browning, 143.
17. Griffith, as told to Povich, "My Biggest Baseball Day," 17.
18. *Ibid.*
19. Browning, 149.
20. *Ibid.*
21. Shirley Povich, "50 Years of Baseball," *Washington Post*, February 12, 1938, X15.
22. Walter Johnson, as told to Lillian Barker, "Walter Johnson's 20 Years on the Mound," *Washington Post*, February 1, 1925, SM9.
23. Harris, 212.
24. Griffith, as told to Povich, "My Biggest Baseball Day," 17.
25. *Ibid.*
26. *Ibid.*
27. Johnson, as told to Lillian Barker, SM9.
28. Harris, 215.
29. Browning, 151.
30. Griffith, as told to Povich, "My Biggest Baseball Day," 17.
31. Judge, 131.
32. *Washington Post*, October 11, 1924, 1.
33. Judge, 132.
34. *Washington Post*, October 11, 1924, 3.
35. Browning, 153.
36. Judge, 133.
37. Browning, 154
38. Griffith, as told to Povich, "My Biggest Baseball Day," 17.
39. *Washington Post*, October 11, 1924, 1.

40. Judge, 134.
41. Browning, 156.
42. Carroll, 111.
43. Browning, 153.

Chapter 15

1. Browning, 156.
2. *Ibid.*
3. Census records indicate that Clark Griffith's mother-in-law was named Jeanne and his sister-in-law, Jane. However, later records, including Ann Robertson's obituary, indicate her sister was also named Jeanne, though she may have gone by Jane to avoid confusion when she lived with her mother in Washington.
4. Clark Griffith, as told to J. G. Taylor Spink, "50 Golden Years in the American League," *The Sporting News*, July 30, 1952, 12.
4. "Baseball Notes," *Baseball Magazine*, June 1913, 86.
5. John Kerr, *Calvin: Baseball's Last Dinosaur* (Dubuque: William C. Brown, 1990), 8.
6. *Ibid.*, 7.
7. *Ibid.*, 8.
8. Clark Griffith III, telephone interview with author, September 24, 2010, Chevy Chase, MD. He maintains that Calvin Griffith's recollection of his adoption — relayed in the book by James Kerr — is flawed. He claims that Calvin had his name changed on his own in later years rather than by Clark Griffith upon his arrival in the mid 1920s.
9. "Clark Griffith Brings Home 5 More Children to Adopt," *Washington Post*, November 24, 1925, 5.
10. "Building Is Booming in Gallaudet Park," *Washington Post*, May 31, 1925, R3.
11. Clark Griffith III, author interview.
12. Kerr, 8.
13. Clark Griffith III, author interview.
14. *Ibid.*
15. *Ibid.*
16. *The Pantagraph*, August 17, 1921, 11.
17. Kerr, 9.
18. *Ibid.*
19. Mark Armour, *Joe Cronin*, 34.
20. Kerr, 12.
21. *Ibid.*, 6.
22. *Ibid.*, 21.
23. Bill James, *The New Bill James Historical Baseball Abstract*, 129.
24. *Ibid.*, 120.
25. Armour, 33.

22. Shirley Povich, *The Washington Senators*, 243.

Chapter 16

1. "Young Blood in Decided Minority," *Washington Post*, June 21, 1925, 22.
2. Thomas, 254.
3. *Ibid.*
4. *Ibid.*, 262.
5. "President Coolidge and 32,000 Fans See Nats Beat Yankees," *Washington Post*, April 23, 1925, 1.
6. *Ibid.*
7. *Ibid.*
8. "His Champions Are In Again," *Washington Post*, July 11, 1925, 15.
9. *Ibid.*
10. Frank H. Young, "Harrismen Are Always Behind," *Washington Post*, June 12, 1925, 12.
11. Thomas, 267.
12. Shirley Povich, "50 Years in Baseball," *Washington Post*, February 13, 1938, X3.
13. Carroll, 118.
14. Frances P. Daily, "25,000 Cheer Champions in Triumph," *Washington Post*, September 2, 1925, 15.
15. *Ibid.*
16. Thomas, 265. Baseball-reference.com inexplicably lists Orel Hershiser's .356 average in 1993 as the highest average for a pitcher despite Hershiser having only 73 at-bats that year. Johnson recorded his .433 average over 97 at-bats in 1925, with two home runs.
17. *Ibid.*
18. Thomas, 269.
19. Charles C. Alexander, *John McGraw*, 303.
20. Thomas, 271.
21. Grantland Rice, "Bull Fight Has Something on Series," *Washington Post*, October 4, 1925, 26.
22. Will Rogers, "Walter Johnson Showed Smarts Going to the Ballpark Instead of to the Capital," *Washington Post*, October 4, 1925, sm2.
23. Thomas, 273.
24. Hugh Jennings, "Jennings Declares Smart Playing Won," *New York Times*, October 11, 1925, s1.
25. Carroll, 128–131. His account of the catch is the best I found and his recounting of Rice's letter is a must read for any Nationals aficionado.
26. Thomas, 278.

27. N. W. Baxter, "Big Train Refuses to Quit, Although Virtual Cripple," *Washington Post*, October 12, 1925, 1.

28. *Ibid.*

29. *Washington Post*, October 16, 1925, 20.

30. Povich, *The Washington Senators*, 145.

31. Lawrence Ritter, *The Glory of Their Times* (New York: Macmillan, 1966), 285.

32. Thomas, 282.

33. Ritter, 285.

34. Stuffy McInnis, "Fighting Club Wins," *Washington Post*, October 16, 1925, 19.

35. Povich, 147.

36. "Beaten But Unbowed," *Washington Post*, October 16, 1925, 6.

37. Frank H. Young, "Two Pitchers Get $1,000 Bonuses," *Washington Post*, October 17, 1925, 13.

38. *Ibid.*

39. Povich, "50 Years of Baseball," *Washington Post*, February 13, 1938, X3.

Chapter 17

1. *Washington Post*, February 2, 17.

2. *Washington Post*, January 20, 1926, 17.

3. *Ibid.*

4. Frank H. Young, "Griff Yields to Bucky's Demands," *Washington Post*, January 27, 1926, 13.

5. "In the Press Box with Baxter," *Washington Post*, June 7, 1926, 11.

6. *New York Times*, April 13, 1926, 20.

7. Frank H. Young, "Griff Plans Scouting Trip," *Washington Post*, July 3, 1926, 3.

8. *Washington Post*, September, 26, 9.

9. Irwin Howe, "Hot Stove League," *Washington Post*, January 29, 1926, 16.

10. Frank H. Young, "Nationals Pay Out 115,000 for Rookie Mound Talent," *Washington Post*, October 31, 1926, M24.

11. *Washington Post*, February 1, 1927, 1.

12. *Ibid.*, 2.

13. Thomas, 292.

14. *New York Times*, March 11, 1927, 17.

15. Thomas, 297–298.

16. *Ibid.*

17. *Ibid.*, 92.

18. *Ibid.*, 98.

19. *Ibid.*, 132.

20. Armour, 29.

21. Povich, *The Washington Senators*, 154.

22. *Ibid.*

23. *Washington Post*, October 3, 1928, 15.

24. Frank H. Young, "End of Bucky May Have String," *Washington Post*, October 7, 1928, M20.

25. Thomas, 305–306.

26. Povich, *The Washington Senators*, 158.

27. Frank H. Young, "$88,000 Paid for 6 Young Pitchers," *Washington Post*, January 6, 1929, M16.

28. *Washington Post*, April 14, 1929, SM1.

29. Frank H. Young, "Manager Not Discouraged by Trouncing in First Game," *Washington Post*, April 14, 1929, 13.

30. *Ibid.*

31. Thomas, 311.

32. Armour, 39.

33. Thomas, 312.

34. Frank H. Young, "Nat's Failure Not Blamed on Walter," *Washington Post*, August 18, 1929, M17.

35. Thomas, 313.

36. *Washington Post*, June 6, 1929, 13.

37. *Ibid.*

38. Frank H. Young, "Source of New Talent Is Problem," *Washington Post*, June 23, 1929, M15.

Chapter 18

1. Frank H. Young. "1929 Talent Cost Nats $154,500," *Washington Post*, January 8, 1930, 17.

2. Charles C. Alexander, *Breaking the Slump* (New York: Columbia University Press, 2002), 23.

3. *Ibid.*, 24.

4. Charles C. Alexander, *Breaking the Slump*, quoting *Baseball Magazine* article, 17.

5. *Ibid.*, 19.

6. Armour, 40.

7. Frank H. Young, "Holdout Overpaid Even With Slash of $7,000 Says Owner," *Washington Post*, March 9, 1930, M19.

8. Don B. Reed, "Hoover Hurls First Ball as 23,000 Watch," *Washington Post*, April 15, 1930, 1.

9. Carroll, 164.

10. Frank H. Young, "Johnson Men Lead League in Slugging," *Washington Post*, May 27, 1930, 17–18.

11. Shirley Povich, "Player Swap Sends Outfielder in Slump to St. Louis," *Washington Post*, June 15, 1930, M15.

12. Frank H. Young, "Manager Sees Pennant With New Punch," *Washington Post*, June 15, 1930, M17.

13. Alexander, 16.

14. Shirley Povich, "Nats Acquire Art

Shires in Trade for Two," *Washington Post*, June 17, 1.

15. *Ibid.*
16. Thomas, 317.
17. *Ibid.*, 318.
18. Alexander, 29.
19. *Ibid.*
20. *Ibid.*, 16.
21. Frank H. Young, "Nats Buy Weaver, Oriole Pitching Ace," *Washington Post*, July 30, 1931, 11.
22. *Washington Post*, August 19, 1931, 16.
23. Alexander, 45.

Chapter 19

1. Carroll, 168.
2. Nicholas Dawidoff, *The Catcher Was a Spy* (New York: Random House, 2004), 34.
3. Alexander, 48.
4. Alexander, 36.
5. *Ibid.*, 37–40.
6. *Ibid.*, 49.
7. Frank H. Young, "Griffith, Cronin Bemoan Lack of Pitchers by Nats." *Washington Post*, April 6, 1932, 11.
8. Shirley Povich, "Griffith Ends Johnson Term as Nats' Pilot," *Washington Post*, October 5, 1932, 1.
9. Armour, 50.
10. Alexander, 52.
11. *Washington Post*, December 7, 1932, 13.
12. *Ibid.*
13. *Ibid.*
14. Al Hirshberg, *From Sandlot to League President, The Story of Joe Cronin* (New York: J. Messner, 1962), 77.
15. Alexander, 62.
16. *Ibid.*, 61.
17. Clark Griffith, "Foster Alone Named From Dim Past," *Washington Post*, March 19, 1933, 14.
18. *Washington Post*, March 5, 1933, 16.
19. "High Priced Rookie Is Gone Forever, Says Clark Griffith," *Washington Post*, March 27, 1933, 17.
20. *Washington Post*, April 7, 1933.
21. *Ibid.*
22. Alexander, 39.
23. *Ibid.*, 60.
24. Westbrook Pegler, "Cheers Greet Roosevelt's Presence," *Washington Post*, April 13, 1933, 11.
25. Armour, 56.
26. Shirley Povich, "This Morning," *Washington Post*, July 4, 1933, 11.

27. Westbrook Pegler, "Griffith Is Strong on Keeping Game Romantic," *Washington Post*, July 17, 1933, 15.
28. Frank H. Young, "Chapman Joins Nats, McAfee Released," *Washington Post*, August 2, 1933, 17.
29. Alexander, *McGraw*, 310.
30. *Ibid.*, 323.
31. *Washington Post*, October 3, 1933, 17.
32. Shirley Povich, "Odds Shifted as Nats Bow to Giants 4–2 in Opener," *Washington Post*, October 4, 1933, 1.
33. Gary A. Sarnoff, *The Wrecking Crew of '33* (Jefferson, NC: McFarland, 2009), 116.
34. Armour, 60.
35. Sarnoff, 190.
36. Westbrook Pegler, "Nats' Dispute With Umpires Is High Light of Giant Victory," *Washington Post*, October 7, 1933, 17.
37. *Ibid.*
38. *Washington Post*, October 9, 1933, 15.
39. *Ibid.*
40. *Washington Post*, October 11, 1933, 28.
41. Shirley Povich, "This Morning," *Washington Post*, October 11, 1933, 11.

Chapter 20

1. *Washington Post*, December 7, 1933, 16.
2. *Washington Post*, December 17, 1934, 14.
3. *Washington Post*, January 9, 1934, 17.
4. *Ibid.*
5. *Washington Post*, January 13, 1934, 20.
6. Shirley Povich. "Old Age Creeping Up on Nats, Four Star Pitchers Are Now 33," *Washington Post*, March 20, 1934, 16.
7. Armour, 67.
8. *Washington Post*, September 8, 1934, 15.
9. Shirley Povich, "Price tag on Nats' Gem Sets a Record in Diamond Sales," *Washington Post*, October 28, 1934, B1.
10. *Ibid.*, B7.
11. J. G. Taylor Spink, "50 Golden Years in the American League," *The Sporting News*, July 30, 1952, 12.
12. *Ibid.*
13. *Ibid.*
14. "Joe Cronin Sold to Red Sox in Game's Biggest Cash Deal," *Washington Post*, October 27, 1934, 1.
15. Armour, 71.
16. *Washington Post*, November 18, 1934, M18.
17. Shirley Povich, "Club 'Nearly Broke

Even' Is Report," *Washington Post*, January 3, 1935, 15.

18. Kirkpatrick, 39.

19. Shirley Povich, "Harris Is Recalled As Nats' Manager," *Washington Post*, November 14, 1934, 1.

20. Lewis F. Atchison, "Griffith to Go South; Will Spur Drive for Top-Notch Hurler," *Washington Post*, January 18, 1935, 19.

21. *Washington Post*, March 8, 1935, 21.

22. Bill James, *The New Bill James Historical Baseball Abstract*, 159.

23. Kerr, 24–25.

24. Brad Snyder, *Beyond the Shadows of the Senators,* 66.

25. Snyder, 70–71. Snyder reiterates the many broad claims about Estallela's heritage but the claim of the ballplayer himself after his playing days seems to undercut the controversy.

26. S. L. Price, *Pitching Around Fidel* (New York: Harper Collins, 2000), 218.

27. Snyder, 70.

28. *Ibid.*, 68.

29. Bill James, *The New Bill James Historical Baseball Extract*, 164–165.

30. William J. Dwyer, "Evolution From Sport to National Million Dollar Industry," *Washington Post*, April 24, 1935, FS4.

31. *Washington Post*, May 18, 1936, 15.

32. Wayne Corbett, The SABR Biography Project, www.sabr.org.

33. *Washington Post*, April 11, 1936, 11.

34. Clark Griffith III, personal interview with author, September 24, 2010.

35. Shirley Povich, "Clark Griffith, 50 Years in Baseball," *Washington Post*, February 17, 1938, X19.

36. Thomas, 333.

37. Robert Gregory, *Diz* (New York: Penguin Books, 1992), 334.

38. *New York Times,* August 15, 1940, 14.

39. Bob Considine and Shirley Povich, "Old Fox, Baseball's Red-Eyed Radical and Archconservative, Clark Griffith," *The Saturday Evening Post*, August 15, 1940, 14.

Chapter 21

1. Shirley Povich, "This Morning," *Washington Post*, December 9, 1941, 26.

2. Bob Considine, "On the Line," *Washington Post*, December 13, 1941, 23.

3. www.baseballalmanac.com

4. Snyder, 94.

5. Shirley Povich, "WMC Order May Absorb All Players," *Washington Post*, February 3, 1943, 10.

6. Shirley Povich, *The Washington Senators*, 212.

7. *Washington Post*, February 16, 1943, 16.

8. Shirley Povich, "This Morning," *Washington Post*, October 2, 1942, 13.

9. John Kerr, *Calvin,* 27.

10. Al Costello, "Opening Day Throng Pays Tribute to Late President," *Washington Post*, April 21, 1945, 6.

11. Povich, *The Washington Senators*, 220.

12. Shirley Povich, "This Morning," *Washington Post*, September 29, 1945, 8.

Chapter 22

1. Snyder, 2.

2. *Ibid.*, 3.

3. *Ibid.*, 78. This incident is not corroborated by any press accounts that the author could find, even in the African American press of the day. Snyder details numerous incidents between African American fans at Griffith Stadium that colored Griffith's view of the potential problems that occurred when white and black players took the same field, but he directly links the ban on interracial exhibitions to this one incident, which is why it is included.

4. *Ibid.*, 74.

5. Sam Lacy, "Looking 'em Over in the Tribune," *Washington Tribune*, December 25, 1937 12.

6. *Ibid.*

7. Snyder, 76.

8. *Ibid.*, 90.

9. *Ibid.*, 123–124.

10. Bob Kirkpatrick, *Cecil Travis of the Washington Senators* (Lincoln: University of Nebraska, 2009), 124.

11. Snyder, 170.

12. Lee Lowenfish, *Branch Rickey: Baseball's Ferocious Gentleman*, 352.

13. Snyder, 108.

14. *Ibid.*, 131.

15. *Ibid.*, 156.

16. Bob Considine, "On the Line With Considine," *Washington Post*, August 15, 1942, 15.

17. Lacy, 12.

18. Snyder, 165.

19. Lowenfish, 352.

20. *Ibid.*

21. *Ibid.*, 353.

22. Snyder, 199.

23. Clark Griffith, as told to J. G. Taylor Spink, *The Sporting News*, July 23, 1952, 12.

24. *Ibid.*

25. Snyder, email, December 2010.

26. *Ibid.*, 284.

27. Lowenfish, 353.

28. Snyder, 219–220

29. Lacy, 12.

30. Snyder, 289.

Chapter 23

1. Lowenfish, 365.

2. Shirley Povich, "This Morning," *Washington Post*, September 29, 1945, 8.

3. *Ibid.*

4. *Ibid.*

5. *Washington Post*, April 30, 1946, 1.

6. *Ibid.*

7. *Washington Post*, January 3, 1946, 10

8. *Washington Post*, May, 5, 1946, M7.

9. *Washington Post*, June 14th, 1946, 12.

10. Povich, "Hi Amigo," *Washington Post*, February 24, 1946, M6.

11. *Washington Post*, March 11, 1946.

12. Merrill W. Whittlesey, "Watching Williams Kept Fans and Players Well Entertained," *Washington Post*, April 17, 1946, 9.

13. Shirley Povich, *The Washington Senators*, 224.

14. Thomas, 348.

15. Bob Kirkpatrick, *Cecil Travis*, 135.

16. *Washington Post*, September 25, 1953, 32.

17. *Washington Post*, December 22, 1953, 14.

18. Povich, Shirley, "This Morning," December 25, 1953, 14.

19. Philip Lowry, *Green Cathedrals*, 246–247.

20. Al Hailey, "Draft Shuffle Irks Griff Celebrating His 82nd Birthday," *Washington Post*, November 21, 1951, 2.

21. *Ibid.*

22. James T. Farrell, "Clark Griffith Watches Ball Game," *The Redwood Rancher*, May 1963, 22.

23. *Ibid.*

24. Bob Addie, *The Sporting News*, April 6, 1974, 18.

25. *Washington Post*, October 20, 1955, 21.

26. Shirley Povich, "Griffith Always Played It Hard Til the Final Out," *Washington Post and Times Herald*, October 28, 1955, 46.

27. *Ibid.*

28. *Washington Post and Times Herald*, October 28, 1955, 46.

29. *Ibid.*

30. *Ibid.*

31. From Thomas, 163, and *Washington Post*, June 10, 1942, 10.

32. *Ibid.*

33. *Washington Post and Times Herald*, November 1, 1955, 1.

34. *Ibid.*

35. Povich, *The Washington Senators*, 229.

Epilogue

1. Bob Considine, "Aunt Addie Had Spirit, Charm," Un-sourced document in the Baseball Hall of Fame player file for Clark Griffith.

2. *Ibid.*

3. Bob Addie, "It's Wonderful News Says Mrs. Griffith," *Washington Post*, October 20, 1956, A10.

4. Snyder, 288.

5. Kerr, 49.

6. *Ibid.*, 48.

7. Snyder, 289.

Bibliography

Books

Achorn, Edward. *Fifty-nine in '84.* New York: Harper Collins, 2010.

Alexander, Charles. *Breaking the Slump.* New York: Columbia University Press, 2002.

_____. *John McGraw.* Lincoln: University of Nebraska, 1988.

Armour, Mark. *Joe Cronin.* Lincoln: University of Nebraska, 2010.

Axelson, Gustaf W. *Commy: The Life Story of Charles A. Comiskey.* 1919. Reprint, Danvers, MA: General Books, 2009.

Bealle, Morris A. *The Washington Senators: An 87-year History of the World's Oldest Baseball Club and Most Incurable Fandom.* Washington, D.C.: Columbia, 1947.

Browning, Reed. *Baseball's Greatest Season: 1924.* Amherst: University of Massachusetts, 2003.

Carroll, Jeff. *Sam Rice.* Jefferson, NC: McFarland, 2008.

Ceresi, Frank, and Mark Rucker. *Baseball in Washington, D.C.* Charleston, SC: Arcadia, 2002.

Connor, Anthony J. *Baseball for the Love of It.* New York: Macmillan, 1982.

Dawidoff, Nicholas. *The Catcher Was a Spy.* New York: Random House, 2004.

Deford, Frank. *The Old Ball Game.* New York: Atlantic Monthly Press, 2005.

Deveaux, Tom. *The Washington Senators, 1901–1971.* Jefferson, NC: McFarland, 2001.

Eig, Jonathan. *The Luckiest Man: The Life and Death of Lou Gehrig.* New York: Simon & Schuster, 2005.

Einstein, Charles, ed. *The Second Fireside Book of Baseball.* New York: Simon & Schuster, 1958.

Felber, Bill. *A Game of Brawl.* Lincoln: University of Nebraska, 2007.

Fleitz, David. *Cap Anson.* Jefferson, NC: McFarland, 2008.

Frommer, Frederick J. *The Washington Nationals: 1859 to Today.* Lanham, MD: Taylor Trade, 2005.

Gregory, Robert. *Diz: The Story of Dizzy Dean and Baseball During the Great Depression.* New York: Penguin Books, 1992.

Harris, Stanley. *Playing the Game.* New York: Grosset and Dunlap, 1925.

Hirshberg, Al. *From Sandlot to League President, The Story of Joe Cronin.* New York: J. Messner, 1962.

James, Bill. *The New Bill James Historical Baseball Abstract.* New York: Free Press, 2001.

Judge, Mark Gavreau. *Damn Senators.* San Francisco: Encounter Books, 2003.

Kerr, John. *Calvin: Baseball's Last Dinosaur.* Dubuque: William C. Brown, 1990.

Kirkpatrick, Rob. *Cecil Travis of the Washington Senators.* Lincoln: University of Nebraska, 2009.

Lowenfish, Lee. *Branch Rickey: Baseball's Ferocious Gentleman.* Lincoln: University of Nebraska, 2007.

Lowry, Philip J. *Green Cathedrals.* Reading, MA: Addison-Wesley, 1992.

Lynch, Michael. *Harry Frazee, Ban Johnson and the Feud That Nearly Destroyed The American League.* Jefferson, NC: McFarland, 2008.

Macht, Norman L. *Connie Mack, and the Early Years of Baseball.* Lincoln: University of Nebraska, 2007.

Mead, William B., and Paul Dickson. *Baseball: The Presidents' Game.* Washington, D.C.: Farragut, 1993.

Pajot, Dennis. *The Rise of Milwaukee Baseball: the Cream City from the Midwestern Outpost to the Major Leagues.* Jefferson, NC: McFarland, 2008.

Povich, Shirley. *All Those Mornings: At the Post.* New York: Public Affairs Books, 2005.

_____. *The Washington Senators.* New York: Putnam's, 1954.

Price, S. I. *Pitching Around Fidel.* New York: Harper Collins, 2000.

Ritter, Lawrence S. *The Glory of Their Times.* New York: Macmillan, 1966.

Sarnoff, Gary A. *The Wrecking Crew of '33.* Jefferson, NC: McFarland, 2009.

Snyder, Brad. *Beyond the Shadow of the Senators.* New York: McGraw-Hill, 2003.

_____. *A Well-Paid Slave.* New York: Viking, 2006.

Stout, Glenn. *Yankees Century: 100 Years of New York Yankees.* New York: Houghton Mifflin, 2002.

Thomas, Henry W. *Walter Johnson, Baseball's Big Train.* Lincoln: University of Nebraska, 1995.

Williams, Paul K. *Greater U Street, Images in America.* Charleston, SC: Arcadia, 2002.

Zimbalist, Andrew. *Baseball and Billions: A Probing Look Inside the Big Business of Our National Pastime.* New York: Basic Books, 1992.

Personal Interviews

Brad Snyder, telephone interview by author, September 19, 2010, Chevy Chase, MD, as well as subsequent email correspondence.

Clark Griffith, III, telephone interview by author, September 24, 2010, Chevy Chase, MD.

Articles from Magazines and Periodicals

Ahrens, Arthur, R. "The Chicago White Sox of 1900." *Baseball Research Journal*, 1978, 87–92.

"Baseball for Our Soldiers and Sailors." *Baseball Magazine*, 1917, 372.

Callahan, Jimmy. "Griffith's Superstition." *Baseball Magazine*, January 1917, 16–18.

"Chick Gandil, The Man Who Started the Famous Seventeen Straight." *Baseball Magazine*, August 1914, 69–75.

Considine, Bob. "On the Line With Considine." *Washington Post*, August 15, 1942, 15.

Considine, Bob, and Shirley L. Povich. "Old Fox, Baseball's Red-Eyed Radical and Arch-conservative, Clark Griffith." *Saturday Evening Post*, Parts 1 and 2, April 13, 1940, 14–15, 120–137, 20; April 1940, 18–19, 91–97.

"Critics of the Federal League." *Baseball Magazine*, June 1915, 53–57.

Denlinger, Ken. "There Used to Be a Tree, and a Ballpark, and a Team." *Washington Post*, July 10, 1985.

Donovan, Carrie. "Shaw's Vibrant History, Revisited." *Washington Post*, April 2, 2006.

"Famous Feats of Baseball." *Baseball Magazine*, April 1912, 33.

Farrell, James T. "Clark Griffith Watches a Ball Game." *The Redwood Rancher*, May 1963, 16–22.

"Good To Be Back To Home Town." *The Pantagraph*, 17 August 1921, 11.

Griffith, Clark. "Building a Winning Baseball Team." *The Outing Magazine*, May 1913, 131–141.

_____. As told to J. G. Taylor Spink. "Clark Griffith's 50 Golden Years in the American

League: 'Doesn't Sigh for Good Old Days Return.'" *The Sporting News*, July 23, 1952, 12–13.

_____. As told to J. G. Taylor Spink. "Clark Griffith's 50 Golden Years in the American League: 'Griff's Adopted Son Cal Trained to Take Over.'" *The Sporting News*, August 6, 1952, 12–13.

_____. As told to J. G. Taylor Spink. "Clark Griffith's 50 Golden Years in the American League: 'Sale of Son-in-law Cronin Nat's Salvation.'" *The Sporting News*, July 30, 1952, 12–13.

_____. "Foster Alone Named From Dim Past," *Washington Post*, March 19, 1933, 14.

_____. "High Priced Rookie Is Gone Forever, Says Clark Griffith," *Washington Post*, March 27, 1933, 17.

_____. As told to Shirley Povich. "My Biggest Baseball Day." Unsourced clipping, circa, 1942, Clark Griffith clippings file, National Baseball Hall of Fame Library.

_____. "Twenty-Five Years of Big League Baseball: Milestones of the Game." *The Outing Magazine*, May 1914, 164–171.

_____. "Twenty-Five Years of Big League Baseball: Stars of Yesterday and Today." *The Outing Magazine*, June 1914, 35–42, 163.

_____. "Why I Went to Washington." *Baseball Magazine*, January 1912, 62.

_____. "Why the Spitball Should Be Abolished." *Baseball Magazine* 19, no. 3, 1917, 371–390.

Johnson, Walter. "Why I Signed With the Federal League." *Baseball Magazine*, April 1915.

Kofoed, J.C. "The Field Marshall of the Washington Club." *Baseball Magazine*, June 1915, 33–36.

Lacy, Sam. "Looking 'em Over in the Tribune." *The Washington Tribune*, December 25, 1937, 12.

Lane, F.C. "Baseball's Bit in the World War." *Baseball Magazine,* March 1919, 386–437.

_____. "The Emery Ball, Strangest of All Freak Deliveries." *Baseball Magazine*, July 1915, 58–72.

_____. "The Little Old Fox of Baseball." *Baseball Magazine*, July 1912, 21–25.

_____. "Winning Streaks and Losing Slumps." *Baseball Magazine*, 1919, 323–325, 374–378.

McBride, George, "How Baseball Looks to Me." *Baseball Magazine*, July 1912, 51–53.

Meaney, P. A. "Who Invented the Spitball." *Baseball Magazine*, May 1913, 59–60.

Morse, Jacob C. "Startling Changes in Big League Circles." *Baseball Magazine*, April 1912, 9–12.

Phelan, William A. "Baseball History Up To Date." *Baseball Magazine*, April 1916, 15–24, 110–112.

Smith, Red. "The Pay-Off on Griffith." *New York Herald Tribune*, 26 September 1945, 11.

Soden, E. D. "On the Eve of Battle." *Baseball Magazine*, November 1912, 67–76.

Spink, J. G. Taylor. "50 Golden Years in the American League," *The Sporting News,* 30 July 1952, 11–12.

Steinbacher-Kemp, Bill. "Baseball Hall of Famer Griffith Started Here." *The Pantagraph*, April 16, 2006, 83.

Walsh, Ed. "The Spitball." *Baseball Magazine*, February 1912, 84.

Young, Fred. "Griff's Rival All but Beat Him." *The Pantagraph*, 5 May 1940, 4.

Newspapers

Chicago Tribune, 1890–1902.
New York Globe and Merchandiser, 1903–1906.
New York Times, 1901–1940.
Sporting Life, 1896–1917.
Washington Post, 1911–1959.
Washington Tribune, 1937–1943.

Encyclopedias

Thorn, John, and Pete Palmer, eds. *Total Baseball.* New York: Warner Books, 1989.

Archival Sources

Clark Griffith Player File, Giamatti Research Center, National Baseball Hall of Fame Library, Coopertown, N.Y.
Moorland-Spingarn Research Center, Howard University, Washington, D.C.
U.S. Census Records, 1890, 1900, 1910, 1920, 1930. National Archives and Records Administration, Washington, D.C.

Web Sites

Ballparksofbaseball.com
Baseballalmanac.com
Baseball-reference.com

Index